JAPANESE DIPLOMACY
IN
A DILEMMA

JAPANESE DIPLOMACY
IN
A DILEMMA

NEW LIGHT
ON JAPAN'S CHINA POLICY, 1924-1929

BY

NOBUYA BAMBA

University of British Columbia Press

VANCOUVER

ISBN 0-7748-0018-6

First published 1972
by MINERVA PRESS CO., LTD.
1 Tsutsumidani-cho, Hinooka, Yamashina
Higashiyama-ku, Kyoto, Japan

Printed in Japan
by Tenri-jihosha
© NOBUYA BAMBA 1972

To

My Parents

and

Kyoko

PREFACE

Japan in the latter half of the 1920's, having achieved the diplomatic objectives of the Meiji period — national security and diplomatic equality — was at a crossroads in determining her future goals in world politics and history. Over this issue arose much incompatibility and conflict between the two key diplomats of the period, Shidehara Kijūrō (1872–1951) and Tanaka Giichi (1863–1929). This conflict led them to differing perceptions of more immediate national goals and the general international environments, such as the League of Nations, the Washington System, rising Chinese nationalism, and the Manchurian problem. Their conflict exemplified Japan's dilemma in ascertaining her own identity in the world.

This monograph attempts to investigate how Shidehara's and Tanaka's "subjective perceptions," arising from contrasting personalities and cultural identities, influenced Japanese diplomacy, especially toward China. Through this study, I hope to probe some crucial problems in the study of Japanese diplomatic history: the essential meaning and differences of the traditionally accepted contrast between the "Shidehara Diplomacy" and the "Tanaka Diplomacy"; Japan's dilemma in her China policy prior to the Manchurian Incident; and two distinctly different lines of development in Japanese diplomacy, which are often, and rather superficially, contrasted in terms of military versus civilian leadership.

Methodologically, I have ventured to introduce a sociopsychological approach to the study of Japanese diplomatic history and to emphasize the importance of the study of leadership vis-à-vis the contemporary domestic and international milieu.

Shidehara Kijūrō and Tanaka Giichi, while searching for their own personal identities in a rapidly changing world, also tried to construct an identity for their nation. Today, when a sense of impotence and hopelessness hangs over many men in their struggle to find an inner identity, a study of Shidehara and Tanaka may give us an opportunity to reconsider the scope as well as the limits of the role an individual can play in the making of politics and history.

I wish to thank Professor Robert N. Bellah for giving me not only his kind and painstaking guidance but also his moral support throughout my research; Professors Delmer M. Brown, George De Vos, and the late Professor Joseph R. Levenson for their inspiring ideas at the initial stage of this research; Dr. Irwin Scheiner, Dr. Frederic E. Wakeman, and Dr. Thomas R. H. Havens, who have read the entire manuscript and given me invaluable suggestions; Japanese Professors Takahashi Akira, Etō Shinkichi, and Usui Katsumi for helping me greatly in dealing with Japanese materials; and Mr. Kurihara Ken and Mr. Baba Akira for assisting me in my research at the Document Office of the Foreign Ministry. I would also like to acknowledge the financial support for my research which I received from the Center for Japanese and Korean Studies at the University of California at Berkeley.

I would also like to thank many friends who gave me generous assistance for my research in various ways: Dr. Thomas Swift, Dr. W. K. Cummings, Miss Dorothy Stroup, Mr. A. Hamish Ion, Mr. Donald James Haslam, Mr. Wayne Leduc, Mr. Yutani Eiji and Mr. Miyazaki Makoto of the East Asiatic Library, University of California, Berkeley, Mr. and Mrs. Yamada Toshio, students at Tsuda-Juku College, and Mr. Sugita Nobuo and Mr. Terauchi Ichirō of the Minerva Press, Kyoto, who made the publication of this monograph possible.

Finally I would like to acknowledge my gratitude to Dr.

Tabata Shinobu, the former President of Doshisha University, whose humanism and pacifism have had a great influence on my life.

NOBUYA BAMBA

Tokyo, Japan
December 1971

CONTENTS

LIST OF APPENDIXES

INTRODUCTION

A STRUGGLE IN
NATIONAL-CULTURAL IDENTITY

Hitherto, many researchers have observed the contrasting character of the policies pursued by Shidehara Kijūrō (1872–1951) and Tanaka Giichi (1863–1929), leaders in Japanese diplomacy in the latter half of the 1920's. Shidehara's policy was often called "co-operative diplomacy" (*kyōchō gaikō*), "weak-kneed diplomacy" (*nanjaku gaikō*), "negative diplomacy" (*shōkyoku gaikō*), and "peaceful diplomacy" (*heiwa gaikō*), in contrast to Tanaka's "autonomous diplomacy" (*jishu gaikō*), "strong diplomacy" (*kyōkō gaikō*), "positive diplomacy" (*sekkyoku gaikō*), and "expansionistic or aggressive diplomacy" (*hadō gaikō*). Beneath these apparent differences, however, one can recognize that there were more fundamental conflicts in their national-cultural identities. This study attempts to analyze how the personality and cultural identity of these diplomats influenced Japan's diplomacy, and it also attempts to survey Japanese diplomatic history in the light of her struggle to ascertain her national-cultural identity ever since the nation entered modern international politics.[1]

---

[1] See, for example, Sadako N. Ogata, *Defiance in Manchuria: The*

INFLUENCE OF CULTURAL TRADITION
ON DIPLOMACY

The goals of diplomacy may roughly be classified into three
categories: the fundamental, the intermediate, and the ultimate.
The first goal includes such objectives as the guarantee of national
survival, the defense of national independence, and the preservation of territorial integrity. The ultimate goal is, as Kamikawa

---

Making of Japanese Foreign Policy, 1931–1932 (Berkeley, 1964), Chap. 1; Etō
Shinkichi, *Higashi Ajia Seiji-shi Kenkyū* (A study of East Asian political history;
Tokyo, 1968), Chaps. 4, 5; Ōhata Tokushirō, *Kokusai Kankyō to Nihon Gaikō*
(International environments and Japanese diplomacy; Tokyo, 1966), 240–260;
Shigemitsu Mamoru, *Shōwa no Dōran* (Upheavals of Shōwa: Tokyo, 1952), I,
22–57; Usui Katsumi, "Shidehara Gaikō Oboegaki" (A note on the Shidehara
diplomacy), *Nihon Rekishi*, No. 126 (Dec. 1958), 62–68; Usui Katsumi, "Shōwa
Shoki no Chū-Nichi Kankei: Hokubatsu e no Kanshō" (Sino-Japanese relations
during the early Shōwa period: The intervention in the Northern Expedition),
Kokushi Ronshū, II (Kyoto, 1959), 1657-1672; Usui Katsumi, "Tanaka Gaikō
ni tsuite no Oboegaki" (A note on the Tanaka diplomacy), *Nihon Gaikō-shi
Kenkyū: Shōwa Jidai*, (A study of Japanese diplomatic history: the Shōwa
period), ed. Nihon Kokusai Seiji Gakkai (Tokyo, 1959), 26–35; Ishii Itarō,
Gaikōkan no Isshō (A life of a diplomat; Tokyo, 1950); Horiuchi Tateki,
Chūgoku no Arashi no Naka de (Amid the storms of China; Tokyo, 1950);
Kiyosawa Kiyoshi, *Nihon Gaikō-shi* (A diplomatic history of Japan; Tokyo, 1942),
423–440; Baba Tsunego, *Gendai Jimbutsu Hyōron* (Comments on contemporary
figures; Tokyo, 1930), 38–81, 273–289; Togawa Isao, *Shōwa Gaikō-shi* (A diplomatic history of the Shōwa period; Tokyo, 1962), 3–61.

In fact, their policies were so different in nature that they have come to
be considered two major "types" of Japanese diplomacy, called "The Shidehara
Diplomacy" and "The Tanaka Diplomacy." After World War II, many people
argued that Shidehara's type of diplomacy was the normal one in contrast to
Tanaka's, and that Japan should have followed Shidehara's type of diplomacy.
See the editorials of *The Asahi Shimbun* and *The Mainichi Shimbun*, March 11,
1951; Ujita Naoyoshi, *Shidehara Kijūrō* (Tokyo, 1955), 9–10; and Ishii, 460.
In opposition to this view of the majority, however, Iriye Akira and Marxist
historians contend that there was not much difference between Shidehara's and
Tanaka's policies toward China. The former by taking the international system
approach argues that if there was any difference between the two, it was due
to the changing international environments. The latter, Imai Seiichi for example, asserts that both policies were "imperialistic." Shidehara's was economic, while Tanaka's was military imperialism. See Akira Iriye, *After Imperialism:
The Search for a New Order in the Far East* (Cambridge, Mass., 1965); Imai Seiichi, "Seitō Seiji to Shidehara Gaikō" (Party politics and the Shidehara diplomacy), *Rekishigaku Kenkyū*, No. 219 (May 1958), 20–26.

Hikomatsu has pointed out, to fulfill national aspirations and ideals and to create an ideal world according to her world design.[2] Between the two goals various intermediate objectives can be arranged in preferential hierarchical order. These may include the expansion of foreign markets, the security of strategic positions, and the protection of established rights and interests abroad. Although the fundamental goal is identical for all nations except self-abnegating ones,[3] the ultimate and intermediate goals vary from nation to nation. To secure the fundamental goal is the main prerequisite for any nation.

However, a nation is not always exposed to the real danger of national survival. When the fundamental goal is secured, the nation aspires to a higher goal. In the goal hierarchy, to attain a lower end is a means for achieving a higher end. Conversely, obtaining the means for achieving a higher end becomes an end in itself for the immediate purpose. In the final analysis all intermediate goals are means for achieving the ultimate goal. Hence, the guiding principle of a nation's diplomacy is determined by what the nation's ultimate goal is. And the ultimate goal of each nation is largely determined by her cultural tradition, i.e., her beliefs and myths, primary values and norms, principles and ideologies, her ethos and idiosyncracies. Why does it become so in reality? In the final analysis, a nation's diplomacy is determined by her chief executive or her Minister of Foreign Affairs. But when these diplomats formulate policies, they do so in the light of achieving the ultimate goal. In other words, they choose appropriate intermediate goals in the hope of attaining that which their nation aspires to most. And the national aspiration is

---

[2] Kamikawa Hikomatsu, "Nihon Gaikō e no Puroregomena" (A prolegomena of Japanese diplomacy), *Nihon Gaikō no Bunseki* (Analyses of Japanese diplomacy), ed. Nihon Kokusai Seiji Gakkai (Tokyo, 1957), 9.

[3] This case is very rare, but Haas and Whiting observe this attitude of self-abnegation in Mohandas K. Gandhi's policy of non-cooperation with the Japanese troops which invaded India in 1942. Gandhi opposed military countermeasures. See Ernst B. Haas and Allen S. Whiting, *Dynamics of International Relations* (New York, 1956), 68.

largely determined by the nation's dominant values, principles, beliefs and Weltanschauung — in short, her cultural tradition.

But if a key diplomat's perception of the ultimate goal differs from that of the general population, what will happen? To begin with the conclusion: So far as the nation maintains a relatively cohesive culture, such a case rarely arises. Even if it does, the "deviation" will eventually be corrected and the nation's diplomacy returns to a "normality" reflecting her general cultural tradition.[4] In most cases the diplomat shares the same cultural tradition with the general public. He is also strongly controlled by the realization that he is working in the service of the nation as well as for the particular Cabinet (or government) which he represents. Furthermore, he is constantly checked by the public through various means, such as public opinion, pressures from other decision makers, and the threat of political ostracism — the form of the punishment may vary depending upon the indigenous political culture and constitutional framework — perhaps by a general election or recall, by public accusation, assassination, coup d'État, or even by a revolution.

A nation's diplomacy still may change temporarily — from person to person and from time to time — in the selection of

---

[4] The following studies are good examples to illustrate how nations' cultural traditions are extended in their diplomacies. The best example will be Haas and Whiting's study introduced above; with regard to the reflection of Confucian cultural tradition upon China's traditional diplomacy, Immanuel C. Y. Hsü, *China's Entrance into the Family of Nations: The Diplomatic Phase, 1858–1880* (Cambridge, Mass., 1960) is good, see especially Chap. 1; concerning the influence of cultural tradition upon the West German diplomacy, see Karl Deutsch and Lewis Edinger's "Foreign Policy of the German Federal Republic," *Foreign Policy in World Politics*, ed. Roy C. Macridis (Englewood Cliffs, N. J., 1962), 91–132; on the Soviet diplomacy see Anthony T. Bouscaren, *Soviet Foreign Policy: A Pattern of Persistence* (Philadelphia, 1961) and Margaret Mead, *Soviet Attitudes toward Authority: An Inter-disciplinary Approach to Problems of Soviet Character* (New York, 1955); with regard to more recent bibliography on this subject, see David J. Singer (ed.), *Human Behavior and International Politics* (Chicago, 1965), especially Pt. II and its bibliography, and John R. Raser, "Personal Characteristics of Political Decision-Makers: A Literature Review," *Peace Research Society (International) Papers*, V (Philadelphia Conference, 1965), 177–181.

intermediate goals. For instance, according to diplomats' varying predispositions, some may choose more aggressive policies than others.[5] Or, depending upon different environments, a nation may rely on economic means at one time, and at another on military means. And yet, these changes are only in nuance and not in fundamental nature. In the overall historical perspective, diplomats' personality differences are nullified, and the nation's cultural tradition tends to be projected in her diplomatic history. As Haas and Whiting point out, a nation's diplomacy always tends toward a "common denominator" of the generally accepted values, beliefs, and Weltanschauung of the nation.[6] So far as nations endeavor to achieve their ultimate goals according to their cultural traditions, the history of international relations may be understood as "cultural" as well as "power" struggles among nations.

Split National-Cultural Identity

If a nation's culture disintegrates, what will happen to the nation's diplomacy? In the Age of Nationalism in the nineteenth century, most of the "late-coming" nations, including Germany, Japan, Russia and China, wished to become "rich and strong." The Japanese slogan of the Meiji Restoration, "*fukoku kyōhei*" (enrich the nation and strengthen the army), and the Chinese echo of the same slogan, "*fu-kuo ch'iang-p'ing*," clearly indicated these sentiments. In the twentieth century, most developing

<hr />

[5]   In this regard, see Nihon Kokusai Seiji Gakkai (ed.), *Nihon Gaikō-shi Kenkyū: Gaikō Shidōsha Ron* (Studies of Japanese diplomatic history: Treatises on Japanese diplomatic leaderships; Tokyo, 1967); Alexander L. and Lulietta L. Georges, *Woodrow Wilson and Colonel House* (New York, 1956); Alan Bullock, *Hitler: A Study in Tyranny* (New York, 1961); Frederick Wyatt and William B. Willcox, "Sir Henry Clinton: A Psychological Exploration in History," *William and Mary Quarterly*, XVI, 3rd series (January 1959), 1–26; and John R. Raser.

[6]   Haas and Whiting, 55–57.

nations have hoped to become "advanced and modernized" as well as "rich and strong." These late comers have been striving to transform themselves from "traditional" to "modern" nations with high standards of living, widespread literacy, modern science and technology, industrialization and urbanization. Yet, as S. N. Eisenstadt states, "Western European modernization and its direct off-shoots — that of the United States and the English-speaking Dominions — were the only cases of modernization that developed mostly through internal developments from within the society." All other cases of modernization came about in response to the "impingement" of international forces from outside. In other words, the modernization of non-Western nations must be understood as their acculturation and assimilation to the modern culture which originated and developed in the West. Consequently, the more the late comers incline toward modern culture, the more they have to experience the disintegration of their own cultural traditions.[7]

Nevertheless, their aspirations toward modernity emanate from nationalistic sentiments, which simultaneously contain a directly opposite aspect. Namely, nationalism tends to drive nostalgic people back to their tradition. Moreover, it also urges them to assert to the world something unique about their nation. For this reason, too, the nation's indigenous tradition must be not only preserved but also promoted. Consequently, those who cherish this kind of traditionalistic, nationalistic sentiment protest against the dilution and disintegration of their tradition. Thus a nation falls into a serious dilemma between two opposing camps: one hopes to make the nation a part of the modernized world and the other endeavors to resist it. A nation is divided between those individuals, groups, and institutions which tend to identify themselves with the Western oriented modern values, norms and

---

[7] S. N. Eisenstadt, *Modernization: Protest and Change* (Englewood Cliffs, N. J., 1966), 67–68. The term "split-up" national personality was introduced by the same author. On this theme, see *ibid.*, Chap. 4.

symbols, and those which identify themselves with the nation's past tradition.[8] The two competing forces often fight over domestic as well as the foreign policies, in order to determine the nation's future goal and identity.

Of course, no nation is completely polarized into two camps to this extent. Instead, some elites and the majority of the general public constantly vacillate between the two. Sometimes the general aspirations of a nation incline toward modernity, and at other times shift in the other direction. In this regard, Japan's case is typical. Modern Japanese nationalism began with the Meiji Restoration in 1868. From the outset, however, it has contained these two diametrically opposed forces, i.e., restoration of the old (*fukko*) and reformation in a progressive spirit (*ishin*). The Charter Oath of March 1868 called for the abandonment of the evil customs of the past and the seeking of knowledge throughout the world on the one hand, and the strengthening of the foundations of Imperial Polity on the other.[9] Since then, Japan

---

[8] In Japan, this "split" has been observed to some extent — though not precisely so — between the urban area and the rural area, and between the Ministry of Foreign Affairs and the Army. Clearer distinctions are found between individuals, for example between Fukuzawa Yukichi (1835–1901) as a modern philosopher and Nishimura Shigeki (1828–1902) as a traditionalist, between Ienaga Saburō (1913–   ) and Watsuji Tetsurō (1889–1960), and between Ōkubo Toshimichi (1830–78) and Saigō Takamori (1827–77). Robert N. Bellah makes a good comparison between Ienaga and Watsuji in his works, "Ienaga Saburō and the Search for Meaning in Modern Japan," *Changing Japanese Attitudes toward Modernization*, ed. Marius B. Jansen (Princeton, 1965), 369–423, and "Japan's Cultural Identity: Some Reflections on the Work of Watsuji Tetsurō," *Journal of Asian Studies*, XXXIV, No. 4 (August 1965), 573–594; on Nishimura Shigeki see Donald H. Shively, "Nishimura Shigeki: A Confucian View of Modernization," *Changing Japanese Attitudes toward Modernization*, 193–241; an interesting comparison of Ōkubo Toshimichi, Kido Kōin (Takayoshi, 1833–77), and Saigō Takamori is done by Tōyama Shigeki (ed.), *Kindai Nihon no Seijika* (Statesmen of modern Japan; Tokyo, 1964), and by Albert M. Craig, "Kido Kōin and Ōkubo Toshimichi: A Psycho-Social Analysis," delivered at the Colloquium of the Center for Japanese and Korean Studies, University of Galifornia, Berkeley, February 28, 1969; Irwin Scheiner's *Christian Converts and Social Protest in Meiji Japan* (Berkeley, 1970) and Kenneth B. Pyle, *The New Generation in Meiji Japan: Problems of Cultural Identity, 1885–1895* (Stanford, 1969) are interesting concerning the problems of the Meiji period.

[9] Ryūsaku Tsunoda, Wm. Theodore De Bary, and Donald Keene

has constantly vacillated between modernity and traditionalism. Furthermore, interestingly enough, the general tendency of national aspirations has shifted in cycles of fifteen to twenty years.

The years 1872–73 marked Japan's initiation into wholesale modernization. "Civilization and enlightenment" (*bummei kaika*) was on everybody's lips. In the 1880's Japan's craze for Westernization further increased. The Rokumeikan — a novel Western-style red brick building where foreign diplomats and Japanese officials were entertained by everything Western including music, dance, food and drink — symbolized Japan's desire to westernize in the eighties. Then came repercussions from the traditionalists. A number of factors came into play. Some of the major ones were the popular awareness of things Japanese stimulated by the injection of foreign elements into the indigenous society; increased national consciousness due to economic progress, development of education, communication and transportation, and greater political centralization; the humiliating Triple Intervention after the first Sino-Japanese War (1894–95) — the intervention by Russia, France and Germany over Japan's claim on the Liaotung Peninsula —; and the Russian threat on the Continent. Hence, popular enthusiasm for the West gradually shifted to skepticism, and the traditionalistic leaders taking advantage of this opportunity strongly attacked superficial imitation of the West. Thus the "Japanism" movement (*nihon-shugi*) began to grow.[10]

Japan's victory over Czarist Russia in 1905 marked another turning point. Although nationalistic exaltation still lingered for a few years thanks to the victory, Westernization was accelerated once again. This period was called the period of Taishō Democracy (1912–26). However, Japan's learning about the West grew much more reflective than before. For the first time,

---

(comps.), *Sources of Japanese Tradition* (New York, 1965), II, 137.
[10] With regard to more discussion on the Japanism movement, see Delmer M. Brown, *Nationalism in Japan: An Introductory Historical Analysis*, (Berkeley, 1965), Chap. 7.

"Westernization" and "modernization" were distinguished. In the Japanese vocabulary such expressions as "modern" ideas and "modern" living were introduced, instead of the conventional adjective "Western."[11] Simultaneously, people in general became interested not only in Western technology but also in Western philosophy and culture. Hence, modernization and Westernization penetrated Japanese society much more deeply than in the period between 1872 and 1890. Proportionately the traditionalists' protests also increased. The transition from the Taishō to the Shōwa (1925-27) was the watershed between the enthusiasm for modernization and the upsurge of traditionalism.[12] Some extremists began to attack parliamentarism which had swayed the minds of the "Taishō Liberals." As a consequence, the debate on "parliamentarism" (*gikai chūshin-shugi*) versus "emperorism" (*tennō chūshin-shugi*) became vocal between the two rival groups concerned with the future political system of Japan. This issue paralleled the contemporary diplomatic issue, "co-operative diplomacy with the West" (*kyōchō gaikō*) versus "autonomous diplomacy" (*jishu gaikō*). Shidehara Kijūrō was an advocate of the former, as Tanaka Giichi was of the latter.

Eventually the traditionalists overcame their opponents, and Japan entered a period of "ultranationalism." Within the nation, parliamentarism was destroyed by a series of assassinations and coup d'État, while abroad Japan pursued her "autonomous diplomacy" by withdrawing from the League of Nations in March 1933.[13]

---

[11] Masao Maruyama, "Patterns of Individuation and the Case of Japan: A Conceptual Scheme," *Changing Japanese Attitudes toward Modernization*, 507.

[12] Concerning a general survey on the Japanese attitudes toward modernization, see Marius B. Jansen, "Changing Japanese Attitudes toward Modernization," *Changing Japanese Attitudes toward Modernization*, 43-89. A more detailed survey on this period will be made in the next chapter.

[13] See Richard Storry, *The Double Patriots; A Study of Japanese Nationalism* (Boston, 1957).

The Aims Of This Study

When national-cultural identity splits as in the case of Japan — though this is a common enough phenomenon in many late-coming and developing nations today — the nation tends to fall into a dilemma in determining her ultimate goal and identity to be attained through diplomacy. This study attempts to investigate how such a national identity struggle was reflected in the course of Japanese diplomacy, and by doing so to survey the major trends of modern Japanese diplomatic history. The dilemma had existed ever since Japan's encounter with the West, but it became most conspicuous in the period under study, 1924–29, for a number of reasons: the national-cultural identities of the two most outstanding leaders of this period, namely, Shidehara Kijūrō and Tanaka Giichi, were so different that the contrasting nature of their leadership was clear even to the public;[14] the precarious balance of power between the traditionalists and modernizers intensified their competition; and finally, since by that time Japan has attained the fundamental goals, i.e., her national security, independence, and international equality, the major issue of the nation's diplomacy now revolved around the question of what her ultimate goal was, namely, what Japan's national destiny was in world politics and history.

At the same time, I also hope to find out a deeper meaning in the hitherto commonly accepted distinction between the so-called "Shidehara Diplomacy" and "Tanaka Diplomacy." A careful research of their different socializations and perceptions of domestic and international problems will indicate that the difference between

---

[14] One can detect a fairly clear distinction between those who supported Shidehara and those who supported Tanaka. Usui Katsumi also observed this point. See Nihon Kokusai Seiji Gakkai (ed.), *Gaikō Shidōsha Ron*, 119.

the two types of diplomacy was not just a matter of style. The two contradicted one another more fundamentally in principles, values and Weltanschauung, and their confrontation was a crystallization of the nationwide search for national identity in the rapidly changing international and domestic world of the twenties.

With regard to the methodology of the study of diplomatic history and international relations, I would like to make a new suggestion: that four aspects of analysis — the international, the decision making, the social and cultural "milieu" created by the public, and the key diplomat's subjective perception of the objective world — may be more proper than the traditionally prevalent dichotomous approaches, i.e., "the international or the national system as a level of analysis." Although both analyses contain other variations — for example in the first group we may count the multistate system and the game-theory approaches; and in the second group the minds-of-men approach and the decision-making approach — those who take the first approach in general focus upon international circumstances external to each nation. They tend to regard objective, external factors as the determinant of the nation's diplomacy formulation, and concentrate their attention upon such aspects as the world power configuration, alliance systems, geographical setting, the history of the region, and the characteristics of neighboring nations. The proponents of the second approach, on the other hand, turn their eyes to the internal state system: the constitutional setting for issuing foreign policies, the power relations among decision makers, forces from various pressure groups and lobbyists.[15]

---

[15] David J. Singer, "The Level of Analysis Problem in International Relations," *World Politics*, XIV (1961), 77–92; Hedley Bull, "International Theory: The Case for the Classical Approach," *World Politics*, XVIII (1966), 361–367; Arnold Wolfers, "The Actors in International Politics," *Theoretical Aspects of International Relations*, ed. William T. R. Fox (Notre Dame, 1959), 83–106. With regard to some actual studies particularly related to the Far Eastern diplomatic history, Hosea B. Morse and Harley F. MacNair, *Far Eastern International Relations* (New York, 1931) would be a classical example of the first group, and Akira Iriye's *After Imperialism* would be a more recent example

There are some shortcomings in both approaches. An obvious shortcoming of the first group is, as those in the second group point out, that they are inclined to regard international relations as a system of "billiard balls" or the "black box." External power relations necessitate a nation to pursue a certain policy, and the whole "system" of international relations can be rationally analyzed and accurately predicted like a problem of physics.[16] Against this kind of understanding of international relations, the exponents of the second approach insist that diplomatic decisions cannot be understood unless one understands individual decision makers. Take the Korean War, for example. The American intervention was not a foregone conclusion regardless of who the decision makers were at that particular time. It was people like Truman, Stimson, and Acheson, and the various events around them which made the United States pursue that particular course of action instead of other alternatives. This argument of the second group against the first sounds pertinent.[17]

Nevertheless, there is also an inherent shortcoming in the second group. They tend to overlook the significant role the non-elite population plays by influencing the decision makers' perception of national interests and international relations. The proponents of the decision-making approach state:

> It is one of our basic methodological choices to define the state as its official decision makers — those whose authoritative acts are, to all intents and purposes, the acts of the state. State action is the action taken by those acting in the name of the state. Hence, the state is its decision-makers. State X as actor is translated into its decision-makers as actors.[18]

---

of the same group. James W. Morley's *The Japanese Thrust into Siberia, 1918* (New York, 1957) and Ogata's work may be classified into the second group.

[16] See, for example, Morton A. Kaplan, *System and Process in International Politics* (New York, 1957); George Liska, *International Equilibrium: A Theoretical Essay on the Politics and Organization of Security* (Cambridge, Mass., 1957); and Richard E. Quandt, "On the Use of Game Models in Theories of International Relations," *World Politics*, XIV (1961), 69–76.

[17] Richard C. Snyder and Glenn D. Paige, "The United States' Decision

Obviously, the key decision makers, even including pressure groups, are not the sole components of the nation. The general public must be included in the entity of what is called a nation, not simply because of its being a compositional part of the nation, but also because of its actual influence upon the decision makers. When the nation's national-cultural identity is "split," the rise and fall of diplomats is greatly influenced by the vicissitudes of dominant popular sentiments and aspirations in the society. What the society hopes for, needs, and demands in diplomacy determines to a great extent the kind of diplomatic leadership. Hence, the social and cultural "milieu" becomes a critical area to be investigated in the study of diplomatic history.[19]

In this regard, Shidehara Kijūrō and Tanaka Giichi serve as good barometers of the general social trend, for both of them were consistent in their identities throughout their careers. Shidehara rose to power in the middle of the 1920's at the height of the liberal and democratic atmosphere in the society. Tanaka's emergence, on the other hand, indicated a gradually ascending traditionalism. When the balance of power in society shifted toward traditionalism in the 1930's, Shidehara lost his popularity completely and had to spend fifteen years in adversity and obscurity. Then after World War II, with the new rise of popular sentiments toward Westernization and modernization, he once more came to the fore politically. On the other hand, if a diplomat, unlike Shidehara, hopes to swim with the tide, he is obligated to change the general tone of his diplomacy from time to time. So, for

---

to Resist Aggression in Korea," *Administrative Science Quarterly*, II, No. 3 (1958), 341–378; Wolfers, 92.

[18] Richard C. Snyder, H. W. Bruck, and Burton Sapin, *Foreign Policy Decision-Making; An Approach to the Study of International Politics* (Glencoe, Ill., 1962), 65.

[19] Etō Shinkichi stresses the importance of this aspect and introduces an interesting statistical analysis of Japanese public opinion toward China between 1925 and 1928. See Etō Shinkichi, "Nikka Kinchō to Nihonjin" (Sino-Japanese tension and the Japanese), *Chūgoku o meguru Kokusai Seiji* (International politics and China), eds., Banno Masataka and Etō Shinkichi (Tokyo, 1968), 183–235.

example, Uchida Kōsai (1865–1936) who became famous for his aggressive "autonomous diplomacy" in the early thirties, had advocated international co-operation in the early twenties.

However, the key diplomat's subjective perception is still the most crucial. Depending upon the diplomats' different national-cultural identities their understandings of ultimate national interests and international environment, such as the Washington System, Bolshevism, and the Manchurian problem, may differ greatly. In fact, this was the case with Shidehara Kijūrō and Tanaka Giichi.[20] Thus I conclude this discussion with the methodological proposition: to understand a nation's particular policy at a particular time requires the student to investigate all four aspects, the international, the decision making, the milieu, and the key diplomat's perception, in the light of their intricate mutual inter-actions.[21]

A question remains. Why does one person identify himself with one culture as opposed to another? To answer this question, one has to probe into the problem of socialization and the social cultural milieu. By socialization I mean the individual's personal experience, such as his family background, education, and the character of his home town; by milieu, I mean the contemporary national experience common to all within the nation. And

---

[20] To give an example that two persons' perceptions of the same objective object are different: when a Westerner and a Japanese poet look at beautiful cherry blossoms, they might express entirely different feelings because of their different subjective perceptions. The Westerner will perhaps become cheerful at the beautiful sight and act accordingly, while the Japanese poet might feel melancholy and might even start to sob, realizing that the blossoms are evanescent. These different feelings and responses to the same object are caused by the perceivers' different cultural backgrounds: one with a Buddhist ephemeral view of life and the other without such a tradition. The same thing can be said of Shidehara's and Tanaka's perceptions in diplomacy due to their different cultural identities. The classic of phenomenology is Edmund Husserl's *Ideas: General Introduction to Pure Phenomenology*, trans. W. R. Boyce Gibson (New York, 1958); the original was published in 1913 under the title *Ideen zu einer reinen Phänomenologie und Phänomenologischen Philosophie*. See also Alfred Schutz, *The Phenomenology of the Social World*, trans. George Walsh and Frederick Lehnert (Evanston, Ill., 1967); George H. Mead, *The Philosophy of the Act* (Chicago, 1964); Karl Zener *et al.* (eds.), "Inter-relationships between Perception and Personality: A Symposium," *Journal of Personality*, XVIII (1949), 1–266. More references on this subject are listed in n. 30 of Chap. 5.

yet, according to their different socialization Shidehara Kijūrō and Tanaka Giichi had formed clearly different identities by the time of their maturity, and each was inclined to identify himself with only those aspects of the milieu that were congenial to him. What George De Vos has termed "selective permeability"[22] seems to have functioned in both Shidehara's and Tanaka's perceptions.

---

[21]   My methodology can be illustrated by the following diagram:

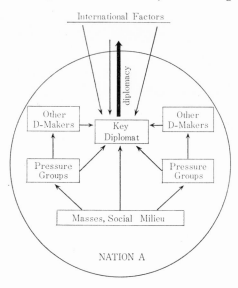

[22]   The term "selective permeability" is more broadly used as "reference groups" in various disciplines of social sciences. However, De Vos draws a distinction between the two terms, and defines the term "selective permeability" as "the mechanisms within the ego that are concerned with selective cognitive perception and interpretation of the outer social reality."   See George De Vos and Hiroshi Wagatsuma, *Japan's Invisible Race; Caste in Culture and Personality* (Berkeley, 1967), 226–227.

PART ONE

CHAPTER 1

JAPANESE DIPLOMACY
IN
A DILEMMA

TRADITIONALISM AND TRADITIONALISTS
BEFORE TANAKA

The core idea of Japan's traditionalism in the modern age is *kokutai*, the national polity. Traditionalists are those nationalists who wished to maintain and even to promote it against Japan's increasing Westernization and modernization.[1]

The term *kokutai* literally means national body. It had been called *kuniburi* (national features) or *kunigara* (national character). The term *kokutai* began to be used in about the eighteenth century by Shintō scholars, "National-learning" scholars (*Kokugakusha*), and some Confucian scholars. It was understood as the embodiment of indigenous ethics, values, ideas, customs and manners, and as a political system. Toward the end of the Tokugawa regime, the idea of *kokutai* became more popular, as

---

[1] See a further account of traditionalism in the Introduction and the Conclusion.

the Japanese national consciousness sharpened against China, India and the West. The idea was expressed by Yamazaki Ansai (1618–82) in Suika Shintō, Yamaga Sokō (1622–85) in Shidō, the Mito School's treaties on Taigi Meibun (loyalty and patriotism), Hirata Atsutane (1776–1843) in Fukko Shintō (Restoration Shintō), and by Yoshida Shōin (1830–59) in the Kōson Aikoku (revere the Emperor and love the country) movement.[2]

The downfall of the Tokugawa regime and its diplomacy, *sakoku*, gave a new opportunity to the *kokutai* movement. Traditionalists had to search for a "new" tradition, and yet one they could still call "indigenous" and "old." They found it in the idea of direct Imperial Rule, the ancient politico-religious system which had existed prior to the feudal regime. They called this political change the "Restoration." All schools related to the study of *kokutai* during the Tokugawa period were now loosely organized into a study called Kōkokugaku (Imperial Country Learning). In early Meiji, Kōkokugaku was taught by ex-samurai in many private schools (*juku*). Such private schools were still prevalent even after the introduction of the compulsory educational system by the Meiji Government in August 1872. Tanaka Giichi, for example, was strongly influenced by Kōkokugaku during his early education at these shools.

The idea of *kokutai* took a clearer form during the period of the Japanism movement after Japan's initial craze for Westernization. It was expressed in the Imperial House Law of 1889, the Constitution in the same year, and the Imperial Rescript on Education in 1890.[3] Through the promulgation of these laws and edicts,

---

[2] See David M. Earl, *Emperor and Nation in Japan: Political Thinkers of the Tokugawa Period* (Seattle, 1964); and H. D. Harootunian, *Toward Restoration: The Growth of Political Consciousness in Tokugawa Japan* (Berkeley, 1970).

[3] The Imperial Rescript on Education declares:
"Know Ye, Our subjects:
Our Imperial Ancestors have founded Our Empire on a basis broad and everlasting, and have deeply and firmly implanted virtue; Our subjects ever united in loyalty and filial piety have from generation to generation illustrated the beauty thereof. This is the glory of the fundamental character of Our

the quintessence of Japan's *kokutai* was firmly established. There are two major aspects in the idea of *kokutai*: the politico-religious aspect dealing with beliefs and ideas, and the aspect of national character dealing with values and ethics. The core of the first aspect is Imperial Rule and Shintō, which teach the doctrines that the Japanese nation was founded by the Divine Ancestors, that it is to be governed eternally by a successive line of Emperors (*bansei ikkei*), and that the Imperial Prerogatives were bestowed upon the Imperial Descendants by the Will of Divine Ancestors. The second aspect in *kokutai* stresses such values as loyalty, filial piety, obedience, self-sacrifice, courage, frugality and sincerity. The core is *bushidō* (the way of the warrior) and *Yamato gokoro* (Yamato spirit).[4]

Empire, and herein also lies the source of Our education. Ye, Our subjects, be filial to your parents, affectionate to your brothers and sisters; as husbands and wives be harmonious, as friends true; bear yourselves in modesty and moderation; extend your benevolence to all; ... should emergency arise, offer yourselves courageously to the State; and thus guard and maintain the prosperity of Our Imperial Throne coeval with heaven and earth. So shall ye not only be Our good and faithful subjects, but render illustrious the best traditions of your forefathers.

"The Way here set forth is indeed the teaching bequeathed by Our Imperial Ancestors, to be observed alike by Their Descendants and the subjects, infallible for all ages and true in all places. It is Our wish to lay it to heart in all reverence, in common with you, Our subjects, that we may all attain to the same virtue." Tsunoda, De Bary, and Keene (comps.) II, 139–140.

And the Meiji Constitution proclaims: "Having, by virtue of the glories of Our Ancestors, ascended the Throne of a lineal succession unbroken for ages eternal; desiring to promote the welfare of, and to give development to the moral and intellectual faculties of Our beloved subjects, the very same that have been favoured with the benevolent care and affectionate vigilance of Our Ancestors; and hoping to maintain the prosperity of the State, in concert with Our people and with their support, We hereby promulgate, in pursuance of Our Imperial Rescript of the 12th day of the 10th month of the 14th year of Meiji, a fundamental law of State, to exhibit the principles, by which We are to be guided in Our conduct, and to point out to what Our descendants and Our subjects and their descendants are forever to conform.

"The rights of sovereignty of the State, We have inherited from Our Ancestors, and We shall bequeath them to Our descendants. Neither We nor they shall in future fail to wield them, in accordance with the provisions of the Constitution hereby granted." The translation is taken from the Appendix of Tatsuji Takeuchi's *War and Diplomacy in the Japanese Empire* (Chicago, 1935), 477.

[4] *Bushidō Sōsho* (Bushidō library), eds. Inoue Tetsujirō and Arima

Japan's victory over Czarist Russia in 1905 was a very significant event in her diplomatic history. The victory indicated that her survival was no longer at stake, at least immediately. It also cleansed the stain of national humiliation caused by the Triple Intervention. Japan's military power which had been demonstrated in the war eased the way for her to abolish the unequal treaties.[5] Her success in making an alliance with Great Britain in 1902 had also raised her international prestige. During World War I, Japanese industries made great progress. As a result, after the war, Japan became one of the most powerful nations in the world. Her initial goals, i.e., security and equality — the former being the fundamental goal and the latter the intermediate — having been achieved, Japan could now work for the materialization of her ultimate goal. As a consequence, Japanese nationalism also made a remarkable turn during this period: from a "crisis consciousness" to a deliberation of her *raison d'être* in world politics and history. What could Japan be proud of before the world? Was there anything unique in Japan which she could contribute to the world? These concerns naturally drove traditionalists to assert the significance of the Japanese *kokutai*, the quintessence of her tradition, to the world.

The decade after the period of Taishō Democracy was a transition in which the idea of *kokutai* was to be transformed into the

---

Sukemasa (Tokyo, 1905), 3 vols., is the first systematic study of *bushidō* and *Yamato gokoro* (or *Yamato damashii*). The book contains not only many works on *bushidō* written ever since the mediaeval period and various codes of important military houses, but also good reference materials. See also Furukawa Tesshi, *Bushidō no Shisō to sono Shūhen* (Bushidō thought and related problems; Tokyo, 1957); Fukuchi Shigetaka, *Gunkoku Nihon no Keisei: Shizoku Ishiki no Tenkai to sono Shūmatsu* (The formation of militant nation, Japan: The development and decline of samurai consciousness; Tokyo, 1959); Fukuchi Shigetaka, *Shizoku to Shizoku Ishiki* (Samurai caste and samurai consciousness; Tokyo, 1956); Watsuji Tetsurō, *Nihon Seishin-shi Kenkyū* (A study of the development of the Japanese spirit; Tokyo, 1940), 2 vols.; and Inazō Nitobe, *Bushidō, the Soul of Japan* (New York, 1905).

[5] In 1911, having terminated extraterritoriality and regained complete control over its tariffs, Japan finally attained her diplomatic equality with Western powers.

idea of *kōdō* (the Imperial Way), which was the external expression of *kokutai* and which became the ultimate goal of Japanese diplomacy in the 1930's. However, the idea of *kōdō* was not established over night. Ideas are things that grow and develop. In the 1920's, before Japan's domestic principles, *kokutai*, were crystallized into the guiding principles of the nation's diplomacy, *kōdō*, various terms such as *ōdō* (the king's way), *tendō* (the way of heaven), *hadō* (expansionism) as well as *kōdō* were used. Kita Ikki (1883–1937) in *Nihon Kaizō Hōan Taikō* (An Outline Plan for the Reorganization of Japan, written in 1918 and published in 1923) was one of the first to give some theoretical framework to Japan's ultimate diplomatic goal based upon *kokutai*. He asserted:

> At the time when the authorities in the European and American revolutionary creeds have found it completely impossible to arrive at an understanding of the "gospel of the sword" because of their superficial philosophy, the noble Greece of Asian culture [Japan] must complete her national reorganization on the basis of her own national polity [*kokutai*]. At the same time, let her lift the virtuous banner of an Asian league and take the leadership in a world federation which must come. In so doing let her proclaim to the world the Way of Heaven [*tendō*] in which all are children of Buddha, and let her set the example which the world must follow.[6]

Kita, together with Ōkawa Shūmei (1886–1957), a professor at Tokyo University, profoundly influenced the young officers who

---

[6]   Tsunoda, De Bary, and Keene (comps.), II, 269. Subsequent development of *kokutai* and *kōdō* since Tanaka Giichi, and the distinction between the Confucian-oriented *ōdō* and the Shintō-oriented *kōdō* will be discussed in the Conclusion. Kōno Seizō and Kiyohara Sadao have done good works on the development of *kōdō* and *kokutai*. See, Kōno Seizō, *Nihon Seishin Hattatsu-shi* (A history of the development of the Japanese spirit; Tokyo, 1939); Kōno Seizō, *Kokutai Kannen no Shiteki Kenkyū* (A historical study of the concept of national polity; Tokyo, 1943); Kiyohara Sadao, *Kokutairon-shi* (A history of *kokutai* treatises; Tokyo, 1939); Kiyohara Sadao, *Kokushi to Nihon Seishin no Kengen* (National history and manifestation of the Japanese spirit; Tokyo, 1942); Daniel C. Holtom, *Modern Japan and Shintō Nationalism; A Study of Present-day Trends in Japanese Religions* (New York, 1963); Tsunetsugu Muraoka, *Studies in Shintō Thought*, trans. Delmer M. Brown and James T. Araki (Tokyo, 1964), especially Chaps. 6–7; and Delmer M. Brown.

carried out "patriotic" coup d'État and assassinations in order to put their ideals into practice in the 1930's.

Japanese Diplomacy in A Dilemma

The first national conflict between modernization and traditionalism in Japanese diplomacy took the form of "open the country" (*kaikoku*) versus "expel barbarians" (*jōi*). Generally speaking, the more people were exposed to Western influence, the more they tended to hold universalistic and rational views. Even in the early nineteenth century, the Dutch-learning scholars (*Rangakusha*) had more cosmopolitan views than others. Shiba Kōkan (1748–1818)[7] criticized the Tokugawa authorities as follows:

> They have kept the Russian mission at Nagasaki and have not let them land for half a year. And yet, their reply to the mission is very impolite, saying that the mission has displeased them.... Rezanov [Nikolai Petrovich Rezanov, 1764–1807] is the envoy of the Russian king. A king is a king just as in our country. Decorum is the beginning of all teaching and all humanity. The attitude of our authorities toward the mission is like standing naked in front of the well-dressed mission. I am sure that the Russians will regard us as beast-like creatures. What a regrettable thing![8]

Many who did not know the Western world, on the other hand, had a strong sense of cultural superiority due to their naiveté. Shionoya Tōin (1809–1867), an important Confucian scholar, typified such attitudes in his raging anger against Western culture and morality. Tōin was scornful about everything Western including Western writing, of which he wrote:

---

[7]   Shiba Kōkan's official occupation was Western painting, but he was also a philosopher with a good knowledge of the West.

[8]   Shiba Kōkan, "Shumparō Hikki" (Memoirs at Shumparō), *Hyakka Setsurin* (Treatises of a hundred philosophers), ed. Yoshikawa Kōbunkan (Tokyo, 1905), 1173.

It is confused and irregular, wriggling like snakes or the larvae of mosquitos. The straight ones are like dog's teeth, the round ones are like worms. The crooked ones are like the forelegs of a mantis, the stretched ones are like slimy lines left by snails. They resemble dried bones or decaying skulls, rotten bellies of dead snakes or parched vipers.[9]

The same attitudes were observed over the issue between *kaikoku* and *jōi*. Those who knew the quality of Western civilization, its military power in particular, advocated that Japan open the country for her own survival and to make Japan catch up with advanced Western technology. The traditionalists, however, asserted that Japan had to adhere to *sakoku* (closed country) in order to fortify her superior tradition against the West. Fujita Tōko (1806–55), an adviser to Mito (Tokugawa) Nariaki, explained the attitude of his lord, a leader of the Jōi Movement:

> The Hōjō cut down the Mongolian mission, and the first three Shōguns burnt foreign boats and crucified the people [Christians]. All of these deeds were to make our people determined [to reject foreign influences]. If we are determined, we can protect ourselves from enemies, even though our military preparations are not quite ready.... Those bold and crafty barbarians with all kinds of tricks and through heresy will demoralize and enfeeble our people. This is as crystal clear as looking into a mirror. If people are demoralized and neglect our military preparations, and if the heretic religion spreads, no matter how much we regret it, it will be too late. [Literally, even if we make such a hard effort as to try to bite our own navels, still we cannot mend our course once we are headed in the wrong direction.][10]

Other feudal lords (*daimyō*) who supported the *sakoku* and *jōi* policies were more unsophisticated, or ridiculous.

---

[9] Quoted from Jansen, "Changing Japanese Attitudes toward Modernization," 57–58.

[10] Fujita Tōko, "Hitachi Obi," *Fujita Tōko Zenshū* (A complete collection of Fujita Tōko's works), ed. Takase Yoshijirō (Tokyo, 1935), I, 420–431.

Some asserted that they should reach the Black Ships by small boats and cut down the canvas-ropes with Japanese swords like they cut noodles. Some advocated that they should slice the enemies as they do watermelons. Some said that they should float rubbish down to the Black Ships from the upper stream and stop the operation of making steam. And some contended that they should send many small boats loaded with fired dry grasses from the windward to the enemy ships to set fire to them.[11]

Opinions about how to expel barbarians varied, but traditionalists were all xenophobic and were never interested in establishing "international" relations with other powers. They saw no need of exchanging goods, to say nothing of culture. Nariaki said, "To open our country for trade is not only unnecessary, but also is greatly harmful to our Divine Country (*shinkoku*)."[12] Their common concern was "unchange," as Townsend Harris wrote in his diary: "As in everything else in Japan, the motto is *Quieta non movere*."[13] A court noble requested the Tokugawa Shogunate, "not to change our *kokutai*."[14] They were naive and ignorant, and their methods were impractical and irrational. Katsu Kaishū (1823–1899), who was in charge of naval defense and therefore was more aware of advanced Western culture and civilization, explained:

In short, this is because traditionally the authorities have prohibited people from reading Western books and from making Western instruments. People's ears and eyes have been closed and those who had some contacts abroad have been ordered not to speak out. Should some one speak out, he is severely punished. Without know-

---

[11]   Kiyosawa, I, 18.

[12]   *Ibid.*

[13]   Townsend Harris, *The Complete Journal of Townsend Harris* (Garden City, N. Y., 1930), 363.

[14]   The letter from Shoshidai Wakisaka Awaji-no-Kami to the Bakufu, dated September 22, 1855, quoted by Inau Tentarō, "Bakumatsu ni okeru Kōbu no Jōyaku Rongi" (Discussions on treaties by samurai and court nobles toward the end of Tokugawa), *Nihon Gaikō-shi Kenkyū: Bakumatsu Ishin Jidai* (Studies of Japanese diplomatic history, during the end of Tokugawa and the Restoration period), ed. Nihon Kokusai Seiji Gakkai (Tokyo, 1960), 84.

ing foreign affairs, people only imagined what they were and became suspicious. Hence, when foreigners came to ask for water and fuel, our people thought that they were harming our traditional knowledge. If they came to measure the depth of the ocean, our people accused them of humiliating our *kokutai*. Our people disliked them like snakes and scorpions, and despised them like dogs or pigs. These are all because our people did not know them.[15]

The policy of *sakoku* was finally destroyed by the West. The Japanese had to come out of their confinement of ignorance and naïveté, and the nation joined the international community. Nevertheless, Tokugawa legacies, especially samurai dispositions, still remained strong in the Meiji period, and its spirit was "Eastern Ethics and Western Technology," the slogan which Sakuma Shōzan (1811–64) had originally propounded. Hence, as many samurai wished to demonstrate their military strength, Japan's urge for war and conquest appeared again and again: the conquest of Taiwan in 1874, the debate on the Korean expedition (1872–77), the first Sino-Japanese War in 1894–95, and the Russo-Japanese War a decade later. The imperialistic atmosphere in the world further precipitated Japanese leaders toward such deeds. A motivation for Japan to carry out these military adventures was to increase her military prestige abroad, though it was not the sole cause. Various other factors also came into play such as Japan's concern with defense and her hope to gain international equality by demonstrating her military strength. But if defense had been the major aim, it was not rational to wage war against powerful Russia. It might have resulted in national destruction. The rational solution for national defense should have been compromise and negotiation with Russia, as Itō Hirobumi (Shunsuke, 1841–1909) insisted against the then military leaders. The latter, however, like many samurai who preferred sword

[15] Katsu Kaishū, "Rikugun Rekishi" (A history of the army), *Kaishū Zenshū* (A collection of Katsu Kaishū's works), ed. Kaishū Zenshū Kankō-kai (Tokyo, 1928), VII, 55–56.

fights to compromise, chose war instead of diplomatic solutions.[16]

In this connection, there is an interesting episode. In the
Imperial Conference (a conference of the highest leadership in
the presence of the Emperor) on August 28, 1905, to decide
Japan's conditions for peace with Russia, Admiral Yamamoto
Gonnohyōe (1852–1933) asserted that Japan did not have to
receive an indemnity, "for Japan had not fought for money." The Admiral declared, "We don't want a penny of indemnity! But as to territory, the Japanese Army had already con-
quered the whole of Sakhalin. If the Russians ask us to withdraw from the area we occupied, their request contradicts established fact. So we shall never give up Sakhalin. We must accomplish our original purpose in fighting the war."[17] Thus,
in the peace negotiations with Russia, Japan took territory instead
of money. Like Tokugawa samurai, many Japanese leaders including Admiral Yamamoto felt it base to be overly concerned
with money. The conquest of people and territory had been their
primary concern. It is also important to note that these wars
were fought during the patriotic period of Japanism. Dominant
traditionalistic sentiments in the society and Japan's engagement
in wars were interrelated. The shift toward traditionalism beginning in 1890 became a cause of the Sino-Japanese War, and the war
further stimulated traditionalistic nationalistic sentiments which
invited still another war.

It has been observed that one of important behavioral characteristics in traditional Japan is the extreme sense of shame. Moreover, the Japanese sense of shame is closely related to a sense of
proper hierarchy. They feel extremely "shamed" when they are
looked down upon, or laughed at, or scorned by others. The
sense of shame, therefore, is equivalent to a sense of humiliation.[18]

---

[16] See more discussion on this issue in Chapter 3.

[17] Shidehara Kijūrō, *Gaikō Gojū-nen* (Fifty years of diplomacy; Tokyo,
1951), 12.

[18] This point has been observed by Robert N. Bellah in *Tokugawa Religion; The Values of Pre-Industrial Japan* (Glencoe, Ill., 1957), *passim*; Ruth

The Japanese achievement orientation was strongly motivated by this "shame-humiliation" consciousness. To catch up to more advanced or superior ones and to supersede them was the individual as well as the national goal. Naturally, then, they considered the unequal treaties as great national humiliations, and to get rid of them became a major purpose of their diplomacy during the Meiji era. The whole of the national energy was exerted to achieve this goal. Likewise, the people in Meiji felt the Triple Intervention was a great national humiliation. The entire country became enraged. "*Gashin shōtan*" (endurance and hard work for the achievement of future revenge) expressed Japan's determination to wipe out this humiliation. Compensation for an extreme shame can be done either in a negative or in an affirmative way. Many samurai had either committed *seppuku* or attempted revenge. The Russo-Japanese War was Japan's "revenge" against Russia. Russian ambitions toward Korea gave Japan an opportunity to act.

Irrationality and the lack of pragmatism, observed among Tokugawa traditionalists, are also found among the Meiji leaders who advocated war against Korea. Saigō Takamori (1827–77), Soejima Taneomi (1828–1905) and Itagaki Taisuke (1837–1919)[19] reasoned that the Koreans "insulted" Japan and so Japan had to admonish the "impudent" Koreans.[20] They also suggested to

Benedict, *The Chrysanthemum and the Sword; Patterns of Japanese Culture* (Boston, 1946), *passim*; Edwin O. Reischauer, *The United States and Japan* (Cambridge, Mass., 1965), Pt. III, *passim*; John W. Hall and Richard K. Beardsley (eds.), *Twelve Doors to Japan* (New York, 1965), Chaps. 2, 8, *passim*. With regard to more recent works on Japanese character and personality, see Albert M. Craig and Donald H. Shively (eds.), *Personality in Japanese History* (Berkeley, 1971); Bernard S. Silberman (ed.), *Japanese Character and Culture; A Book of Selected Readings* (Tucson, 1962); Chie Nakane, *Japanese Society* (Berkeley, 1970).

[19] Itagaki later became a leader of political modernization by carrying out the Jiyū Minken Undō (Liberty and Civil Rights Movement). This change of his was partly motivated by his grudge against the government dominated by his rivals at the time of the debate.

[20] Tanaka Giichi and his Vice-Minister of Foreign Affairs, Mori Kaku, made the same kind of argument, when they carried out military interventions to China. And during the Second Sino-Japanese War (1937–1945) General

the government that such a military adventure would satisfy the discontented ex-samurai who had been deprived of their swords and status. When national survival against Western threats was at stake, this was an absurd argument. Iwakura Tomomi (1825–83), Ōkubo Toshimichi (1830–78), and Kido Kōin (1833–77), who had visited the United States and Europe, knew the world better than these adventurers and were strongly opposed to the idea of the Korean expedition. Instead, they stressed the priority of nation-building through the modernization of Japan. In Meiji diplomacy, this was the first sharp conflict between the two contesting groups. The contrast between the two groups can be seen not only in their different ideas about this particular issue but also in their life-styles and Weltanschauung.[21]

Throughout the Meiji era, however, Japan's national identity was not yet clearly divided. Consequently the conflict over national identity did not sharply reflect upon diplomacy. This was due to various reasons: most Meiji leaders were ex-samurai with traditionalistic values and concepts; Japan's modernization was still superficial. It was limited to large cities, while most rural areas were left largely untouched; the leaders of modernization themselves did not clearly discern their own national goal. Lastly and perhaps most importantly, in the Meiji era Japan's preoccupation in diplomacy was with her national survival. In terms of our diplomatic goal hierarchy, it was still the period when Japan had to accomplish the fundamental goal. In order not to be reduced to a "semi-colonized" status similar to that of China or into an actual colony like most Asian nations, the whole country

---

Matsui Iwane asserted, "Japan had to *chastise* China in order to make her behave properly." (Italics mine.) The quotation is taken from Masao Maruyama's *Thought and Behaviour in Modern Japanese Politics*, trans. and ed. Ivan Morris (London, 1963), 95. See more discussion on traditionalists' mind and view of international relations in Chap. 7 and the Conclusion.

21 Kiyosawa, Chap. 3; Tōyama; and Craig. With regard to more detailed account of the Korean expedition, see Tabohashi Kiyoshi, *Kindai Nissen Kankei no Kenkyū* (A study of recent Japanese-Korean relations; Seoul, 1940), I, Chaps. 4–10, and Ōhata, 79–89.

had to strive for nation-building. *Fukoku kyōhei* was the new national policy, replacing *sakoku*. *Fukoku*, to enrich the nation, suggested an economic goal, whereas *kyōhei*, to strengthen the army, implied a military goal. In other words, in the Meiji era, both the "military-feudal" goal and the more modern "economic" goal coexisted side by side, and both "modern" and "traditional" forces had to be fully utilized for the immediate purpose of nation-building. The two concerns mutually supported the achievement of the same goal.

During the Taishō era, popular aspirations for modernization and internationalism were high, owing partly to the victory of democratic powers in World War I, partly to Japan's war boom, and partly to the rising new generation. Such international and domestic "milieu" could not but influence Japan's diplomacy. For example, on March 12, 1922, Prime Minister Takahashi Korekiyo (1854–1936; in office, November–June 1922) stated that the diplomatic principle of his government was to contribute to peaceful coexistence. His government was determined to carry out those decisions which had been concluded by the Washington Conference and which, he thought, cultivated "a bright new epoch in the history of international relations."[22] In January of the next year, at the Forty-sixth Imperial Diet, Foreign Minister Uchida Kōsai emphasized: "The Imperial Government makes it its diplomatic principle to exert itself for the construction of peaceful policy which has been the supreme international aspiration since the Great War."[23] The construction of world peace, international co-operation and the faithful observation of the Washington treaties; these became the fundamental principles of Japanese diplomacy toward the latter part of Taishō. The successive Cabinets following the Takahashi Cabinet — those of Katō Tomo-

---

[22] *The Asahi Shimbun*, March 13, 1922.
[23] *Dai Nihon Teikoku Gikai-shi* (The diet record of Great Japanese Empire), ed. Dai Nihon Teikoku Gikai-shi Kankō-kai (Tokyo, 1930), XIV, 442–443.

saburō (1861–1923), Yamamoto Gonnohyōe, and Kiyoura Keigo (1850–1942) — also stressed the same principles.

Then came the period of Shidehara Diplomacy, as the culmination of this whole movement toward modernization and internationalism in Japanese society. Shidehara had a clear vision of the future Japan as a modern nation. He supported as the main principles of Japanese diplomacy, international co-operation, especially with Western democratic powers, eternal world peace, the strengthening of Japan's economic foundation through diplomacy, compromise and negotiation instead of military aggression, and non-intervention in Chinese domestic affairs. Thanks to his cosmopolitan (universalistic) and peaceful attitude, both his and Japan's prestige ascended to a high position in the international community. Thus, a new epoch was created in the diplomatic history of Japan.

Even during the Taishō era, however, traditionalistic nationalistic influences were observable in Japan's Twenty-One Demands of 1915 and her dispatch of troops to Siberia in 1918. Indeed, there was a clear contest between modernizers and traditionalists in the debate over the Siberian expedition. In this issue, again one finds a distinction between two clusters of leaders: Genrō Saionji Kimmochi (1849–1940), Seiyūkai's President Hara Kei (Satoshi, 1856–1921), Kokumintō's President Inukai Tsuyoshi (Tsuyoki, 1855–1932), and a member of the Peers, Makino Nobuaki (1861–1949), were in one group, while Vice-Chief of the General Staff Tanaka Giichi, Genrō Yamagata Aritomo (Kyōsuke, 1838–1922), Foreign Minister Gotō Shimpei (1857–1929), Prime Minister and General Terauchi Masatake (1852–1919), and War Minister Ōshima Ken'ichi were in the other. The former group was opposed to the idea of military intervention, because it was anti-democratic in principle, too costly, and impractical. They thought it impossible to give a major blow to the Bolshevik Revolution by sending a small number of troops. They were also concerned with the damage which might be done to Japan's

Russian trade by such a military adventure. The latter group, on the other hand, hoped to raise Japan's military prestige, to deter future Russian expansion toward the south, and thereby to protect Japan's *kokutai* against communism.[24]

The former group finally yielded to the strong pressure from the latter, but with one condition: namely, a joint expedition according to the original American proposal. They hoped to build a coalition with the United States. The latter, on the contrary, asserted that the action was "a contest against" the United States. For traditionalists, sending troops was another "contest" within the context of their superior-inferior mentality. In this regard, Foreign Minister Gotō's answer to Inukai at the Advisory Council of Foreign Relations is most significant. Gotō emphasized that he had no intention of limiting the number of troops. He reasoned that to do so would injure Japan's pride (*jisonshin*), and that he could not foresee the future development of such an intervention "until the action was taken in reality." A rational-minded person might wonder if the future consequences were so unpredictable why Japan still had to risk such a military adventure. Furthermore, according to Nagai Matsuzō's, a diplomat, recollection, when the American Government made a protest because Japan sent in many times the number of troops originally agreed upon, Gotō answered, "Force is spirit!" Nagai says that Gotō's answer was so "Orientally mystic" or like a Zen dialogue that the American Ambassador could never make sense out of his reply.[25]

Since the beginning of Shōwa (1926–   ), traditionalists once

---

[24] See fuller accounts of the Siberian expedition in Morley; and Takeuchi, Chap. 18.

[25] The original Japanese goes, *"Hei wa Ikioi nari !"* (兵は勢なり) *Ikioi* has various meanings, such as "force," "spirit," and "trend." I am not sure myself, either, what Gotō meant exactly, but perhaps he meant that when one sends troops, one must take advantage of the circumstances. See Nagai Matsuzō's recollection in "Shoka no Shidehara Kan" (Various people's views on Shidehara; Shidehara Heiwa Bunko, Tokyo), 132–135; Tanaka Giichi Denki Kankō-kai (ed.), *Tanaka Giichi Denki* (A biography of Tanaka Giichi; Tokyo, 1958), II, 21.

again began to assert themselves strongly. Deep and penetrating influences from Western democracy and Marxism-Leninism stimulated a defense of Japanese tradition. Nationalistic associations and secret societies began to mushroom in the latter half of the 1920's and became an increasingly powerful movement in the 1930's. Undoubtedly Shidehara's insistence on pursuing his policy of internationalism which, for his opponents, looked overly subservient to the West, irritated them. His conciliatory attitude toward the Chinese rights-recovery movements especially incited anger in the Army, the Seiyūkai, the Privy Council, and among the Japanese industrialists trading with China. Calling the new era the "Shōwa Restoration," traditionalists advocated the promotion of the national spirit, and some even advocated the ancient political system, i.e., direct rule of the Emperor rather than party government. It was under such circumstances that Tanaka Giichi emerged.

Tanaka, in contrast to Shidehara, emphasized the propagation of *kokutai*, especially *bushidō* and *Yamato damashii*, and hoped to demonstrate it to the world through what he called the "autonomous" and "positive" diplomacy, namely, being independent of and opposed to the West. In Tanaka's policy similar characteristics to those of former traditionalists which I have illustrated above, were also observed. Furthermore, being one of a few leaders of the 1920's who had been born in Tokugawa, Tanaka served as the vital link between the Meiji traditionalists and the Shōwa ultranationalists. In fact, he was the *protégé* of Genrō Yamagata Aritomo and simultaneously a teacher of the young ultranationalistic officers who emerged in the thirties.

CHAPTER 2

FROM TAISHŌ DEMOCRACY TO THE SHŌWA RESTORATION

The period under study, particularly between the end of Taishō and the beginning of Shōwa (1926–27), witnessed a transition in general popular aspirations which gradually shifted from a desire for modernization to one emphasizing traditionalism. The emergence of Tanaka Giichi was a symptom and simultaneously a result of such social change. However, the opposing forces to traditionalism were still strong enough to maintain a precarious balance of power throughout the twenties. From the time of the Bolshevik Revolution, a third choice had been offered to some of the Japanese elite; namely, to follow the Soviet example. This movement also became fairly strong during this period. Nevertheless, as traditionalism came to sway the scepter of the society, the movement was completely suppressed by the government. As the result it did not become a major force in Japan until the end of World War II, though it played an important role in inciting the protest of traditionalists.

Emergence of the Masses

The Taishō era saw a remarkable social phenomenon, the rise of the masses. For most people in the Meiji era, politics had still been the business of the *okami*, the people above them, and was beyond their concern and comprehension. They were "a-political" in the sense of what Riesman characterizes as "tradition-directed indifference."[1] Moreover, to them politics was a matter of obligation rather than participation. Nevertheless, from about the last decade of the Meiji era Japan began to see a spectacular development in mass movements. After the Russo-Japanese War, the masses, displeased with Japan's "modest" gains from Russia through the Treaty of Portsmouth, rioted in the capital, and peace was restored only through the use of martial law. In the last year of Meiji (1911), 6,000 Tokyo streetcar workers went on strike. In the Taishō political crisis there were mass riots around the Diet which became a force bringing down the Katsura Cabinet (December 1912–February 1913).[2] In June 1914 the citizens

---

[1] Riesman explains: "Characteristic of the tradition-directed indifference is an attitude that politics is someone else's job. ... the political indifference of this type, though excluded from direct political participation, has no cause to feel at sea. Having no sense of personal responsibility for the political sphere, such a person seeks no power over, and therefore seldom feels frustrated or guilty about politics." David Riesman, *The Lonely Crowd* (New Haven, 1960), 185.

[2] Various other factors also contributed to the fall of the Katsura Cabinet. Backed by the massive rallies and many small ones against the government which had spread over the entire nation, the Seiyūkai introduced a motion of impeachment against the government. As many as 234 Dietmen in the House of Representatives supported the motion. Then, there were intricate power struggles among Katsura Tarō (1847–1913), Hara Kei (Satoshi, 1856–1921), Saionji Kimmochi (1849–1940), and Yamagata Aritomo. Especially fatal to Katsura was Yamagata's enmity, which was caused by Katsura's establishment of a political party, Dōshikai. Yamagata felt this move of Katsura as if his former protégé tried to overshadow his authority. An ill feeling had also existed in the Navy ever since Katsura had attempted to retrench the Navy as well as the Army to solve financial difficulties. Admiral Yamamoto Gonnohyōe criticized Katsura

of Gifu, opposing the increase of electricity rates, took off meters and blacked out the city. Many other mass riots and rallies followed, and finally in 1918 the rice riots took place involving more than 700,000 people.[3]

Various internal and external factors caused this change. A change took place in Japan's international status. Japan having grown into a major power by the end of World War I, such a platform as *"gashin shōtan"* (the Meiji slogan of perseverance and self-sacrifice for the sake of the Emperor and the nation) became no longer necessary. The slogan even sounded absurd to many intellectuals and young people in the Taishō era. This sentiment was aptly expressed by the conversation between Daisuke and his sister-in-law in Natsume Sōseki's novel, *Sorekara* (Since then):

> 'And what on earth did father find to scold you about today?'
>
> 'That's hardly the point. He always finds something. What really did surprise me was to hear that father has been serving the nation. He told me that from the age of eighteen until today he has gone on serving the country to the best of his ability.'
>
> 'I suppose that's why he's been such a success.'
>
> 'Yes, if one can make as much money as father has by serving the nation, I wouldn't mind serving it myself.'[4]

---

for taking advantage of the new Emperor for his own interests by issuing many Imperial Rescripts to overcome his personal crisis. Ozaki Yukio (1859–1954) also criticized Katsura and his supporters by saying, "They conceal themselves behind the Throne and snipe at their political enemies. Do they not indeed seek to destroy their enemies by using the Throne as a parapet and Imperial Rescripts as bullets?" All of these forces, encouraged by the mass movement for the constitutional government, acted against Katsura. With regard to the interplay of power struggles among these politicians, see Peter Duus, *Party Rivalry and Political Change in Taishō Japan* (Cambridge, Mass., 1968), 38–49; Tetsuo Najita, *Hara Kei in the Politics of Compromise: 1905–1915* (Cambridge, Mass., 1967), 80–162; Oka Yoshitake, *Yamagata Aritomo* (Tokyo, 1958), 109–132; Kawahara Jikichirō, *Katsura Tarō* (Tokyo, 1959), 143-158.

[3] A detailed study on the rice riots has been done by Inoue Kiyoshi and Watanabe Tōru (eds.), *Kome Sōdō no Kenkyū* (A study of rice riots; Tokyo, 1959–62), 5 vols.

[4] Quoted by Masao Maruyama in *Thought and Behavior in Modern Japanese Politics*, 7.

There was also a natural time lapse. Half a century had elapsed since the Restoration, and a new generation had emerged. As the above quotation indicates, there was a definite generation gap between the people of the Meiji and the Taishō eras. Serving the nation and the Emperor had been a public obligation for the older generation, but Daisuke and his sister could sneer at such an attitude, and openly pursue their own interests. The death of the Meiji Emperor (December 7, 1912) who had been the embodiment of Meiji absolutism, and General Nogi Maresuke's (1849–1912) *junshi* (suicide in loyalty to the Emperor), signified to many Japanese the end of the "Old era." The *sensei* in Sōseki's *Kokoro* says:

> On the evening of the Emperor's funeral I sat in my study as usual and heard the signal gun. To me it sounded as a signal announcing the passing for good of the Meiji Era. Later I found that it had also marked General Nogi's death. With an extra edition of the newspaper in my hands I unconsciously repeated to my wife, "He followed the Emperor to the grave."[5]

The "emergence of individualism" and the "awakening of individuality" were expressions of the new Taishō spirit as contrasted with the Meiji *étatisme* which had stressed "loyalty to the Emperor and patriotism."

Coupled with this socio-psychological trend, there were democratic intellectual stimuli at home and abroad. The World War I accentuated this mood in Japanese society. The popular image of the war was, as Albert Craig puts it, that of "the Punch stereotypes: the bearded Kaiser of German militarism fighting the beautiful goddess of liberty, who represented the Allied cause."[6] Western political theory — such as Rousseau's theory of social contract, Locke's idea of inalienable natural rights of the individual, and Bentham's utilitarian concept of the government —

---

    5 Natsume Sōseki, *Kokoro*, trans. Ineko Kondō (Tokyo, 1956), 280.
    6 Edwin O. Reischauer, John K. Fairbank, and Albert N. Craig, *East Asia: The Modern Transformation* (Boston, 1965), 568.

had become extremely influential, and was greatly damaging to the traditional concept of the state and Imperial authority based upon Shintō mythology. Yoshino Sakuzō's (a liberal professor of Tokyo University, 1877–1933) theory of *"mimpon-shugi,"* a Japanese version of democracy, caused a sensation among the so-called "Taishō jiyūjin" (Taishō liberals).[7] The Reimeikai (Society of Enlightenment) which was organized by democrats like Yoshino Sakuzō and Asō Hisashi (1891–1940) in 1918, asserted "the extirpation of 'obstinate' and 'dangerous' thought (traditional and feudalistic thought) which goes against the general trend of the world," and "the stabilization of people's life in accordance with the new trend of the postwar world."[8] In literature the Naturalist School advocated emancipation of the individual and iconoclasm, and the Shirakaba-ha (White Birch Group), which followed the Naturalists, emphasized the pursuit of the individual self.

The record-breaking economic prosperity of the early Taishō was another important factor. Due to the war, Japan's trade and industries had progressed enormously. Net wartime earnings on international account amounted to 2,800 million yen, from the favorable balance of trade and from invisible trade. Japan was transformed overnight from a semi-permanent debtor to a creditor nation.[9] Her total number of steamships and motor vessels doubled, from 1.5 million tons in 1914 to 3 million tons in 1918. The profit ratio to the paid capital of various businesses and industries also rose sharply. For example, that of the cotton industry increased from 25 percent in 1915 to 92 percent in 1917. In terms of actual investment between 1911 and 1921, the transportation business expanded from 167 million yen to 826 million yen,

---

[7] Yoshino's *"mimpon-shugi"* was first introduced in *Chūō Kōron* in 1916.

[8] Kodama Kōta, *et al.* (eds.), *Zusetsu Nihon Bunkashi Taikei: Taishō Shōwa Jidai* (Illustrated Japanese cultural history: Taishō and Shōwa periods; Tokyo, 1956), XII, 150.

[9] *Ibid.*, 94; W. G. Beasley states 3,000 million yen in all — see W. G. Beasley, *The Modern History of Japan* (New York and Washington, 1964), 215.

and the machine industry from 630 to 3,551 million yen.[10] Such economic prosperity gave people in general financial and psychological "room to think" beyond the problems of bread and butter. Particularly important was the fact that it created a large wage-earning middle class with good educational background which constituted a politically enlightened group.

Rapid progress in education expanded people's horizons in the political world and gave them more confidence, self-respect, and responsibility. In 1873, 39.9percent of the male and 15.14 percent of the female population received compulsory education. But by 1925 the figures had increased to 99.47percent and 99.38 percent respectively. Higher education had also advanced. Between 1895 and 1925 the number of students in high school had increased almost tenfold. The number of universities had increased from 2 to 34 during the same period.[11] Education advanced not only in terms of numbers of schools and students but also in content. Confucian-style education which had emphasized mechanical memorization had been supplanted by Western-style education which stressed scientific, positivistic and rational methods. The number and kind of academic periodicals likewise increased remarkably, and international exchange of academic information became more active from the time Japan joined the International Association of Academies in 1906.

The period from late Taishō to early Shōwa has often been called the "age of mass media." All kinds of magazines and journals were sold by the millions. Newspapers were read extensively. The first issue of *Kingu*, a popular monthly magazine published in January 1925, sold out its 740,000 copies at once and *Yen-bon*

---

[10] Ōshima Kiyoshi, *Nihon Kyōkōshi-ron* (A treatise on the history of Japan's panics; Tokyo, 1952–55), II, 31; Okazaki Jirō, Kajinishi Mitsuhaya, and Kuramochi Hiroshi (eds.), *Nihon Shihonshugi Hattatsu-shi Nempyō* (The chronological table of the development of Japanese capitalism; Tokyo, 1949), Table 6, 441. See Appendix I, IX, XXI and XXII.

[11] Naikaku Kambō, Japan (ed.), *Naikaku Seido Sichijūnen-shi* (Seventy-year history of the Cabinet; Tokyo, 1955), Tables 40 and 41. See Appendix X.

(collections of famous novels and poems sold at the popular price of one yen for each volume) came into fashion after 1926.[12] Radio broadcasting also began in March 1925. The progress of transportation was equally remarkable. In 1907, the railway development was only 30.3percent of what was to be constructed by 1955, but by 1927 it had reached 76.0percent covering the entire nation.[13] Streetcars were introduced into major cities in the first, and buses in the second decade of this century. Such progress in communication and transportation systems also played an important role in enlightening the people and emancipating them from the "fetters" of small traditional communities and associations.

However, politicization requires a transformation of people themselves. Political consciousness presupposes self-consciousness. A traditional human nexus, such as *oyabun-kobun* (boss-followers) relations and paternalism, generated an attitude of conformity, cohesiveness and blind obedience. In such a traditional social structure it was difficult for the individual to have his own independent view of life and the world, to say nothing of an individual, critical view of politics. Various socio-economic changes, however, began to disrupt this traditional community and its values.

Industrialization and urbanization recruited millions of people from villages for work in the cities. Between 1909 and 1919, for example, the number of factory workers doubled. In 1925 there were 20 cities which had a population greater than 100,000.[14] This meant about one-sixth of the entire population lived in these cities. Due to these developments even in rural areas large families controlled by the absolute power of the family-head (*kachō*) were declining. In 1927 the average size of the agrarian family was

---

[12] Maruyama in Jansen, 518. See also *Asahi Nenkan, 1928,* 305-306, and *Mainichi Nenkan, 1928,* 508.

[13] Naikaku Kambō, Japan (ed.), Diagram VII.

[14] The actual number increased from 1,012,000 to 2,025,000. *Ibid.,* Table 5.

between six and eight members, mainly composed of parents and children.[15] In cities, the size was even smaller than the figure for rural areas. Moreover, many people such as factory workers, female workers in various jobs — restaurants, inns, dance halls, streetcars and buses, etc. — and students lived alone, separated from their families in the villages. Hence in urban areas the destruction of traditional family ties was more extensive. The atomization of workers was already seen in the 1900's in mining industries, shipbuilding and steel industries.

The progress of capitalism and bureaucratization also helped destroy traditions to a great extent. In big banks, trading companies, department stores, and government organizations, such human relations as kinship, the *oyabun-kobun*, and master-apprentice relationships began to disappear; and instead, wage-earning, more individualistic workers were created. The disintegration of these associations could not but bring about the same effect upon the values which had regulated such associations. People sought more individualistic and private lives, unbound by traditional notions of loyalty, obedience, self-sacrifice, and irrational obligations such as *giri* and *ninjō* (a traditional sense of fulfilling personal obligations and of compassion). Moreover, the new trends — capitalism, industrialization, commercialization and bureaucratization — themselves oriented people toward more scientific and rational thinking. They also introduced new values, such as efficiency, independence, and individualism. These anti-traditional modern values and ways of thinking were gradually fostered for the first time on Japanese soil and were further accentuated by Western, especially American, pragmatism, introduced by intellectual leaders such as Tanaka Ōdō (1867–1932). The populace, which had been submerged in traditional communities and

---

[15] According to a survey by the Ministry of Agriculture and Forestry, the average size of independent farmer-families was 7.6, that of half independent and half tenant families was 7.3, and that of tenant families was 6.6. Ono Michio, *et al.*, *Nihon Nōgyō Kyōkō Kenkyū* (A study of Japan's agrarian panic; Tokyo, 1932), 39.

absorbed in self-abnegating values was being transformed into independent, self-conscious individuals.

It was from such socio-economic conditions in the Taishō era that the masses began to emerge. Takayama Chogyū (1871–1902), a novelist, wrote in the *New Japan* in 1899:

> What is then the so-called New Japan? Internally, it is a Japan where the great Genrō figures are fading. It is a Japan where new personalities, educated in the atmosphere of the new Japan, are taking hold of the reins in such areas as politics, law, literature, and religion. It is a Japan which tries to wipe out the family-system through new Civil Codes. It is a Japan where the idea of rights is replacing the traditional morality based on piety. It is a Japan where workers' unions are emerging in the industrial world....[16]

As Chogyū predicted, the Taishō liberals hoped to establish a "new" Japan replacing the "old," and one of their strongest aspirations was to create a popular government which would reflect public opinion more than before. Hence, a movement toward the establishment of "constitutional government" took place.

MOVEMENT TOWARD CONSTITUTIONAL GOVERNMENT

A radical political change began with the "Taishō Crisis." On December 21, 1912, replacing Saionji Kimmochi, the chairman of the Seiyūkai and a liberal democrat, the Army General, Katsura Tarō, became Prime Minister for the third time. Katsura's return looked to many people as if the "old" politics controlled by the Genrō, by the Chōshū-Satsuma clique, and by the military was sure to continue in the new age. Parties, intellectuals, workers and some businessmen rose up demanding a constitutional government. The League for the Protection of the Constitution (Kensei Yōgo-kai) called for a "Taishō Reformation," advocating sweep-

---

[16] Quoted by Maruyama in Jansen, 506.

ing reforms directed towards a modern and democratic Japan. On February 10, 1913, when the Diet was opened, thousands rioted outside the building, destroyed the offices of pro-government newspapers, and burned police boxes. Katsura was forced to resign. On this day Hara Kei, a leading member of Seiyūkai, wrote in his diary, "If Katsura had not resigned, a revolution might have occurred."[17] This was the first case in Japan's political history in which the masses played a decisive role in the fall of a Cabinet.

The destruction of the Katsura Cabinet, however, did not bring about party politics immediately. Genrō Yamagata Aritomo, the military, and the bureaucracy were still strong. The masses were disorganized, the parties were not strong enough, and above all there was no clear idea of democracy. The years from 1913 to 1918 were a transitory period between the "old" politics and the "new." Cabinets were organized on the basis of a balance of power between the old forces and the new. Yamamoto Gonnohyōe, a Satsuma admiral, succeeded Katsura, but was soon ousted again by angry rioters incited by disclosures of naval bribery. General Terauchi Masatake's Cabinet (October 1916–September 1918), which followed the Yamamoto and Ōkuma Cabinets, was toppled by the rice riots.

By this time both mass power and the people's understanding of democracy had greatly increased. Yoshino Sakuzō's *mimpon-shugi* (1916) gave the parties and the people their guiding principle of democracy. From then on, the term *mimpon-shugi* began to be used frequently in the discussions of the Diet. The establishment of the Dōshikai (Kenseikai) under Katō Takaaki's (1860–1926) leadership increased the strength of the political parties against the "old" forces. As the economy progressed, the size of the industrial and commercial middle class increased, forming a strong base for the party movement. Businessmen and industrialists began to organize themselves into pressure groups against the govern-

---

[17] Hara Kei, *Hara Kei Nikki* (Hara Kei's diary; Tokyo, 1950–51), V, 191 (February 10, 1913).

ment. Furthermore, the Genrō were becoming old. Both Yamagata Aritomo and Ōkuma Shigenobu (1838–1922) died in 1922,
leaving only Saionji. Mass power had also become formidable,
as demonstrated in the rice riots.[18]

Thus Hara Kei, the chairman of the Seiyūkai, was appointed
the new Prime Minister to succeed the Terauchi Cabinet. Hara
was celebrated as the "Great Commoner," since he had established
his power as a party-man without any peerage. Besides, all
members of his Cabinet, except the men holding the portfolios
of Foreign Affairs, War and Navy, were selected from the Seiyūkai.
Therefore, his government was hailed by many in the party movement as the beginning of a new era of party government in Japan.
However, Hara was, as Craig says, at best a half-hearted liberal.[19]
Above all, he was deeply suspicious of the merit of universal suffrage, which was now being demanded by a mass movement.
The victory of the democratic powers in World War I further
stimulated this movement. Intellectuals, students, and workers
organized the League for the Promotion of Universal Suffrage
and the National Student League for Universal Suffrage in February 1919, and declared, "Democracy is the dominant trend in
world politics. *Mimpon-shugi* is the trend of today." Opposition parties also joined the movement against the Hara Administration.[20]

---

[18] In terms of labor strikes, the number increased from 64 cases in 1915
to 398 in 1917, and the number of participants in these strikes from 7, 852 to 57,
309 during the same period. See Okazaki, Kajinishi, and Kuramochi (eds.),
386; Horie Yasuzō, *Nihon Keizai-shi* (An economic history of Japan; Tokyo,
1942), 279–280. See Appendix XIV.

[19] Scalapino says, "Hara's policy toward the Genrō was deferential;
toward the militarists, ambivalent; toward the Privy Council and Peers, conciliatory; toward the Seiyūkai rank and file, arbitrary; and toward the opposition
parties and the general public (except certain industrial and landed elements),
unconcerned." See Robert A. Scalapino, *Democracy and the Party Movement in Prewar Japan* (Berkeley, 1962), 212; Reischauer, Fairbank, and Craig,
572.

[20] Peter Duus gives a good survey on the political scene during this
period. See Peter Duus, 68–81 on Hara Kei, and 107-161 on the popular
movement toward constitutional government during Hara's leadership.

After Hara's assassination by a rightist youth in 1921, the
government was once again turned over to the "old" hands,
Admiral Katō Tomosaburō (June 1922-September 1923), Admiral
Yamamoto Gonnohyōe (September 1923-January 1924), and the
74-year-old President of the Privy Council, Kiyoura Keigo (January-June 1924). Popular hostilities against these governments
controlled by the bureaucratic-military complex broke out into
violent mass movements for the defense of constitutional government. The movement for universal suffrage was now incorporated
into this nation-wide movement. Three major parties, the
Seiyūkai, the Kenseikai, and the Kakushin Club, united in
order to carry out their common goal. The mass-media also
enthusiastically supported the movement. Hence the zenith of
popular movements toward party government and parliamentary
democracy took place in the middle of 1924. In the general
election of May 1924 the three parties won an overwhelming
victory over the Seiyū Hontō which had supported the Kiyoura
Administration.[21] Thus, Katō Takaaki, the chairman of the leading Kenseikai party, organized his three-party Coalition Cabinet.
The Taishō liberals thought this to be the popular triumph of
parliamentary democracy. It was in this government that Shidehara Kijūrō first became Minister of Foreign Affairs.[22]

---

[21] 283 seats went to the three parties, 116 to the Seiyū Hontō, and 65
to the neutrals.

[22] Albert M. Craig considers the Katō Administration was the "high-
water mark of parliamentary government in prewar Japan." Reischauer,
Fairbank, and Craig, 574; and Scalapino describes Katō's general outlook:
"Of all political leaders, Katō was the one who had been, in many respects,
the most faithful to the cause of democratic institutions in prewar Japan. As
a great admirer of English institutions he had long championed the concepts
of 'pure party' Cabinets, subordination of bureaucratic forces, and the importance of political opposition and debate.... Certainly there were few others
of his own group who could reach his degree of understanding and acceptance
of democratic principles." Scalapino, 228–229.

POPULAR ASPIRATIONS FOR MODERNITY

The emergence of the masses, the establishment of parliamentary democracy, and the growing tendency toward privatization and individualization were only some of the most conspicuous aspects of Taishō society. Beneath them there was a new spirit. New slogans such as "Democracy," "Freedom," and "Modernization" were exalted. Bourgeois-democratic culture and civilization seemed triumphant in the urban areas. Expressing this spirit, Western-style rooms for entertaining were added to homes. Red or blue, instead of traditional black, tile-roofed houses began to attract people's attention. A study group for opera was born in 1903 and developed into the popular Asakusa Opera, which performed Verdi's *Rigoletto*, Bizet's *Carmen*, and many others. The girls' musical revues at Takarazuka and in Tokyo became a new attraction. Dance halls mushroomed. The so-called *mobo* and *moga* (modern boys and modern girls) with Western-style hair and clothes strolled through the streets.[23] In accordance with such Western fashions, new businesses such as beauticians and barbers specializing in Western hairstyles, and restaurants serving Western dishes also flourished. It was in this kind of lively, liberal and modern milieu that popular demands for parliamentary democracy and internationalism became vocal, which in turn were to result in the "Shidehara Diplomacy."[24]

---

[23] The typical style of the *mobo* in Taishō Japan was to grow long hair, whiskers and beard and to wear thick, black-framed Lloyd glasses and bellbottomed trousers, a practice which reminds us of today's hippies.

[24] As to more account of Taishō culture and social atmosphere, see Minami Hiroshi, *Taishō Bunka* (Taishō culture; Tokyo, 1965); Yanagida Kunio, *Meiji Taishō-shi: Sesōhen* (Meiji Taishō history: social features; Tokyo, 1931); and Yanagida Kunio and Ōfuji Tokihiko, *Sesō-shi* (A history of social features; Tokyo, 1943).

THE WATERSHED

As we have seen, modernity and democracy were popular in the Taishō era, but this does not mean traditionalism subsided completely. On the contrary, as modern and Western influences penetrated more deeply, to that extent the vociferous protests of the traditionalists increased. Toward the end of Taishō, Yabuki Keiki (1879–1939), a noted journalist and historian, candidly observed this contest between the two forces and wrote:

> Today's Japan, where airplanes exhibit the excellent invention of the twentieth century, fly in the sky and where farmers still use farming tools several hundred years old, has produced an interesting society from various view points. To begin with, the Meiji Restoration was a combination of restoration and reformation — the Imperial Restoration on the one hand and the opening of the country with a progressive spirit on the other. "Restoration" means to turn back and "progressiveness" means to advance forward. In other words, the former is to reflect upon our history and the latter is to cherish the future ideal. Japan at the time of the Meiji Restoration stood at such a crossroads of national destiny. However, the same currents of conflicting thoughts still continue today. For fifty-eight years, through the eras of Meiji and Taishō, like ever-changing pictures on the Japanese revolving lantern, Japan has been vacillating between reflection on the past and on progressiveness in the future.... Through a number of changes in art, literature, customs, and manners Japan is still vacillating between the two. This vacillation is not contained in just social and ideological problems....[25]

---

[25] Yabuki Keiki, "Kanreki no Toshi ni Chikazuku Shin-Nihon" (A new Japan soon to celebrate her sixty-first birthday), *The Asahi-Shimbun*, January 1, 1926. Yamakawa Hitoshi (1880–1958), a socialist-communist leader, also observed two opposing forces existing in Japan during this time: the force of "feudalistic-traditionalism" and that of "progressive-reformation." Yamakawa further classified the latter force into modernization (or Westernization) and

The latter half of the 1920's was the peak of popular aspirations for democracy and modernization on the one hand and the upsurge of traditionalism on the other. The fact that Shidehara Kijūrō and Tanaka Giichi alternated in the Foreign Ministry — Shidehara was Foreign Minister from June 1924 to April 1927, and from July 1929 to December 1931, and Tanaka came in between the two terms of Shidehara — itself reflected the see-saw competition within the society.

PROTESTS FROM TRADITIONALISTS

In December 1926, the insane Taishō Emperor died and the young Crown Prince was enthroned. Traditionalists proclaimed it the "Shōwa Restoration," and began to turn back the social tide which had opposed them. A number of factors contributed to this reaction.

The end of the Great War soon brought the end of Japan's war boom. The Great Kantō Earthquake of September 1923, which destroyed more than 400,000 houses and either killed or injured about 1.5 million people, caused further economic hardships. From that time a chronic depression developed. In the spring of 1927 came a financial crisis in which many banks, including such major ones as the Bank of Taiwan, collapsed. Accompanying these economic difficulties was the problem of increasing unemployment. In 1927 the percentage of unemployed

---

proletarian revolution. But, he stated, the attempts at national reformation by Westernization and modernization exhibited in such activities as "wearing Western suits instead of Japanese *haori*...or eating bread at breakfast ..., etc.," were trifling matters. In between the two major contesting forces, one to reform the nation thoroughly, i.e., the proletarian revolution, and the other to preserve the "old" Japan, those small attempts at modernization would soon be blown away "just like papers or leaves in a storm." See Yamakawa Kikue and Yamakawa Shinsaku (eds.), *Yamakawa Hitoshi Zenshū* (A complete collection of Yamakawa Hitoshi's works; Tokyo, 1968), V, 78.

white-collar workers was 5.79; that of blue-collar workers was
7.51; and that of day-laborers as high as 40.45. The total number
of unemployed in 1930 reached between 2.4 and 2.6 million.[26]
Even those fortunate enough to have jobs also had to suffer economic hardships. The most graphic account of depression during
this period is given by the steady fall of prices. *The Asahi Shimbun* of May 12, 1926, recorded:

> It is the fall of prices of various commodities that clearly indi-
> cates the economic depression of these days. At this time last year,
> the price of raw silk was about ¥ 1,888; now it is about ¥ 1,500.
> Rice which was on the 40-yen level, now has fallen below the 37-yen
> mark. The price of cotton yarn declined from 280-90 to 240–50 yen.
> According to an investigation by the Bank of Japan, the general
> wholesale price index declined from 264 last April to 239 this April.

If the salary scale remained the same, life would have been
very good for wage earners. However, the loss of profit to business
caused by the fall of commodity prices directly affected workers

---

26   In 1927, in terms of the length of unemployment, 12.6 percent of the
unemployed had to look for jobs for more than one year, and 12.9 percent of them
had waited for over six months before they could obtain any job. Abe Isoo
(1865–1949), a Christian leader of labor-socialist movements reported the
acute sense of unemployment crisis as follows:
    "Hitherto, the jobless workers at the City Employment Security Office
    waited quietly for their turn when job-tickets were distributed. But
    nowadays, because people are suffering the 'unemployment-hell,' and
    because they can at best barely obtain work every seven or ten days,
    workers storm offices at Kotobashi, Tamahime and Shinjuku from about
    three o'clock in the morning. At seven o'clock, when the door is opened,
    they dash into the office screaming and outdoing one another, scrambling
    for the hundred or so tickets available. No matter how many police are
    in attendance, the struggle gets out of control. It is said that blood is
    often shed in the fight for tickets at the Kotobashi office. Yet, more
    than half cannot get any job and have to go home empty-handed."
Not only unskilled workers, but college graduates had an equally difficult time
in finding jobs. In March 1923, 72 percent of the college graduates in the
liberal arts found jobs, but in 1926 the figure dropped to 52 percent and in 1928
to 46.7 percent. Even in scientific fields, the figure declined from 88 percent in
1923 to 73.3 percent in 1928. Ōhara Shakai Mondai Kenkyū-sho (ed.), *Nihon
Rōdō Nenkan, 1929* (Japan Labor Yearbook), 4–5; *Ibid., 1927*, 4; Abe Isoo,
Shitsugyō Mondai (Problems of unemployment; Tokyo, 1929), 34–37; Ōuchi
Hyōe, "Keizai-shi" (Economic history) in Yanaihara Tadao (ed.), *Gendai Nihon
Shōshi* (A short history of modern Japan; Tokyo, 1953), 109–121. See Appendix
XII and XIII.

whose salaries were lowered or who were discharged. According to *The General Survey of Japan's Economic Statistics*, the salary index of 47 different kinds of jobs in Tokyo dropped from 115.8 in 1924 to 108.8 in 1926. The government survey of 1926–27 indicates that laborers had to spend 81.15percent of their income for the absolute necessities of life, i.e., food, rent, fuel, electricity, clothing and medicine; the families of white-collar workers, 76.86 percent. Furthermore, out of 3,210 working-class families 624 (= 19.75percent) were in debt; among white-collar workers, 20.38 percent were in debt.[27] Moreover, the growing unemployment created an abundant labor supply, which in turn worsened the working condition of workers. Even the governmental research program on the working conditions of female workers in the spinning industry had to report:

> Workers must suffer that monotonous job all day from dawn to seven or eight o'clock at night.... Having finished the job and eaten supper, taken a bath, when they reached the dormitory, it is already about nine o'clock and it is time to turn off light.... Even if they have one or, rarely two hours, because of their exhaustion they have no energy to read or to write...to say nothing of time to go out for exercising or sun bathing. Two days off in a month are spent even more busily by doing washing and other necessary work.... Indeed, we cannot but sympathize with them.[28]

The mass-media also revealed a dark "image" of society.

---

[27] Ōmichi Hiroo (ed.), *Nihon Keizai Tōkei Sōkan* (A general survey of Japanese economic statistics; Osaka, 1930), 920; *Nihon Rōdō Nenkan, 1929,* 8–10.

[28] In November 1925, 6,500 workers at the Fuji Gas Spinning Factory at Kawasaki entered into a labor dispute. Workers said, "The factory is like a prison and female workers are treated even worse than prisoners." In this factory, it was reported, the staple food was composed of 70percent wheat and only 30percent rice. At breakfast the side dishes were only a bowl of soup and pickles. Out of 21 meals a week, unskinned potatoes and cooked seaweed were served at 16 meals, and nothing else. The workers' average monthly income was 20 yen (the national average income of families with four members was 76.56 yen in 1921). The working condition of miners in Kyushu and Hokkaido was particularly miserable. The Engel's Coefficient was 50.5percent among diggers, and 55.6percent among carriers in 1925. Mori Kiichi, *Rōdōsha no Seikatsu* (Laborers' life; Tokyo, 1963), 126–128.

The Asahi Shimbun of August 4, 1926, for example, wrote in an editorial:

> Among various social incidents those which have particularly drawn our attention are the suicide of a total family in Nakano, the murder of a wife and children by a husband in Kyoto, the case of using forged notes at Takada, the robbery of a man by another man and his wife. Although they chose different ways, they have all suffered the same misery, hard living which drove them to those crimes. It is obvious that the extreme difficulty of living leads people either to suicide or to crime.... Such suicides are very different in nature from the ordinary suicides of *taedium vitae*. Children are victimized by the misery. The incidents at Nakano and Kyoto are examples of such cases. The man who used forged notes was renting a room in another person's house, and the robbery couple were loafers without settled habitation. All lost jobs and many were forced to commit crimes in order to survive. It is obvious that none have committed crimes in order to enjoy extravagance, but rather for the sake of compelling necessities of life.

The Labor Yearbook of 1926 also reported a sense of crisis:

> Skilled workers are being discharged. Unemployed skilled workers are forced to become day laborers. This situation itself is miserable. And yet, this year even the unemployment of day laborers has increased. Authorities are at a loss in their struggle to discover some temporary measures. When things have come to this pass, it is more than just misery. In this way, this year has turned into the next without even a slight sign of hope in the future.[29]

Owing to such aggravated economic conditions, the bright, gay and exciting atmosphere of the Taishō era gradually disappeared and dark, gloomy conservatism began to prevail.[30]

The leftist movements which had gradually become powerful since the end of Meiji more directly stimulated the traditionalists'

---

[29] *Nihon Rōdō Nenkan, 1926*, Preface i-ii.

[30] With regard to the economic conditions during this period, see Ōshima, II, 107–191; Kajinishi Mitsuhaya *et al.* (eds.), *Nihon Shihonshugi no Botsuraku* (The decline of Japanese capitalism; Tokyo, 1960), III, 207–233.

protest. Toward the end of the era, as if foretelling the end of Meiji absolutism, a group of anarchists and socialists plotted to assassinate the Emperor (the Kōtoku Shūsui Incident). A similar *lèse-majesté* affair occurred again in December 1923, when an anarchist attempted to kill the Crown Prince (the Toranomon Incident). To anarchists the Emperor was the symbol of all the authority that had to be destroyed. Communists and socialists also attacked the Imperial Institution, though for different reasons. To them the Emperor was the symbol of "feudal relations," the destruction of which was the first prerequisite for their revolution. In addition to this, they also regarded the Emperor as the spearhead of imperialism. They believed that the Emperor had always instigated Japan's imperialistic wars. So, for example, the communist organ, *The Red Flag* declared:

> Through the people's struggle against imperialistic wars, through their struggle for the protection of the Soviet League and of the Chinese Revolution, let us destroy the Emperor and the Buddhist priests who instigate imperialism![31]

Either way, both anarchists and communist-socialists directly challenged the *kokutai* which the traditionalists revered.

In the first year of Taishō (1912) the Japanese Federation of Labor, Yūaikai (the Friendly Society), was organized. In December 1920 the Japan Socialist League (Nihon Shakaishugi Dōmei), in the next year the Dawn Communist (Gyōmin Kyōsantō), and in the summer of 1922 the Japan Communist Party was organized. Many leftist journals, such as *Studies of Socialism* (*Shakaishugi Kenkyū*), *The Vanguards* (*Zen'ei*), *The Proletariat* (*Musan Kaikyū*), *The Labor Union* (*Rōdō Kumiai*) were published and widely circulated. Between 1922 and 1924 the conservative governments headed by Admirals Katō, Yamamoto, and the President of the Privy Council, Kiyoura, conducted mass arrests of communists and destroyed the Communist Party. From the middle of 1924

---

[31] *Akahata*, I, 264.

to early 1927, however, the party governments headed by Katō Takaaki and Wakatsuki Reijirō (1866–1949) took more liberal attitudes toward the leftists, and their activities once again revived.[32] In 1926, the Communist Party was reorganized and the leftist journals flourished. In the same year, an anarchist group raided the Ginza, the shopping center of Tokyo.[33] Many other leftist parties and associations mushroomed for the first general election based upon the Universal Manhood Suffrage Bill scheduled for 1928.[34] Labor disputes (including sabotage) increased from 584 cases with 85,909 participants in 1922 to 1,260 with 127,267 workers in 1926. Labor unions swelled as well. In 1921 there were 300 unions with 103,412 members, but the figure increased to 505 with 309,493 members in 1927.[35]

---

[32] The Katō Cabinet abolished Article 17 of the Public Peace Police Law which had made it illegal to strike, passed a National Health Insurance Law, a Factory Law and a Labor Disputes Conciliation Law. However, it is also noteworthy that the same government simultaneously introduced the so-called Peace Preservation Law as well.

[33] After the Amakasu Incident of 1923 — in which Ōsugi Sakae, an anarchist leader, his wife and a nephew were killed — anarchist activities declined partly due to the government's pressure and partly due to the Japanese Bolshevists' victory over the anarcho-syndicalists. However, Ōsugi's followers like Mizunuma Kūma and Iwasa Sakutarō still continued disruptive activities. This particular case was caused by an anarchist group called the Black Youth League (Kokushoku Seinen Renmei) on January 31, 1926. *The Asahi Shimbun* described the incident, "The Ginza became a war-front. Tough gangs raged through the street wildly, as if there were no police force to stop them."

[34] Such leftist parties as the Socialist Mass Party (Shakai Minshutō), Japan Labor-Farmer Party (Nihon Rōnōtō), and the Labor-Farmer Party (Rōdō Nōmintō) were organized. The first party was a democratic socialist party established by Abe Isoo and Yoshino Sakuzō, and the last one was the most radical one among the three, basically under the communist control. In April 1924 the Japan Fabian Society was founded, and the Labor Union Council of Japan (Nihon Rōdōkumiai Hyōgikai), a more leftist union league than the Fabian Society, was organized in May of the next year. Labor-socialist youths established the All-Japan Proletarian Youth League (Zen Nihon Musan Seinen Dōmei) in December, 1925. The proletarian cultural movement, too, became powerful, and the All-Japan Federation of Proletarian Artists (Zen Nihon Musansha Geijutsu Dōmei) — commonly known as NAPF — was organized during the same month. After 1923, leftist student associations also mushroomed at various universities and high schools. They were respectively incorporated into the Socialist Students Federation (Gakusei Shakai Kagaku Rengōkai) and the High School Alliance (Kōtō Gakkō Renmei) in 1924.

Agrarian society had been the repository of old traditions. And yet, even in this area dangerous situations were brewing, which aggravated the traditionalists' anxiety. Since they highly valued order and harmony, one of the most distasteful symptoms was the growing unrest caused by tenant disputes. An even more obnoxious phenomenon for them was the penetration of leftist influence into the villages. Also disturbing was the impoverishment of the agrarian population. Traditionalists were angry, because they believed that the peasants were the most hard-working of the people and the core of *kokutai*, and yet they were unjustly suffering. Lastly, among agrarian youth there was a growing tendency to yearn for modern urban life. Many had left villages for cities to enjoy the "gay" and "frivolous" Western civilization. Even those who remained in the villages tended toward "extravagance," forgetting the traditional virtues of hard work and frugality. Traditionalists were afraid that if such conditions continued unchecked, their rural stronghold would eventually be undermined.

The effects of the depression were observed in villages as well as in cities. This period is often called the period of "agrarian panic." Peasants suffered from the steady decline of farm prices. The price of rice, for example, taking the average for three years from 1911 to 1913 as 100, was 114 in 1925, but dropped to 98 in the next year and to 87 in 1928. The general index of farm prices declined from 118 in 1925 to 93 in 1928.[36] In terms of actual income, the average price of one sack of rice (about 2 bushels) cost only about 6–7 yen in 1928. This meant that about 40

---

[35] Okazaki, Kajinishi, and Kuramochi (eds.), I, 385–386, Table 61 and 62. See more information about the leftist movements during this time in Shihōshō, Japan, *Wagakuni ni okeru Kyōsanshugi Undō-shi Gairon* (An outline of the communist movement in Japan; Tokyo, 1939); George M. Beckmann and Genji Ōkubo, *The Japanese Communist Party: 1922–1945* (Stanford, 1969); Robert A. Scalapino, *The Japanese Communist Movement: 1920–1966* (Berkeley and Los Angeles, 1967); and concerning socialist-labor movements, see George O. Totten, *The Social Democratic Movement in Prewar Japan* (New Haven, 1966).

percent of the agrarian population earned less than 60 yen from the rice crop after having paid rent to the landlord. This was worse than even the lowest income group of urban workers.[37] On the other hand, industrialization and the penetration of money economy into villages greatly harmed the self-sufficient agrarian economy. Small house-industries in villages, such as spinning and weaving, sake-brewing and soy-making, were destroyed by the neighboring big industries. To purchase these and other necessary goods, not less than 60 percent of the average farmer's produce had to be sold for cash. In addition to all this, the mounting unemployment in the cities drove many workers who had left for cities during the war boom back to the villages. As a consequence, the villages had to act as "shock absorbers" for urban unemployment.[38]

---

[36]

Table I   Price Index of Farm Products*

	1925	1926	1927	1928
Rice	114	98	94	87
Wheat	151	123	112	113
Fruits	100	98	96	106
Cocoon	138	110	83	92
General Index	118	102	95	93

* The average price of each item for three years from 1911 to 1913 is taken as 100. Kimura Seiji, *Nihon Nōgyō Kyōkō no Bunseki* (An analysis of agrarian panic in Japan; Tokyo, 1948), 25.

[37] Furthermore, the nation-wide statistics taken in 1929 indicates that about 70 percent of the farming population were either full or partial tenants, and the rent was as high as 50 percent of the crop. According to other data, 82.6 percent of the farming families in the north-east and 93.8 percent in south-western Japan had to do side jobs in order to support themselves. They worked part time for mining companies, forestry works, and various other temporary jobs, often as day-laborers. Many male farmers became emigrants (*dekasegi-nin*) during off seasons, and daughters worked in factories or even became prostitutes to borrow small amounts of money for their families. See Ōuchi Tsutomu, *Nihon Shihonshugi no Nōgyō Mondai* (Agrarian problems in Japanese capitalism; Tokyo, 1948), 13 ff.; Ono Michio, *et al.*, 39.

[38] The largest expenditure was spent for fertilizer. In 1925 a tenant farmer spent 22 percent of his total expenditure for fertilizer, but by 1929 it had increased to 25.4 percent. Moreover he had to pay 70–80 percent of this expense in cash. According to the investigation of the Ministry of Commerce and Industry, chemical fertilizer consumption increased greatly in comparison to natural organic fertilizer. For instance, in 1920 the ratio between bean-refuse and ammonium sulfate was about 31 : 4, but the ratio had increased in favor of the latter steadily and by 1928 it reached a ratio of 30 : 12. Moreover, the price of chemical fertilizer was controlled by the monopoly of a few giant companies — as

It was because of these circumstances that agrarian unrest grew. In 1917, there were only 85 cases of tenant disputes, but in 1926 the number increased to 2,751 cases involving more than 151,000 peasants.[39] Moreover, peasant riots were often instigated by Marxist-oriented tenant unions, which also grew rapidly. In 1911 there were only 41 unions, but by 1920 the number had increased to 352, and then to 3,926 with 346,693 members in 1926. Many of them were integrated into the Japan Farmers Union (Nihon Nōmin Kumiai) which was established in April, 1922 by Sugiyama Motojirō (1885–1964) and Kagawa Toyohiko (1888–1960).[40] The leftist-oriented tenant movement was menacing to traditionalists not only because of its increasing size but also because of its increasing radicalization. In 1922,

---

indicated earlier, the monopolization of industries through cartel, trust and concern systems advanced greatly during this period.

Table II   Increase of Chemical Fertilizer

	Bean-refuse	Ammonium Sulfate
1920	31, 051*	4, 140
1921	33, 660	4, 549
1922	36, 941	4, 473
1923	40, 681	6, 409
1924	34, 421	6, 780
1925	31, 560	8, 111
1926	40, 269	10, 655
1927	35, 712	10, 273
1928	30, 991	12, 174

* million *kan* unit. Kimura Seiji, 15.

[39] See Appendix XVI.

[40]

Table III   Japan Farmers Union**

	Branches	Members
1922	96	6, 131
1923	304	25, 711
1924	694	51, 806
1925	—	
1926	3013	239, 329

** Kuroda Toshio and Ikeda Tsuneo, *Nihon Nōmin Kumiai Undō-shi* (A history of the Japanese farmers' union movement; Tokyo, 1949), 60.

Table IV   Tenant Union***

	Unions	Members
1920	352	—
1921	681	—
1922	1114	—
1923	1534	163, 931
1924	2337	232, 125
1925	3496	307, 106
1926	3926	346, 693

*** *Ibid.*, 17.

Sugiyama Motojirō, the founder of the Japan Farmers Union, stated the reason for the necessity of organizing the union as follows:

> To produce rice and wheat is the main occupation of Japanese tenants. Yet, we are not eating rice or wheat contently.... After pain and toil we finally harvest the crops, only to put them into the granaries of the landlords who do not work, and we have to eat grass and millet.[41]

However, already in 1925, the Japan Farmers Union had become much more radical and called for "the eradication of landlordism and the nationalization of all farm land." In December of the same year, the Union organized its own political party, the Farmer-Labor Party (Nōmin-Rōdōtō) and advocated, "The emancipation of the proletariat!"[42]

The long-awaited "parliamentary democracy" by the Taishō liberals was not working as well as had been expected, either. As soon as party government began, it fell into the abyss of scandal and corruption. Representatives in the Diet shouted, heckled and exchanged rootings, causing frequent pandemonium, and the newspapers daily reported the struggles among parties with plentiful ugly cartoons. The period between 1926 and 1927 is often called "the years of unprecedentedly ugly strife" in modern Japanese political history.

To sketch the political scene during this period: The coalition government already began to collapse in the late spring of 1925 for a number of reasons. The government was by nature a precarious one, since each party tried to seek its own exclusive power against others. Moreover, the parties, having finally succeeded in establishing the party politics and having achieved the enactment of the Universal Manhood Suffrage Law (May 5, 1925), lost the common ground with which to continue the united front. Now the major fight had to take place among parties rather than

---

[41] *Ibid.*, 28–45; Aoki Keiichirō (Keiichi), *Nihon Nōmin Kumiai Undō-shi* (A history of the Japanese farmers' union movement; Tokyo, 1931), 24.
[42] *Ibid.*

against the old nonpartisan elements. In addition to these, there was the personnel problem. The coalition government had been barely supported by three pillars, Katō Takaaki (1860–1926) of the Kenseikai, Takahashi Korekiyo (1854–1936) of the Seiyūkai, and Inukai Tsuyoshi (Tsuyoki, 1855–1932) of the Kakushin Club. However, it was set on a shaky foundation, when aggressive Tanaka Giichi became the Seiyūkai's chairman replacing more moderate Takahashi in April 1925, and when the Kakushin Club, the mediating organ between the Seiyūkai and the Kenseikai, split and Inukai joined the Seiyūkai.[43]

The two major contesting parties clashed headlong over the tax reform plan, and in August 1925, Katō formed the Kenseikai's one-party Cabinet. In January 1926, due to Katō's death, Wakatsuki Reijirō, who had been the Minister of Home Affairs in the Katō Administration, was appointed to be the new Prime Minister, in spite of the Seiyūkai's assertion that their chairman, Tanaka, should have been appointed. Out of vexation and resentment the Seiyūkai's attack upon Wakatsuki's Kenseikai Government became more frantic than before. The Seiyū Hontō's participation in this power struggle made the situation even more complicated. This party was just as antagonistic as the Seiyūkai toward the Kenseikai, but at the same time mutual enmity between the Seiyū Hontō and the Seiyūkai had been deep ever since the two split from the original Seiyūkai. Finally, the parties, having exhausted their long-term aims, i.e., the establishment of party politics and the enactment of the Universal Manhood Suffrage Law, could not find new slogans to identify themselves with and with which to discipline their members within each party. Such goal-less situations tended to produce the induction of party mem-

---

[43] Tanaka, as we shall see, had an uncompromising spirit and strong ambitions. Not being satisfied with his position as the head of the number two party, he was determined to come into power. On June 20, 1925, according to the new militant leadership of Tanaka, the Seiyūkai held an extraordinary meeting and declared that from now on the party would never modify its own policies for the sake of maintaining the coalition government.

bers by bribery and frequent splits and alliances, resulting in bitter enmities among parties.[44] Moreover, the parties could not but worry about their future status in the next general election under the Universal Manhood Suffrage Law.

Under these circumstances, competition among parties became increasingly tense. And yet, without concrete goals and principles of their own, the parties did not know what to compete for, except in the matter of denouncing their opponents. Hence, their desire for power, anxiety, and the aimless situation tended to drive them into the senseless conduct of disclosing their opponents' scandals and corruption, both "true" and "false," instead of debating the real political problems. A slander begot a slander and disclosure of scandal led to the disclosure of another scandal, and the political mud-slinging struggle among the Dietmen reached a climax in March of 1926. Just to illustrate the actual operation of "Japanese" parliamentary democracy during this period: On March 7, 1926, for example, under the heading "Tanaka (Giichi) Incident Placed on the Agenda: Ferocity Reigns Over the House!" *The Asahi Shimbun* reported that for the anticipated physical fights the Seiyūkai changed the order of seats so that young strong members could sit in front. The Kenseikai, in response, ordered all young Dietmen to wear Western clothes instead of long-sleeved Japanese clothes so that they could move quickly when a fight occurred. Simultaneously both parties smuggled

---

[44] In January 1924, the Seiyūkai split, over the issue of whether it should support the Kiyoura Cabinet, into the Seiyūkai and the Seiyū Hontō. The Kakushin Club also split in May 1925, due to its internal schism and Chairman Inukai gave up his seriously-weakened party and joined the Seiyūkai. In late 1925 twenty-three members of the Seiyū Hontō led by Hatoyama Ichirō (1883–1959) withdrew, organized an independent party called the Dōkōkai, made an alliance with the Seiyūkai, then finally in February 1926 joined the Seiyūkai. As the result, the total seats of the Seiyūkai in the House of Representatives increased from 135 to 160 — two members from a minor party also joined the Seiyūkai at the same time with the Dōkōkai —, and became only four seats short of the Kenseikai. The rivalry between the Seiyūkai and the Kenseikai naturally became extremely tense on the one hand, and the relations between the Seiyūkai and the remaining members of the Seiyū Hontō, on the other hand, became more bitter than ever before.

March 7, 1926 *Ōsaka Asahi*

March 9, 1926 *Ōsaka Asahi*

many rough nonparliamentary men into the hall for the fight. On March 9, the indignant Seiyūkai, in retaliation for the Kenseikai's and the Seiyū Hontō's action of putting the Tanaka Incident on the agenda, charged that Nakano Seigo (1886–1943) of the Kenseikai had received some political funds from the U.S.S.R. and called the Kenseikai as well as the Seiyū Hontō members "a bunch of traitors!" Excitement increased in the House, and because the Seiyūkai appeared to attack Nakano physically, his seat was changed from the center of the hall to the rear corner, making the seats of the Seiyū Hontō as the "buffer zone" against the direct attack from the Seiyūkai.[45] On March 11, the same newspaper reported that after repeated pandemonium the session was resumed for the fourth time. It was already after ten o'clock at night. But the Seiyū Hontō once again tried to bring forward a disciplinary motion against the Seiyūkai's speaker who called his opponents "traitors." The Seiyūkai members at once stood up and many rushed to attack the Seiyū Hontō. The House Speaker desperately rang the bell to restore order, but in vain. Pandemonium increased. Some Dietmen escaped from the hall, only to find another fight which had been started by nonparliamentary members outside of the hall. Some Dietmen were hit on the head by clubs and others by shoes. Guards tried desperately to intervene among Dietmen fighting with overcoat racks and other articles nearby. The Japanese parliament became a bloody arena.[46]

---

[45]   On the next day *The Asahi Shimbun* printed a cartoon of Dietmen fighting in feudal suits of armor and ridiculed them by giving a satirical verse: "*Ikani rikken kokkai no tōin mo koreja te ga todokumai*." The verse had two meanings, "No matter how big a swing a man might have, he cannot reach [Nakano] in this situation," and "Even though a constitutional Diet was introduced to Japan as a system, it would be hardly attainable in reality under these circumstances."

[46]   On the following day, in the meeting of the Seiyūkai Dietmen, the floor leader, Yamamoto Jōtarō (1867–1936) thanked the members for their "courageous fight" and said, "Due to the irrational action of our opponents, the session was thrown into an unexpected confusion. But, thanks to your temperance and brave deeds, our party could preserve our honor. I hope you will attend more diligently to your duties with this spirit and courage." In the meantime, the Kenseikai Dietmen at their assembly spoke excitedly that the time had come

In the interval between this and the next session of the Diet (the Fifty-second, December 1926-March 1927) the newspapers were filled with investigations of scandals and corrupt acts committed by the representatives. To introduce only some of the most important incidents: In the so-called Three Million Yen Incident, Tanaka Giichi, the chairman of the Seiyūkai, was suspected of having collected his political funds by promising to make the donors members of the House of Peers and giving them various bribes when he became Prime Minister. In the Umeda Kan'ichi Incident, General Yamanashi Hanzō (1864–1944), a close friend of Tanaka Giichi, asked Umeda, a member of the Seiyū Hontō, to induce members of the Seiyū Hontō to join the Seiyūkai by giving them a considerable amount of money. The money used for this was believed to have come from the Army secret service funds. The Matsushima Licenced Quarter Incident was perhaps the worst of all, involving all three major parties, the Kenseikai, the Seiyūkai, the Seiyū Hontō, bankers, realty brokers and the governor of Osaka. According to the original accusation by a minor party, cadres of the three major parties and government officials had made arrangements to let some realty companies make huge profits by moving the licenced quarter at Matsushima to places owned by the realty companies. In return, the bankers and brokers paid remuneration to those politicians who had helped them.

In these and other scandals many leading party members were suspected. And yet clear evidence was never brought forth except to produce some victims among minor officials, which made the public more dissatisfied. By the winter of 1926, the public had become completely disgusted with and alienated from the existing party politics. Except for scandals, bloody strife,

to prepare for the open physical fight, and that they could no longer give ears to staffs' request for "perseverance." The members of the Seiyū Hontō agreed that they would prepare for self-defense against "the roughs and scoundrels" who destroyed the constitutional government.

and the so-called *machiai-seiji* — a Japanese political custom in which important decisions were made secretly at *machiai* (secret meeting place) instead of in the Diet — nothing tangibly beneficial had been offered them by their representatives. And yet, the Fifty-second session was no different from the previous one. Hisses and hecklings were tirelessly repeated. Proceedings were incessantly disrupted and the Diet was often thrown into chaos.[47] Although many people still cherished a hope of finally executing the Universal Manhood Suffrage Law which, they thought, would destroy these corrupted "old" parties, traditionalists, taking advantage of this opportunity, began to persuade people that a Western-style political system was unsuitable to the Japanese nature and tradition. Even Ozaki Yukio (1859–1954), known as the leading proponent of parliamentary democracy, lamented, "Since my youthful days, I have dreamed of founding a political party. But under present circumstances, party politics itself can choose no other course but its own destruction."[48]

---

[47] For example, *The Asahi Shimbun* reported the pandemonium of March 25, 1927:
"The Seiyūkai strongly hooted at Kiyose Ichirō, the Speaker, and made big noises. Tazaki of the Shinsei Club [of which Kiyose was a member] reviled the Seiyūkai in support of Kiyose. Then, Itano, a member of the Seiyūkai, threw paper-stones at Tazaki, and the latter angrily dashed to the seats of the Seiyūkai to denounce the party. At that time, Kaihara, another Seiyūkai member, suddenly jumped over his desk to strike Tazaki. The guards intervened between the two fighting men. But, Kaihara once again tried to beat Tazaki and at the same time ten odd Seiyūkai members ran after the escaping Tazaki in the Diet hall ...[the Diet was thrown into complete chaos]. Several members of the Seiyūkai fell on Kiyose.... Horikiri and Hirose hit Kiyose hard on the head, while another Seiyūkai member tore Kiyose's notes into pieces, and a few more dashed to the floor...."

[48] *The Asahi Shimbun* also bitterly criticized the existing political parties: "The whole people acutely observe the corruption of existing political parties. They are only concerned with their own interests, and not the people's welfare. The Diet is like a bullring, and partisans gather only to satisfy their own private interests. They completely disregard political principles and fidelity in their pursuit of material interests. Their constant combination and separation according to their changing interests is like the behavior of prostitutes [who run after money and patrons.]... They are either egoistic utilitarians incarnate or inhuman machines which only function in the scramble for political power. Nobody, except themselves, would dare to respond to their frantic acts and slogans. Their activities are nothing but a political play in which the people

In addition to all of these factors which incited the tradition-alists' anger, there were some distasteful "mass phenomena" developing in the larger cities, especially Tokyo. Moderniza-tion had brought the "Age of Enlightenment" to the Taishō society, but at the same time had worked as a "disruptive" force by cutting off individuals from the traditional community. A trend from "development to decay" was observed after the Great Kantō Earthquake, a tendency which further degenerated in the early 1930's. Japanese society in the 1920's saw "the beginning of radio broadcasting; the proliferation of *baa* (bars), *kafue* (cafés), *kissaten* (tearooms); the rapid growth of street buses and suburban railways; the beginning of the subway system (1927); the growth of department stores and modern business offices — all of these were," as Maruyama points out, "*après-la-sismique* phenomena."[49] All events pointed to the full-fledged growth of "mass society" and the emergence of the "glob of humanity." The rapid transformation of society, and injection of "modern" and "foreign" thoughts and values created a keen sense of atomiza-tion, alienation and *anomie* among sensitive intellectuals and the younger generation.[50] The *lèse-majesté* affairs, the earthquake,

---

are completely disinterested." *The Asahi Shimbun*, January 1, 1926. The above section on the political scene is based upon the day by day reports of *The Asahi Shimbun, The Mainichi Shimbun* as well as *The Asahi Nenkan, The Mainichi Nenkan, The Jiji Shimpō*, and *Dai-Nihon Teikoku Gikai-shi* (The Diet record of Great Japanese Empire), ed. Dai-Nihon Teikoku Gikai-shi Kankō-kai (Tokyo, 1930), VIII–XVII. See also Peter Duus, 214–235; Scalapino, *Democracy and the Party Movement in Prewar Japan*, 227–235; Naikaku Kambō, Japan (ed.), 85–119; Rōyama Masamichi, *Seiji-shi* (A political history; Tokyo, 1940), 389–465.

[49] Maruyama in Jansen, 518.

[50] The following poems of Ishikawa Takuboku (1885–1912) vividly express this sense of loneliness and alienation in rapidly developing urban socie-ties.

こみ合へる電車の隅に	In the corner of a crowded streetcar
ちぢこまる	Cramped
ゆふべゆふべの	Night after night
我のいとしさ	Only myself to love
浅草の夜のにぎはいに	At night in Asakusa
まぎれ入り	Wandered in among the noisy crowd

and the chronic depression further increased the general sense of uneasiness, anxiety and crisis.

Under these circumstances, various new phenomena began to appear in the society. In the summer of 1926, for example, *The Asahi Shimbun* reported:

> Bloody incidents like murders and suicides have continuously occurred from late spring to early summer, every year. This is clearly indicated by the daily incidents reported on the third page of the newspapers. But this year these incidents have not decreased even during the midst of summer.... Furthermore, we have noticed that these incidents are deeply rooted in the extreme hardships of life.[51]

In December the same newspaper reported that the number of insane people was increasing, amounting to 5,290 in police custody in Tokyo alone. All 13 mental hospitals in Tokyo were filled and had no capacity even for a single additional patient. Statistics verify the truth of these observations. The total number of suicides increased from 13,377 in 1923 to 15,639 in 1927 (in terms of percentage from 0.023 to 0.026 in relation to the total population of respective years). Particularly significant was the fact that among various causes which motivated these people to take their own lives, weariness of life or extreme pessimism about the future was the dominant factor.[52]

Another new phenomenon was the creation of mass amuse-

まぎれ出で来し   Wandered back out
さびしき心   Even lonelier now*

*Ishikawa Takuboku, "Ichiaku no Suna" (A handful of sand), in *Gendai Nihon Bungaku Zenshū* (A collection of modern Japanese literature; Tokyo, 1954), 78. Satō Haruo in his *Tokai no Yūutsu* (Ennui of urban life, written in 1922) described the boredom and nihilistic despair of a lost urban dweller. Because the author skillfully described painful personal and social alienation, and the nervous prostration of a sensitive man, the book won the popular acclaim among the urban youths and intellectuals who shared the same feeling with the hero of the novel.

    [51]   *The Asahi Shimbun*, August 4, 1926.

    [52]   The number of suicides caused by this factor increased from 1,286 in 1923 to 1,863 in 1927, and 2,058 in 1930. *The Asahi Nenkan, 1931,* 255. The original investigation was done by the Ministry of Internal Affairs. See Appendix XVIII.

ment centers like Asakusa in Tokyo and Sennichimae in Osaka. Tremendous numbers of people gathered in the noise and confusion of these places, to forget their daily hardships, economic as well as psychological. They were motivated by some unrestrainable inner urge to "laugh" and to "drink." For example, at a *manzai* (idiotically comical talk) theater in Osaka, 530,000 people came during the year of 1929. This meant about 1,500 people a day. At a small bar in Sennichimae on a national holiday of 1928, 1.4 *koku* (about 67 gallons) of sake was consumed by about 600–700 people. In 1930, the number of people who had come to Asakusa during the year reached the 100 million mark.[53] Gonda Yasunosuke (1887–1951), a cultural anthropologist, explained the attraction of these flourishing mass-centers:

> Those who are not satisfied with the present life, those who are afraid of losing their jobs, come here to get excited, to get angry, or to share the same feeling with others. That is the world of "Asakusa."[54]

A decadent and nihilistic atmosphere prevailed over these amusement centers. *Ero kafue* (erotic cafés) and *ero baa* (erotic bars) thrived. Dance halls were filled with students, workers, and young urban dwellers. The music to which they danced was jazz imported from America. The situation was exactly like the verse of *Tokyo Kōshinkyoku* (The Tokyo March, a popular song): "dance with jazz drunk with liquor." In these bars, cafés, and dance halls, obscene and nonsensical conversations were exchanged. In theaters idiotic talks and dramas (*acharaka*) won popularity. In women's journals and magazines, the "disclosure" (*bakurokiji*) of divorces and triangular relationships became popular. Thus came the period of *ero-guro-nansensu* (eroticism, grotesqueness, and nonsense). As Katō Hidetoshi states, it was like the situation

---

[53] Katō Hidetoshi, "Atarashii Sakariba: Asakusa to Sennichimae" (New mass amusement centers: Asakusa and Sennichimae), *Shōwa-shi no Shunkan* (Great moments of Shōwa history), ed. *The Asahi Journal* (Tokyo, 1966), I, 67.

[54] *Ibid.*, 61.

in which the individual confined in a cell without any exit imagines that there is an exit. There he could dream any kind of fantasy he wished. The society of *ero-guro-nansensu* was created by this vacant delusion and hope of desperate people. Those who could not forget themselves by such "delusions" of reality — those who could not imagine this exit in the cell — became frustrated, desperate, and insane, or committed suicide.[55]

The above illustration is a general picture of Japanese society in the latter part of the 1920's: the earthquake, the *lèse-majesté* affairs, the chronic depression, the corruption of partisans, the growing agrarian unrest and labor disputes, the increasing leftist influence, the daily news of suicides, robberies, and murders, and the generally decadent, hedonistic atmosphere of urban society. In addition to this, over-population and food shortage were also recorded by the mass media. And abroad the Chinese rights-recovery movement and civil war became more and more menacing to Japan's vested interests. Shidehara's policy still remained conciliatory to the Chinese. Lastly, the youth who were to bear the burden of national responsibility were indulging themselves in "rampant individualism" and "frivolous Western fashions." From these observations traditionalists thought that the good old Japan was falling to pieces. They keenly felt the sense of "deadlock." It was from this base that their frantic efforts to "restore" the nation began: to restore the order and harmony, to restore the traditional Japanese spirits, and above all to restore the prestige of the Imperial Family. The enthronement of the young Crown Prince which they called the "Shōwa Restoration" provided them with the initial opportunity for their task.[56]

---

[55] Katō Hidetoshi, "Ero, guro, nansensu" (Eroticism, grotesqueness, and nonsense) in *Shōwa-shi no Shunkan*, I, 103–104. Many others who could neither forget themselves in the world of delusion nor commit suicide, submitted to religious power in their hope of being "saved." After late Taishō, all kinds of new — and often delusive — religions were founded in Japan. According to a survey by the Ministry of Education, there were 98 new religions and religious associations with 31, 995 believers in 1924. By 1930, the figures had increased to 414 and 281, 259 respectively.

THE RISE OF TRADITIONALISTS

It was in this environment that many powerful traditionalists emerged into the limelight: Tanaka Giichi and Ishiwara Kanji (1886–1949) from the Army; Gondō Seikyō (Seikei, 1868–1937) and Katō Kanji (1884–1965) in the rural area; Tokutomi Sohō (1863–1957), Gotō Shimpei (1857–1929), Kita Ikki (1883–1937), Ōkawa Shūmei (1886–1957), Mitsukawa Kametarō (1888–1936), Tsukui Tatsuo (1901– ?), Mori Kaku (1882–1932), to name only some of the prominent figures in the late 1920's. Some traditionalists like Tsukui Tatsuo, an intellectual leader of the new Japanism movement, strongly criticized corrupted "parliamentarism" (*gikai-chūshin shugi*) and advocated "emperorism" (*tennō-chūshin shugi*) instead. He contended:

> The concrete political expression of the Shōwa Restoration is to overthrow party politics and to establish a politics of the Imperial Way. The present purpose of the Japanism movement is to carry out this Shōwa Restoration.[57]

According to the protagonists of "Emperorism," democracy was unsuitable for Japan for two reasons: because of its inherent self-contradiction and because of its direct conflict with *kokutai*. With regard to the first cause, Western individualism, the very base of

---

[56] Traditionalists were not the only people who felt this sense of "deadlock" and "crisis." Yamakawa Hitoshi said, "What I felt during my visit to the countryside was social unrest and the uneasiness that accompanies it. This uneasiness, which is an indirect reflection of the instability of capitalism, now in the period of decline, is overflowing among the masses both in farm villages and small towns. They are seeking for something...but do not know what." From these observations the leftists as well as traditionalists felt the need of national reconstruction, though entirely in the opposite directions. George M. Beckmann and Genji Ōkubo, 69.

[57] Tsukui Tatsuo, *Nihonshugi Undō no Riron to Jissen* (Theory and practice of the Japanism movement; Tokyo, 1935), 58.

democracy, necessarily induces conflicts among individuals, between the individual and the state, and among states, for it regards
each individual's interest, happiness and freedom as the highest
values. In fact, the operation of democracy presupposes such
conflicts. The contemporary troubles of Japan's democracy were
nothing but the reflection of this innate contradiction of the system
itself. The traditionalists argued that party politics necessarily
falls into "mobocracy" (*shūgu seiji*) or "hypocritical politics"
(*giman seiji*).

With regard to the second cause, democracy contradicts the
inherent spirit of the Japanese nation. The Emperor had been
the national center from ancient times. The Japanese nation
was the united soul of the Japanese race and its nucleus of expression had always been the Emperor. Japan's politics, economics, and ethics had all to be built upon this assumption. And
the individual should be taken into consideration only for the
purpose of attaining this goal. Democracy was also unconstitu-
tional. Article 1 of the Meiji Constitution clearly states that
Japan is governed by "the line of Emperors unbroken for ages
eternal." The Emperor "granted" the Constitution to his subjects, and received the supreme power to govern Japan from his
ancestors. His power does not rest upon the theory of social
contract. Hence there is no room for a democratic interpretation
in the Meiji Constitution. Lastly, the election system is against
the Japanese virtue of modesty. Tsukui said:

> The candidate must speak much of himself as if he were the
> best person in the world and has to beg votes from people as a beggar
> would do, or otherwise he has to buy votes like a mean merchant.
> Is this really a thing for a gentleman (*kunshi*) to do? Therefore,
> candidates who stand for the election are most un-Japanese.... Thus,
> thoughtful Japanese would prefer not to join politics, and parliament
> then becomes a gathering place for scoundrels.[58]

---

[58]   *Ibid.*, 70, 18 ff.

Gotō Shimpei carried out a nationwide "Moralization Campaign," Rinrika Undō. On April 20, 1926, in the first speech of his campaign, he asserted that the most shameful events had been occurring in society, and that the Japanese nation had arrived at a deadlock. Western-oriented materialism had eroded the foundation of society and the people were indulging in frivolous fashions, forgetting the great spirit of Japanism. He said he was obliged to rise up, in spite of his age — he was sixty-eight years old — in order to create honest and sincere youths who would sacrifice themselves for the Emperor and the nation. In order to achieve this great task, traditional ethics — *jin* (Confucian love), *gi* (justice and loyalty), *wa* (harmony) and *rei* (decorum) — had to be restored to replace the Western idea of individual rights and egoism. More than one million youths were recruited to his movement.[59] Equally energetic, Kita Ikki wrote and distributed patriotic articles among the masses. He declared:

> At present the Japanese empire is faced with a national crisis unparalleled in its history; it faces dilemmas at home and abroad. The vast majority of the people feel insecure in their livelihood and they are on the verge of taking a lesson from the collapse of European societies, while those who monopolize political, military, and economic power simply hide themselves and, quaking with fear, try to maintain their unjust position...even our neighbour China, which long benefited from the protection we provided through the Russo-Japanese War, not only has failed to repay us but instead despises us.... The entire Japanese people..., should, in planning how the great Japanese empire should be reorganized, petition for a manifestation of the imperial prerogative establishing "a national opinion in which no dissenting voice is heard, by the organization of a great union of the Japanese people." Thus, by homage to the Emperor, a basis for national reorganization can be set up.[60]

---

[59] *The Asahi Shimbun*, April 21, 1926, and *The Mainichi Shimbun* of the same date. See also Gotō Shimpei, *Seiji no Rinrika* (Moralization of politics; Tokyo, 1926), *passim*.

[60] Tsunoda, De Bary, and Keene (comps.), II, 268–269.

In the Diet, too, the attack upon "frivolous Westernization" and "egoistic individualism" became vocal, and the restoration of traditional order and morality was emphasized. Shimizu Koichirō (1854–1932) in the House of Peers, for example, stressed the need for national moralization and for disciplining school children, youths as well as all teachers through military training. Another Dietman stated:

> Since about the time of the Great Kantō Earthquake a frivolous atmosphere and egoistic thoughts are filling up all quarters of our Empire. Attacks upon various existing social orders and systems have become extreme. There has been no time in our history when popular thoughts are so deteriorated and confused as they are today. Especially in the cities this tendency is strong, but even in villages where people traditionally have been simple and honest, the degradation of thoughts is gradually penetrating.

He, then, continued to assert that the traditional national spirit and morality had to be restored. "Otherwise," he warned, "these extremely frivolous fashions will be even more aggravated and the youths will no longer be able to maintain their vigor for bearing the responsibility of supporting the *kokutai*."[61]

Gondō Seikyō and Katō Kanji were the vanguards of the "Save the Village!" campaign. Katō established the Japan People's High School (Nihon Kokumin Kōtō Gakkō) in 1926. In this high school Katō made ancient Shintō the principle of education and taught Japanism to agrarian students. He was violently opposed to both Western-types of democracy and communism. He taught students that men who had *Yamato damashii* were absolutely loyal to the Emperor and to the nation, and were pure, sincere and devoted. Katō especially favored the Tokugawa men like Yoshida Shōin (1830–59), leader of the "Revere the Emperor and Love the Nation" movement; Fujita Tōko (1806–55), a leader of the "Expel the Barbarian" movement; and (Mito) Mitsukuni

---

61 *Dai Nihon Teikoku Gikai-shi*, XVI, 53–54, 59 (January 26 and February 1, 1926).

(Tokugawa Mitsukuni, 1628–1700), who sponsored the patriotic history, *Dai Nihonshi* (The Great History of Japan). Katō also advanced agrarianism, advocating "even with the threat of death not to abandon farming for the sake of the Emperor's nation." His doctrine was soon spread all over Japan. His high school produced more than 300,000 agrarian youths who went to the Continent as Volunteer Soldiers for the Cultivation of Manchuria and Mongolia (Man-Mō Kaitaku Giyū-dan).[62]

Gondō was the leader of the agrarian "Self-help" movement. He, too, strictly rejected industrialization and commercialization and exalted pure and simple agrarianism. His ideal was to estabish idyllic, autonomous communities where the Emperor and farmers could rule themselves together without various oppressive intermediary bodies, such as the central government, bureaucracy, and big industry. He was most concerned with the question of how to restore primitive and contented agrarian communities to Japan. Many who were annoyed by recent agrarian disorders and distress enthusiastically supported Gondō's "Self-help" movement. His books, *Kōmin Jichi Hongi* (The fundamental principle of self-rule by the Imperial subjects, written in 1921) and *Jichi Mimpan* (Self-government by the people, published in 1932) were considered the "bibles" of the young ultranationalists together with Kita's *Nihon Kaizō Hōan Taikō* (An Outline Plan for the Reorganization of Japan). In these books, Gondō bitterly attacked all things Western, capitalism, parliamentarism, and socialism, and instead praised indigenous Japanese tradition.[63]

---

[62] See Takeda Kiyoko, *Dochaku to Haikyō* (The indigenous and the pervert; Tokyo, 1961), 271–324; Thomas R. H. Havens, "Katō Kanji (1884–1965) and the Spirit of Agriculture in Modern Japan," *Monumenta Nipponica*, XXV, Nos. 3–4 (1970), 249–266. See also their bibliographies on Katō Kanji.

[63] Various right wing associations also became active in villages. Hirao Rikizō for example, established the All Japan Farmers Union League (Zen Nihon Nōmin Kumiai Dōmei) in March 1926 against the leftist-oriented Farmers Union. By the end of 1927, this organization already had 282 branches and 26,0000 active members. The Veterans Association and the Youths Association which Tanaka Giichi had helped to establish, were equally vociferous in protest. The former group, by revising its platform in

There was also the rise of traditionalism with deep roots in the social milieu, in concert with and to support these leaders. On February 11, 1926, a grand festival celebrating the founding of the nation based upon the Shintō myth (*Kenkokusai*) was held for the first time in Japanese history. More than forty thousand people gathered at Shiba Park, sang the national anthem, and cried "*Banzai* (Long Live the Emperor)!" According to Nagata Hidejirō (1876–1943), the former mayor of Tokyo and the promoter of the festival, the celebration was to exalt nationalistic spirit all over the nation. Japan which had been corrupted by Westernization, he thought, had to return to the ancient spirits of the time when Emperor Jimmu founded the nation two thousand five hundred and eighty-six years earlier. The general tendency of publications, too, indicated the changing popular taste. In place of translated Western novels and philosophies, books on Japanese history and on historical heroes like the Soga brothers, the forty-seven rōnins, Saigō Takamori, and Minamoto no Yoshitsune (1159–89) became popular. These were the heroes who had demonstrated *bushidō* and absolute loyalty to the Emperor.[64]

1925, made a declaration to fight against "dangerous thoughts," "frivolous Westernization," and for the preservation of *kokutai*. The latter group was also reorganized into the Greater Japan Youths Association League (Dai Nihon Rengō Seinendan) and began active campaigns against "degeneration" of rural communities. Against fierce tenant movements, landlords also stood up and held the national landlords convention. They declared themselves to fight those who instigated the "class struggle" among tenants and to make the best effort to promote the national destiny by uniting the Emperor and His subjects. *The Mainichi Shimbun*, April 23, 1926.

[64] *The Mainichi Nenkan* made the following significant report on the general tendency of publication between 1926 and 1927:

"During this period, a great number of valuable studies on Japanese culture have been published. Not only the reproduction of classics which have been well-known, but many rare books have also been published.... Simultaneously, many studies of our own culture and history based upon these classics have also been made public. These books (both original texts and commentaries) range from *Nihon Shoki* and *Manyōshū* to the Meiji Restoration covering practically every period of our history.... It is a joyful phenomenon both in terms of general development of our culture and of self-recognition of our own people that the study and publication of our classics has flourished to such an extent. This tendency seems to be heightened since the death of the Taishō Emperor and the enthronement of the present Emperor, giving an impression that a trans-

One can also observe a gradual shift in the general trend of popular amusement. The so-called Asakusa Opera came to its peak in 1923, but since then its popularity declined and the theaters had to switch to comedy. With this, the *"peragoro* culture" — the culture which was produced by students and intellectual loafers who loved opera — also faded away, and more traditional melancholy melodies like *Karesusuki* (decaying miscanthus) became popular, instead of the bright Western melodies taken from operas and Broadway shows. Enoken (Enomoto Ken'ichi) who performed *"acharaka"* — idiotic and topsy-turvy comedies — rose to stardom in Asakusa. *Acharaka* meant *achira kara ka*, "Is this really from *achira*, overseas?" What *acharaka* comedians wanted to say was that the dramas which had been performed at Asakusa may have originated in the West, but that what "we" were playing now were "Japanese" comedies, based entirely upon Japanese taste. The same tendency was recognized in the *genre* of films. The period from the end of Taishō to early Shōwa was called the "golden age of samurai movies." The samurai moviestars like Bandō Tsumasaburō, Ōkōchi Denjirō, and Hayashi Chōjirō (Hasegawa Kazuo) became the heroes of the day. In the movies they not only demonstrated their excellent swordmanship, but also such traditional values as loyalty, bravery, and self-sacrifice.[65]

formation has taken place." *The Mainichi Nenkan, 1928*, 501–508; Kikuchi Kan (Hiroshi, 1888–1948) also noticed the same "conservative" and "reactionary" tendency in the literary world. See his comments on current literature in *Chūō Kōron* (January, 1927), 267–268.

[65] Myriad traditionalistic-nationalistic associations were also organized during this period. Only to give some prominent names: In August 1919, the Yūsonsha was formed by Kita Ikki, Ōkawa Shūmei and Mitsukawa Kametarō. They swore that they would make a fundamental reform of the nation by promoting *Yamato damashii*, and by "emancipating" all Asian people from the yoke of the West. In April 1920, the Taika-kai was organized by Iwato Tomio to rebuild the nation centering around the Imperial Household, as did the ancient Taika Reform (645). Two months later, Gondō Seikyō established the Jichi Gakkai. In the same year patriotic students at Tokyo University formed the Association of Sun (Hi no kai). In the latter half of the 1920's the Gyōchi-kai by Ōkawa Shūmei; the National Essence Association (Kokuhonsha) by Hiranuma Kiichirō (1867–1952) and Mazaki Jinzaburō (1876–1956);

82 PART ONE

It was from this kind of social milieu that Tanaka Giichi first emerged as the champion of traditionalism in the Army. He, too, strongly advocated *ōdō seiji* (the Imperial Way or King's Way) and the promotion of *kokutai*. In 1923, for instance, Tanaka in his article entitled, "Exterminate All Evil Thoughts Wherever the Veterans Association Marches!" chided soldiers by saying:

> We declare that if we lose our loyalty to the Emperor and love of nation [*chūkun aikoku*], the greatest crisis will befall our Empire. In comparison with this danger, all other dangers are trifling. In my judgement of the popular trend of thought, our people today seem to be advancing toward this great danger.... Disrespecting the Veterans Association whose fundamental principles are stateism [*kokka-shugi*] and emperorism [*tennō-chūshin shugi*], recalcitrant men like traitors and anarchists are rampant. In the final analysis, this is all because we are spiritless. We must say that this is to our deep dishonor.... Now, together with all fellow-soldiers, we must ride at the head of the "thought" campaign. We must be determined to exterminate all evil thoughts which may impair the majesty of our *kokutai*. To do this is our duty during peace-time.[66]

the Yūkō-kai by Kyoto University students; the Self-Sacrificing Society for Greater Japan (Dai-Nihon Junkoku-kai) by the Used Clothes Association; the Association of One Soul (Isshin-kai) by the students at Tokyo Agricultural University; the Association of the Spirit (Tamashii-no-kai) by Takuhoku University students; all were established one after another between 1925 and 1926. In the year 1927, Shioya Keiichirō organized the Moralization Association (Meitoku-kai) with the slogan, "materialization of the Imperial Way," and Endō Tomosaburō a former anarchist now converted to an ultranationalist, formed the Imperial Flag Association (Kinki-kai). It is equally noteworthy that many prominent liberals and Westernites converted themselves to enthusiastic promoters of traditionalism: Tokutomi Sohō (Iichirō, 1863–1957) who had received a Christian education at Dōshisha (though the beginning of his conversion had already been noticed in the period of the Meiji Japanism movement); Katō Kanji, a former Christian; Uchida Kōsai who had stressed Japan's international co-operation during the Taishō period, now advocating the "autonomous diplomacy" by all means; and Takabatake Motoyuki (1886–1928), a former socialist intellectual. With regard to more information about the rightist movements, see Arahara Bokusui, *Dai-Uyoku-shi* (The great history of right wings; Tokyo, 1966), 47–138; Arahara Bokusui, *Nihon Kokka-shugi-dantai Meikan* (A dictionary of Japanese nationalist associations; Tokyo, 1963), *passim*; and Kawamura Tadao (ed.), *Shisō Mondai Nempyō* (A chronological table of ideological problems; Tokyo, 1936), 21–105.

[66] Tanaka Giichi, "Exterminate All Evil Thoughts Wherever the Veterans Association Marches!" in *Senyū* (Fellow-soldiers; December 1923).

In 1925, thanks to his rising popularity among the traditionalists, Tanaka Giichi was recruited by the Seiyūkai, which had increasingly been inclining toward the right, to head the party. After the fall of the Wakatsuki Cabinet in April 1927, as the chairman of the second largest party, Tanaka became Prime Minister, and took the leadership of Japan's diplomacy until July, 1929. Through his "positive" (*sekkyoku*) foreign and domestic policies, Tanaka was now to put his long-time aspirations into practice: the demonstration of his own type of *bushidō*, the promotion of the Imperial Way abroad and the preservation of *kokutai* at home.

The above was a brief study of the general social background — according to my methodological scheme proposed in the Introduction, this chapter is the survey of the third level, i.e., the social milieu — from which Shidehara Kijūrō and Tanaka Giichi arose. The international system approach, namely, the study of power relations abroad, alone is not sufficient to understand a nation's diplomacy. Equally important is the investigation of the domestic milieu or popular sentiments which expect and produce certain kinds of leadership, and which influence the leaders' policy making.[67] A foreign policy is determined at, as it were, "a point of contact" in mathematical terminology between the international environments and domestic circumstances. And how or in what direction the foreign policy is actually determined at that point of contact depends in the final analysis upon the elite's sub-

---

[67] Siegfried Kracauer did an interesting study of the trend of German films, in order to investigate the social milieu from which a leader like Hitler emerged. See Siegfried Kracauer, *From Caligari to Hitler, A Psychological History of the German Film* (Princeton, 1947). See also Sebastian De Grazia, *The Political Community, A Study of Anomie* (Chicago, 1948); Émile Durkheim, *Suicide, A Study in Sociology*, trans. John A. Spualding and George Simpson, ed. with an intro. George Simpson (Glencoe, III., 1962); Abram Kardiner, *The Psychological Frontiers of Society* (New York, 1959); William Kornhauser, *The Politics of Mass Society* (Glencoe, III., 1959); Hannah Arendt, *The Origins of Totalitarianism* (New York, 1951); Karl Mannheim, *Man and Society in an Age of Reconstruction* (London, 1940); Eric Hoffer, *The True Believer* (New York, 1951) and David Riesman already introduced, as theoretical references for this chapter.

jective perception of various internal and external forces and problems. In such contexts the key diplomat makes a policy so as to define his own, and at the same time his nation's identity. From this point of view there was a fundamental difference between Shidehara's and Tanaka's policies, for their personal as well as national cultural identities were mutually incompatible.

Before closing this chapter, however, it is to be noted that this period was the "watershed." The democrats and Westernites still remained powerful during this period. Among them were Yoshino Sakuzō, Genrō Saionji Kimmochi, Inoue Junnosuke (1869–1932), a democratic financier, and Kiyosawa Kiyoshi (1890–1945), an international-minded scholar of diplomatic history. Their continuing struggle against the traditionalists and Tanaka's failure in his aggressive China policy brought about the comeback of the "Shidehara Diplomacy" which lasted from July 1929 to December 1931. The competition between the two forces intensified, resulting in the assassination of Prime Minister Inukai Tsuyoshi on March 15, 1932 by a radical traditionalistic-nationalistic group called, the Blood Brotherhood League (Ketsumei-dan). The event marked the end of party politics and Japan's entrance into the period of ultranationalism. At the same time abroad, the Kwantung Army started the Manchurian Incident on September 18, 1931; established a puppet regime, Manchukuo; and Japan pushed herself on toward the "autonomous diplomacy" by withdrawing her membership from the League of Nations, in order to propound her Imperial Way to the world: the goal which Tanaka Giichi first set out to achieve.[68]

---

[68] In fact Matsuoka Yōsuke (1880–1946) who was chiefly responsible for this historical act of Japan, was Tanaka's most trusted protégé. With regard to the trend toward ultranationalism in the 1930's, see Richard Storry; Shigemitsu Mamoru; Sadako N. Ogata; Nihon Kokusai Seiji Gakkai (ed.), *Taiheiyō Sensō e no Michi* (The road to the Pacific War; Tokyo, 1962–63), I-VII; Akira Iriye, 254–303; Masao Maruyama, *Thought and Behaviour in Modern Japanese Politics*, Chaps. 1–4; Yale C. Maxon, *Control of Japanese Foreign Policy: A Study of Civil-Military Rivalry, 1930–1945* (Berkeley and Los Angeles, 1957).

PART TWO

CHAPTER 3

TANAKA GIICHI
THE MAN AND HIS IDEAS

THE MAN

Baron and retired-general Tanaka Giichi was Prime Minister
and concurrently Minister of Foreign Affairs from April 20, 1927
to July 2, 1929.[1] As a child he dreamed of becoming a person

---

[1] Some of the major works related to Tanaka's biography are: Tanaka
Giichi Denki Kankō-kai (ed.), 3 vols.; Hosokawa Ryūgen, *Tanaka Giichi* (Tokyo,
1958); Kawai Tsuguo, *Tanaka Giichi-den* (A biography of Tanaka Giichi, Tokyo,
1929); Hori Shika, *Saishō to narumade no Tanaka Giichi* (Tanaka Giichi till he
became Premier; Tokyo, 1928); Miyake Setsurei, "Tanaka Giichi-ron" (Treatise
on Tanaka Giichi), *Chūō Kōron*, (June 1927), 121–124; Oyamada Kennan,
"Tanaka Giichi-ron" (Treatise on Tanaka Giichi), *Nihon oyobi Nihonjin* (September 15, 1925), 47–58; Baba Tsunego, *Gendai Jimbutsu Hyōron*, 38–81; Baba
Tsunego, *Seikai Jimbutsu Fūkei* (A sketch of political figures; Tokyo, 1931),
396–418, 327–330; Kiya Ikusaburō, *Seikai Gojūnen no Butai-ura* (Behind the
scenes of a fifty-year political world; Tokyo, 1965), 32–127; Kokuryū-kai (ed.),
Tōa Senkaku Shishi Kiden (Records of pioneers in East Asia; Tokyo, 1966), I,
726–738, II, 743–815, III, 40–139, 264–266; Tōa Dōbun-kai (ed.), *Taishi Kaiko-
roku* (Reminiscences of China policy; Tokyo, 1936), I, 374–423, 517–607, II,
1313–1336; Ishigami Ryōhei, *Seitōshi-ron: Hara Kei Botsugo* (A history of a
political party, Seiyūkai, since the death of Hara Kei; Tokyo, 1960), *passim*;

Tanaka Giichi

like Toyotomi Hideyoshi (1536 –98) who from peasant beginnings ascended to dominate the whole of Japan, Saigō Takamori (1827–77), the samurai incarnate, and Yoshida Shōin (1830– 59), a passionate loyalist and the spiritual father of all Restoration leaders who emerged from Chōshū (present Yamaguchi Prefecture), Tanaka's birth place. Yoshida's influence upon Tanaka was especially profound: his heroism; his peasantry life-style with earnest and unsophisticated heart, but alive with the raw energy of the earth; his belief in Japan's mis-

Yamaura Kan'ichi (ed.), *Tōa Shintaisei no Senku, Mori Kaku* (A forerunner of the new order in East Asia, Mori Kaku; Tokyo, 1940), *passim;* Yamamoto Jōtarō-ō Denki Hensan-kai (ed.), *Yamamoto Jōtarō Denki* (A biography of Yamamoto Jōtarō; Tokyo, 1942), *passim;* Yamasaki Kazuyoshi, *Kuhara Fusanosuke* (Tokyo, 1939), *passim;* "Kuhara Fusanosuke-shi ni Mono o Kiku Zadan-kai" (A conversation with Mr. Kuhara Fusanosuke), *Bungei Shunjū* (April 1932), 168–184; Kuroda Kōshirō (ed.), *Gensui Terauchi Hakushaku Denki* (General and Count Terauchi's biography; Tokyo, 1920), *passim;* Tokutomi Iichirō (ed.), *Kōshaku Yamagata Aritomo-den* (A biography of Prince Yamagata Aritomo; Tokyo, 1933), 3 vols, *passim,* especially vols. II and III; Kawahara Jikichirō, *passim;* Mitarai Tatsuo, *Yamagata Aritomo* (Tokyo, 1958), *passim;* Matsushita Yoshio, *Nihon no Gumbatsu-zō* (Japanese military cliques; Tokyo, 1969), 199–232; Matsushita Yoshio, *Nihon Riku-Kaigun Sōdō-shi* (A history of disputes in the Japanese Army and Navy; Tokyo, 1966), 277–282; Matsushita Yoshio, *Nihon Gumbatsu no Kōbō* (The rise and fall of the Japanese military cliques; Tokyo, 1967), II, 165–192, III, 59– 79; Harada Kumao, I and II, *passim;* Ugaki Kazunari, *Ugaki Kazunari Nikki* (Ugaki Kazunari's diary; Tokyo, 1954), *passim;* Mitani Taichirō, "Tenkan-ki, 1918–1921, no Gaikō Shidō — Hara Kei oyobi Tanaka Giichi o Chūshin to shite" (Diplomatic leadership in a transitional period, 1918–1921 — Hara Kei and Tanaka Giichi), *Kindai Nihon no Seiji Shidō* (Political leadership of modern Japan), eds., Shinohara Hajime and Mitani Taichirō (Tokyo, 1965), 293–374; Etō Shinkichi, "Kei-Hō-sen Shadan Mondai no Gaikō Katei — Tanaka Gaikō to sono Haikei" (Diplomatic process concerning the problem of intercepting the Peking-Mukden line — Tanaka Diplomacy and its background), *ibid.,* 375–429.

sion to turn back the West and found a world empire under the
Imperial Rule; and his direct actionist attitude characterized by
some spectacular act of bravery.[2]

Tanaka was nicknamed "Don Quixote" or "*Oraga Shushō.*"
Like Don Quixote, he was ambitious and somewhat of a megalomaniac. He always dreamed of things on a grand scale and disliked petty things. "*Oraga Shushō*" means "I, the Prime Minister" in the Yamaguchi dialect. Most Prime Ministers spoke or
at least tried to speak standard Japanese, but Tanaka did not
bother about such a trifling matter. This nickname connoted
his unrefined, rural, and vulgar style, but it also suggested his
optimistic, amiable character. He drank a great deal and made
grand splurges. He was rough and magnanimous. His adoration
for *bushidō*, aspirations for promoting *kokutai* and the Imperial
Way, preference for hierarchical values, unyielding spirit, good
knowledge of Chinese and Japanese classics, physiocratic ideals,
his powerfully built body, valor, aggressive attitudes, and contempt
for money — all these traits in his personality and cultural identity
indicate that he was typically a traditionalistic leader[3] with all
the samurai virtues and vices.

HAGI, THE CONSERVATIVE CASTLE TOWN

Tanaka Giichi was born on June 22, 1863, at least a decade
before Japan's initiation of modernization. His birthplace, Hagi,

---

[2] This account of Yoshida Shōin is taken from *Sources of Japanese
Tradition* which gives a concise but excellent sketch of Yoshida Shōin. See
Tsunoda, De Bary, Keene (comps.), II, 109–115. See also Naramoto Tatsuya,
Yoshida Shōin (Tokyo, 1951); Henricus Van Straelen, *Yoshida Shōin, Forerunner
of the Meiji Restoration* (T'oung Pao Monograph; Leiden, 1952).
[3] I should like to draw a distinction between "traditional" and "traditionalistic." By the term, traditionalistic, I mean those who have nostalgic
feeling or almost romantic yearning for the past tradition and wish to restore
it.

was the castle town of Chōshū and was one of the centers of the "Revere the Emperor and Expel the Barbarians" (*sonnō-jōi*) movement. Under the influence of Yoshida Shōin, Chōshū produced such Restoration leaders as Kusaka Genzui (1840–64), Takasugi Shinsaku (1839–67), Katsura Kogorō (Kido Kōin or Takayoshi, 1833–77), Itō Shunsuke (Hirobumi, 1841–1909), and Yamagata Kyōsuke (Aritomo, 1838–1922). Chōshū, being predominantly rural and remote, was the stronghold of provincialism and xenophobia. Its provincialism was exemplified by the notorious Chōshū clique in the government which had among its members such traditionalistic leaders as Yamagata Aritomo, Nogi Maresuke (1849–1912), Katsura Tarō (1847–1913) and Terauchi Masatake (1852–1919). It was to these senior compatriots that Tanaka looked avidly for inspiration and from whom he received great favors. A few days after Giichi's birth, Chōshū attacked an American vessel in the Shimonoseki Straits. In the next month, July, Chōshū steamers again bombarded French and Dutch vessels. As a result, in September of the next year, 1864, Chōshū suffered a heavy joint retaliation from the British, the French, the Dutch and the Americans. This was the environment into which Tanaka Giichi was born.

ADORATION FOR BUSHIDŌ

Otokuma — as Giichi was called in his childhood — was the third and last son of a *bushi* (samurai) family.[4] Although his father, Nobusuke, was only a *rikushaku*, a samurai of the lowest rank, he was very proud of his *bushi* status and was absolutely loyal to his lord, Mōri Takachika (1819–71). Nobusuke kept

---

[4] *Bushi* (武士) means military gentleman and samurai (侍) means attendant, as the Chinese characters suggest. The former has more formal connotation than the latter. *Bushi* also emphasizes the ethical aspect.

hammering into his children not only an awareness of their *bushi* origins, but also a knowledge of *bushidō* ideals. Otokuma was a notoriously unruly boy. One day when he was eight years old his mischievous deeds in Okada Juku (a private school) went beyond the master's tolerance, and Otokuma was expelled from the school. At that time, Nobusuke told his son:

> "Otokuma, how do you explain your expulsion by master Okada? For a man, there is nothing so shameful as this. Poor as we are, you are still the son of a *bushi* house. Being expelled due to your own bad manners, how can you dare to live on under such a shame! I have nothing more to say to you. It's useless for you to live on. You will only make your parents and brothers feel sad. Here is our ancestral short sword. The least you can do is to commit suicide with this sword in a manly manner."[5]

Otokuma was prepared for *seppuku* (disembowelment), when his mother came out to rescue him from the next room.

Otokuma himself dreamed of becoming a strong *bushi*. From his childhood, he was big and wild, and was fond of violent games. *Ishigassen* (the stone fight) was one of his favorites. In this game two groups of children gathered on the dry riverbed, threw pebbles at each other, then fought with bamboo sticks, and finally grappled with one another. Otokuma always made himself the leader of one camp. His strategy was to take the offensive and his camp usually won. He was the *oyabun* (the boss) among neighboring children. He used to strut down the street with several *kobun* (followers). Some were older than Otokuma. But thanks to his physical strength and magnanimity, he enjoyed absolute obedience from his *kobun*. One day, having found a boy bullying a girl, Otokuma's chivalrous sentiments were aroused. He ordered his *kobun* to bring the boy over to him. Several henchmen immediately caught the boy. The *oyabun* then took by the scruff of the neck of the captive, who was a couple of years older

---

[5] Kawai, 14–15; Hosokawa, 10.

than he, and forced him to grasp some wet dog's droppings. He told the boy just as he had been reminded by his own father, "You are a son of a *bushi* house. And yet you bullied a poor girl. You deserve dog's shit!" At another time, a certain Takasu had done something against Otokuma's sense of *bushi* righteousness. Having ordered his *kobun* to pick up a Chinese date which had fallen from the tree into a compost pond, Otokuma tried to coerce Takasu into eating it. Takasu cried and begged pardon of the *oyabun*.[6]

Based upon his father's daily preaching on *bushidō*, Otokuma assumed his own version of this Japanese tradition. He understood it symbolically as physical strength, often violence, chivalry, manliness, unyielding spirit, magnanimity, righteousness, absolute loyalty and obedience. However, his was assuredly the style of country samurai (*inaka zamurai*), as illustrated by the dog's manure and the Chinese date in the compost pond episodes. His style of *bushidō* lacked in urbane refinement. Nevertheless, he was so proud of his *bushi* origin that he always carried a tobacco pipe which was disguised as a short sword, even after the Meiji Government had abolished the practice of carrying the two swords as the *bushi* symbol. Hence, Tanaka Giichi's identity with *bushidō* began early.

As his *oyabun-kobun* relations indicate, Otokuma already visualized his surrounding human relations in terms of the traditional hierarchical order. Within his immediate circle, he always had to sit at the top. He was too proud to yield to anyone. However, in his school, Ishibe Juku, there was a boy named Shibata Kamon (1862–1919) who later became Minister of Education in the Third Katsura Cabinet (December 1911–February 1912). Kamon was a very intelligent boy and was always ahead of Otokuma in the class. Vexed by this, Otokuma was waiting for an opportunity to make Kamon kneel down before him. A chance came on a hot summer day. Otokuma invited Kamon out for a swim in the river Hashi-

---

6 Kawai, 20–21.

moto. Knowing that Kamon was not good at swimming, Otokuma took him to the deep river and suddenly attacked him. Kamon was no match for an enemy as strong as Otokuma and was almost drowned. Fortunately he was saved, but his foot was seriously injured in the fight.

Nevertheless, Otokuma also won the reputation of being the most dutiful son in his neighborhood. His mother, Miyo, was crippled after giving birth to Otokuma. It was said that her misfortune was caused by the hard labor, for the baby was unusually big. In the hope of curing his ailing mother, Otokuma used to visit Kasuga Shrine and bring back holy water for her. One day he was attacked by several boys on his way home from the shrine. Unlike the usual Otokuma, he offered no resistance at this time. He was struck and kicked, but firmly protected the holy water. Having taken the water safely to his mother, however, he immediately returned to the boys and beat them up. Ōtawa Shinsuke, who lived next to the Tanakas and who later became a Lieutenant General, recalls his early days when his mother used to say, "Otokuma is really a filial son. A very admirable boy!" Shinsuke's mother often told her son to follow Otokuma's good example.[7]

Otokuma also faithfully observed *hōon* (returning favors), another traditional practice. After the Meiji Government abolished the *bushi* caste,[8] Otokuma's family was impoverished and he had to work in a town office as a janitor. His work was very heavy, but an old janitor was always helpful to him. Later, when Tanaka

---

[7] Tanaka Giichi Denki Kankō-kai (ed.), I, 34; Hori, 1–16.

[8] I should also like to make a distinction between "caste" and "class," though in Japanese history the term *bushi* (or samurai) class is more commonly used than *bushi* caste. I understand "class" in terms of economic distinction, whereas "caste" more in terms of status with some distinctive life-styles and symbols. The term, caste, does not necessarily suggest the economic elite nor economically deprived people. In this sense, the *bushi* caste sounds more proper than the *bushi* class. See Max Weber's distinction between caste and class in his essays, *From Max Weber: Essays in Sociology*, trans., ed., and with an introduction by H. H. Gerth and C. Wright Mills (London, 1947), Chaps. 7 and 16.

returned home for a visit after having become a general, he discovered that the old man had died. The general's disappointment was great. He visited the old man's tomb and thanked him for his kindness in the past, offering incense sticks. Tanaka then invited the old man's son and his wife over to his house for a great feast. Remembering the past favors of the old man, General Tanaka said, "Indeed, I received great favors from your aged father...."[9] Thus Tanaka returned *on*, thanks, to the old man's children.

As noted above, Tanaka's identification with *bushidō*, his propensity for violence, his orientation toward hierarchical relations, and his adherence to traditional ethics like filial piety and *hōon*, were already developed in his childhood. These traditionalistic personality traits took a firmer shape through his education.

Learning in Japanese and Chinese Classics

After his seventh birthday, Otokuma entered a popular private school in Hagi conducted by Okada Kendō. Master Okada had won fame in the town because of his rich knowledge of Chinese classics and Kōkokugaku. Okada's devotion to Kōkokugaku later led him to his position as a Shintō priest. Under such a master's guidance, Kōkokugaku was drummed into the head of young Otokuma. In addition, Hagi itself had been rich in loyalist atmosphere. Tanaka's devotion to the Emperor and his belief in the divine nature of the Japanese nation were fostered already during this time. At the age of fourteen, Giichi became a disciple of Ishibe Seichū, an ex-activist in the Restoration, under whom he continued his study of Kōkokugaku and Confucianism. Ishibe's teaching method was typically traditional: "Acquire

---

[9] Kawai, 30; Hosokawa, 11–12.

knowledge through mental discipline and physical training." All
disciples had to participate in drawing water from the well, sweep-
ing and mopping the floors, chopping firewood, and even cooking.
"Learn the teachings of the sages through living experience," was
his motto. A *sumō* (Japanese wrestling) ring was set in the front
yard and the disciples had to compete with one another. When
they were frustrated in learning, the master ordered them to recite
classical Chinese poems aloud. Ishibe used to tell his disciples,
"Once you are born a man, conquer the four seas by following a
courageous ambition for your life, then leave your great name for
eternity after death. This is the real way of man."[10]

Ishibe encouraged Giichi to go, not to the West, but to China,
to improve his study of Chinese classics and to investigate Chinese
national affairs. In his judgement, Japan and China were destin-
ed to fight in the near future. Consequently, the young patriots,
upon whose shoulders rested the destiny of Japan, had to know
China thoroughly. Ishibe told Giichi that this was the way to
serve the nation and the Emperor. Ishibe introduced Giichi
to his fellow compatriot Kasahara Hankurō, who was a judge in
Nagasaki. According to Ishibe's original plan, Giichi was to
prepare himself for the trip to China in Nagasaki, then was to be
introduced to another Chōshū compatriot, Shishido Tamaki, who
was minister plenipotentiary to China. In the early morning
of April 9, 1879, when Giichi was sixteen, he left his home town
for the first time and proceeded to Nagasaki. Thus Tanaka
Giichi became the disciple of Kasahara Hankurō. Giichi's new
master never fell behind Okada and Ishibe in his loyalist and
patriotic spirit. He had received his education at the *han* academy
of Chōshū, Meirinkan, where Yoshida Shōin had taught, and had
played an important role in the Restoration. He was especially
well-learned in Chinese classics and poetry. Meanwhile, Minister Plenipotentiary Shishido was ordered by the government to

---

[10] Kawai, 45.

return to Japan. Accordingly, Giichi was obliged to give up his original plan of going to China. Instead, he continued his stay with the Kasaharas.

Unfortunately for Giichi, Kasahara was soon appointed to the judgeship of Tsushima, and in April 1880, out of loyalty to his master, Giichi followed Kasahara to the farthest tip of Japan. At the time, it took one full day to go to Tsushima from Nagasaki by boat. While Westernization was proceeding at a rapid rate in the cities, Giichi, for one year, spent his most sensitive adolescence on this isolated island. Since there was not much to do at Tsushima, he devoted himself to the study of Chinese classics. Giichi not only finished reading the three hundred fifty-four volumes of *Tzu Chih Tung Chien* (Central Mirror for the Aid of the Government) but also took careful notes on this book. By the time he left the island, the notebooks had piled up to more than two feet high. From about this time, Giichi started to write all his letters in Chinese. His Chinese compositions were very good. And when someone complimented Giichi on his Chinese, he said, "Well, writing is something like shitting. As long as you eat, it will come out naturally."[11] After the year at Tsushima, Giichi followed Kasahara to Matsushima in Shikoku, and there he spent another year before he entered the Army.

As shown above, Tanaka Giichi received a very thorough traditional education. Although the Meiji Government issued the modern Elementary School Order in 1872, Tanaka never attended an official elementary school. Instead, he was educated in *juku* by former samurai-masters, through whom he absorbed the essentials of *kokutai* and *bushidō* teaching. Kōkokugaku taught him that "Japan is ruled by an Emperor descended in one line for ages eternal from a Kami ancestor," that "the supreme divinity of the Sun Goddess is a historical reflection of the augustness of the Emperor who, as a descendant of the divine Sun Goddess,

---

[11]   *Ibid.*, 66.

is considered manifest Kami," that "the subjects must show, therefore, an absolute and unconditional reverence for the Emperor," and that "since Japan was the Father Country (*sokoku*) of all countries, Shintō likewise should be considered the source of all religions and the Emperor the supreme ruler of all countries."[12] In the mind of young Giichi, the concept of *kokutai* seemed to have taken a concrete shape. He was also steeped in Motoori Norinaga's (1730–1801) theory that an absolute reverence for the Emperor, in contrast to the Confucian theory of revolution (Mandate of Heaven) is the superior way of bringing happiness to the world. Later, Prime Minister Tanaka pursued his "Manchuria-First" policy partly due to this kind of conviction and his hope to establish a Utopia under the Imperial Way.[13]

In addition to Kōkokugaku, Giichi's study of Chinese classics increased his knowledge of Chinese history and traditional Oriental virtues. *Tzu Chih Tung Chien* provided him with a good knowledge of ancient Chinese history. It is noteworthy, however, that along with these Neo-Confucian texts, Tanaka liked *Han Fei Tzu*, an important text of Legalist teachings, which openly advocated war as a means of strengthening the power of the ruler, expanding the state, and making the people strong, disciplined, and submissive. The same text emphasized that agriculture, as the basis of the economy, had to be promoted intensively, while commerce and intellectual endeavor were to be severely restricted as nonessential and diversionary and that the people would live frugal and obedient lives devoted to the interests of the state in peace and war.[14] Hence, Giichi gradually acquired the ideals

---

[12] Muraoka, 11–22, 46–48.

[13] With regard to Manchuria, Tanaka had a similar idea to that of Ishiwara Kanji. His policy toward Manchuria will be discussed in Chapter 7. As to Ishiwara's biography, see Takagi Seiju and Takagi Junko, *Tōa no Chichi Ishiwara Kanji* (The father of Asia, Ishiwara Kanji; Tokyo, 1954); Saigō Kōsaku, *Ishiwara Kanji* (Tokyo, 1937); Yamaguchi Shigeji, *Higeki no Shōgun, Ishiwara Kanji* (A tragic general, Ishiwara Kanji; Tokyo, 1952).

[14] This explanation of *Han Fei Tzu* is taken from Wm. Theodore De Bary, Wing-tsit Chan, and Burton Watson (comps.), *Sources of Chinese Tradition* (New York, 1968), I, 137.

of physiocracy and the Confucian concept of economy, i.e., agriculture, frugality and diligence being the foundation of wealth.

His knowledge from these textbooks notwithstanding, Giichi also learned traditional virtues through the living examples of his masters: paternalism, self-sacrifice, comradeship among compatriots were especially impressive. With regard to the last virtue, Ishibe and Kasahara were perfect examples for Giichi. As the reader will recall, Ishibe entrusted his beloved disciple to his fellow compatriots Kasahara in Nagasaki and Shishido in China. Giichi was to be trained through a network that extended through these senior compatriots. Like Ishibe, Kasahara also demonstrated this particularistic virtue by welcoming Giichi, who had been a complete stranger to him. With only one letter from his compatriot, Kasahara had decided to accept Giichi and introduced him to his wife, saying, "This man is from Hagi and used to live near your home. So please take care of him."[15] Mrs. Kasahara simply obeyed her husband's decision. In this kind of association, compatriots self-sacrificingly extended mutual aid and favor almost to the extent of an ethical obligation. Nevertheless, from a modern viewpoint, such relations are nothing but a feudalistic vice, for they contain, by nature, a narrow exclusive view and attitude toward outsiders, to say nothing of foreigners. In extreme cases, such prejudicial views against outsiders drove people into violent fights against various opposing groups.[16]

Paternalism was another virtue which Giichi absorbed through his association with his masters. For example, Ishibe gave five yen each to Giichi and another disciple who also went to Nagasaki. Ishibe was not rich, and five yen was not a small amount of money

---

15   Kawai, 54; Hosokawa, 17–19.

16   Stronger provincial ties were observed among Chinese guilds and clans in the traditional society. *Hsieh tou* (fight with arms), which was commonly observed among traditional Chinese villages, would be a typical example of this. See exclusive and hostile attitudes of Chinese guilds and clans against "others" in Niida Noboru, *Chūgoku no Nōson Kazoku* (Chinese agrarian families; Tokyo, 1954) and *Chūgoku Shakai to Girudo* (Chinese society and guilds; Tokyo, 1951).

during that time, for one yen was the approximate monthly wage of an assistant teacher of an elementary school. Even from this fact alone, we can conjecture that theirs was not an ordinary teacher-student relationship in a modern sense. Giichi's masters extended rich paternalistic love to their disciples. The latter in return wholly trusted the former. Their fellowship was not based upon calculated, individualistic interests; rather it was dependent on the assumption of mutual self-sacrifice. The disciples were ready to do whatever they could for their masters, while the latter demonstrated benevolence toward the former. On neither side, however, was there established the independent realm of the individual. On neither side was there a full assertion of the individual ego, volition, and interest. Both parties were inseparably fused. Full development of individuality was impossible. A similar relationship is also observable between *oyabun-kobun*, *sempai-kōhai* (senior-junior) and many other hierarchical human relations.

For young Tanaka, the influence of the so-called Yōgaku (Western-learning) was almost nil. Universalistic and egalitarian concepts both in personal and international relations were alien to Tanaka Giichi. The democratic order both in the public and private sense was heresy to Tanaka's ideal viewed through his hierarchical spectacles. Economic-oriented rationalism (the Weberian sense of *Zwecksrationalität*), individualism based upon self-interest, and free volition of the independent being, all of these ideas considered to be "modern" contradicted Tanaka's ethical ideals which were composed of loyalty, filial piety, obedience and self-sacrifice. Such a traditionalistic orientation as Tanaka's was reinforced by environmental experiences in his adolescence. While most ambitious youths were heading toward Tokyo, the capital of Japan, where the impact of modernization was tremendous, Giichi was heading in the opposite direction. He spent his formative adolescent years in the most remote and backward parts of Japan, such as Hagi, Tsushima and Matsuyama.

Career Soldier

Tanaka Giichi was literally a career soldier. From 1883, when he entered the School of Noncommissioned Officers (Kyō-dōdan) at the age of twenty, to 1925, when he retired from the Army to take the chairmanship of the Seiyūkai — for more than forty years he had spent his life in the Imperial Army of Japan. And it was the Army which surpassed all other institutions in preserving the samurai tradition. Tanaka, however, was not only passively influenced by such an environment but also actively exerted himself to enhance what he believed to be the "flower and essence" of the Japanese tradition, *bushidō*, within the Army and the nation. Since it is impossible to describe his long military career thoroughly in a limited space, I will attempt to focus my discussion on only some of the most significant aspects of his personality development and his activities during this period.

In the School of Noncommissioned Officers and in the Military Academy (1883–1889), Tanaka was still the *oyabun* among rough soldiers, many of whom themselves might have been local bosses in their childhood. Tanaka was more magnanimous, more overbearing, and more aggressive than they. "One of the most remarkable aspects of Tanaka," recalls his instructor, "was his *oyabun* temperament. He was not suited for petty internal jobs within barracks." "Tanaka always talked big," says a former classmate, "and did not bother himself with small things. He was so broad-minded that he looked as if he would have swallowed up everybody." Tanaka's juniors also admitted that he was their *oyabun* and said, "Tanaka was simple and yet full of the feeling of *giri* and *ninjō*. We all admired him and were obedient to him."[17]

---

[17]   Tanaka Giichi Denki Kankō-kai (ed.), I, 61–65.

The episode that Tanaka as a mere student of the Military
University (1889–1892) took care of seven *shosei* (students or
disciples who live with the master and do errands) may also show
his *oyabun* temperament as well as his feeling of *giri* and *ninjō*
towards his compatriots, relatives, and friends. It was impossible
for Tanaka to refuse, when his friends asked him to look after
their children, or nephews or brothers. Most of these *shosei*
came to Tanaka with hopes of entering the Military Academy.
Tanaka taught his disciples that self-discipline is the fundamental
principle of a good soldier, and said, "Even if you feel pain, don't
say it is painful. Even if you are suffering, don't say so. Even
if you are cold or hot, don't say so. Under any circumstances
complaints are prohibited. The issue of a battle may be decided
by your perseverance during the last five minutes."[18] His teaching reminds us of the samurai posture expressed by the popular
saying, "the samurai betrays no weakness when starving," (*Bushi
wa kuwanedo takayōji*). War was Tanaka's preoccupation and
in war self-discipline and spiritual power are the most crucial
factors. Tanaka, like many samurai, sought fame and power as
man's greatest glory and identified Japan's ultimate goal with her
expansion of power by successive victories.

Soon after his graduation from the Military University,
Lieutenant Tanaka hoped to show his aged father his own success
as well as the astoundingly modern city, Tokyo, by inviting him
from Hagi. Tanaka, being always fond of show and disliking
small things, had to find a nice house to give his father a good
impression. After a long effort in searching for a suitable house
within his poor budget, he finally found one which was unbeliev-
ably inexpensive to rent, for it had a bad reputation as a haunted
house. Tanaka, scoffing at such a rumor, was not bothered
at all. Strangely, however, both Tanaka and his father soon
became ill in that house and his father passed away while Tanaka

---

18   *Ibid.*, 76.

was in the hospital. His natural inclination to aim at big and impressive things even beyond his capacity turned out to be ruinous in spite of his good intentions to make his father happy. Similarly, as we shall see, his chauvinism in war and diplomacy ironically resulted in the ruin of Japan's international prestige as a peace-loving and international law-abiding nation, the image built painstakingly by his predecessor, Shidehara Kijūrō.

On August 1, 1894, the first Sino-Japanese War broke out. Lieutenant Tanaka went to the war front and was soon promoted to the rank of Captain due to his meritorious services in war. It was in this war that he began to distinguish himself in the Army and it was his Tōkichirō-ism that gave him fame.

Tanaka regarded Toyotomi Hideyoshi (his youthful name was Kinoshita Tōkichirō) as his symbolic hero. He always reminded himself of the story of Tōkichirō who, as the sandal carrier of Oda Nobunaga (1534–82), warmed his lord's slippers in his own bosom on cold winter days. Tanaka believed that wholehearted devotion to his duty and absolute loyalty to his superiors were the fundamental principles of all soldiers, and he himself demonstrated this principle in the war. His commander, Major Nishi Kanjirō (1846–1912), was notorious for being overly fastidious. Before Tanaka entered Nishi's Brigade, he was cautioned by another major general about Nishi's hot temper. But Tanaka answered:

> Master Yoshida Shōin told us that everyone is moved by true sincerity. So I will also serve Commander Nishi with true sincerity.... My most important responsibility now in the war is to keep the Commander from flying into a passion. If I cannot do this, I will know that my sincerity is not yet sufficient, and I will be prepared to make further efforts.[19]

And so he did. For instance, when Tanaka heard that his commander loved *tempura*, he went to the river to catch fish in his spare time, cooked them by himself, and served them at the table.

---

[19]   *Ibid.*, 92.

To such an extent, including food and personal care, Tanaka served the commander with the greatest possible care. Thus Tanaka won Nishi's trust and was called the great adjutant by the same commander.

Tanaka further hoped to propagate Tōkichirō-ism within the Army as the motto of all soldiers. So he instructed his subordinates:

> Act according to Tōkichirō-ism. When you are a sandal carrier, become the best sandal carrier in Japan. When you are an *ashigaru* [foot soldier], become the No. 1 *ashigaru* in Japan. In this way in each situation Kinoshita Tōkichirō devoted himself to his duty. Thus, you see, he finally became Kampaku [the Chief Advisor to the Emperor] and Dajō Daijin [Prime Minister] and took the world.[20]

Tōkichirō-ism was a traditional ethic which emphasized loyalty to one's superiors and devotion to one's own duty. Devotion to one's duty, however, was not understood in the modern bureaucratic sense, but rather in the sense of the samurai's ethics. In other words, it was not so much the fulfillment of one's own official function as it was personal obligation to one's superiors. In this devotion, too, achievement was emphasized as in a modern bureaucracy which aims to attain the highest efficiency. Both Tanaka's Tōkichirō-ism and the Weberian concept of modern bureaucracy are achievement-oriented. Nevertheless, the most noteworthy point in the former case is that it is strongly politically oriented. For Tanaka, achievement was ultimately directed toward the attainment of political power.[21]

In 1898, Major Tanaka was sent by the Imperial Army to Russia to investigate the Czarist Army, as a confrontation between the two countries had been anticipated. With regard to

---

[20] *Ibid.*, 95; see also Hosokawa, 21–32; Hori, 47–66.

[21] Bellah also observes the importance of particularistic political values in the traditional social system of Japan. See more discussion on this point in Robert N. Bellah, *Tokugawa Religion*, Chaps. 1 and 2.

the question of whether Japan should wage war against Russia, the nation was sharply divided. Genrō Itō Hirobumi was the leader of the camp which opposed risking such a danger. Tanaka was an activist in the opposite camp. In November 1901, Itō went to Russia via the United States and France with hopes of concluding a Russo-Japanese entente by giving Manchuria to Russia in return for allowing Japan to take Korea into her sphere of influence. By doing so, the Genrō tried to avoid a direct conflict with powerful Russia. Tanaka visited Itō at his hotel and frankly criticized his plan as a "useless" and "unthinking" conciliatory measure which would eventually, but totally, destroy Japan. Under normal circumstances a minor officer like Tanaka could hardly challenge this famous Genrō of the Meiji Restoration. In fact, Itō was infuriated by Tanaka's insolence, and reprimanded him saying that Itō had no ears to listen to a "foolish greenhorn's impractical argument." Like many Restoration leaders — Itō himself was one of them — who acted with determination according to their own sense of *taigi meibun* (for a just and great cause), it was now Tanaka's turn to challenge the Genrō. He reacted to Itō by answering, "Your Excellency was also a 'greenhorn' when you were busily engaged in the great task of the Restoration." Itō hurled back at Tanaka, "A man like you staying here in Russia is an obstacle in normal relations between Japan and Russia. I'll send a cable to Tokyo to summon you back. Be prepared!"[22]

Having returned to the General Staff in Tokyo, Tanaka — far from being threatened by Itō — became more active in advocating war against Russia. He organized a secret association called the Kogetsu-kai, composed of middle ranking warlike officers and diplomats. The members of Kogetsu-kai were determined to persuade military and political leaders into opening the war. Yamaza Enjirō, a diplomat, who had been assigned to prevail on Genrō Itō Hirobumi, reportedly said that he would cut down the

---

22 Tanaka Giichi Denki Kankō-kai (ed.), I, 175–176; Hori, 66–81.

Genrō if he would not yield to his persuasion and that he himself would also commit *seppuku* on the spot, in order to further the destiny of the Japanese Empire.[23] Simultaneously, Tanaka while in the General Staff was in charge of the mobilization plan for the Russo-Japanese War. According to his subordinate's investigation of the transportation capacity of the Siberian Railway, the Russian railway could handle eight trains a day for troops and ammunition. Of these eight trains, two would be used for carrying ammunition and the rest for transporting troops. Tanaka on the other hand, estimated that Japan's daily troopship capacity to the Continent was about equal to the Russian capacity of six troop trains. This meant Japan was short two trains of ammunition a day in comparison with the Russian capacity of mobilization. Moreover, Russia had already stationed six divisions in Manchuria.

He knew that Genrō Itō Hirobumi, Yamagata Aritomo, and General Ōyama Iwao (1842–1916), the supreme commander of the war, would never agree to Tanaka's proposal to wage war against Russia, should they be informed about such an enormous gap in the mobilization capacity of the two countries. Tanaka therefore ordered his subordinate to change the report. But the latter declined to do so, because the report would be presented to the Council in the presence of the Emperor and the reporter would be charged with having committed a great treason by making a false mobilization report.

The subordinate asked: "But Sir, if we open war based upon such a false report and we should lose, what would you do?"

Tanaka replied, "No! If we should lose? No! Never do we lose."

"That's what you think. But contrary to your expectation, Sir, *if* we lose, there would be no remedy, even if you and I commit *seppuku*."[24]

---

[23] For a more detailed account of the Kogetsu-kai, see "Kogetsu-kai Sensō Sokushin Undō" (Kogetsu-kai's promotion of war), Kokuryū-kai (ed.), I, 726–738.

[24] Tanaka Giichi Denki Kankō-kai (ed.), I, 232–233.

Tanaka became furious and gave his subordinate a final order to change the report. Hence a false report on the Russian mobilization capacity was made. It was reported that the Russians could carry only six trains a day on the railway instead of eight. The next morning Tanaka brought the false report to the Imperial Council. Both men had promised to disembowel themselves if Japan should lose.

The above episode indicates various significant points in regard to Tanaka's behavior and way of thinking. If absolute loyalty and devotion were virtues in *bushidō*, the defiance of authority was the worst vice, which could be expiated only by death. Nevertheless, the defiance of authority was allowed under extraordinary circumstances — at a time of crisis, for instance, or for noble causes. Therefore, in 1860, a group of Mito *rōnin* assassinated Tairō (the Great Elder) Ii Naosuke (1815–60) of the Tokugawa Shogunate, who had confined their lords, neglected the Imperial approval for the Harris commercial treaty, and endangered Japan. Again in the name of *taigi meibun* many Restoration leaders withdrew their *han* registrations, *dappan*, and ran to serve the Emperor and the nation against Western threats. Likewise, it was now Tanaka's turn to defy the Genrō for a national crisis, because he firmly believed that Russia, like most nations, was a power-hungry lion and consequently Japan's eventual clash with her was inevitable.[25] If this were the case, Tanaka insisted, Japan should declare war as soon as possible, before Russia could swallow up Manchuria and Korea, then Japan would be forced to "beg" Anglo-American interference in the Far East. For him, war was constant and peace was only temporary, and hence diplomatic means and compromise were of no avail for solving international conflicts. Foreign policy had to be ultimately determined in terms of overall national strategy, and strategy should always

---

[25] Similar reasoning was asserted by many wartime leaders. Hence the Manchurian Incident and the Marco Polo Bridge Incident (July 7, 1937) broke out in defiance of authority by minor officers.

be "positive and offensive," (*sekkyoku shinshu*), his lifetime motto.[26] His advocacy of war also demonstrated both the direct-actionist and "sink or swim" attitude. In contrast to Itō who hoped to solve the problem through negotiations and compromises with Russia, Tanaka demanded war, just as many samurai preferred sword fights to compromise or conciliation. To gamble the whole national destiny on war, itself, is risky. But when one realizes that there was an enormous gap in the mobilization capacity between Japan and Russia, Tanaka's assertion was irrational or even "quixotic." His attitude was similar to that of the samurai who, wielding swords, fought their way into powerful enemy camps and risked their lives on one spectacular charge against the enemy. They, like Tanaka and his colleagues of the Kogetsu-kai, prepared themselves for death, instead of for shameful escape and surrender. The samurai thought their action heroic and valorous. As Nitobe Inazō (1862–1933) pointed out, however, their action was only "superficially" heroic. One must distinguish between the real valor of *bushidō* and what Shakespeare called "valour misbegot." "To run all kinds of hazards, to jeopardize one's self, and to rush into the jaws of death" says Nitobe, "is a dog's death (*inujini*)." It is the act of country samurai (*inaka zamurai*) and not that of refined *bushi*.[27]

Tanaka and the war advocates in the Kogetsu-kai fortunately did not have to commit *seppuku*. Japan won the Russo-Japanese War. Tanaka, who was a prime mover for war, instead of being punished for his false mobilization report was decorated by the Emperor with the third-class Order of the Golden Kite (Kinshi Kunshō) in recognition of his war services. Furthermore, thanks to his chauvinistic activities throughout this period from war preparations to the end of the war, and thanks to strong support

---

[26] For a detailed account of this episode, see Tanaka Giichi Denki Kankō-kai (ed.), I, 174–242; Hosokawa, 35–40; Hori, 81–92.

[27] With regard to Nitobe's distinction between real samurai and that of *inaka zamurai*, see Inazō Nitobe, 29–30.

from the Chōshū clique within the Army, Tanaka began to stand
as a giant among his fellow soldiers. At the same time, Japan's
victory further strengthened his conviction of the importance
of spiritual power in the Army. Tanaka could unhesitatingly
advocate war against Russia for two main reasons: the Russian
expansion toward the south was so definite that Japan was doomed
to fight Russia sooner or later; and because the Japanese Army's
morale was far better than that of the Russian Army under the
corrupt Czarist regime, Japan's spiritual power could overcome
the Russian material power such as her large territory, great size
of troops, and superior armament. The result of war seemed to
have proved that Tanaka's judgment had been correct. Japan's
successful war against China had already indicated the same point.

Thus, after the Russo-Japanese War, in order further to
strengthen non-material spiritual power within the Army, Tanaka
became the commander of the Third Infantry Regiment on his
own request. He was convinced that one of the important elements of spiritual power was the spiritual solidarity between officers and enlisted men. To achieve this, paternalism would be
the best tool. He had probably reached this conclusion because
of his faith in the traditional Japanese family system, his rich
experience with his ex-samurai masters, and his knowledge of
Japanese and Chinese classics acquired in his youth. Hence, as
soon as he took command, he spoke to the commissioned officers
in his regiment:

> Parental affection should be the attitude of the commanders
> toward their soldiers. This is the secret of how to control men
> under your command. As Master Yoshida Shōin's poetry, which
> he composed just before his execution, teaches us:
>
> > "My affection toward my parent...,
> > But even greater is their love toward me.
> > I wonder how they received today's news...."
>
> Parental love is far deeper than children's affection toward their
> parents. If you face your men with parental love, they will surely

obey you wholeheartedly.... Parental love toward soldiers is the fundamental by which our military life can be made into a familial life. And by doing so, we can improve our military education. In the final analysis, the commander-soldier relationship should be based upon paternalism and filial piety.[28]

Tanaka apparently did succeed in disciplining his soldiers. Even a socialist who had been a troublemaker in the Army was firmly controlled by Tanaka. His troops were regarded as a model brigade in the Army. Tanaka, proud of this, invited Genrō Ōkuma Shigenobu (1838–1922) to visit his troops. Ōkuma during this time was strongly opposed to Yamagata and his military clique. Nevertheless, even Ōkuma was reportedly impressed by Tanaka's well-disciplined troops. As a consequence, Ōkuma subsequently agreed to become the president of the Supporters' Association for the Veterans.

In the Army, Tanaka was also a good example of the Japanese soldier who was endowed with all the samurai virtues. Even the previously mentioned socialist in Tanaka's regiment had to admit that his commander's courage and aggressiveness were impressive. He described how Tanaka conducted maneuvers:

---

[28] Tanaka Giichi Denki Kankō-kai (ed.), I, 387–388. Tanaka's conviction that Japanese paternalism would be the best spiritual discipline never changed throughout his career. In 1910, after his service in the Army Administration as the Section Chief of Military Affairs, Colonel Tanaka became the Second Brigade commander. At that time he reemphasized the same principle before his commissioned and non-commissioned officers:

"True military discipline is a spiritual thing which springs out naturally from the heart of the people. If this cannot be attained, how can we expect to exhibit military excellence under the rain of bullets and glittering swords? Military discipline is not just a formality but also a real spiritual unity.... This can be fostered by two things: affection from above and loyalty from below.... Now, by what means can we seek such deep and rich feeling? We can do so by our warm feeling and benevolence to soldiers. For if your subordinates feel that they owe you *on* and love, they will serve you with the heart which they serve their own parents. Only by doing so can we obtain the real unity of the spirit. This is real military discipline. A company is a family..., the company's commander is the father, officers are the mother, and soldiers are the children. Children who have been brought up in a good family are sincere and honest. So the soldiers who have been educated in the warm and friendly familial atmosphere of a company are ideal." Kawai, 245–246.

In the morning both forces drew up on the field of battle. The
time had come for fighting. Major General Nagaoka fiercely commanded his troops to charge the enemy. All the troops were ready
to make an attack. The third infantry regimental commander,
Colonel Tanaka, occupied the position of backbone for all the troops.
He quietly beckoned to the reserves in the rear. The first company
quietly but quickly joined us anew. Then swiftly alighting from
his horse, holding the colors in his arms, and commanding the crack
troops, Colonel Tanaka dashed roaring and brandishing his saber.
In all of these actions he was so swift that it was as if a squall had
swept over the field. He was so powerful that it was as if raging
billows had struck against a precipice. At that time I happened to
be in the reserve corps and near the Colonel. I simply gazed at his
huge physique. His countenance was courageous and manly. He
dashed down the hill almost rolling, roaring like a god or a demon.
All the soldiers were so impressed by Colonel Tanaka's vigor and
valor that they forgot that it was only a manuever. With bloodshot
eyes and breathing fire from their mouths in their excitement, all
followed the Colonel in the charge. It was like a flood running down
from a broken bank.[29]

On August 29, 1910, Japan annexed Korea. Taking advantage of this opportunity, Tanaka as Bureau Chief of Military Affairs proposed his plan for an increase of divisions to Genrō Yamagata and Ōkuma as well as Generals Katsura and Terauchi.
Always preoccupied with strategic problems, he was convinced
that Japan had to increase her forces considerably in order to
defend her much enlarged territory, now including Korea in addition to Sakhalin. Through his consultation with these leaders
and in view of their evaluation of Japan's economic difficulties
after the Russo-Japanese War, Tanaka felt obliged to satisfy himself with, for him, a rather modest plan of an increase of two army
divisions. Nevertheless, Saionji Kimmochi, then Prime Minister,
rejected even this "modest" proposal. He was an anti-military

---

[29] Tanaka Giichi Denki Kankō-kai (ed.), I, 394.

liberal and his party, the Seiyūkai, was talking of a retrenchment policy. Hot words were exchanged between Saionji and Hara Kei, Minister of Internal Affairs on the one hand, and Tanaka and War Minister Uyehara on the other. Tanaka insisted that upon the Imperial Army's "honor" he was determined to carry out the plan. On December 1, 1912, after long debate, Saionji finally concluded in his Cabinet meeting that because he could not accept the Army's demand under any circumstances, if the Army still insisted on the demand he would be obliged to change the War Minister.

Throughout this fight, Tanaka was busily engaged in agitating support for his plan within the Army and from the public at large. He frequently met Yamagata, Ōkuma and military leaders. Another powerful figure whom he hoped to recruit on his side was Marquis Inoue Kaoru (1835–1915). Inoue had been very influential to the Seiyūkai as the Party elder, and had many friends in the Mitsui, Mitsubishi Companies, and other big business firms. Tanaka, having skilfully won Inoue's backing, tried to turn his opponents over to his side. However, the Saionji-Hara faction in the Seiyūkai was too strong for Tanaka to win in this scheme. He succeeded only in alienating his patron, Inoue, from the Seiyūkai and in discrediting Inoue's prestige among financial circles. Nevertheless, Saionji still had to suffer the ultimate defeat, when he met Genrō Yamagata's adamant refusal for his request to select a new War Minister. As the result, the second Saionji Cabinet (August 1911-December 1912) was toppled. Rumors spread that Yamagata and the Army plotted to destroy the liberal Cabinet, and that the chief schemer was Tanaka Giichi.[30]

Another contest between the Saionji-Hara group and the Yamagata-Tanaka group arose over the Siberian dispatches. In late July 1917, at the Inter-Allied Conference in Paris, France had suggested

---

[30]   Hosokawa, 74–91; Hori, 108–121.

a Japanese expedition to the Russian Front, and in November Britain talked with the United States about the possibility of Japanese and/or American intervention in revolutionary Russia. Although during this time the Japanese Army officially rejected the Allied proposal of the "European Expedition," the Vice-Chief of the General Staff, Tanaka Giichi, was from the outset all for the idea of sending expeditionary troops to Russia. Tanaka felt it absolutely necessary for Japan to make a strong buffer zone consisting of Siberia, Mongolia, Manchuria, and Korea against the Russian southern expansion. As we have already seen, in Tanaka's thinking Japan's strategic concerns always came first to his mind. Consequently, he tried hard to separate Siberia from Russia and to make it an autonomous and independent region. The Russian revolution provided him with the excellent excuse to fulfill his life-long strategic scheme. In this connection, we must note that later on Tanaka as the Prime Minister and concurrently the Foreign Minister, by taking advantage of Chinese civil wars, once again maneuvered to set Manchuria aside from China proper and to incorporate it into Japan's defense zone.

With the above plan in his mind, Tanaka first approached the Chief of the General Staff, Uyehara Yūsaku (1856–1933), and the latter succeeded in persuading War Minister Ōshima Ken'ichi (1858–1947). Foreign Minister Gotō Shimpei also endorsed Tanaka's assertion. Meanwhile Genrō Yamagata Aritomo and Prime Minister Terauchi Masatake gradually inclined to support their most trusted protégé and virtual "heir apparent" of the Chōshū clique, Tanaka Giichi. Thus came a headlong clash between these interventionists who gave no heed to the Russian sovereignty and territorial integrity, and Genrō Saionji Kimmochi, the Seiyūkai president Hara Kei and the Kokumintō chairman Inukai Tsuyoshi, the liberals, who hoped to maintain democratic principles in international relations. The latter group finally made a compromise with the former when the American invitation to the joint dispatch came (July 8, 1918), in order to build a coalition with the United States. Tanaka, then, asserted Japan's independent action and dispatch of much more troops than the original American proposal of 7,000 each to the Russian front. It was Tanaka's argument that Japan had to seek the initiative and "autonomy" in her diplomacy and that even if she was obliged to "co-operate" with other powers in the final analysis, the commander-in-chief of allied forces had to be provided from the Japanese Army, and that to do so, she had to send the largest number of troops.[31]

For Tanaka in his competitive mind, like Gotō, the dispatch of troops to Siberia was a "contest" against rather than a "co-operation" with the United States. Just as he hoped to place himself at the top and to make himself the *oyabun* in his private affairs, so he wished Japan to take the initiative and the leadership in world diplomacy. In the same manner, when foreign residents' lives and property in north China were exposed to possible danger due to the Chinese civil war in the 1920's, Prime Minister Tanaka went right ahead to send troops to Shantung without seeking cooperation with the United States and Britain. Tanaka's assertion of "autonomous diplomacy" (*jishu gaikō*) thus demonstrated made a good contrast with the "co-operative diplomacy" (*kyōchō gaikō*) of his predecessor, Shidehara Kijūrō.

Throughout the period of Taishō Democracy, Tanaka carried out a vociferous protest against Japan's increasing Westernization and modernization. He emerged strong as a champion among traditionalistic nationalists. His most remarkable activities in

---

[31] According to Morley, the interventionists had more ambitious plans than just strategic concerns. In the original plan, the interventionists had prepared the way for a large expedition to the Amur basin to bolster a pro-Japanese Government in the Russian territories, gain control of the Chinese Eastern Railway and the Siberian Railway east of Irkutsk, and harness the region to the Japanese economy. Morley, 308. See fuller accounts of this incident in Morley; Tatsuji Takeuchi, 204–218; Seki Kanji, "Harubin Kakumei, 1917, Shiberia Shuppei-shi Josetsu" (Harbin revolution, 1917, a prelude to the Siberian dispatch), *Nihon Gaikō-shi Kenkyū, Taishō Jidai* (Studies of Japanese diplomatic history, the Taishō period), ed. Nihon Kokusai Seiji Gakkai (Tokyo, 1959), 97–104.

this regard were the efforts to establish the Veterans Association and the Youth Association. He endeavored to promote *kokutai* within the Army and throughout the nation by dint of these organizational weapons. From such activities and his speeches addressed to these associations, one can observe his ideas on the soldier's function, the economy and the state.

SOLDIER AND STATE

For Tanaka, *bushidō* personified a personal as well as national identity. He was convinced that Japan's *kokutai* represented Imperial Rule with the spirit of *bushidō*. Should Japan lose this great tradition, then Japan would no longer be Japan. Should a Japanese forget this national cult, he would no longer be a Japanese. This tradition was not only the fountain-head of Japan's national power and prosperity but also the very thing which she could be proud of before the whole world and by which she could demonstrate her unique *raison d'être* among nations. On November 3, 1910, when the Veterans Association was established in commemoration of the Emperor's birthday, Tanaka wrote in the manuscript of the presidential address:

> It is our national essence that all subjects of the Imperial Nation are rich in the spirit of *bushidō*. This, the whole universe and all nations admire. It goes without saying that our great victories in recent wars [the first Sino-Japanese War and the Russo-Japanese War] are mainly owed to our spirit of *bushidō*.[32]

Nevertheless, Tanaka thought, this essence and the ultimate power-source of the Japanese nation had been threatened by the invasion of modern-Western as well as socialist-communist influences. In July 1911, while Tanaka was still the Commander

---

[32] Tanaka Giichi Denki Kankō-kai (ed.), I, 411.

of the Second Brigade, he chided the veterans, "Our unique *Yamato damashii* and *bushidō*, these have been deeply rooted in our nation. Until recently, at least, this was a historical fact which had lasted for over three thousand years. Yet, nowadays, these are being eroded and they are disappearing." And in May 1923, at the Conference of the All-Japan Divisional Chiefs of Staff, War Minister Tanaka stated:

> The spirit of self-sacrifice must be made the core of the national spirit.... Recently, the whole people tend to indulge in luxury and extravagance and have weakened the virtue of frugality. They are dispirited. And not a few are bewitched by dangerous thoughts.... I believe that the best remedy for correcting the abuse of this age is to envigorate the people and to stir up the notion that we must courageously sacrifice ourselves to the nation and to the Emperor.[33]

It was from this conviction that Tanaka was determined to restore the old Japan, the only Japan which he could think of, and that he carried out a grand plan of national reconstruction. According to this plan, *kokutai* was to be promoted through four stages: first, among school children, then among youth (between the ages of fifteen and twenty) through the Youth Association, then in the Army, and lastly among the veterans through the Veterans Association.

In this plan Tanaka conceived of soldiers as the vanguard of national reconstruction, and as teachers of the whole nation. Consequently, in 1912 when Tanaka was Bureau Chief, he obtained the Emperor's special permission to incorporate the following instruction into the Ordinance of Military Education:

> The military man is the flower of the nation and takes the highest and most important position in the nation. Therefore the education of the military man directly influences other people. Military education exerts a great influence upon the entire spirit of the nation. Moral qualities acquired in the Army will surely elevate the traits of society, and will surely be a good example for the nation. It

---

[33] Kawai, 173–175.

cannot but bring about the spirit of fortitude and vigor (*shitsujitsu gōken*), and promote the prosperity of the nation. Consequently, those who have the responsibility of providing military education must know that to foster good soldiers is to create good subjects, and must be resolved to form the model for the nation.[34]

Tanaka's idea resembled the idea of Yamaga Sokō (1622–85) expressed in his book, *Shidō* (the way of the warrior, written in 1663–65). Like Sokō, Tanaka believed that soldiers — in Sokō's case *bushi* — were models for the nation, and that by maintaining this principle the "proper order" of the nation could be established: soldiers should enjoy the highest rank in the society.[35] Tanaka asserted:

> Good soldiers are good subjects. And the veterans are the backbone of the people. However, we should not be contented only among ourselves with this assertion. We must make the whole nation assent to our proclamation and we must truly realize this. By doing so, we shall be able to maintain the proper order of our nation.[36]

This was because they (or *bushi* in Sokō's case) were the people who strictly observed traditional morality. Tanaka proclaimed:

> The purpose of military education is to train soldiers so that they cherish the military spirit and the lawful mind and observe a strict military code: so that they enjoy physical strength and become proficient in military arts. Military spirit is composed of five warps, namely loyalty, decorum, bravery, fidelity and simplicity, and of three woofs, namely co-operation, obedience and self-discipline. Sincerity

---

34   Tanaka Giichi Denki Kankō-kai (ed.), I, 470–471.

35   Yamaga Sokō was the first to write a systematic treatise on *bushidō*. He especially emphasized samurai's moral disciplines and loyalty to his lord. In his later years Sokō was more and more convinced that Japanese civilization was better than Chinese and, in fact, came to believe that Japan was the center of all culture and civilization. In *Chūchō Jijitsu* (The true facts concerning the central kingdom, 1669), he wrote that "Japan was divinely created and ruled over by an imperial line coeval with heaven and earth," Tanaka's favorite phrase. It is small wonder that Tanaka's idea resembled Sokō's, for Sokō gave a profound influence to all Restoration leaders who hoped to utilize *bushidō* for the service of the Emperor and the nation against the Shōgun and the West. Yoshida Shōin, Tanaka's spiritual master, devoted himself to the precepts of Sokō. Tsunoda, De Bary, and Keene (comps.), I, 384–401, II, 109–115.

36   Kawai, 173.

pierces all of these elements. Consequently to foster good soldiers means to create good subjects. And by doing so, we make models of the nation and train our national character.[37]

Thus the first step of his national reconstruction had to begin within the Army. Once soldiers had absorbed these traditional virtues in the Army, then each of them should know that he had the mission to promote *kokutai* among all of the Japanese people. Tanaka called this principle "Good-Soldiers-are-Good-Subjects-ism," (Ryōhei soku Ryōmin-shugi).

Even if this "mission" of the soldier was extolled aloud within the Army, Tanaka realized, it would end up with hardly more than self-complacency among soldiers unless the common people also were made to assume this idea. Unless the exhortation of *kokutai* prevailed among all the Japanese, the diseases of society would infect even the Army itself, and soon the whole of the nation would be destroyed from within. To promote *kokutai* in the entire nation, non-military people as well had to be like soldiers. Tanaka called this second principle "All-Japanese-are-Soldiers-ism," (Kokumin Kaihei-shugi). The Veterans Association was the best means for achieving this end. In the presidential declaration to the Veterans Association which Tanaka drafted for General Terauchi Masatake (1911), he wrote:

> It is the bounden duty of veterans to exert their best effort in furthering this spirit (*bushidō*), to promote military knowledge, to become the shield for the Imperial Household and to endure the

---

[37] *Ibid.*, 472. Sokō explains in *Shidō*:
"The business of the samurai consists in reflecting on his own station in life, in discharging loyal service to his master if he has one, in deepening his fidelity in associations with friends, and, with due consideration of his own position, in devoting himself to duty above all.... The samurai dispenses with the business of the farmer, artisan, and merchant and confines himself to practicing this Way; should there be someone in the three classes of the common people who transgresses against these moral principles, the samurai summarily punishes him and thus upholds proper moral principles in the land.... The three classes of the common people make him (samurai) their teacher and respect him. By following his teachings, they are enabled to understand what is fundamental and what is secondary." Tsunoda, De Bary, and Keene (comps.), I, 390.

burden of becoming the bulwark of the nation. There is no other purpose for this Association but to make the veterans perform their real duty as military men..., and thus make them the best examples of the nation.[38]

Tanaka then realized (originally inspired by Nogi Maresuke shortly before his death) that the Army and the Veterans Association were still not enough. If he really wanted to be thorough about national reconstruction, he had to start it among youths before they entered the Army. His close observation of youth activities abroad during his military inspection tour (from December 1913 to August 1914, Manchuria-China-Russia-Europe) further convinced him that Japan needed more vigorous youth activities for nation-building. After the tour, Tanaka decided to establish a powerful nationwide youth association and busied himself negotiating with the Ministries of Internal Affairs and of Education, meeting local youth leaders, and distributing pamphlets about his plan. He originally intended to name the association "The Patriotic (or Self-Sacrificing) Youth Corps," (Seinen Giyū-dan).

Tanaka clearly stipulated his idea in the draft plan for the establishment of the Patriotic Youth Corps (August 1915):

Principles:

1. To revere the Imperial Household, to bear *kokutai* in mind, and to fulfill the great obligation of loyalty and filial piety.

2. To observe strict discipline and temperance, and to esteem the ethics of obedience and co-operation.

3. To train one's physical strength, to keep fidelity and to overcome traits of timidity and cowardice.

Regulations:

4. To esteem the spirit of frugality and militarism and to cherish progressive ambition.

6. To place high value on the sense of honor, to respect one's seniors and to be honest to friends.

---

[38]   Tanaka Giichi Denki Kankō-kai (ed.), I, 411.

8. To confront the troubles of others voluntarily and to endeavor to make contributions to public affairs.

10. To not neglect physical training such as gymnastics, athlet-
ics and martial arts without reason.

11. To be simple and plain in choosing daily necessities such
as food, clothing and shelter.

12. Not to enjoy entertainment which would cause frivolous
and extravagant desires.[39]

In 1917, due to Tanaka's efforts, the National Youth Association
was founded. Tanaka Giichi as Vice-Chief of the General Staff
and then as War Minister in the Hara Cabinet was chairman of
both the Veterans Association and the Youth Association until
the spring of 1919.

In the meantime, Tanaka was aware of the need for *kokutai*
education to begin with elementary and middle school children.
This idea was expressed in his plan for revising universal compulsory education (1916):

It must be a great concern to our school education that educated
people lack the spirit of sacrifice and are poor in military knowledge.
... The cultivation of the sacrificing spirit and the improvement of
military knowledge among the educated people must be sought in
middle school and in elementary school education. The most important thing in our national education is to bring up good and loyal
subjects who are rich in the spirit of wanting to fight gloriously for
their country, to cultivate their morality, to develop their intellectual
faculties, and to strengthen their bodies. Clearly this is the intention of the Imperial Rescript on Education. Nevertheless, the reason
why satisfactory results have not been obtained up to now is that
this principle of education is not throughly carried out. The system
is provided, but is not accompanied by its execution. The curriculum
of military drill is established in school. Its purpose is not to train
soldiers, but to strengthen the subjects' bodies, to envigorate their
spirit, to cultivate their moral sense, and to strengthen fortitude and

[39] *Ibid.*, 606–607.

manliness. This is the quality of good soldiers. In a country where the universal conscription system is enforced, it is necessary to cultivate such a quality. Only the subjects who are educated under this principle can be victors not only in military but also in other affairs. This fact has been proved by the example of the Great European War. Indeed, there is no need of distinction between the education for soldiers and for ordinary subjects. This is the quintessence of the All-Subjects-are-Soldiers-ism.[40]

Thus Tanaka's grand plan of promoting *kokutai* was firmly established. According to this plan, all Japanese children were to be exposed to the idea of *kokutai*, i.e., self-sacrificing devotion to the Imperial Household, and traditional virtues, especially *bushidō*; later, they were to be recruited into the Youth Association; at the age of twenty they would be drafted and the idea of *kokutai* and military education would be drummed into their heads; after leaving the Army they were to propagate *kokutai* in society through the Veterans Association.[41]

---

[40]   *Ibid.*, 476.

[41]   Both the Veterans Association and the Youth Association contributed greatly to Tanaka's national reconstruction. For example, in the famous communist purge of the March Fifteenth Incident (1928) which Prime Minister Tanaka carried out, all branches of the Veterans Association made a declaration at once to fight against "dangerous thoughts and for the preservation of *kokutai*." The Association played an important role in villages by assisting the Tanaka Administration's suppression of communism. In the same way, the Youth Association was reorganized into the Great Japan's Youth Association League (Dai Nihon Rengō Seinen-dan) in 1926, and began active protests against "degeneration" of rural communities. From this organization thousands of volunteer soldiers for the cultivation of Manchuria and Mongolia (Mam-Mō Kaitaku Giyū-gun) were sent to the Continent.

Yamakawa Hitoshi, a socialist leader, was already aware of this danger in 1923 and wrote an article entitled, "The Youth Association and the Veterans Association," in *Kaihō* (Emancipation, September 1923), saying:

"The Japanese governing class has organized all young people in Japan into a government-controlled Youth Association. The youth are always on the progressive side, everywhere the budding revolutionaries. To crush budding movements is the safest way to destroy the revolutionary movement.... It [the Youth Association] is a skillful trick to crush this.

"However, the Japanese governing class has a greater ambition. They are not satisfied with just crushing the egg, from which hatches a cock that is to announce the dawn of the new life and the new society. They even hope to produce a new rooster which will highly exalt the preservation of the status quo and which will attack progressive thoughts and movements."

However, Tanaka's "All-Japanese-are-Soldiers-ism" had another important purpose — to transform Japan into a garrison-state. Not to be confused with Tanaka's "All-Japanese-are-Soldiers-ism (Kokumin Kaihei-shugi)" is Kokumin Kaihei-seido, the universal conscription system. The latter is a system in which all subjects may be drafted once during their life. Tanaka himself confused these two terms and often used them as synonyms. What he actually meant by using the two terms synonymously was that all subjects regardless of their own occupations always had to assume that they were soldiers. In the previously quoted plan for revising universal compulsory education, Tanaka stated:

> In our country, the universal conscription system (Kokumin Kaihei-seido) was introduced in early Meiji, and the Imperial Rescript on Education was granted in the 23rd year of Meiji (1890). Thus, what the Emperor meant by saying: "Should an emergency arise one should courageously sacrifice oneself to the public good and should support the Imperial destiny which is coeval with heaven and earth" was to remind us of the principle of national education in which all subjects are soldiers (Kokumin Kaihei-shugi). The military system, therefore, is concurrently the basis of our national system. This is the essence of our *kokutai* which is unsurpassed in the world.[42]

Tanaka was preoccupied with defense problems. In order for a small country like Japan to win successive wars, all Japanese had to be made into soldiers. As early as 1898, he expressed this conviction to his colleagues:

> In the future a small country like Japan will always be required to fight great powers as we fought against China. There is no comparison between those powers and Japan both in terms of the number of soldiers and general population. Consequently, as war is protracted, we must send reservists to the front. Therefore, it is very important for us to train reservists so that they will meet this grave responsibility.[43]

Yamakawa Kikue and Yamakawa Shinsaku (eds.), V, 259.

[42] Tanaka Giichi Denki Kankō-kai (ed.), I, 472.

[43] *Ibid.*, 399.

In December 1915, before more than 10,000 representatives of
the Veterans Association who had assembled at the Yasukuni
Shrine, Vice Chief of General Staff Tanaka expressed the same
idea:

> Now Europe is in the midst of war and every nation is expending
> its maximum physical strength, military capacity and financial re-
> sources. We ought to be mindful of this fact. Should a national
> emergency arise, we must know that our country also has to confront
> the same situation.... In the next war, the nation will not fight only
> with soldiers and warships. The whole nation with all its might and
> main has to fight to win the final battle. We must know that the
> next war will be a total national war.... Hence in future wars we
> cannot expect to win if only our soldiers are strong. The people, in
> general, must become strong. It goes without saying that a strong
> nation must be endowed with robust health, strong physique and with
> a virile spirit. But these qualities are not enough. The nation has
> to be rich in loyalty to the Emperor, love of nation, and in the spirit
> of co-operation, obedience and good order.

With this hope to make Japan a garrison-state, Tanaka declared:

> From now on,...the reservists are the main body of the Japanese
> Army and the soldiers on active duty are only the supplement.
> Therefore, Japan's future fighting power is chiefly dependent upon
> reservists and not upon soldiers on active duty.... Our country
> intends to reorganize the Army so as to make the reservists its base
> instead of the soldiers on active duty.[44]

In Tanaka's conception of international relations, each nation
by nature sought its self-aggrandizement, which led the powers
inevitably to violent wars. Japan with her samurai tradition not
only had to demonstrate her readiness to fight at any time, but
also had to strive to win all wars. By doing so, like samurai and
like Tanaka, who himself constantly struggled to win power and
prestige, Japan had to exalt her national prestige among the powers,
and ultimately to establish her military hegemony over the world.

---

[44] Kawai, 136–145.

This was, as he said, "the essence of Japan's *kokutai* which was unsurpassed in the world." His national reconstruction based upon *kokutai* and plan for the establishment of a garrison-state were, in the final analysis, to propagate this *kokutai* in the world, which was the natural destiny of the Imperial Way believed to be "coeval with heaven and earth."

Nevertheless, Tanaka had no clear ideas on modern economy to facilitate his hope for Japan's military expansion. Because of this, his whole scheme seems rather "quixotic" or fantastic, just as his nickname suggested. In September 1919, War Minister Tanaka addressed the Youth Association:

> Traditionally, what has made the Japanese different from Westerners is that the Japanese are not influenced by money. Transcending money, transcending materials, we consider spiritual things the most important. This is the unique character of the Japanese people. We are completely different from the people of mammon. And yet, Westerners are trying to seduce us and convert us into a belief that money is the greatest thing in the world. If we become unable to hold up our heads before money, our unique national character will be extinguished.[45]

As Tanaka had taught his *shosei* the samurai spirit of perseverance, and as he had attempted to carry out paternalism and Tōkichirō-ism in the Army, he still believed that the essential element of national strength was "spiritual power," and not money nor material power. Furthermore, for Tanaka, to think them unimportant as such meant precisely to preserve the beauty of Japan's *kokutai*.

As a capitalistic mode of economy began to flourish in Japan during the Taishō period, Tanaka was even more convinced that Japan had to maintain her traditional spiritual identity. To be indifferent to money matters and to despise merchant's attitude of profit-making was the way of samurai, and therefore it was also the way of the modern Japan. Hence Tanaka, instead of

---

[45] Kawai, 396.

advocating the importance of commerce and industry, encouraged people to engage in thrifty life, which was the best means of cultivating people's character as well as the national wealth. In August 1919, War Minister Tanaka addressed the veterans:

> In these times, the people are very clamorous about food problems. But generally speaking, under these circumstances, it is the best time and the most urgent for us to work for thrift and saving. The encouragement of thrift and saving will restrain the people's extravagance on the one hand and will rouse the sense of prudence among those who tend to become flippant on the other. Furthermore, it will increase our national resources. If all people restrain themselves from becoming too extravagant with food, such a situation as we see today will not come about.... I believe it very important to investigate how lavishly the people are spending for food and to stamp out such an evil for the solution of food problems.[46]

Following the same line of argument, he encouraged saving through frugality in order to prepare for a national crisis. To the representatives of the Veterans Association who gathered at the Military Academy in September 1921, Tanaka said:

> This public service bag (*hōkō-bukuro*) is to make soldiers prepare themselves daily without a flurry, when they receive their induction papers. This is exactly the same idea as in the past when *bushi* saved their war funds in their armour cases and never took out the money in ordinary times, no matter how much they were pressed. Thus, today...everybody should reduce his expenses of life greatly, and I hope this effort will spread to all the villages and towns. Unless the whole people are awakened and become frugal, our country will return to poverty as before. Nevertheless, nobody has been willing to put this into practice and no association or group has taken charge of this problem. This is most regrettable. Under the present condition of our country, I believe it most proper and effective for the branches of the Veterans Association to take the initiative in this task. Therefore, I urge you to consider this problem.[47]

---

46 Hosokawa, 66–67.
47 Tanaka Giichi Denki Kankō-kai (ed.), I, 435.

It is not surprising, then, to find that Tanaka as a believer in a traditional economy advocated agrarianism. He preached to the youth:

> To make a country rich and strong, agriculture must be our first consideration. There is no doubt about this. Especially, for a country like Japan, we must regard agriculture the most important. Nevertheless, young farmers tend to regard such jobs as raising cattle, carrying manure, cultivating land, as something mean to them, as soon as they come to the city from the village. They even feel ashamed to be called farmers. Formerly in Japan, people used to call farmers "respectful farmers" (*ohyakushō-sama*) and this word had significance. They laid in a stock of manure, which was just like saving money. To take care of cattle is the most valuable thing. The words, respectful farmers, were to remind people of such ideas. Even if one wears dirty clothes in engaging himself in agriculture, it does not affect his dignity.[48]

Tanaka's promotion of agriculture instead of commerce and trade, his encouragement of thrift and saving in place of profit making, and his personal conduct of *hōon*, returning *on* (favors or thanks) — all are reminiscent of the teachings of Ninomiya Sontoku (1787–1856). He also seemed to have been profoundly influenced by the Chinese Legalist text, *Han Fei Tzu*, which he studied in his youth.

The following speech of his (1917) would best summarize Tanaka's whole idea of economy, national power, and character building:

> The most important thing in the spiritual part of education for youth is to cultivate the traditional soul...which our nation has had for several thousand years, to envigorate the spirit of heroic sacrifice for public service, to observe discipline and abstinence without falling into license, and to cultivate the lawful mind to abide with law and order, with the moral sense of obedience and the idea of co-operation. Furthermore, they must be educated to have the spirit of

---

[48] Kawai, 361.

fortitude and manliness, to gain strong self-confidence, to practice simplicity and frugality, to not become frivolous and flippant, to strengthen endurance, and to overcome every kind of difficulty and scarcity. And with such ideas, thoughts must be unified. Only the person with such character and personality can overcome the temptations of society, can succeed in various businesses, can win world trust in commercial dealings, can become excellent soldiers, and can take the great burden of cultivating the national destiny and to make the nation strong and prosper. Even if one reads millions of books, if he is flippant and frivolous, effeminate and timid, poor in character and physique, he can hardly bear the burden for the nation in the future.[49]

CLIMBING TO THE TOP OF THE POWER-PYRAMID

Tanaka was an extremely ambitious man. He dreamed of becoming a Kinoshita Tōkichirō, who from peasant beginnings had built up his power by wits, machinations and manipulation, and finally came to control the whole of Japan. In 1909 he became Section Chief of Military Affairs. After his efforts to propagate paternalism in his Second Brigade, he became Bureau Chief in 1911, the Vice Chief of the General Staff and Lieutenant General in 1915, and then War Minister in 1918 under the Hara Cabinet. After that between 1921 and 1925 he became War Minister two more times, Council of Military Affairs, Chairman of the Seiyūkai, and finally in April 1927 Prime Minister.

Various factors came into play for this success: his ambition, unyielding spirit, overbearing and *oyabun* temperament, distinguished activities within the Army. However, perhaps the most remarkable endowment of his was the political skill of mani-

---

[49]   *Ibid.*, 316–317; with regard to Tanaka's activities in the Youth Association and the Veterans Association, see also Hori, 121–134; Hosokawa, 48–73, 87–89.

pulation. He was a genius, not in the intellectual sense, but in winning the hearts of the people. His emotional eloquence, boldness, courage, organizational skill and leadership, magnanimity, loyalty, and devotion to seniors — all of these were attributes of his political skill, especially suitable in the Army. Thanks to this ability, Tanaka enjoyed strong support from many powerful figures within and without the Army: Genrō Yamagata Aritomo, Generals Nogi Maresuke, Katsura Tarō, Terauchi Masatake; Genrō Ōkuma Shigenobu and Inoue Kaoru. It is noteworthy that all of them except Ōkuma were Tanaka's senior compatriots from Chōshū. Tanaka also had many followers who backed him, including Matsuoka Yōsuke (1880–1946), Tanaka's protégé who furthered Tanaka's aggressive "autonomous diplomacy" by withdrawing Japan's membership from the League of Nations and who became the main schemer of the Tripartite Pact; Mori Kaku, who became Parliamentary Vice Minister of Foreign Affairs in the Tanaka Cabinet and a forerunner of the advocates for the Greater East Asia Co-prosperity Sphere; and Ishiwara Kanji, who was a chief promoter of the Manchurian Incident as the Staff Officer of the Kwantung Army.

Among all these supporters, Tanaka, perhaps, owed his success most to General Nogi — the hero of the first Sino-Japanese War and the Russo-Japanese War — and Genrō Yamagata, the "Tycoon" of the Army. Just to give brief episodes to show their intimate relations: During Tanaka's misfortunes in the haunted house, it was Nogi who looked after him in the hospital and took care of his father's funeral. In the first Sino-Japanese War, Nogi had a severe cold, but he never accepted his subordinates' repeated requests to wear a warm coat specially made for him, because, Nogi said, he alone could not enjoy such comfort while his soldiers were suffering. And it was Tanaka, Nogi's favorite, who finally succeeded in the "mission" to persuade the stubborn commander. Nogi also helped Tanaka in establishing the Veterans Association and the Youth Association. When Nogi committed *junshi,* he left notes behind to a few close friends, among them Tanaka Giichi.

Both Yamagata and Tanaka himself considered Tanaka to be the heir apparent of Yamagata as the chief of the Chōshū clique. Tanaka won Yamagata's recognition during the Russo-Japanese War. Since then, through Tanaka's activities in planning for an increase of divisions during the Saionji Cabinet (August 1911-December 1912), establishing the Veterans Association and the Youth Association, their close relationship increased to the extent that Yamagata was convinced that he trusted Tanaka the most. Tanaka frequently visited Yamagata at home, and they drank together. It is reported that on such occasions Yamagata accepted Tanaka's arguments and expressed them to the public as his own. When Hara was to organize his Cabinet, he trusted Genrō Yamagata with the selection of the War Minister. Yamagata naturally chose his protégé, and Tanaka became War Minister. After this, Yamagata entrusted Tanaka with the selection of successive War Ministers. Hence when Tanaka resigned from the Hara Cabinet and Hara asked Yamagata to choose the next War Minister (June 9, 1921), Yamagata told Hara to ask Tanaka, and Tanaka chose his good friend since his life in the Military Academy, Yamanashi Hanzō (1864–1944). As the reader might recall, Yamanashi in return worked hard to support Tanaka as the chairman of the Seiyūkai by inducing the Seiyū Hontō[50] members to join the Seiyūkai, which caused the notorious scandals.

On January 10, 1922, Genrō Ōkuma Shigenobu died, and three weeks later Genrō Yamagata Aritomo passed away. Generals Katsura Tarō and Terauchi Masatake had already died (the former in 1913 and the latter in 1919). Tanaka lost, in quick succession, his most powerful patrons, but it also gave him a good opportunity to build his own power. Within the Army, Tanaka had no rival except General Uyehara Yūsaku who was his senior. Tanaka's

---

[50]   Hosokawa, 89–94; Hori, 134–154.

ambition for supremacy in the Army could not but drive him into a bitter power struggle against Uyehara. The confrontation between the two generals was so severe that even the public knew the Army was split into two camps. In addition to their own ambition, various other factors were involved. Tanaka, considering himself to be the legitimate successor of Yamagata, hoped to maintain the dominant Chōshū clique under his leadership. Uyehara directly opposed Tanaka's scheme, partly because he was from Satsuma, Chōshū's traditional rival, but also because he had more universalistic ideals in order to establish a more modern efficient Army, unbound by factions and cliques. Intellectually, too, the two were opposite. Uyehara was better versed in modern ideas than was Tanaka, whose mentality was, according to some critics, equal to the level of Shimizu Jirochō or Kunisada Chūji (traditional *oyabun* of ne'er-do-well gangs).

The two rivals came to a direct showdown over the selection of War Minister in the Kiyoura Cabinet (January-June 1924). Tanaka arbitrarily and against Uyehara's desires chose Ugaki Kazushige (1868–1956), a junior to other ranking generals who were candidates on the list. Indignant, Uyehara demanded that Tanaka resign from the Army, and those candidates who missed the opportunity to become War Minister publicly attacked Tanaka.[51]

At about the same time there had also been a factional struggle within the Seiyūkai after Hara Kei's powerful leadership. In the Hara Seiyūkai Cabinet there were several future leaders of the party, including Minister of Commerce and Agriculture Yamamoto Tatsuo (1856–1947) and Minister of Finance Takahashi Korekiyo, who had been competitors for a long time. Owing to Hara's assassination, on November 13, 1921, Takahashi was appointed Prime Minister by the Genrō. Simultaneously he

---

[51] For more detailed accounts of this event, see Araki Sadao (ed.), *Gensui Uyehara Yūsaku-den* (General Uyehara Yūsaku's biography; Tokyo, 1937), II, 196–212; Matsushita Yoshio, *Nihon no Gumbatsu-zō*, 199–232 and *Nihon Gumbatsu no Kōbō*, II, 165–192, III, 59–79; *The Asahi Shimbun*, March 14–21, 1926; Baba Tsunego, *Gendai Jimbutsu Hyōron*, 52–55.

became chairman of the Seiyūkai, because the majority of the
party cadres thought it advantageous for the party for the Prime
Minister to be concurrently the leader of the party.   Other elders
of the party like Yamamoto and Tokonami Takejirō (1866–1935),
who had been Minister of Internal Affairs in the Hara Cabinet,
felt alienated from the main faction.   The struggle became more
complicated when Takahashi tried to reshuffle Cabinet members
according to his own leadership.   The schisms of the Takahashi
Cabinet became uncontrollable, and the government was obliged
to resign.   On June 9, 1922, Admiral Katō Tomosaburō organized a new Cabinet.   Within the Seiyūkai Takahashi could not
but be blamed, because the party lost power to the military-
bureaucratic clique due to his lack of strong leadership.   Over
the issue of whether the Seiyūkai should support the Kiyoura
Cabinet headed by the aged Chairman of the Privy Council, the
ever aggravating factional struggles came to a culmination.   Yamamoto and Tokonami in alliance organized a new party, the Seiyū
Hontō (literally meaning the main faction of the Seiyūkai), and
supported the Kiyoura Cabinet.

After the split, the remaining cadres of the Seiyūkai realized
that they needed a powerful leader who could control all factions.
Takahashi himself expressed his desire to resign, partly because
of his wish to take responsibility for mismanagement of the party,
and partly because of his exhaustion from his efforts to control
the long-lasting schisms.   Furthermore, the Seiyūkai advocated
"positive" policies to all problems and was increasingly leaning
toward the right, in contrast to its rival, the Kenseikai, which took
on more liberal policies.   Tanaka during this time was in trouble
in the Army, and aimed at a higher goal — to dominate the whole
of Japan instead of just the Army.   Having been War Minister
in the Hara Cabinet, Tanaka had had close connections with the
Seiyūkai.   Tanaka's organizational skills which had been demonstrated by his establishment of the Veterans Association and the
Youth Association, his *oyabun* temperament, his motto of "being

positive and offensive," and his traditionalistic leadership all met Seiyūkai needs. Hence on May 13, 1925, after complicated maneuvers within the party, and between Tanaka and the Seiyūkai, Tanaka was invited to become Chairman of the Seiyūkai. The Seiyūkai needed a leader like Tanaka, and the latter had to have a strong party backing in order to become Prime Minister during the time when the popular movements for party government and universal suffrage were prevailing in society.[52]

The coalition Cabinet headed by the Kenseikai's Katō Takaaki had been in power since June 1924. The Prime Minister hoped to continue his coalition with the new Chairman of the Seiyūkai. But Tanaka, unlike Takahashi, refused to co-operate with Katō. As a result, an "unprecedented bitter struggle" developed among the three major parties — the Kenseikai, the Seiyūkai, and the Seiyū Hontō — and a number of minor parties. In his inaugural speech, Tanaka said he would commit *seppuku* if he could not make his party grasp power.[53] Upon Tanaka's entrance into the Seiyūkai, the whole tone of the party changed drastically. Militant members like Yamamoto Jōtarō (1867–1936), Mori Kaku and Hatoyama Ichirō (1883–1959) began to dominate the party.[54] The Seiyūkai under Tanaka's leadership and backed by these members opposed every policy of the Kenseikai Government, especially Shidehara's "weak-kneed" and "negative" foreign policy. Finally in April 1927, unable to solve the financial crisis, the Kenseikai Cabinet resigned. Thus on April 19 the Imperial Mandate to organize a new Cabinet fell upon Tanaka Giichi, leader of the second largest party.

---

[52] Ishigami's account is the best on this event, Ishigami, 9–255; 343–376. See also Matsushita Yoshio, *Nihon Riku-Kaigun Sōdō-shi*, 277–282.

[53] Yamaura Kan'ichi (ed.), 565.

[54] *The Asahi Shimbun* also noticed this point. The newspaper stated that it was an unhealthy situation for the Seiyūkai that the party was filled with right-wing patriots without left-wing or liberal groups to balance the general tone of the party. See *The Asahi Shimbun*, July 2, 1926.

Going Home

The Tanaka Administration lasted for a little over two years. His aggressive "autonomous or uncooperative" policy set off strong international criticism, and violent anti-Japanese movements in China which resulted in a sharp decline of Japan's China trade.[55] The assassination of Chang Tso-lin (1873–1928) made his son, Chang Hsüeh-liang (1898–   ), bring Manchuria under the Nationalist unification. Hence Tanaka even failed in his well advertised "Manchuria-First" policy, by which he had hoped to increase Japan's territorial and military control over Manchuria. In response to these failures, mounting criticisms against the Tanaka Administration came from all parts of society. On top of that and because of Tanaka's successive blunders, the Emperor admonished him, especially for his indecisiveness in punishing Kōmoto Daisaku who killed Chang Tso-lin. Tanaka's shock was great, for in spite of all his titles — retired general, Prime Minister, Minister of Foreign Affairs, Minister of Colonial Affairs, and Chairman of the Seiyūkai — and in spite of his indomitable character, to him the Emperor was still absolute. He told his friends that his heart was benumbed by the Emperor's reproof and that he no longer had courage to maintain his administration.[56]

Tanaka's statement of resignation read:

An incident which broke out abroad last year [Chang's assassination] became the cause for political strife and finally resulted in a political problem for our nation. I deeply regret this development for the sake of the nation and of the Imperial Government. In the light of my grave responsibility to assist the Imperial Rule, my apprehen-

---

[55] See the table of the Chinese boycotts and the Japanese trade to China in the Appendix.

[56] Tanaka Giichi Denki Kankō-kai (ed.), II, 1035–1043.

sions are beyond measure.... I believe that under the present circumstances of domestic and international affairs a change of Cabinet will
bring about a turn of the wheel and an advancement of the national
destiny. Hence I hereby reverently present my resignation to the
Emperor.

My soul and body, all is for the Imperial Nation. Whether in
or out of the government this resolution of mine is the same. Today
facing national difficulties, the nation is increasingly busy with
domestic and external affairs. All I must do in the last remaining
few years of my life is to devote this old man's flesh and spirit entirely
to the country of the Emperor.[57]

Having visited the Ise Shrine, the ancestral shrine of the Imperial
Household, and the Imperial Tombs at Momoyama, on July 26
this old loyal subject left Tokyo for Hagi.

The "homecoming" always meant a great deal to Tanaka,
who stressed an ascriptive tie to his birthplace. He was still the
oyabun among his Yamaguchi (Chōshū) compatriots. At all
stations and meeting halls he received great receptions. At one
place his *kobun* who was himself the local boss of the Seiyūkai
brought several thousand school children to the station and gave
repeated "*banzai*" to the retired Prime Minister, waving the
national colors. At another station another follower led local
politicians and crowds, and presented two hundred fresh *ayu*
(sweetfish which are considered a rare delicacy in summer time).
At still another station, a henchman of Tanaka brought villagers
and townsmen and presented huge ice pillars containing all kinds
of beautiful summer flowers to Tanaka.

Day and night, grand receptions were held for the great *oyabun*
of Yamaguchi. At one place a special night-fishing party was
sponsored by the local people to entertain Tanaka. When Tanaka
caught a big fish, everybody in the boats hailed "*banzai*" and
"*banzai*" for him. At Hagi grand scale fireworks were displayed
to welcome the local hero — and so on and so forth. Tanaka

57 *The Asahi Shimbun* and *The Mainichi Shimbun,* July 3, 1929.

Giichi contentedly remarked, "the happiest thing in the world is to come home and meet compatriots and old friends and to talk about the old days." He complained, but with satisfaction, "nobody leaves me alone. People follow me one after another like the excrement of goldfish." In spite of such busy and excited parties, Tanaka never forgot to give offerings to his ancestors and to conduct grand Buddhist services for them, nor did he neglect to pay a visit to the former lord of Chōshū, Prince Mōri Motoaki (1497–1571). On September 29, 1929, only a little over two months after his resignation from the premiership, either because of serious grief from being chided by the Emperor or because of uproarious festivities extended by his faithful followers in Yamaguchi, Tanaka Giichi died of a heart attack. He was sixty-six years of age.[58]

To those who aspired at Japan's political modernization, the Tanaka Cabinet was one of the most abhorrent ones. According to Baba Tsunego, the best contemporary critic of politics and political figures, the Tanaka Administration was a typical case of bad politics, injudicious policy and corrupt government. Baba said, "Tanaka looks just as if the hero of feudal story books (kōdanbon). His thought and behaviour is no more than that of the oyabun of traditional ne'er-do-well gangs, except he does not have the long sword which the ne'er-do-well gangsters used to wear. Unfortunately, Tanaka appeared in a wrong age. He should have lived in the feudal age, but not in the age of Shōwa (literally meaning bright and peaceful).... In view of present day, he is nothing but a Don Quixote of the East. But the most pitiful thing is the fortune of the Japanese people who must sing and dance together with this Don Quixote."[59]

With all of his defects, however, many people still liked or even loved Tanaka, for he was very human. In contrast to Shi-

---

58 Hosokawa, 206–234.
59 Baba Tsunego, Gendai Jimbutsu Hyōron, 64.

dehara who was a highly rational but rather austere lawyer-bureaucrat, Tanaka's life is filled with interesting anecdotes. During his stay in Russia before the Russo-Japanese War, for instance, he competed with Russian soldiers in drinking, became completely drunk, and could not get up the next morning. In his farewell party, Tanaka was shouldered by the Russian soldiers of the Alexander III Regiment, and became so enraptured that he kept scattering 5 rouble coins over the soldiers till he was carried over to his carriage. Tanaka used to take many soldiers to the story-telling house, and being deeply impressed by the story of filial sons or loyal samurai he could not resist crying, and was awfully embarrassed before his subordinates. No matter how many times he was deceived, Tanaka gave money away generously to those who came to him for pecuniary help. When his aides reminded him that many of them were swindlers, Tanaka used to say, "It's all right, don't say that. They, too, are thinking of me. Sometime, I might be able to use them." Because of his optimistic, magnanimous and chaotic character, he left phenomenal debts when he died. Even his own house had been in mortgage. But he also had friends of a kind who were willing to pay all of his debts back. Such was the man and the life of Tanaka Giichi.

CHAPTER 4

SHIDEHARA KIJŪRŌ
THE MAN AND HIS IDEAS

THE MAN

Baron Shidehara Kijūrō,[1] who became Foreign Minister

---

[1] Major works related to Shidehara Kijūrō's biography are: Shidehara Heiwa Zaidan (ed.), *Shidehara Kijūrō* (Tokyo, 1955); Shidehara Kijūrō, *Gaikō Gojūnen*; Ujita Naoyoshi. There are also abundant unpublished materials in Shidehara Heiwa Bunko (Shidehara Peace Library) within the Library of Congress in Tokyo; especially important are "Shoka no Shidehara-kan" (Various people's views on Shidehara); Shina Mondai Kankei (Problems related to China); "Gaikō Kanken" (My view on diplomacy); "Shidehara Keizai Gaikō Shiryō" (Materials on Shidehara's economic-oriented diplomacy); "Manshū Mondai" (Manchurian problems). Shidehara himself wrote several reminiscent articles, such as "Watakushi no Yōshō Jidai" (My childhood), *The Yomiuri Shimbun Gakkō-ban*, November 27, 1950; "Wasure e nu Hitobito" (Unforgettable people), *Bungei Shunjū* (Jan. 1951), 54–65; and the article on his stay in Holland in *The Yomiuri Shimbun*, November 15, 1950, the evening edition. Other related works are: Baba Tsunego, *Gendai Jimbutsu Hyōron*, 273–289; *Seikai Jimbutsu Fūkei*, 305–326, 331–395, 419–456; Horiuchi Tateki, *passim*; Ishii Itarō, *passim*; Tabata Shinobu, *Teikō-ken* (Right of resistance; Kyoto, 1965), 352–356; Katō-haku Denki Hensan Iinkai (ed.), *Katō Takaaki* (Tokyo and Osaka, 1929), 2 vols., *passim*, especially vol. 2; Aoki Tokuzō, *Wakatsuki Reijirō, Hamaguchi Osachi* (Tokyo, 1958); Wakatsuki Reijirō, *Kofūan Kaiko-roku* (Reminiscences at Kofūan;

Shidehara Kijūrō

twice — both preceding and following the Tanaka Cabinet (from June 1924 to April 1927 and from July 1929 to December 1931) — was a man with a personality and cultural identity entirely different from his competitor, Tanaka Giichi. If Tanaka was a man with a sword, Shidehara was a man with a Webster's Dictionary. If the former loved to quote sayings of Japanese and Chinese sages and patriotic leaders, the latter liked Western fairy tales and words of Western statesmen. Tanaka was praised for his excellent classical Chinese compositions, while Shidehara's English was called a "national treasure" by his colleagues.[2] Tanaka adored the *shishi* of the Restoration, whereas Shidehara respected British and American diplomats.[3] Tanaka enjoyed *yōkyoku* (Noh recitation) and *kōdan* (storytelling about such traditional heroes as loyal subjects, courageous samurai, and filial sons), while Shidehara loved to recite beautiful English passages. The two were different even in their tastes for liquor: Tanaka preferred Japanese *sake*, and Shidehara liked good whisky, brandy, and cognac.

Shidehara's love of the West was thorough. For example,

Tokyo, 1950), *passim;* Harada Kumao, I, II, and the separate additional volume (*bekkan*), *passim*; Ishii Kikujirō, *Gaikō Yoroku* (Reminiscences of my diplomatic career; Tokyo, 1930), *passim;* KiyosawaKiyoshi, II, Chaps. 2 and 3.

[2] "Shoka no Shidehara-kan", 277.

[3] Shidehara especially admired Henry W. Denison (1846–1924), an American advisor to the Foreign Ministry; Sir. Edward G. Grey (1862–1933), the Foreign Secretary of Great Britain (1905–1916); and James Bryce (1838–1922), the British Ambassador to the United States (1907–1913) and the author of *The American Commonwealth*.

when he took a walk, he always had a gentleman's cane and wore a bowler hat like a British gentleman.[4] He ate a British-style breakfast with tea and toast, wearing a dressing gown. He ordered his suits from one of the best tailors in London and chose the best British materials.[5] He was so well informed on things Western that even within the Foreign Ministry, where there were many Western-oriented diplomats, he won a reputation for his thorough knowledge of Western etiquette.[6] Shidehara felt so much at home with English that he usually prepared manuscripts of diplomatic documents first in English and then later translated them into Japanese.

Once an American soldier, through Shidehara's barber, asked Prime Minister Shidehara (his premiership: October 1945-May 1946) to give him an autograph. The Prime Minister wrote the following passage:

> The quality of mercy is not strained:
> It droppeth as the gentle rain from heaven
> Upon the place beneath. It is twice blest;
> It blesseth him that gives, and him that takes.

The American soldier might have expected some fancy calligraphy such as most Japanese statesmen would have done, but Shidehara wrote a passage from Shakespeare's *The Merchant of Venice*. And he did so from memory without making a mistake.[7] To give some explanation of the passage: The barber and the soldier were good friends since the former had offered a night's shelter at his house when the soldier, being drunk, lost his way to the camp. The passage had a double meaning: the friendship between the barber and the soldier, and the friendship between Japan and the United States. In the former case the barber was to give and

---

[4] Ishii Itarō, "Shidehara-dan no Omoide" (My recollection of Baron Shidehara), "Shoka no Shidehara-kan", 275-276.
[5] Kishi Kuramatsu, "Shidehara Kijūrō-shi no Omoide o Kataru" (Reminiscences of Mr. Shidehara Kijūrō), "Shoka no Shidehara-kan", 25-35.
[6] Ishii, "Shidehara-dan no Omoide," 276.
[7] Shidehara, *Gaikō Gojūnen*, 315-321.

the soldier to take, and in the latter case the position was reversed. The United States was to give aid to Japan devastated by the war.

In personality and national-cultural identity the difference between the two diplomats was also profound. Tanaka was a born *oyabun* attended by many faithful followers, while Shidehara was a loner. Tanaka was closely tied to various cliques and factions, whereas Shidehara was a modern "free-floating" man. Tanaka loved competitive games and had an inner urge to dominate others. Shidehara disliked any kind of game and enjoyed taking a walk, instead. The former was a country man speaking in the vulgar Yamaguchi dialect, whereas the latter seemed surrounded by an urbane aristocratic atmosphere. Being nicknamed "Don Quixote," Tanaka liked exaggeration and aggrandizement. Shidehara, on the other hand, was a rigid and self-restrained lawyer-bureaucrat who attached great importance to orderly procedure, lawfulness, and rationality. Tanaka esteemed Japanese traditional values such as loyalty, filial-piety, and obedience, whereas Shidehara emphasized freedom, equality, and individuality. Tanaka considered politico-military interests as the highest diplomatic goal; Shidehara, on the other hand, emphasized economic interests. Above all, the former hoped to maintain *kokutai*, while the latter wished to promote democracy. Few statesmen in modern Japanese history both enjoyed and suffered such extreme public praise and censure simultaneously as did they. This was because their values, principles, and aspirations were entirely opposite, which in a sense represented Japan's dilemma in searching for a national-cultural identity.[8]

Why and how was such a personality and cultural identity of Shidehara Kijūrō created? Why was his so different from Tanaka's? First of all, the two were born and brought up in dif-

---

[8] Kanamori Tokujirō, "Shidehara-sensei no Omoide" (Reminiscences of Mr. Shidehara), *Shoka no Shidehara-kan*, 278. See also various remarks on Shidehara by Ashida Hitoshi, Itō Jusshi, Nagai Matsuzō, and Kiyosawa Kiyoshi in *Shoka no Shidehara-kan*.

ferent circumstances. Tanaka was born in Hagi, a conservative castle-town of Yamaguchi, in late Tokugawa, while Shidehara was born in Kadoma near Osaka, the busiest commercial city of the day, several years after the Restoration. Tanaka spent his youthful days in remote and tradition-bound areas, while Shidehara spent his adolescence in the largest cities and centers of modernization, Osaka, Kyoto, and Tokyo. Their educational backgrounds make another interesting contrast. After the educational reform of the Meiji Government, Shidehara attended regular public elementary schools where the pupils were educated to acquire a new and broad knowledge of world geography and international affairs. At Tokyo Imperial University, Shidehara specialized in the study of law, particularly Anglo-American law and international law. Tanaka, on the contrary, attended private *juku* conducted by ex-samurai and devoted himself to the study of Kōkokugaku and Chinese classics. The two also differed in their occupational backgrounds: Tanaka Giichi was a career soldier, and Shidehara a career diplomat with a broad cosmopolitan perspective. All of these and other differences in their socialization made up their individual personalities and cultural identities. Now, let us turn our closer attention to Shidehara's biography.

Preparation for a Diplomatic Career

On August 11, 1872, five years after the Restoration, Shidehara Kijūrō was born at Kadoma near Osaka. The new government was carrying out a wholesale modernization program. "Civilization and Enlightenment" was the slogan of the day. As a commercial center Kijūrō's birthplace, Osaka, had been relatively free from the oppressive feudal atmosphere of a castle-town like Hagi. Moreover, the Shidehara family was not of the *bushi* caste, but belonged to the village landlord class. This background seemed to have made it relatively easy for Kijūrō to free himself from *bushidō*. Financially, however, the Shideharas were much better off than the Tanakas. While Giichi's father was reduced to becoming a poor umbrella maker after the Restoration and Giichi himself had to help his family finances with janitorial work, Kijūrō's father was wealthy enough to give all of his children the best education. Kijūrō's older brother, like Kijūrō, was graduated from Tokyo Imperial University and later became the president of Tōhoku Imperial University and a councilor of the Privy Council. His younger sister was graduated from a medical school — a very rare accomplishment for a Japanese girl at that time — and became the first female doctor in Osaka Prefecture.

The family had a large house surrounded by a white wall which looked as if it reigned over a dozen or so small farming houses around it. The Shidehara children distinguished themselves from other village children by their aristocratic style. Whenever they went out, they were formally dressed in *haori* and *hakama*, with white *tabi*, and *chasen* hair style. The parents were so strict in their etiquette training that they even prohibited their children from mingling among the ill-mannered peasant boys. As a result, Kijūrō usually had to play alone in his large yard. Such a lonely childhood might have influenced Kijūrō in developing his individualistic personality. Even during the prime of his life, Shidehara did not have any really close friends, though many people respected him.

In 1878 when Kijūrō was six years old, a public elementary school was established at Kadoma. The first chapter of his primer started with the statement that there were five different races on earth, the Asian, the European, the Malay, the American, and the African. The inaccuracy of such a statement notwithstanding, it is obvious that students in an insular Asiatic nation, which had been secluded from the rest of the world for more than two centuries, were surprised at the new knowledge about different races and the geography of the world. Clearly, the government's intention was to expose the students to international affairs. Kijūrō's teacher at the elementary school, Takeda Ten, had a good background in Chinese classics like most teachers during this period. But, unlike most Confucian teachers, this young teacher had very progressive views. He later became a liberal novelist and a reporter for *The Asahi Shimbun*. Being taught by such a teacher and with modern textbooks, Kijūrō, from the outset had a very different educational background from that of Tanaka Giichi.[9]

In 1883 Kijūrō was graduated from elementary school and entered the Osaka Middle School. He was eleven years old. This school was one of the first middle schools established by the government and was famous for its high academic standards and its special emphasis on the study of English. Students learned English from American and British teachers. Kijūrō's father, Sinjirō, sent his children to this school because he was convinced that the learning of Chinese classics was no longer useful for a new Japan. Thus, Kijūrō's training in English and exposure to Western culture and civilization began. In this school an incident occurred which Shidehara long remembered. During the first several sesssions of his English class no students could understand what the American teacher was talking about. Rather dismayed, the teacher asked them to say anything in English. Still the class was silent. Then suddenly somebody exclaimed, "See the moon!" Both the teacher and students were surprised and the whole class burst into laughter. But Kijūrō, who had broken the silence, was serious. He thought that he had to say something in English and shouted a line he remembered from the English textbook. The American teacher was very happy and after the class he came down from the platform to shake hands with

---

9 Ujita, 12–16; Shidehara Heiwa Zaidan (ed.), 1–13; Shidehara, "Watakushi no Yōshō Jidai."

Kijūrō. The teacher encouraged him to further study English.[10]
The Osaka Middle School changed its name to the Third
Senior Higher Middle School (Daisan Kōtō Chūgakkō) and was
shifted to Kyoto. After his graduation from this school, Kijūrō
went to Tokyo to study law at Tokyo Imperial University.
Throughout his school life, Kijūrō had lived in school dormitories,
separated from his parents. Furthermore, from eleven to twenty-
three, Kijūrō spent his student life in the largest cities of Japan.
He also received the most advanced education in the country.
Hence, to Kijūrō's personality, an urbane and sophisticated quality
was added to the aristocratic upbringing of his childhood. His
lonely childhood experience and his early separation from his
parents might have further fostered Kijūrō's individualistic and
independent personality. At the university, too, Kijūrō was a
quiet student with few close friends. Avoiding social activities,
he studied hard. The professors' general impression of him was
that of a very serious and intelligent student with good common
sense and a rational intellect.[11]

In 1895, at age of twenty-three, Kijūrō was graduated from
the university with the degree of Bachelor of Law. Although
Shidehara had planned to take the national examination for the
diplomatic service, he was obliged to postpone the idea due to
serious illness. Consequently, his professor, Hozumi Nobushige
(1856–1926), arranged jobs for him since it was a custom for *onshi*
(one's former teacher) to look after or even determine the future
of his disciples. Kijūrō was so determined to become a diplomat,
however, that he kept declining the *onshi's* recommendations. In
the decision of his own future course, Shidehara was not bound
by such traditionalistic sentiments as *giri* and *ninjō*.[12] In fact,

---

[10] Shidehara, *Gaikō Gojūnen*, 228–229.
[11] Shidehara Heiwa Zaidan (ed.), 20.
[12] Hozumi obtained a teaching position at Sendai Senior High School
for Shidehara, but the latter declined the offer without any hesitation. Tanaka,
on the other hand, faithfully followed his masters' advice until he entered the
Army. See Ujita, 15.

in order to realize his ambition, Shidehara was obliged to disgrace his *onshi* by resigning from the Department of Commerce and Agriculture, to which Hozumi had recommended him. Such independence of will was later demonstrated in his conduct of diplomacy.

CAREER DIPLOMAT

The new diplomatic service examination system was announced in 1892 by the Second Itō Cabinet (the Foreign Minister was Mutsu Munemitsu (1844–97). Shidehara passed the fourth one in 1896, a year after the Sino-Japanese War. He was one of the first to become a diplomat through this new system. Later, Yoshida Shigeru (1878–1967) and Ashida Hitoshi (1887–1959) followed the same course from career diplomats to Prime Ministers. Before Shidehara became the Minister of Foreign Affairs in the Katō Cabinet in June 1924, for approximately three decades, he had been engaged in various diplomatic services at home and abroad. During this period he met countless foreign diplomats, attended many international conferences, and participated in concluding a number of international treaties and agreements. Furthermore, it is noteworthy that in this long diplomatic career Shidehara had spent half of the time abroad, of which about eight years were in Great Britain and the United States. Especially precious were his experiences as Ambassador to the United States and as a plenipotentiary to the Washington Conference between 1919 and 1922, during one of the most democratic and idealistic periods of world history. As we shall see, through these rich international experiences, Shidehara Kijūrō had attained the position of a career diplomat with a broad international knowledge, universalistic perspective, and liberal, democratic principles.

After passing his examination in 1896, Shidehara was first

sent to the Japanese consulate at Inchon, Korea, with the title of
consular assistant. During this period he mainly worked on
matters related to international judicial problems. His English
ability was already very good and impressed Consul Ishii
Kikujirō (1866–1945, subsequently the Minister of Foreign Affairs
in the Ōkuma Cabinet from April 1914 to October 1916). Later,
when Ishii was the chief of the Communications Bureau in the
Ministry of Foreign Affairs and Shidehara was working under
him, Ishii was convinced that when English cablegrams had to
be prepared, Shidehara was the best of all subordinates.[13]
Having finished a training period of a little over two years at
Inchon, Shidehara was assigned to London. He was now twenty-
seven years old. Life at the Consulate General in London was an
exciting one for the young Japanese diplomat. London was not
only in the fore-front of international activities, but also a most
important place for Japan, because the Anglo-Japanese Alliance
would soon be concluded. Furthermore, for Shidehara, to visit
England had been a long-cherished dream. During his two-year
stay in London he avidly learned English, the British way of life,
the parliamentary system, and international customs and pre-
cedents.

At his lodging house, he was much impressed by the British
way of child rearing. The landlord, when learning that his tenant
had treated his son to lunch several times, prohibited Shidehara
from continuing the practice, in order to cultivate the self-reliant
spirit of his son who had just started to earn by himself. The
father did not impose his own wish upon his son to enter a high
school, when the son wanted to work instead. Shidehara thought
that Japanese parents had to learn such British child rearing so
as to cultivate a child's independent will and freedom, which are
the social bases of parliamentary democracy. At another time,
Shidehara attended a gathering of workers at White Chapel, a

---

    [13] Ōta Tamekichi, "Shidehara-san o Kataru" (Comments on Mr. Shi-
dehara), "Shoka no Shidehara-kan", 217.

slum area in London at that time. Again, the young Japanese diplomat was impressed by the sight of painters, factory workers, and even day-laborers seriously discussing economic and political problems with the visiting lecturer. He was convinced that for Japan to carry out a rational diplomacy her public first had to be educated as in England.[14]

Shidehara also committed himself to the study of English. His English tutor ordered him to memorize a few pages of the classics every day. On the train, in the bus, while walking to and from the office, and even in bed, Shidehara memorized those passages. Every night after work, he went to the tutor to recite the lines he had memorized, and the tutor corrected his accent, intonation, and pronunciation. Thanks to this training, even in his later years it became his practice to memorize good articles and lines from newspapers and magazines. This practice eventually became such a favorite hobby that even sick in bed he dictated Enlgish sentences he had memorized. If he made only a few mistakes out of several pages or an article, he would learn that his sickness was not serious.[15]

Above all Shidehara endeavored to study the British parliamentary system. He read many reference books on the subject and almost all major newspapers and journals. Furthermore, he made scrapbooks from clippings of all important news and articles. Whenever important problems were discussed in the Parliament, Shidehara without fail went to audit the discussion. Moroi Rokurō, a colleague in London, commented on Shidehara:

> First, I only thought that Shidehara was a grind, but later I came to realize that if one wished to become a diplomat who achieved great tasks for the nation, he, like Shidehara, must attend to the promotion of national interests and welfare with the greatest possible care and effort, instead of only talking big.[16]

---

[14] Shidehara, *Gaikō Gojūnen*, 220–240.
[15] *Ibid.*
[16] Shidehara Heiwa Zaidan (ed.), 32–33.

Itō Jusshi, the former chairman of the Information Bureau of
Foreign Ministry, agreeing with Moroi, aptly put it: in contrast
to the more "Oriental" and traditionalistic diplomats like Gotō
Shimpei, Ijūin Hikokichi (1864–1923) and Hayashi Gonsuke
(1860–1939), Shidehara was a "new type of diplomat in a new
age for Japan."[17]

After London, in December 1900, Shidehara was sent to
Antwerp, Belgium, as consul, and in September of the next year
back to Pusan, Korea. During this period there were two interesting episodes in his life.

On his way back to Tokyo from Antwerp, Shidehara passed
through Osaka. At the station, his father, relatives, and villagers
had assembled to welcome their hero. They had intended to have
a big party for the successful compatriot. However, Shidehara
only met them at the platform and went directly to Tokyo by the
same train. His friends felt betrayed because he did not join
their "own group." But Shidehara was not interested in such
provincialism. He, unlike Tanaka, made a clear distinction between private obligation (*giri*) and public duty (*gimu*), which is an
important criterion for political rationalization. As a public
figure, he always considered public duty first. He even felt it
more important to go to the Foreign Ministry than to visit his
ancestors' graves.[18]

Another episode relates to his marriage. Shidehara fell
in love with a British woman, a sister of the British consul with
whom he had become acquainted during his service in Inchon.

---

[17] Itō Jusshi, "Nihon no Shingaikō to Shidehara-san" (Japan's new diplomacy and Mr. Shidehara), "Shoka no Shidehara-kan", 279.

[18] Shidehara Heiwa Zaidan (ed.), 38–39. When Shidehara became
Prime Minister in October, 1945, he took the same attitude to his local people
wno came all the way to Tokyo from Osaka to congratulate him. At such an
occasion Tanaka might have invited them to a great party, but Shidehara simply
greeted them at the gate of his official residence. Because of his universalistic
perspective, he disliked such provincialism displayed by his local friends. He
also believed that his responsibility as Prime Minister was to promote more
national than local interests.

In London, Shidehara associated with her more closely and hoped to marry her. However, all of his friends including his parents and the Consul General were so strongly opposed to this absolutely unconventional idea — most Japanese never dreamed of marrying Westerners during this time — that he finally was obliged to give up his hope. Perhaps this was the only occasion throughout his life when he curbed his own will. Because of this incident, his marriage was belated. At the age of thirty-one he married Iwasaki Masako, the youngest daughter of the owner of the Mitsubishi Company.

People tend to assume that through this marriage Shidehara established a close tie with the Mitsubishi Zaibatsu and enjoyed its financial backing, as many Japanese politicians did. For example, Katō Takaaki's connection with the Mitsubishi by dint of his marriage to another Iwasaki daughter is well known.[19] However, Shidehara was different. So far as I have investigated various people's reminiscences and biographies of Shidehara, there is no such evidence. A commentator on Shidehara speaks:

> Shidehara was not such a person as to take advantage of his private relations for his political ambition. With regard to money, because he was by nature a negative person, he did not have any intention at all to enter upon a political career by seeking his political funds from the Iwasaki family. Of course, Masako brought some considerable amount of money from the Iwasaki family when she married Shidehara, and received a small amount of spending money from her parents afterward. But he never received a farthing which was not accounted for, or which was unnecessary. On the contrary, some people state that the reason why Shidehara could not become such a powerful politician as Katō Takaaki was because he did not receive even one-thirtieth or -fortieth of the financial backing which

---

[19] Uchiyama Masakuma, "Kasumigaseki Seitō Gaikō no Seiritsu" (The establishment of the orthodox Kasumigaseki diplomacy), *Nihon Gaikō-shi no Shomondai* (Various problems of Japanese diplomatic history), ed. Nihon Kokusai Seiji Gakkai (Tokyo, 1965), 13–15. For Katō Takaaki's biography, see Katō-haku Denki Hensan Iinkai (ed.) and Kondō Misao, *Katō Takaaki* (Tokyo, 1959).

the Iwasaki gave Katō.   To that extent, Shidehara was a man of pure
heart and clean hands.[20]

At the same time, however, Shidehara's marriage introduced him
to the business circle, which might have influenced his "economic-
oriented" policy, though he did not patronize any particular firm
like the Mitsubishi Company.

In 1904, having spent most of the period of the Japanism
movement abroad, Shidehara returned to Tokyo to become the
acting chief of the telegraphic service section within the Foreign
Ministry.   He never lost his enthusiasm for studying international
law and the English composition of diplomatic documents.   His
teacher in Tokyo was Henry W. Denison (1846–1924), an American
adviser to the Foreign Ministry.   Shidehara admired him and
literally "stuck with him from morning till night."[21]   Denison
emphasized that to write correct English was not enough, that
one had to write appealing English in diplomatic transactions, and
that in order to do so, one had to adopt the American and the
British ways of thinking.   Denison also taught Shidehara what
to look for and how to pursue national interests in diplomacy.
Through Denison, Shidehara understood that the primary purpose of diplomacy was to pursue the nation's economic interests
in order to promote people's well-being at home.   As in a commercial transaction, the major principle of diplomacy is honesty.   To
seek power and to utilize all kinds of wiles for that purpose is an
outmoded type of diplomacy.   Bluffing is dangerous because it
not only deceives the enemy but also the very nation which is
bluffing.   In the long run the nation's real substance will auto-
matically be reflected as its real power in world history.[22]

For about eight years, until 1911, Shidehara worked in the
Foreign Ministry in Tokyo.   He ascended from the acting sec-

---

[20]   Ujita, 19–25.
[21]   Ōta Tamekichi, 216.
[22]   Shidehara, *Gaikō Gojūnen*, 239–246; Shidehara Heiwa Zaidan (ed.),
53–60.

tion chief to the bureau chief of telegraphic and investigation services. During this period, the Cabinet changed four times and the Foreign Minister nine times. In Japan, where traditionally the ascriptive tendency was strong, when the head of an office changed, reshuffling of all important personnel tended to follow accordingly. Nevertheless, Shidehara remained in the same position under seven different Foreign Ministers. This fact is significant. The reasons he could stay in the same position in spite of frequent changes in the head office of the Foreign Ministry are that during these days almost all telegraphs had to be written in English, and Shidehara was the best-suited person in such an office; his work in the investigation service was also superb in view of his diligence, accuracy and rationality in research, and good knowledge of international laws and precedent; finally, he was a non-partisan bureaucrat. He did not have any particular tie with various factions and cliques. This fact indicates that Shidehara was a typical modern bureaucrat in the Weberian sense: rational, efficient, and universalistic.[23]

After eight years of training under Denison's guidance, Shidehara was sent to the Japanese Embassy in Washington as a councilor. During his stay in Washington, Shidehara established a close association with the British Ambassador, James Bryce from whom he learned pragmatic and rational ways of thinking in diplomacy. Between 1912 and 1913, Japan was at pains to prevent California's anti-Japanese exclusion law. Great Britain, on the other hand, was protesting to the United States concerning the transit duty charged on ships using the newly opened Panama Canal. In spite of the British protest, the American Congress soon passed the law on the Panama transit duty. Bryce, then, dropped his protest immediately. When Shidehara asked Bryce the reason, Bryce told him that, because Great Britain had no intention of waging war against the United States, she would only

---

[23]   *Ibid.*, 46–66; Ujita, 25–32.

accumulate more shame if she still had continued protesting. The veteran British diplomat, implying Japan's over-sensitive protest against the Californian law, told Shidehara that a clever diplomat should not blind himself to overall national interests by being preoccupied with small things. Later on, while Shidehara was Ambassador to the United States, Bryce once again reminded Shidehara, who was struggling to find a way out of the American anti-Japanese immigration law, that a nation's fortune is eternal and that a diplomat should always perceive his nation's destiny in the long run. In his memoirs Shidehara wrote that he was very much impressed by Bryce's teaching and felt as if he had been taught by his grandfather.[24]

In December 1913, Shidehara was sent to London as a Councilor at the Japanese Embassy. He was forty-one years of age. During his stay in London, the so-called Benton Incident occurred. The factories of the Benton Company, which owned an oil field in Mexico, were burned by Mexican nationalists and the owner was killed in the fire. In response to the incident, and in order to prevent further attacks upon the British interests there, the government had decided to send war vessels to Mexico. However, the American Government, in accordance with its own Monroe Doctrine, intervened. Shidehara was very interested in the way the British Parliament would cope with the problem. Contrary to Shidehara's expectations, the British Foreign Minister, Sir Edward Grey (1862–1933), simply declined to take any countermeasure against the American action. Moreover, both pro- and anti-government newspapers praised the Foreign Minister's decision, because Britain could not fight the United States over such a trifling matter. In his memoirs, Shidehara praised the British pragmatism and wrote that, if he had answered in the same way Grey did, he would have been killed at least two or three times by angry Japanese mobs. Shidehara was convinced that both

---

[24] Shidehara, *Gaikō Gojūnen*, 28–44.

the Japanese public and politicians had to discard their over-sensitivity to such vain issues as "national face" and to concentrate on more concrete ends.[25]

In 1914, having served as Minister plenipotentiary to Holland and Denmark, Shidehara returned to Tokyo to become Vice-Foreign Minister under Ishii Kikujirō (1866–1945), in the Ōkuma Cabinet. Until 1919, when he was sent to the United States as Ambassador, he not only served under five different ministers but also under Motono Ichirō (1862–1928) and Gotō Shimpei who were political rivals of Katō Takaaki, Shidehara's brother-in-law. It was said that Gotō and Katō were "mortal foes." When the Terauchi Cabinet was organized in 1916 and Gotō was regarded as the Vice-Prime Minister, Katō declared himself the new chairman of the Kenseikai and was determined to destroy the Terauchi Cabinet. Shidehara also remained in the same post under the Seiyūkai-controlled Hara Cabinet, again Katō's enemy. These cases reinforce the non-partisan (universalistic) nature of Shidehara Kijūrō. He never entered into the *oyabun-kobun* relations with anybody, nor developed factions supported by his favorite subordinates. While Shidehara was Ambassador to the United States, his subordinates complained that the new Ambassador did not "look after" them. According to the traditionalistic concept of superior-inferior relationships, he was supposed to show generosity and to "take care of" them as if he had been a big brother. He never did such things, because he felt that each individual had to stand alone and to train himself instead of being led by others.[26]

This way of thinking is related to his principle of conducting diplomacy. He was a proponent of what he called "*chōtō gaikō*," (nonpartisan diplomacy). It was his opinion that the best and the

---

[25] Edward G. Grey's *Twenty-five Years, 1892–1916, The League of Nations* and Bryce's *The American Commonwealth* were Shidehara's favorite books. *Ibid.*, 247–251; Baba Tsunego, *Gendai Jimbutsu Hyōron*, 287–289.

[26] Ishii, "Shidehara-dan no Omoide," 274.

most important national interests had to be sought beyond all local and factional interests. Out of this belief, Shidehara himself never belonged to any political party during his service in the Ministry of Foreign Affairs. For this reason his foreign policy is sometimes called the "bureaucratic diplomacy." He also claimed that he did not have any partiality for anybody, and that he would ask the most capable persons to work for him regardless of their political and private affiliations.[27] In fact, he demonstrated this principle by keeping Yoshida Shigeru, who had been the Vice-Minister under the Tanaka Cabinet, as his own Vice-Minister in his second term of foreign ministership. For the same reason, in June 1950 when the Japanese peace conference was placed on the agenda, Shidehara as the president of the House of Representatives endeavored to adjust conflicts among three leading statesmen of the time, Prime Minister Yoshida Shigeru; Chairman of the Democratic Party, Tomabechi Gizō (1880–1959); and Secretary of the Socialist Party, Asanuma Inejirō (1898–1960); in order to achieve the best national interest without partisan conflicts.[28]

As Vice-Minister between 1914 and 1919, Shidehara was engaged in diplomatic transactions with the Allied powers, in the improvement of diplomatic relations with China, which had soured since Japan's Twenty-One Demands in 1915, and in preparation for the Peace Conference. In the meantime he was also active as a member of the economic investigation committee in the Foreign Ministry. Later he received a gold cup from the Emperor in thanks for his distinguished contribution to the committee.

---

[27] Shidehara, "Wasure e nu Hitobito."
[28] Shidehara Heiwa Zaidan (ed.), 757–766. This aspect of Shidehara is a clear contrast to that of Tanaka. For example, Tanaka as Prime Minister made his compatriot and life-long patron, Kuhara Fusanosuke, Minister of Communications, and Yamanashi Hanzō, the Governor of Korea. By doing so, he hoped to return debts to these friends, but these appointments caused tremendous criticisms from many quarters even within his own party, the Seiyūkai. As we shall see, Shidehara's universalistic and Tanaka's particularistic orientations also made a striking contrast in their conduct of foreign policy.

Shidehara had been especially interested in economic matters and had often been in charge of economic transactions between Japan and other nations. In London, he was engaged in promoting Japanese silk trade with Great Britain. In Antwerp, which was a busy international trading port, he was placed in charge of marine insurance for Japanese vessels. In Pusan, Korea, he dealt with all kinds of Japanese goods such as cotton thread, matches, salt, tobacco, porcelain, and bricks. Such previous experience as this, especially connected with economic matters, might have also influenced Shidehara in regard to his belief that Japan's economic interests were the foremost problem in diplomacy.

In September 1919 — the war was over and the Paris Peace Treaty had been concluded — Shidehara Kijūrō once again went out to the world, a world zealous to establish democratic order and peace in the international community. He was assigned as head of the Japanese Embassy in Washington. During his stay in the United States as Ambassador and as a plenipotentiary to the Washington Conference (1921–22), Shidehara met a number of great Western statesmen and diplomats who were democratic idealists. To count only some of them: President Woodrow Wilson, Secretaries of State William J. Bryan and Charles E. Hughes from the United States; British plenipotentiaries to the Conference, Arthur Balfour and Sir Auckland Geddes (Ambassador to the United States, 1920–24); and the French delegates to the Conference, Albert Sarraut and Jules J. Jusserand (Ambassador to the United States, 1902–22). Shidehara was most influenced by Wilsonian democratic idealism and by Lloyd Georgian diplomacy (1919–22). Shidehara's aspirations for establishing world peace and a democratic order, his preoccupation with economic interests, and his orientation toward "conference diplomacy" were all influenced by these Western diplomats.

During his stay in Washington, Shidehara played an important role in Japan's diplomatic history. To sum up his major activities during this period: He contributed to Japan's quick withdrawal of

troops from Siberia. He emphasized to the American delegation
that Japan's real interests in Russia were served by calling for an
equal opportunity for commerce and industry there, observing a
policy of nonintervention and territorial integrity of Russia, rather
than attempting an occupation. He played a major role in the
establishment of the Four Power Treaty by abolishing the Anglo-
Japanese alliance. It was his belief, based upon a universalistic
perspective, that in the new age since the Paris Treaty the days
of any military alliance with a particular country were over. Instead, he drafted a "Consultative Pact" among Japan, the United
States, and Great Britain, in order to maintain the status quo and
to avoid aggression in the Pacific through mutual cooperation
among the three major powers in the region. His draft outlined
the Four Power Treaty, which France was subsequently invited
to join. Admiral Katō Tomosaburō (1861–1923) was Japan's
head delegate to the negotiations of naval reduction. Shidehara,
as a good compromiser, often mitigated conflicts in various technical
problems which arose between the Japanese and the American
delegates.[29]

One of the most difficult problems in American-Japanese
relations which Ambassador Shidehara had to face was the American anti-Japanese immigration policy. His manner of dealing with
this complicated problem indicates that Shidehara was a highly
rational and efficient bureaucrat. Traditionally, Californians were
hostile to Japanese immigrants. In 1913 the Legislature of California had already enacted a law prohibiting Japanese from owning
land. And in 1920, exercising the Initiative, California removed

---

[29] Ujita, 52–73. Gaimushō Hyakunen-shi Hensan Iinkai (ed.), *Gaimushō
no Hyakunen* (One hundred years of the Foreign Ministry; Tokyo, 1969), 787–
845. With regard to more general works on the Washington Conference, see
Yamato Ichihashi, *The Washington Conference and After* (Stanford, 1928);
J. C. Vinson, *The Parchment Peace* (Athens, Ga., 1955); Raymond L. Buell,
The Washington Conference (New York and London, 1922); Mark Sullivan,
The Great Adventure at Washington (Garden City, 1922); A. Whitney Griswold,
The Far Eastern Policy of the United States (New Haven, 1964), Chaps. 6 and 7.

the right of Japanese even to lease land. The exclusionist movement rapidly spread from the west coast to the east. In May
1924, even the American Congress, both House and Senate,
passed a bill containing an exclusionist clause. The Japanese
public was embittered by such American action, and some fanatics
even advocated war against the United States. One nationalist
committed *seppuku* before the American Embassy in Tokyo, being
unable to bear such national "humiliation." Another Japanese
attempted to assassinate the American consul in Yokohama.[30]

In spite of such tension in Japan, Shidehara tried to solve the
problem in a rational way rather than with raging protests. He
got in touch with Roland S. Morris, the former Ambassador to
and a sympathizer with Japan, held many discussions with him,
and hoped to conclude an executive agreement or treaty through
Morris' influence, and thereby possibly curb the California laws.
Shidehara had known that according to the American Constitution
an international treaty or agreement could have a binding force
upon all states. Instead of emotional protests which might cause
serious harm to American-Japanese relations, he took a lawful
measure. His Anglo-Americanophile character might also have
influenced his mild methods against the United States. More
pragmatically, however, Shidehara knew very well that Japan had
to "co-operate" with this powerful nation, not to have a major confrontation, and to promote trade with her. It was most unfortunate
that the fierce exclusionist movement in the United States made
the Shidehara-Morris treaty abortive, aggravating the diplomatic
relations between the two nations.[31]

There is another interesting episode related to the Washington
Conference. Baron and Admiral Katō Tomosaburō, a delegate
to the Washington Conference, was a military man who had inherited the samurai tradition. He felt it cheap to be cheerful and

---

[30] Edwin O. Reischauer, *The United States and Japan*, 147–148; *New
York Times*, June 12, 1924; Griswold, Chap. 9.
[31] Shidehara, *Gaikō Gojūnen*, 28–38.

affable. He intended to meet the American officials who had been sent from the Department of State to greet the Japanese delegates, wearing a naval uniform and a stern face, maintaining his dignity like a samurai. Shidehara, however, knowing the Western diplomatic customs and manners, asked the Admiral to wear civilian clothes and hat, and to wave his hands cheerfully to the welcoming crowds on the streets. By requesting Katō to follow such Western customs, Shidehara hoped to make the Japanese Admiral attractive to other Western delegates and the American people. This was part of Shidehara's calculated plan to carry out the Conference as advantageously as possible to the Japanese interests. This plan was successful. Katō was called a "charming admiral" by the American crowds, though in Japan he was far from "charming." However, the Admiral later complained to Shidehara, "I will never listen to your requests again. I do not like such things!"[32]

On June 11, 1924, having won the general election of May due to the powerful popular support for the establishment of a party government, Katō Takaaki formed a three-party Coalition Cabinet. Shidehara Kijūrō was appointed Foreign Minister. Katō's selection of Shidehara for this post was due not so much to the fact that Shidehara was his brother-in-law as to other factors. It had been an unwritten precedent that former ambassadors to Great Britain or to the United States — those who had attained the highest ranking posts for diplomats — had usually assumed the office.[33] Popular enthusiasm for the democratic West and

---

[32] *Ibid.*, 63–65; Shidehara Heiwa Zaidan (ed.), 148–246.

[33] The following list of Foreign Ministers preceding Shidehara will indicate this point.

Date		Foreign Minister	Former Background
Aug.	1908	Komura Jutarō	Ambassador to Great Britain (1906–1908)
Aug.	1911	Hayashi Tōru	Ambassador to Great Britain (1905–1906)
Oct.	1911	Uchida Kōsai	Ambassador to the U. S. (1909–1911)
Dec.	1912	Katsura Tarō	Prime Minister, concurrently Foreign Minister
Jan.	1913	Katō Takaaki	Former Foreign Minister (1906) Ambassador to Great Britain (1909–1913)

internationalism also matched well with Shidehara's type of diplomacy. Furthermore, Shidehara was a founder of the "Washington System," under which Japan had to cooperate with the powers. In any event, having been given the diplomatic leadership, Shidehara was now to put his ideas into practice. Although I intend to discuss both Shidehara's and Tanaka's policies in actual domestic and international contexts in the following chapters, let us first survey his philosophy of diplomacy.

DIPLOMACY AND NATIONAL INTERESTS

Shidehara's diplomacy was essentially based upon two apparently contradictory principles: idealism and pragmatism. In general terms, idealism and pragmatism often come into conflict. But in Shidehara's diplomacy the two principles were beautifully harmonized. There are three favorite slogans which Shidehara

Feb.	1913	Makino Nobuaki	Former Minister of Commerce and Agriculture (1911–1912)
April	1914	Katō Takaaki	See above
Aug.	1915	Ōkuma Shigenobu	Prime Minister, concurrently Foreign Minister
Oct.	1915	Ishii Kikujirō	Vice-Foreign Minister (1908–1912) Ambassador to France (1912–1915)
Oct.	1916*	Terauchi Masatake	Prime Minister, concurrently Foreign Minister
Nov.	1916	Motono Ichirō	Ambassador to Russia (1910–1913)
April	1918	Gotō Shimpei	Former Minister of Internal Affairs (1916–1918)
Sept.	1918	Uchida Kōsai	See above
Sept.	1923	Yamamoto Gonnohyōe	Prime Minister, concurrently Foreign Minister
Sept.	1923	Ijūin Hikokichi	Ambassador to Italy (1916–1919)
Jan.	1924	Matsui Keishirō	Ambassador to the U. S. (1909) Ambassador to France (1916–1920)
June	1924	Shidehara Kijūrō	Ambassador to the U. S. (1919–1922)

*From 1916 to 1923, except during the period of the Hara Cabinet, as we have seen in Chapter 2, the "old" politics controlled by the military-bureaucratic clique prevailed in Japan. Consequently, Foreign Ministers were also somewhat of the "old" type.

frequently emphasized in his conduct of diplomacy: "Let us establish world peace in co-operation with all mankind"; "Live and Let Live"; and *"Où règne la justice, les armes sont inutiles,"* (If justice reigns, there is no need of weapons).[34] The first slogan expressed his universalistic aspirations, the second his democratic concerns, and the third his moralistic principles. But all of them indicated his belief that Japan and all powers must strive to maintain world peace, and that this is the basic and ultimate principle of diplomacy for all nations.

In his inaugural speech, Foreign Minister Shidehara stressed:

> Now, the age of political maneuver through machination and aggressive policy has passed. The great principles of diplomacy are justice and peace. I am convinced that there is no other principle but these in cultivating our country's way. If we carry out our diplomacy with this conviction, there is nothing for us to worry about, should some unusual difficulties arise....[35]

The next day, before foreign reporters, Shidehara stated that Japan was to base her diplomatic principle upon peace, justice and honor, that he was convinced that there are infinite similarities in the nature of mankind despite their differences in race, religion, and language, and that conflicts arise because some people tend to exaggerate superficial differences. He further emphasized that the world had begun to regard international friendship as of absolute necessity, that to pursue a selfish and exclusive policy in disregard of the legitimate interests of other nations was outmoded, and that the principle of live-and-let-live would begin to win predominant support from all the powers.[36] On July 1, 1924, before the representatives assembled in the Forty-Ninth Diet, Shidehara spoke:

> An international conflict occurs when a nation insists on her narrow selfish view disregarding the justified positions of other nations.

---

[34]   Shidehara, *Gaikō Gojūnen*, 270; Shidehara Heiwa Zaidan (ed.), 3 and 281.

[35]   The Ministry of Foreign Affairs, *Gaimushō Kōhyō-shū*, No. 5.

[36]   *The Asahi Shimbun*, June 12, 1924.

In contrast to this, what we assert is the coexistence and the co-prosperity of all nations. Today, there is a sign that the mind of the people of the world is being awakened in this direction. Undoubtedly an organization like the League of Nations is based upon such an enlightenment of the people. If the powers admit this fundamental principle, I believe, we will find a key for solving all international problems.[37]

To maintain peace, Shidehara's principles for diplomatic method were honesty, lawfulness, and nonaggression. In a public lecture given in October 1928 at Keiō University, Shidehara stated:

What is the real principle of diplomacy? People in general seem to entertain the idea that diplomacy is something treacherous, showy and insincere.... To tell a lie is the worst vice and to rob others is the most shameful crime in the realm of personal morality. And yet many people tend to think that fraud or plunder or any other method is excusable for the sake of the nation.... No matter how base, vicious and wrong their means were, people used not only to excuse, but even to praise and thank those who succeeded in expanding national territory, in obtaining national rights and interests, and in achieving some other profits for the sake of the nation.

From the view of history there are countless examples in which diplomacy by the powers has been conducted by machination. Yet, what was the result? Such means might have contributed to the nation temporarily and popular applause might have been accorded to some immediate success. However, is this the way to make the nation's plan for a century? There is a famous saying of Lincoln, "You can fool some of the people all the time, you can fool all the people some of the time, but you cannot fool all the people all the time." A nation's life is eternal. We must remember, therefore, that machination which was successful temporarily will surely bring about some serious harm to the nation some day. That which Buddhism teaches, the law of rewards in accordance with deeds (*inga ōhō*), is also true in international relations.[38]

---

[37] *Dai-Nihon Teikoku Gikai-shi*, XV, 76–77.
[38] Shidehara, *Gaikō Kanken*.

Obviously Shidehara, who was out of power at this time, was indirectly criticizing Tanaka's diplomacy.

Shidehara also wholeheartedly supported an established world system such as the League of Nations, the International Court of Arbitration, and the idea of a democratic conference among nations. He believed that these were the new ways which were internationally approved to maintain world peace. He said:

> Especially, the horrible lesson of the World War has urged the realization of the League of Nations. Now, organizations like the League of Nations Assembly, the League of Nations Council, the Permanent Court of International Justice, and the International Court of Arbitration and the Deliberative Council of International Disputes which are outside of the League of Nations, all have been established in order to regulate relations among powers by the world's public opinion. As most bacteria cannot survive in sunlight, so the international crimes which have been committed in the dark age must melt away by themselves with the increasing light of the world's just public opinion....
>
> Before the World War such a system of maintaining international peace through the total co-operation of powers was thought to be nearly impossible. However, being impressed by the cruel sight of the great war, the public of the world began to seek seriously for such a system and at last we saw the establishment of the League of Nations. Hence, today, aggressive policies and the might-is-right attitude which were often taken in diplomacy can no longer achieve the goal, being suppressed by the general force of enlightened public sentiments in the world.[39]

Aside from his idealism for establishing world peace, Shidehara also had a definite pragmatic idea of diplomacy. He clearly stated that the first principle of diplomatic policy is to protect and to promote national rights and interests. During the years of the Tanaka Cabinet, while Shidehara was a member of the House of Peers, he stated, alluding to the absurdity of the argument maintained by Tanaka:

---

[39]   *Ibid.*

It is a matter of course that a nation's diplomacy must be determined by a cool judgement of national interests. If a nation's diplomacy is to decide whether the policy is "strong" or "weak," which is a vain emotional argument, the nation's future will be ruined.

The best statement of Shidehara's pragmatism will be found in the following words:

In overestimating the effects of diplomacy, people tend to make unreasonable requests and some often assume that the nation can skilfully succeed in expanding territories and depriving other powers of rights and interests without provoking the excitement of the world, if the nation takes opportune measures in diplomacy. One of the most important qualifications for a statesman is to have the judgement to discern what is possible and what is impossible to bring about....

That which a practical statesman must bear in mind is his obligation to judge rightly the limit of policy and not to attempt a policy which he has discerned impossible, and to establish a systematic plan within the limits which he has considered possible and then make the best effort to attain the goal step by step. Politics is not fantasy.... Diplomacy is not magic....[40]

Shidehara envisioned the future of Japan as a democratic nation with a developed commerce and industry. The famous "economic oriented diplomacy" (*keizai gaikō*) of Shidehara emanated from this conviction. As soon as he assumed the post of Foreign Ministership, he conveyed this idea to Saburi Sadao (1879–1929), the Bureau Chief of Commerce and Trade in the Foreign Ministry. Following Shidehara's instruction, Saburi stated:

The successive Cabinets and political parties in our country have come to emphasize the promotion of our national economy based upon industry. In our small country we are suffering from a population increase of 700,000–800,000 every year. Under such circumstances, in our country there is no other measure but to pro-

---

[40] *Ibid.*

mote our national economy based upon industry so as to adjust our people's economic life. And it naturally follows from this that the procurement of overseas markets becomes a vital necessity. In other words our national policy of promoting an economy based upon industry can be accomplished only by carrying out an economic-oriented diplomacy. However, if we hope to solve our economic difficulties by territorial expansion, we will incur the danger of destroying international co-operation. Hence, there is no other way for Japan but to encourage the growth of domestic industries and to further Japan's overseas trade and commerce. By doing so, gaining national profits, we can expect to stabilize our livelihood in the future.[41]

Shidehara, in contrast to Tanaka, was thoroughly convinced that to save Japan, who is a small insular nation suffering from over-population, he had to promote domestic commerce and industry, and that an economic-oriented policy was the best means for this purpose.

Proceeding from such an understanding of Japan's essential needs, Shidehara in his first term in the foreign ministership either concluded or revised more than ten commercial treaties with both small and large powers, including China, Greece, Ethiopia, Afghanistan, Czechoslovakia, and Mexico, practically covering the whole world. In the meantime, he opened the Near Eastern Trade Conference (December 1925) and the South Pacific Trade Conference (September 1926) in Tokyo, in order to expand Japan's trade in those regions. Furthermore, he negotiated a revision of the Treaty of Commerce and Navigation with Germany; with China to conclude the graduated tariffs for Japanese goods at the Special Conference on Chinese Tariffs in Peking; and with France to cultivate Japan's trade with French Indo-China. Indeed, Shidehara's diplomacy was rightly characterized by such a description as "knocking upon the doors of the world," like modern Japanese

---

[41]   Shidehara Heiwa Zaidan (ed.), 331–332; with regard to more materials on Shidehara's economic-oriented policy, see, "Shidehara Keizai Gaikō Shiryō."

businessmen who look for profitable markets all over the world. Such a global diplomacy indicated Shidehara's preoccupation with the economic issues and his universalistic perspective.[42]

As illustrated above, Shidehara Kijūrō had both an idealistic and a pragmatic view of diplomacy. But, if his idealism and pragmatism could not be reconciled, what would be his solution? Negotiation and compromise was his method. For Shidehara, diplomacy was essentially like a commercial negotiation. If a conflict occurs with another nation, in pursuing national interests, the only solution for both contesting parties is to negotiate and to come to a mutual compromise. In this sense diplomacy is "autonomous" — so far as the nation attempts to pursue her own interest — and simultaneously, "co-operative." It is ridiculous, Shidehara asserted, for traditionalists to argue that a nation's diplomacy should always be "autonomous." Shidehara explained his view:

> It is a matter of course that Japan's diplomacy should protect and promote her rights and interests. However, the other party has the same claim to its rights and interests. In this case the most important principle of diplomacy is to find an agreement between the claims of two parties, but as close to our claim as possible. Nothing is more nonsensical than to distinguish whether a diplomacy is "autonomous" or "co-operative," without understanding this basic principle. Judging from this point of view, any country's diplomacy is autonomous. But at the same time in negotiating with other powers there is no diplomacy which does not make efforts to obtain an agreement with them. In this sense every country's diplomacy must become co-operative. Diplomacy is by nature simultaneously autonomous and co-operative.[43]

In short, Shidehara was convinced that Japan's diplomacy, ideally and in the ultimate sense, had to contribute to the universal task of establishing world peace. But in a more pragmatic and

---

[42] See *Shuyō Monjo*, II, 18–33.
[43] Shidehara Heiwa Zaidan (ed.), 270.

immediate sense, it had to promote and protect the nation's economic rights and interests above all. To do so, practical plans had to be established with careful and rational considerations. And if a conflict arose with other powers in Japan's pursuit of national interests, a peaceful solution had to be sought through negotiations and agreements between them. At that time, however, she had to strive to obtain the best possible national interests.

LATER YEARS

On July 2, 1929, after the fall of the Tanaka Administration, Hamaguchi Yūkō (Osachi, 1870–1931) organized the Minseitō (the former Kenseikai) Cabinet, and Shidehara became Foreign Minister for the second time. In spite of his opponents' criticism of his policy as "weak-kneed" and "subservient to the West," which had destroyed his leadership of the first term, Shidehara still maintained the same diplomatic principles, i.e., international co-operation, pacifism, and respect for Chinese national sovereignty and territorial integrity. He was more faithful to his own conviction than to general public sentiments. This is why his diplomacy is sometimes labeled "bureaucratic" as opposed to "popular." At the same time this was also the very reason why Saionji Kimmochi, the liberal Genrō, praised him, saying that Shidehara pursued a "strong" and "positive" policy rather than a "weak-kneed" and "negative" policy.[44]

Shidehara made the utmost efforts to soothe anti-Japanese sentiments in China, precipitated by Tanaka's aggressive policy. In December, for example, to show his recognition of international equality and his friendly attitudes toward the Chinese people, he

---

[44] Shidehara, *Gaikō Gojūnen*, 269–271. Even a foreign reporter (the A. P.) observed that Shidehara was a man of principle and was an independent individualist, see *Shoka no Shidehara-kan*, 280.

asked for China's *agrément* in appointing Obata Yūkichi (1873–1946) Minister to China. Shidehara was the first in Japan to apply this diplomatic custom to China. Undoubtedly his rational calculation of economic interests in increasing the China trade was also operating in this "friendly" gesture. To his surprise, however, the Chinese Government refused the *agrément*, for the reason that Obata was counselor of the legation when the Twenty-one Demands were presented. Though Obata himself had opposed the demands in 1915, this fact was unknown to the Chinese. Shidehara, therefore, appointed Consul General Shigemitsu Mamoru (1887–1957) at Shanghai chargé d'affaires. Now, his opponents in Japan could not be satisfied with this solution. They complained that Shidehara had simply yielded to the Chinese "insult" without making any protest. The *agrément* problem was the first major difficulty in his second term of leadership.[45]

Shidehara's peace-loving attitude, democratic inclination, and adherence to international laws was best demonstrated by his handling the Russian-Chinese conflicts over the Chinese Eastern Railway. On July 11, 1929, China recovered the Russian controlled railway by force, and a several days later the two countries severed their diplomatic relations. A crisis was posed to Japan which had many residents and vested interests in Manchuria and north China. The situation might have been more dangerous than the period of Chiang Kai-shek's northern expedition. The United States took the diplomatic initiative this time and proposed to put strong co-operative pressure from the United States, Great Britain, Japan, Italy, France, and Germany upon the hostile nations. On July 30, 1929, however, Japan's Foreign Minister, Shidehara, declined this proposal for a number of reasons: the United States and Great Britain did not have any official diplomatic relations with Soviet Russia; the involvement of various nations in the conflict might cause more complications, and per-

---

[45] Shidehara Heiwa Zaidan (ed.), 393–395; Ujita, 112–116.

haps the Japanese military would take advantage of this opportunity in concert with the rising domestic public opinion which
clamoured to "consolidate Japan's special position in Manchuria
and Mongolia"; and finally, because both China and Soviet Russia
had expressed their intention to solve the problem through
direct negotiations instead of asking the good offices of a third
power, other nations should "respect" their willingness to solve
the conflict peacefully.[46]

The Hamaguchi Cabinet hoped to improve the national
economy which had been in a panic ever since the financial crisis
of 1927. Consequently Shidehara, in terms of both his internationalism and curtailing the national budget, whole-heartedly
supported the London Naval Reduction Conference (January-
April 1930). On January 21, 1930, the day when the Conference
was opened, Shidehara spoke in the Fifty-seventh Diet:

> Of course, we must be prepared to face many difficulties before
> the London Conference will establish a satisfactory agreement....
> However, because the world public opinion earnestly hopes security
> and happiness of national life and peace and friendship among nations,
> I believe that the Conference will eventually succeed, if we take this
> ripe opportunity. The participating nations must not fail to meet
> this world public demand. The Washington Conference has opened
> a new epoch in the progressive history of mankind. We expect the
> same result from the Conference which is just opened today in
> London.[47]

Because Great Britain initiated the call for the conference, those
who were concerned with national "face" once again cried that
Japan was "coerced" to attend the conference. Shidehara did
not pay the slightest attention to such criticism, saying "nonsense,"

---

[46] Baba Tsunego conjectured that if Tanaka had still been in power at
that time, almost for sure — "nine out of ten" — Japan would have dispatched
a large number of troops to Manchuria. "Fortunately," he said, "the Tanaka
Cabinet had fallen before that, and we were saved from the danger probably
caused by his 'quixotic' expedition." *Gendai Jimbutsu Hyōron*, 273–274.

[47] Maezawa Hiroaki (ed.), *Nihon Kokkai Shichijū-nen-shi* (Seventy-year
history of Japanese Diet; Tokyo, 1954), II, 67.

and "not worth discussing seriously." When the disarmament negotiation was finally settled with the auxiliary craft ratio of 10 : 10 : 6.975 among the United States, Great Britain, and Japan, the antigovernment forces, especially the Navy and the Privy Council, bitterly attacked the decision-makers. The Prime Minister and the Foreign Minister in close co-operation barely managed to ratify the treaty.

On November 4, however, Hamaguchi was shot by a young ultranationalist, and Shidehara — who endorsed the treaty in the Fifty-eighth Diet in February 1931 — was physically attacked by the Seiyūkai members. Mori Kaku, the Vice-Minister of Political Affairs of the Tanaka Administration, who led the pandemonium, charged that Shidehara violated the "supreme command of the Emperor." The upshot was fatal to Hamaguchi, and in April Wakatsuki Reijirō (1866–1949) replaced Shidehara, who had held the acting premiership during the interval. In spite of the Minseitō Government's economic-oriented policy, Japan's economy never recovered. On the contrary, like many other nations, Japan fell into a severe economic depression. Shidehara's "bureaucratic" or "professional" diplomacy, which paid no heed to irrational mass protest, alienated many malcontents. In addition, the Manchurian problem had never been solved. The anti-Japanese movement in Manchuria under the leadership of Chang Hsüeh-liang was becoming increasingly violent, and the Russians were constantly infiltrating into the region. Under such circumstances, young military officers such as Koiso Kuniaki (1880–1950), Nagata Tetsuzan (1884–1935) and Tōjō Hideki (1884–1948) began to advocate direct action under a military dictatorship. In the Kwantung Army Ishiwara Kanji and Itagaki Seishirō (1885–1948) were convinced that the only solution for Manchuria was a Japanese military occupation. Their "positive" method diametrically opposed Shidehara's principle of respecting Chinese sovereignty and territorial integrity. As the culmination of all these trends, the Manchurian Incident broke out in September 1931, and three months later the Second Wakatsuki Cabinet (April-December 1931) resigned *en masse*.[48]

Liberals, democrats, and modernizers struggled to reassert their power, but the general trend of Japanese society had already shifted toward ultranationalism. From that time on, Shidehara's dark days began. People like him, who were standing on the opposite pole, were either violently attacked as national traitors or cast into complete obscurity.

The movement began with the March and October Incidents of 1931 plotted by the Cherry Blossom Society (Sakura-kai). Agitation and confusion reached their peak in 1932. In January and February of 1932, Japanese and Chinese forces clashed in Shanghai (the Shanghai Incident). Then, stirred by the conquest of Manchuria and by the victory in Shanghai, the "patriotic assassinations" by ultranationalists began. In these incidents, Inoue Junnosuke (a prominent party politician) and Dan Takuma (a Mitsui executive, 1858–1932) were killed. On May 15 Prime Minister Inukai Tsuyoshi, who had succeeded Wakatsuki, and other political figures were assassinated by a group of navy and army officers. Thus the last party government ended in Japan, and governments by two admirals followed. Meanwhile in Manchuria the puppet regime, Manchukuo, was established. The Lytton Commission of the League of Nations condemned Japan as an aggressor. In response to the condemnation Japan led by Matsuoka Yōsuke, Tanaka's protégé, withdrew from the League. As ultranationalism became intensified at home, Japan, took a more and more exclusive and "autonomous" course abroad, the course Tanaka Giichi initiated. Finally on February 26, 1936, a military coup d'État was attempted by young officers. They attacked the Diet, the Imperial Household Ministry, the General Staff Headquarters,

---

[48] See detailed accounts of these events during the second period of Shidehara's diplomatic leadership in Ujita, 107–138; Shidehara Heiwa Zaidan (ed.), 380–491; Gaimushō Hyakunen-shi Hensan Iinkai (ed.), 890–930; Aoki Tokuzō, *Wakatsuki Reijirō, Hamaguchi Osachi*, 87–100, 186–235.

and many other government offices, and murdered a number of important political figures including Cabinet ministers.[49]

Although it is rather difficult to trace Shidehara's activities during this period of semi-retirement, he did keep up an extensive correspondence with Ōhira Komazuchi, a former managing director of the Sumitomo Bank. From those letters one can guess what Shidehara was thinking in his adversity about himself, Japan, and the world. Soon after the final report of the Lytton Commission was made public (October 2, 1932), Shidehara wrote to Ōhira, criticizing the Japanese public's attitude toward the Commission:

> Nowadays in the abnormal international situation, there are many people who propagandize naive anti-foreign ideas in news-papers, speeches and posters, catering to the non-understanding public. I feel our country is also degraded to the same level as China.... To heap abuses upon the Lytton Commission, instead of reflecting upon our own responsibilities, is indeed shameful.

During the crisis of 1935 and 1936, Shidehara in his indignation at the high-handed military wrote:

> With regard to our China diplomacy Miyakezaka [the Army] has seized Kasumigaseki [the Foreign Ministry] both in name and in reality. Not only Kasumigaseki but also Nagata-chō [the Prime Minister] as well is about to raise the white flag.

As Japan plunged herself more and more into the course of ultranationalism, Shidehara could no longer maintain even the spirit of criticism, and only lamented in despair.

> Although an outsider like me can no longer guess at the develop-ment of international relations, the whole situation seems to become even worse than what I have formerly anticipated. Being impotent, just as if we were no longer existing in this world, the only thing we can do is to worry. I am very much ashamed of myself.

---

[49] Nihon Kokusai Seiji Gakkai (ed.), *Taiheiyō Sensō e no Michi*, I-V, is the best source dealing with the period from the Manchurian Incident to the February Twenty-sixth Incident. See also Ogata; Iriye, Chaps. 7–9; Maxon; and Storry.

On March 24, 1938, the National General Mobilization Law was issued by the Konoe Cabinet (June 1937-January 1939), and Japan began to prepare for total war. In October of the same year, Shidehara wrote to Ōhira:

> Things are getting worse and worse, and I writhe in agony day and night. But when I think that I am already a grandfather of two children and another to come by the end of this year, I must recognize that a private soldier like me who has survived the lost war is not qualified to talk about the strategy [meaning that he has lost in the competition against the ultranationalists and the military and that he is not in a position to talk about politics any longer].[50]

At one time, however, Shidehara obstinately opposed the totalitarian movement. The incident reflected great credit on him as a liberal democrat. On July 22, 1940, the Second Konoe Cabinet was established. The new government intended to establish a sort of united front combining all parties and factions, in order to mobilize the whole of national power in the war against China and for the anticipated war with the United States and Great Britain. The plan soon reached fruition and the Imperial Rule Assistance Association (Taisei Yokusan-Kai) was established on October 12. A few weeks before, the Tripartite Pact with Germany and Italy had been signed (September 27). All members of the House of Peers were expected to become members of the Association. But Baron Shidehara declined the invitation from the House of Peers to join the fascist bandwagon. A few days later a young army policeman came and again urged Shidehara to become a member of the Association. The officer warned the stubborn Baron that if the latter still refused the invitation, he would be attacked as a traitor who intended to break the national united front. Shidehara still rejected the demand. Furthermore, he pursuaded the young officer that democracy was far better than fascism by comparing the United States and Germany. The

---

[50] Shidehara Heiwa Zaidan (ed.), 494–508.

officer did not press Shidehara any more and left, saying, "I understand. Because I agree with you, I will not come again to persuade you, though I may be punished by the commander."[51]

On August 15, 1945, the war ended. With the American occupation the democratization of Japan began. The general sentiment and attitude of the populace abruptly changed from anti- to pro-democratization, Westernization, and modernization. Accordingly, the liberal and democratic leaders who had retired into obscurity during the war emerged once again as the vanguard of a new Japan.

It was under such circumstances that Shidehara Kijūrō, who was already seventy-three years old, was drawn from public oblivion into the forefront of politics again. Judging from both his understanding of the United States and his command of English, Shidehara was thought to be the best person to form the new government which had to deal with the Supreme Commander for the Allied Powers (SCAP), General Douglas MacArthur. Hence, on October 9, 1945, by Imperial Mandate, Shidehara Kijūrō was appointed Prime Minister. His inaugural speech ran:

> An old man like me who had been away from politics for a long time unexpectedly received the Imperial Mandate to form a new Cabinet. I am determined to render the last service to the nation and the Emperor at the time of the most unprecedented changes in the nation's

---

[51] Shidehara, *Gaikō Gojūnen*, 197–201. The following anecdote will also give credits to Shidehara as a peace-loving statesman and as a man of principle. Soon after World War II, he was invited to join the compilation committee to write a complimentary biography of Prince Konoe Fumimaro (1891–1945) who had been Prime Minister during the crucial period of the Second Sino-Japanese War and who, as the leading member of the five regent families to the Imperial Household, was very popular even after his death. Most of prominent figures of the day had joined the committee, but Shidehara flatly declined the invitation, because of his conviction that it was Prime Minister Konoe's wavering policy which dragged Japan into a long war with China and finally into the fatal Pacific War. Although the organizers of the committee visited Shidehara many times to induce him by saying that it was very awkward for him alone not to join the group, Shidehara insisted that he saw no reason to become even a nominal member of the committee which hoped to praise Konoe who, Shidehara thought, should actually be blamed for the Pacific War. See also Ujita, 139–173.

history without paying heed to my personal considerations. In the
great difficulties of the nation the responsibility of the new Cabinet
is great. It goes without saying that our responsibility is to work
for the everlasting development and welfare of the nation by establishing a politics based upon universal justice and diplomacy guided
by the great principles of international justice and coexistence of
mankind, and in the final analysis to contribute to the cultural progress of the world. For this purpose I am resolved to make the
best effort so that the whole nation can cherish hopes for a bright
future by carrying out various political reforms, renovating the
public mind, and materializing urgent and necessary policies for the
start of a new Japan.[52]

Since it is impossible to cover all the tasks undertaken by the
Shidehara Cabinet in this period of national devastation, I will
introduce only two events which will be helpful for our further
understanding of Shidehara Kijūrō, the man. One is related to
his view of Japanese security in future international relations;
and the other, the future status of the Imperial Institution.

The new Constitution of Japan is often called the MacArthur
Constitution. However, both Shidehara, the then Prime Minister, and General MacArthur denied such a view as far as the main
body of the Preamble and Article IX were concerned. In these
sections of the Constitution it is stipulated that Japan will renounce
war as a means of settling international disputes and will abolish
armaments. It is said that this peaceful idea contained in the new
Constitution originally came from Shidehara Kijūrō, who had
cherished such hope for a long time. Shidehara approves this
viewpoint in his memoirs:

> When I was unexpectedly ordered to form the new Cabinet...,
> I was firmly resolved that I had to...change the way of politics in the
> Constitution so that Japan should not wage war ever again. In other
> words, the decision that Japan must renounce war, abolish military
> preparations, and adhere to democracy, emanated from my own

---

[52] *The Asahi Shimbun*, October 10, 1945.

conviction, regardless of what other people might have felt [about our Constitution].

...Consequently, there is no other way to make Japan live but by appealing to the public opinion of the world based upon the true law of justice, instead of relying upon armaments.... This is the only way for Japan. I have reached the firm resolution that Japan should abolish her war preparations completely instead of having small forces [which are useless].[53]

General MacArthur, in his testimony before the combined Senate Armed Services and Foreign Relations Committee which was held in early May 1951, supported Shidehara's claim that the pacifist ideal expressed in the Constitution was Shidehara's idea. To Senator McMahon's question whether there was any formula to establish peace, the General answered:

I tried to expound it yesterday, Senator. It is the abolition of war. It takes long decades, of course, before that could be accomplished; but, you have to make a start....

There was great evidence of that in Japan. You spoke of Hiroshima and Nagasaki. So the Japanese people more than any other people in the world, understand what atomic warfare means. It wasn't academic with them. They counted their dead, and they buried them. They, of their own volition, wrote into their Constitution a provision outlawing war. When their Prime Minister came to me, Mr. Shidehara, and said: "I have long contemplated and believed," and he was a very wise old man — he died recently — "long contemplated and believed that the only solution to this problem is to do away with war."

He said: "With great reluctance I advanced the subject to you, as a military man, because I am convinced that you would not accept it, but," he said, "I would like to endeavour, in the Constitution we are drawing up, to put in such a provision."

And I couldn't help getting up and shaking hands with the old man and telling him that I thought that that was one of the greatest constructive steps that could possibly be taken.

---

[53] Shidehara, *Gaikō Gojūnen*, 213–215.

I told him that it was quite possible that the world would mock him — this is a debunking age, a cynical age, as you know — that they would not accept it; that it would be an object of derision, which it was; that it would take great moral stamina to go through with it, and in the end they might not be able to hold the line, but I encouraged him and they wrote that provision in.

And if there was any provision in that Constitution which appealed to the popular sentiment of the people of Japan, it was that provision. There was a warrior tribe which for centuries has pursued war, and successful war; but the great concept, the losses, the great lesson the bomb had taught them, had been understood, and they were trying to apply it.[54]

Hence, Shidehara's life-long ideal of renouncing war and thereby establishing world peace was declared in the Japanese Constitution.[55]

---

[54]   *The New York Times*, May 6, 1951. For further discussion on this point, see the sources of Tabata, 352–356.

[55]   The Preamble of the Constitution states:

"We, the Japanese people,...determined that we shall secure for ourselves and our posterity the fruits of peaceful co-operation with all nations and the blessings of liberty throughout this land, and resolved that never again shall we be visited with the horrors of war through the action of government,...

"We, the Japanese people, desire peace for all time and are deeply conscious of the high ideals controlling human relationship, and we have determined to preserve our security and existence, trusting in the justice and faith of the peace-loving peoples of the world. We desire to occupy an honored place in an international society striving for the preservation of peace, and the banishment of tyranny and slavery, oppression and intolerance for all time from the earth. We recognize that all peoples of the world have the right to live in peace, free from fear and want.

"We believe that no nation is responsible to herself alone, but that laws of political morality are universal; and that obedience to such laws is incumbent upon all nations who would sustain their own sovereignty and justify their sovereign relationship with other nations.

"We, the Japanese people, pledge our national honor to accomplish these high ideals and purposes with all our resources."

And the Article IX stipulates:

"Aspiring sincerely to an international peace based on justice and order, the Japanese people forever renounce war as a sovereign right of the nation and the threat or use of force as means of settling international disputes.

"In order to accomplish the aim of the preceding paragraph, land, sea, and air forces, as well as other war potential, will never be maintained. The right of belligerency of the state will not be recognized."

Another difficult question which Prime Minister Shidehara had to confront was what to do with the Imperial Institution. The Allied Powers had clearly indicated their objection to the existing form of the Emperor system. Great Britain and the United States deeply distrusted the system, and other powers such as the U.S.S.R., Australia and the Philippines demanded that Japan abolish the system completely. In Japan, the conservatives hoped to maintain the tradition intact as much as possible. They advocated the "retention of the national polity," (*kokutai no goji*). The communists, on the other hand, asserted, "Down with the Emperor system and establish the government of the people's republic!" The socialists came somewhere in between the two assertions, and advocated a "democratized Emperor system." The way in which Shidehara handled this difficult problem once again suggests his pragmatism and compromising spirit. His solution was to retain the Emperor system but at the same time to democratize it. In a pragmatic way he satisfied the conservatives by maintaining the form, but changed the substance to give some satisfaction to the radicals.

Since the 1920's, when Shidehara was a leading member of the progressive and modernizing group, two decades had elapsed. New generations had emerged and the society had changed radically since then. Shidehara, now over seventy, came to be called a conservative by the younger generation. After all, he was a man of the Meiji era. Having lived with the nation's rise and fall under the reign of the successive Emperors, Meiji, Taishō, and Shōwa, Shidehara could not but feel nostalgic for this old institution. Not his clear-cut reason, this time, but his sentiment dictated that he not completely brush aside this unique tradition of Japan. Shidehara joined his own generation and shared its sentiment in the hope of retaining the national polity. However, the content of "his" national polity was greatly different from that of most of his conservative colleagues. It was his opinion that democracy could be republican like the United States, or a constitutional monarchy like England, or something else, so far as the people's will can be reflected in the government. The important thing, he thought, was not the specific form but the content. He was convinced that after all a democratic government should absorb the general sentiment and aspirations of the people concerning this problem.

In other words, when he favored the retention of the Imperial Institution, he wanted to do so not because he believed in Shintō doctrine or legends, but because the retention of the Emperor system was based upon the people's will and aspirations. Thinking of the British constitutional monarchy as a model, Shidehara was confident that Japan could form a constitutional and democratic government with the Imperial Institution. On the other hand, he was also convinced that various Imperial prerogatives, especially the prerogative of war, under the Meiji Constitution should be abolished, lest Japan repeat the same mistake in yielding to the military control of the nation. According to the above reasoning, the Prime Minister visited SCAP repeatedly to plead for the retention of the Imperial Institution. At the same time, he drafted the historical Imperial Rescript in which the Emperor declared himself as a "human," instead of the "Manifest Kami," (*arahitogami*). The draft was originally prepared in English as Shidehara used to do. The Rescript was read by the Emperor as his own wishes, but in reality it represented the aspirations of Shidehara himself.

The following is a part of the Imperial Rescript, in which Shidehara's life-long view on the future of Japan, the Emperor, and the world is concisely expressed.

IMPERIAL RESCRIPT

January 1st, 1946

In greeting the New Year, We recall to mind that the Emperor Meiji proclaimed, as the basis of our national polity, the Five Clauses of the Charter-Oath at the beginning of the Meiji Era,...

We have to reaffirm the principles embodied in the Charter,

and proceed unflinchingly towards elimination of misguided prac-
tices of the past, and keeping in close touch with the desires of the
people, we will construct a new Japan through thoroughly being
pacific, the officials and the people alike, attaining rich culture, and
advancing the standard of living of the people.

The devastation of war inflicted upon our cities, the miseries
of the destitute, the stagnation of trade, shortage of food, and the
great and growing number of the unemployed are indeed heart-
rending. But if the nation is firmly united in its resolve to face the
present ordeal and to seek civilization consistently in peace, a bright
future will undoubtedly be ours, not only our country, but for the
whole of humanity.

Love of the family and love of the country are especially strong.
This devotion should we now work towards love of mankind....

We stand by the people and We wish always to share with them
in their moments of joys and sorrows. The ties between Us and Our
people have always stood upon mutual trust and affection. They
do not depend upon mere legends and myths. They are not predicat-
ed on the false conception that the Emperor is divine, and that the
Japanese people are superior to other races and fated to rule the world.

Our Government should make every effort to alleviate their
trials and tribulations. At the same time, We trust that the people
will rise to the occasion, and will strive courageously for the solution
of their outstanding difficulties, and for the development of industry
and culture. Acting upon a consciousness of solidarity and of mutual
aid and broad tolerance in their civic life, they will prove themselves
worthy of their best tradition. By their supreme endeavours in
that direction, they will be able to render their substantial contribution to the welfare and advancement of mankind.

The resolution for the year should be made at the beginning of
the year. We expect Our people to join Us in all exertion in this
great undertaking with an indomitable spirit.[56]

After the war it was recognized that party politics was a *sine qua
non* for the operation of parliamentary democracy. Shidehara

---

[56] Shidehara Heiwa Zaidan (ed.), 670–672; Ujita, 186–233.

for the first time joined a party.   However, he was never successful
as a party politician.   On May 22, 1946, the Shidehara Caibnet
was replaced by Yoshida Shigeru, the chairman of Jiyūtō.   In
February 1949, at the age of seventy-seven, Shidehara Kijūrō was
elected the President of the House of Representatives, the most
honored position for this old devoted statesman.   Two years later,
he died of a heart attack.

Shidehara Kijūrō as a democratic statesman had done as much
as he could within his capacity to make Japan an advanced and
modern nation.   But a new Japan had to wait for another statesman like him with fresh insight and enlightenment from the generation to come.   In mourning his death, *The Asahi Shimbun* wrote
the following editorial:

> The late Mr. Shidehara, throughout the pre- and postwar periods,
> was the most well known abroad as a representative of Japan.   In
> the prewar period he played an active part in diplomacy, and the
> so-called "Shidehara Diplomacy" was more highly valued abroad
> than at home....   His long international experience and trustwor-
> thiness were irreplaceably valuable, and it is a great loss for Japan to
> lose him now, when Japan's international exchange is becoming in-
> creasingly active....
>
> As a diplomat, he tenaciously adhered to his own principles.
> The "Shidehara Diplomacy" was the right course for any diplomat
> to pursue, and yet the military and its sycophants persecuted him
> to the extreme.   In spite of this, he never changed his principles....
> Being a man of high principles, he did not seem to like even the idea
> of skilfully gliding alone in the stream of ever-changing politics.
> But he must have been satisfied, because after the War he returned
> to the highest rank of politics as the Prime Minister and the President
> of the House of Representatives.
>
> Previously, the President of the House of Councilors, Mr. Ma-
> tsunaga Tsuneo, passed away and now the President of the House
> of Representatives, Mr. Shidehara Kijūrō, has died. We feel
> mournful in losing these elders of diplomatic circles who had survived
> the War.   At the same time, if we look at the situation from another

angle, we may state that we are on the verge of a transformation from bureaucratic diplomacy (*kanryō gaikō*) to diplomacy by the people (*kokumin gaikō*). Mr. Shidehara was the embodiment of bureaucratic diplomacy. Throughout his long life he had devoted himself to diplomacy. His contributions to the nation should be highly regarded by the people. But in Japan which has just revived as a democratic nation we must establish a new diplomacy by the people and for this purpose we need a new leader of popular diplomacy. We sincerely mourn the death of our great elder of diplomatic and political circles, Mr. Shidehara. But at the same time in thanking him we should like to take this opportunity to ponder over the way in which our future diplomacy ought to be.[57]

---

[57] *The Asahi Shimbun*, March 11, 1951; Ujita, 233–239.

PART THREE

CHAPTER 5

THE DIFFERENT GOALS
PURSUED BY
SHIDEHARA AND TANAKA

As Herbert Hyman once stated, men are urged to certain ends, but the political scene in which they act is "subjectively" perceived and given various different meanings from person to person.[1] This holds true in the case of Shidehara Kijūrō and Tanaka Giichi. One can observe certain fundamental conflicts in their foreign policies, but those conflicts resulted essentially from their different understandings of national interests and of the domestic and the international world. Having examined the contrasting personalities and national-cultural identities of these diplomats, I would now like to proceed with an analysis of the "cognitive map" that accompanied "their movements toward the ends." First, let us survey the "objective" world in which they were situated.

---

[1] Herbert Hyman stated, "Men are urged to certain ends but the political scene in which they act is perceived and given meaning. Some cognitive map accompanies their movement toward their ends." *Political Socialization* (Glencoe, Ill., 1959), 18.

The International Scene

Anti-imperialism.   Perhaps the dominant note in the international situation after the Great War was the general world aspiration for peace and order.   Anti-imperialism, a democratic order, and international co-operation were common goals among nations.   The Wilsonian and Leninist attacks on imperialism continued strong, and China, which had been a major victim of imperialism, enthusiastically supported both American and Russian assertions.   Wilson emphasized self-determination and the sovereign rights of all people.   In Great Britain, Lloyd George advocated "diplomacy by conference," by which he hoped to bring about "open diplomacy" and the "mobilization of world opinion."   All denounced the "old diplomacy" and agreed on the need of establishing a "new diplomacy."   The main elements of the "new diplomacy" were peaceful settlements, open negotiations, multinational conferences and agreements, the mobilization of world opinion, renunciation of economic and military exploitation of weaker nations, respect for national sovereignty, and the self-determination of all peoples.

The Paris Peace Conference, the establishment of the League of Nations, and the Washington Conference were concrete manifestations of these world aspirations.   This trend lasted for about a decade, until the London Naval Armament Reduction Conference of 1930.   The Geneva Protocol of October 1924 and the Kellogg-Briand Pact (1928) expressed the same spirit.   The Preamble of the Covenant of the League of Nations declared:

THE HIGH CONTRACTING PARTIES
> in order to promote international cooperation and to achieve
> international peace and security
> by the acceptance of obligations not to resort to war,

by the prescription of open, just and honourable relations between nations,

by the firm establishment of the understandings of international
law as the actual rule of conduct among Governments, and

by the maintenance of justice and scrupulous respect for all
treaty obligations in the dealings of organized peoples
with one another,

Agree to this Covenant of the League of Nations.[2]

Japan not only sent delegates to all these conferences, but also
pledged her strict observance of these international agreements.

The Washington system. In addition to the dominant
mood of a world seeking peaceful and democratic diplomacy,
Japan was also regulated by the Washington treaties covering the
Pacific region. In the Nine Power Treaty, Japan agreed:

(1) To respect the sovereignty, the independence, and the
territorial and administrative integrity of China;

(2) To provide the fullest and most unembarrassed opportunity to China to develop and maintain for herself an effective
and stable government;

(3) To use their influence for the purpose of effectually establishing and maintaining the principle of equal opportunity for
the commerce and industry of all nations throughout the territory
of China;

(4) To refrain from taking advantage of conditions in China
in order to seek special rights or privileges which would abridge the
rights of subjects or citizens of friendly States, and from counte-
nancing action inimical to the security of such States.

Japan also signed the Five Power Treaty limiting naval armament,
which prescribed:

The United States of America, the British Empire, France,
Italy, and Japan;

Desiring to contribute to the maintenance of the general peace,
and to reduce the burdens of competition in armament;

---

[2] The Covenant of the League of Nations quoted from Annex A in
David H. Miller's *The Geneva Protocol* (New York, 1925).

Have resolved, with a view to accomplishing these purposes, to conclude a treaty to limit their respective naval armament, and to that end have appointed as their Plenipotentiaries;

[Here follows a list of delegates.]

Who, having communicated to each other their respective full powers, found to be in good and due form, have agreed as follows:

Article I. — The Contracting powers agree to limit their respective naval armament as provided in the present Treaty.

Article II. — The Contracting powers may retain respectively the capital ships which are specified in chapter ii, Part 1. On the coming into force of the present Treaty, but subject to the following provisions of this Article, all other capital ships, built or building, of the United States, the British Empire and Japan shall be disposed of as prescribed in chapter ii, Part 2.

Article IV. — The total capital-ship replacement tonnage of each of the Contracting Powers shall not exceed in standard displacement, for the United States 525,000 tons; for the British Empire 525,000 tons; for France 175,000 tons; for Italy 175,000 tons; for Japan 315,000 tons.[3]

Japan's isolation. The Anglo-Japanese Alliance was replaced by the Four Power Treaty at Washington, which lacked the meaning of an "alliance" in any sense. The Nine Power Treaty which pledged the territorial integrity and equal opportunity for trade in China was in fact aimed at Japan, in order to stop further aggression in China. Japan's imperialism during the war, manifested through the notorious Twenty-One Demands (1915) and the Nishihara Loans to China (1917–18), incited bitter anti-Japanese sentiments among Chinese nationalists. Japan's pacts with Czarist Russia between 1907 and 1916, which guaranteed her a special position in Korea and Manchuria, were now abrogated by the Soviet Union, which strongly criticized Japanese ambitions in East Asia in the light of Leninist anti-

---

[3] With regard to full texts of the Nine Power Treaty and the Five Power Treaty, see Buell, Appendix I, and Ichihashi, Appendix III.

imperialism. Wilson's "New Diplomacy" denied the former American assurances based upon the Taft-Katsura Agreement of 1905 and the Lansing-Ishii Agreement of 1917, which had recognized Japan's special interest in China because of her "territorial propinquity."

The spread of Bolshevism in Asia. Japan's isolation was not the only cause of her precarious position in international society. There was also the spread of Bolshevism in East Asia. Outer Mongolia fell into the control of the Soviet Union in July 1921, and this was to be only a first move toward revolutionizing the whole of Asia. In March 1919, the Communist International was organized and the First World Congress was held in Moscow. Four months later, the Soviets issued a manifesto proclaiming, "All people, no matter whether their nations are great or small, no matter where they live, no matter at what time they may have lost their independence, should have their independence and self-government and not to submit to being bound by other nations." The Chinese and the Korean nationalists rallied to this call, and the Russians upheld this principle by renouncing the unequal treaties with China with their provisions for extraterritoriality and tariff concessions.[4] In the meantime, the Russians kept sending missions to China and Japan: Ignatius Yourin reached Peking in August 1920; A. Abram Adolf Joffe in the same month two years later; and in August 1923, Michael Borodin came to act as Sun Yat-sen's advisor, soon to be followed by Leo Karakhan. Hence began a period of close cooperation between Moscow and Canton. The First National Congress of the Chinese Communist Party was held at Shanghai in 1921, and the Kuomintang-Communists *rapprochement* was reached in January 1924.[5]

The Russians were equally ambitious in Manchuria, and in Japan they established close relations with the increasing num-

---

[4] Harley F. MacNair and Donald F. Lach, *Modern Far Eastern International Relations* (New York, 1955), 207–209.

[5] Hosea B. Morse and Harley F. MacNair, 716.

ber of Japanese communists. Such a situation lasted until about 1928, when Chiang Kai-shek succeeded in his northern expedition in China and the Tanaka Administration carried out ruthless anti-communist campaigns in Japan.

China. There were two major factors in China which influenced Japan's diplomacy: Chinese nationalism and civil war. Both endangered Japan's vested interests in China. In the previous two decades, especially during and after the war, the political and economic modernization of China had progressed greatly.[6] The enlightened Chinese were mobilized in a rights-recovery movement against imperialistic nations. The spirit of the May Fourth Movement, which started in Peking in 1919, soon spread over the major cities of China. On that day over ten thousand students demonstrated in Peking against the Paris decision on the Shantung problem and the Chinese Government's humiliating policy toward Japan.[7] The movement was soon supported by other intellectuals, merchants, industrialists, and workers, and it shifted more and more toward the left, as Russian as well as Chinese communist influence increased. Merchants boycotted Japanese and Western goods, and workers carried out strikes. Sporadic strikes in 1922 — such as the seamen's strike in Hong Kong and the strike in Shanghai shipping industries—became widespread by 1925, covering Tsingtao, Canton, Hankow, Shanghai, and Hong Kong. In 1925 there were 318 strikes, the major cause of which was protests against imperialism.[8] Sun Yat-sen de-

---

6 For example, between 1905 and 1917, the number of new-style schools increased from 4,222 to 121,119, and that of students from 102,767 to 3,974,454; see Chow Tse-tsung, *The May Fourth Movement: Intellectual Revolution in Modern China* (Cambridge, Mass., 1960), Appendix A.

7 Tsi C. Wang, *The Youth Movement in China* (New York, 1928), Chap. 10, 165–166. Chiang Monlin estimated about 15,000 students in "The Student Movement," in *The China Mission Year Book, 1919* (1920), eds. E. C. Lobenstine and A. L. Warnshuis, 46. For more information about the number of schools and students involved in the May Fourth Incident, see Appendix B of Chow's *The May Fourth Movement.*

8 Out of 318 strikes, 141 were caused by patriotic movements, Chow, Appendix D. Of the 119 cotton mills in China in 1929, 73 were owned by Chinese, 42 by Japanese, and 4 by Britain, *China Year Book 1929–1930*, 1073–1078.

nounced extraterritoriality, the unequal treaties, and foreign concessions. In 1923 at Shanghai he announced, "China's paramount and most pressing problem is to achieve national unification and attain full national independence."[9]

The period under study is also well known as a period of incessant civil war in China. Tuan Ch'i-jui, chief executive of the provisional government in Peking, headed the Anfu clique. In Manchuria Chang Tso-lin was dominant leading the Fengtien clique. Ts'ao Kun was in Chihli but was soon dominated by General Wu P'ei-fu. Chang had an ally in Chekiang, Lu Yung-hsiang, and Wu was supported by Ch'i Hsieh-yuan in Kiangsu. In opposition to these warlords, Sun Yat-sen in Canton was seeking an opportunity to unify China under the leadership of the Kuomintang. During Shidehara's diplomatic leadership in Japan, civil wars among these warlords continued in China. In the last few remaining months of Shidehara's leadership and during most of the period when Tanaka took control of Japan's diplomacy, Chiang Kai-shek carried out the northern expedition against the warlords. In June 1928 the Nationalists took over Peking, and in October of the same year the Nationalist Government of the Republic of China was inaugurated in Nanking. With Chiang's success in the northern expedition, the long period of civil war came to an end for the time being, though the struggle soon resumed between Chiang and the communists. Throughout these wars, the lives and property of Japanese residents in China were often in danger.

THE DOMESTIC SCENE

Autonomous diplomacy. As we have observed, there

---

[9] Morse and MacNair, 716.

was a general rise of traditionalism in Japan. This change, in turn, brought a change in popular hopes in diplomacy. Popular sentiment, which had favored internationalism in 1924 when Shidehara Kijūrō became Foreign Minister, gradually shifted toward more exclusive nationalism. "Autonomous diplomacy," independent of the West, was the slogan of 1927. The preface of *Gaikō Jihō* (January 1, 1927) — the most important journal of diplomacy — under the heading of "This Year's Task" stated:

> In sympathy with the Emperor's worries, the whole nation has demonstrated supreme love of and loyalty to His Majesty. Indeed, such virtues as glory, benevolence, and equality manifest themselves in the relationship between the Imperial Household and his subjects. This is truly a grand sight in the world. Though the world is broad, there is no nation which enjoys such a splendid *kokutai* as we. Though there are many races in the universe, there is no race which is so loyal and sincere to the Emperor as we. Japan and the Japanese people must be determined to promote the quintessence of such a splendid *kokutai* in co-operation with heaven and earth, and by doing so must contribute to the progress of mankind ever more....
>
> Hence, any race which shares this ideal with us and which contributes to the progress of the world is our friend. On the other hand, those who hinder our course will meet our burning national indignation which will eradicate any kind of thorn and bramble on our road.[10]

The same article continued to assert that in the year 1927 Japan, instead of Great Britain or the United States, had to take the "initiative" in leading all other nations and that with regard to the China problem Japan — because of her possession of a *kokutai* unsurpassed in the world and because of her long experience with China — was best qualified to lead all other nations in suppressing the Chinese who "manipulated and took advantage of powers which were covetous of China profits." The preface

---

10 *Gaikō Jihō* (Current report of diplomacy; Jan. 1, 1927), preface.

to the journal emphasized that this plan should be the task to be achieved in the coming year of 1927. This journal was not particularly fanatical; it was the most popular journal dealing with all varieties of diplomatic problems. A few years before, it had stressed the importance of Japan's international co-operation. In the next issue it re-emphasized the need of "autonomous diplomacy." The editor stated that the "Kasumigaseki Diplomacy" dominated by the Foreign Ministry did not reflect the real sentiment of the populace. Kasumigaseki (the Foreign Ministry), he continued, was only the keeper of the bird (diplomacy), while the real owner was the people:

> We wonder whether the bird keeper did not switch our excellent bird to a parrot which imitates what the British and the American say?.... Fortunately, these days the bird keeper tries to make our bird sing "economic diplomacy" and "autonomous diplomacy toward China." We must encourage the bird keeper so that our bird sings aloud the new meaning of "Shōwa Diplomacy."[11]

This remarkable change in the editorial principle of this journal can be considered a barometer of the shift in popular sentiment.

In the Diet, too, "autonomous diplomacy" became a major issue. Both the Seiyūkai and the Seiyū Hontō criticized Shidehara's "co-operative diplomacy" with the West. Umeda Kanichi of the Seiyū Hontō stated in January 1926:

> Today the general trend of the world is the omnipotence of white people. Everything is judged by the standard of the white, and all world affairs are decided by them. As a result it is the necessary trend of the world that the sentiment of "anti-Japan" and "reject Japan" is increasing among the powers. It is not too much to say that in the future when the Japanese Empire hopes to maintain and promote its position, prestige and honor in the world, they will cause more difficulties to us.... Under these world circumstances, I believe that Japan must prepare great policies in diplomacy, in education, in industry, and in defense, in order to secure our

---

[11] *Ibid.* (Jan. 15, 1927), preface.

right to live and maintain our position, prestige and honor in the world.

Umeda then stressed the need for bolstering the traditional Japanese spirit which had supposedly been inherited by the Japanese race from the time of the founding of the nation:

> We must promote the spirit of loyalty to the Emperor and love of nation (*chūkun aikoku*), and at the same time must foster our beautiful mores of virility (*shitsujitsu gōken*, one of the most important virtues of the samurai). By doing so, we must clarify the quintessense of *kokutai* and make it impossible for foreign thoughts to erode our people…. In short, first and above all, we must clearly understand the great spirit of founding our nation and *kokutai* which is unsurpassed in the world.[12]

Both within and outside the Diet, the same kind of demands were being made by the traditionalists. We must also remember that Umeda Kan'ichi was a close friend of both General Yamanashi Hanzō and Tanaka Giichi, who were all involved in the scandal of the Umeda Kan'ichi Incident.[13]

Positive diplomacy. Another change in domestic society during the period in which Shidehara and Tanaka alternated as foreign minister was the increasing sense of frustration and uneasiness among the people. This does not mean that in 1924 there was no such feeling in the society. A series of *lèse-majesté* incidents had taken place; the great earthquake had occurred; trade was bad; there were already problems of unemployment, labor strikes and tenant disputes; and communists and anarchists were active in disrupting the social order. However, the whole situation had been greatly aggravated by 1927. The financial crisis at home caused anxiety, and Shidehara's compromising attitude toward the Chinese rights-recovery movement caused more frustration among the public. Further, there was a deep sense of political alienation among an already enlightened public.

---

[12] *Dai-Nihon Teikoku Gikai-shi*, XVI, January 27, 1926.
[13] See page 69 for the explanation of this incident.

Parliamentary democracy was indeed in trouble. Politics as well as the whole society became more corrupt and degenerate. Suicide and crime sharply increased, on the one hand, and the popular indulgence in *ero-guro-nansensu* became more extreme on the other. To the traditionalists it looked as if the whole society was breaking into pieces. Social harmony and order were gone. Thrift and modesty were being replaced by waste and extravagance. Obedience and loyalty were changing to licentiousness and arrogance.

Many people felt that some method had to be found to break through the deadlock on all sides of the society. People like Tanaka Giichi, Gotō Shimpei, and Mori Kaku thought the only way to overcome all these difficulties was to pursue resolutely "positive" policies both at home and abroad. Fanatics like Kita Ikki, Ōkawa Shūmei, and Mitsukawa Kametarō even advocated revolution. The Seiyūkai, especially, made the "positive policy" the party's best tool for attacking what they called the "negative policy" of the Wakatsuki Cabinet. For example, in June 1927, at the Seiyūkai Convention of all Kantō districts, a representative, stressing that the party's fundamental principle was "positive and progressive (or offensive)," declared:

> Sixty years have passed since the Restoration. In the light of the constantly changing situation in the world and of the present situation in people's livelihood, various institutions must now be renewed.... While rejecting the negative and retreating policies, we must carry out "positive and progressive" policies. Official discipline should be enforced, national spirit should be rejuvenated, and the great principle of revering the Emperor and loving the nation must be manifested. While perfecting national power inside, we must demonstrate our prestige abroad.[14]

Anti-Americanism and anti-Westernism. The traditionalists' anti-American and anti-Western feelings were deep-rooted,

---

[14] Kawai, 571.

dating back to the "expel the barbarians" (jōi) movement in the late Tokugawa period. Their pride in Japan's unique tradition and xenophobia were two sides of the same coin. But the core of the matter was their naïveté and ignorance. In addition to these factors, traditionalists held grudges against the West, because Japan had to yield to the Western forces and was coerced into opening the country. Japan's unequal treaties with the West and the Triple Intervention further increased their sense of humiliation. Even after Japan had become a major power in the world, various incidents took place stinging the nagging feelings of the sensitive Japanese. Those incidents in the twentieth century mainly took the form of racial discrimination in the United States. The Japanese delegates at the Paris Peace Conference tried to terminate discrimination once and for all by incorporating the racial equality clause into the Covenant of the League of Nations, but they were defeated by the Western powers. As a result, Japanese enmity toward the West was deepened, and the high-pitched call of Wilsonian democracy looked like a sham to the traditionalists.

Then came the American discriminatory Immigration Act which brought the traditionalists' resentment against the United States to a head. Tokutomi Sohō (Iichirō) asserted in his book, *Yamato Minzoku no Seikaku* (Awake, the Yamato Race!), that the event was the "most unprecedented humiliation in the recent fifty years of Japanese history." He exclaimed, "What can we do about this! How can we restore our national 'face' which was so seriously hurt?" "Persevere. Foster power. Know thy shame and endure it, and think how thou can cleanse thy shame!" Sohō also stated that it was "rampant Americanism" rather than Bolshevism that Japan had to be most concerned with. He reminded the Japanese of the fact that the discriminatory laws were not just against the Japanese, but all the colored races in Asia, the Chinese, the Indians, the Middle and Near Easterners, and that Japan had to become the leader and protector of all these oppressed peoples.[15]

This sense of "racial affinity" was shared by Mitsukawa Kametarō who, in his influential book *Ubawaretaru Ajiya* (Asia that was lost, or deprived, 1921), asserted that the Western people had enslaved the Asian people through all kinds of violence and that they deprived the Asians not only of territories and resources, but also of their good traditions.[16]   Corresponding to this kind of sentiment, in August 1926 an All-Asian Conference was held in Nagasaki, declaring, "We, ourselves, will strive to secure freedom and happiness for all Asian races, based upon equality and justice."[17]

Anti-militarism.   Throughout the twenties strong anti-military sentiment prevailed in Japanese society.   This was also the general feeling abroad, a result of the brutal war.   Taking advantage of this opportunity, intellectuals, students, businessmen, and political parties — especially the Kenseikai — all vehemently criticized the military clique which had been a dominant power in the government and the society.   The Taishō liberals enjoyed being scornful toward the military, and they even thought that such an attitude symbolized their liberal-democratic mindedness. Shigemitsu Mamoru, a veteran diplomat, recalls:

> Wherever soldiers went, passers-by bore a scornful air on their faces.   Even when soldiers rode streetcars, they could not but feel small when they were wearing their uniforms.   For example, in the streetcar people whispered aloud — so that the soldiers would also hear them —, "Are spurs necessary in the streetcar?"   Passengers treated the soldiers' long swords as a nuisance.[18]

The government's reduction of spending on armaments — partly due to the world trend of armament reduction and partly due to

---

[15]   Tokutomi Iichirō, *Yamato Minzoku no Seikaku* (Awake, the Yamato Race!; Tokyo, 1928), 1–46.

[16]   Mitsukawa, *Ubawaretaru Ajiya* (Tokyo, 1921), *passim*.

[17]   The Conference was held between August 1 and 4, see the detailed information in *The Mainichi Shimbun* and *The Asahi Shimbun*, August 1–4, 1926.

[18]   Shigemitsu, *Shōwa no Dōran*, I, 14.

financial necessity in the chronic recession — also caused anger among the military. Between 1920 and 1925 the national military expenditure was reduced from 650 million yen (47 per cent of the total budget) to 434 million yen (27.5 per cent). In 1919 the total number of soldiers was 338,379, but in 1925 it was reduced to 296,237.[19] Because of such a drastic retrenchment of the Army and the Navy, many veteran soldiers were discharged.

Believing that it was the military which had protected the nation and saved her from many crises, and being proud of themselves as the "Imperial" soldiers most loyal to the Emperor, young officers were especially angry about this situation. They were convinced that such a situation was created by party politicians and businessmen — the former asserting liberalism and democracy and the latter selfishly pursuing capitalism — and that all of these were the major sources of social degradation.[20] It was with this conviction that a large number of young fanatic soldiers joined the Tenkentō (Heavenly Sword Society) established by Nishida Zei (Mitsugu, 1901–37) and Kita Ikki in 1926, many members of

---

[19]   Naikaku Kambō (ed.), Tables 32 and 34.

[20]   Tanaka felt the same way. In 1922, for example, General Tanaka stated before the staff officers:

"As a member of the committee of the Veterans Association,... what I am most anxious about in the present situation is that such a tendency will be extremely influential upon the spiritual degradation of the veterans, though it also will weaken the solidarity of soldiers on active duty. In the long run, the former effect will be more serious in harming the high spirit of our military. If people dislike the military, soldiers will injure their pride, and will lose their self-confidence....

"Recently, in reading opinions in newspapers, I have noticed that they tend to connect everything with the reduction of armament. They exaggerate our difficulties, and furthermore they write about them derisively. This is most unpleasant for us. Consequently, soldiers feel small and our traditional prestige has been rooted out almost completely. These days young officers tend to take off their uniforms and wear civilian suits while traveling. This is only a familiar example. In streetcars and trains, when we are wearing uniforms, we feel a certain scorn from the public.... Hence, officers as well as ordinary soldiers cannot but feel disappointed and anxious, which naturally results in losing their vigorous spirit. People's feelings are sensitive and easy to change. In this way, the soldiers' spirit is gradually eroded without being clearly noticed, and their solidarity which had been built at the expense of many years will be cracked, if not destroyed completely." Kawai, 160–161.

which were from Tanaka's Veterans Association. The society proclaimed that in order to realize the Shōwa Restoration the members had to assassinate all recalcitrants by wielding the "Heavenly Swords" as Prince Nakano Ōye (626–671) with the "Heavenly Sword" had killed Soga no Iruka (?–645), and restored the Imperial fortune.[21]

Population increase and food shortage. From about the end of 1925, the mass media began to report a rapid population increase and anticipate food shortages in the near future. In May 1926, for example, the Ministry of Agriculture and Forestry reported that because the population increase was 12.17/1000 a year, within thirty years the total population would amount to more than 85 million, and Japan would have to face the national crisis of a food shortage. In the autumn of 1926 *The Asahi Shimbun* reported that in the year 1925 the population increased by 870,000, the highest increase in history.[22] The problem thus became a major issue in the Diet after 1925. During the Fifty-first Diet in 1925, a Dietman spoke:

> How can we feed our population which is increasing by 600,000 every year, amounting to a six-million increase within ten years? While the population is rapidly increasing, our industry, our wealth, and our economic revenue are not sufficient to feed them. Today's deadlock has come as the result of an imbalance which has been gradually created between the population increase and the progress of our industry. Even if there had been no earthquake, even if there had been no repercussions [of our trade] in 1920, a deadlock would have come in the near future. This is crystal clear. Thus, this problem is of grave importance today and for the near future. Because it will influence our national fortune so greatly, we must find a countermeasure and solve the problem immediately.[23]

The general policy of the Kenseikai Administrations (Katō and

---

[21] Shigemitsu, I, 15–17, Arahara, *Dai Uyoku-shi*, 84–89.

[22] *The Asahi Shimbun*, September 2, 1926.

[23] Yamamoto Teijirō's speech from the record of *Dai-Nihon Teikoku Gikai-shi*, XVI, January 21, 1926.

Wakatsuki) toward this problem was to increase the amount of cultivated land. In early 1926 the Wakatsuki Cabinet set up a second large scale Hokkaidō development project, and the plan was to be begun in 1927. The government also decided to make a thorough investigation of whether there were more arable lands in Kyūshū and Tōhoku. However, many people criticized such policies as too negative and proposed more positive methods. Some people advocated the improvement of rice production. Others saw a need for increasing trade, especially with China, the United States, and South America. Yet others emphasized the importance of more industrialization within Japan. Among these various means, the most noteworthy was the recommendation of sending large amounts of immigrants to the continent, especially to Manchuria and Mongolia.[24] Hence the problem of Manchuria and Mongolia in the eyes of the public became magnified.

The Manchurian-Mongolian issue. As popular concern regarding the rapid population increase and the anticipation of food shortages became more and more serious, Manchuria and Mongolia began to look like Japan's best opportunity for providing land and resources. Chiang Kai-shek's national unification campaign also stimulated Japanese anxiety over the future status of their rights and interests in the region. Most people had forgotten that Japan's "propinquity" to China including Manchuria had been rejected by the powers at the Washington Conference, and that the Japanese delegates had admitted the "open door" policy in China. Even *The Asahi Shimbun*, the most progressive newspaper in Japan, on May 7 and 8, 1926, printed an article which emphasized Japan's special interest in Manchuria. The author stated that the feeling expressed by the popular song saying "Manchuria is several hundred *ri* away [far, far away]" had to be cast away, for Manchuria was a very close problem for Japan. He said:

---

[24] See for example the special issue on how to increase rice production in *Chūō Kōron* (Oct. 1925); *Gaikō Jihō* (Oct. 1, 1926), 15–33; *The Asahi Shimbun*, June 29, 1926.

Japan's special interest in Manchuria and Mongolia was questioned even at the time of the conclusion of the Ishii-Lansing agreement.... The problem has also been asked in the Diet. By Japan's special interest, it means those legal rights and interests which have been guaranteed by the Portsmouth Treaty, the Twenty-One agreements between China and Japan, namely the so-called Sino-Japanese Treaty [the 21 Demands], and by many other treaties. Those special rights and interests are those of Japan which are superior to the claims of other powers.

In this way Japan's "special rights and interests" in Manchuria and Mongolia was asserted everywhere: in the Diet, in newspapers, in magazines like *Gaikō Jihō* and the liberal journal, *Chūō Kōron*, to say nothing of such a traditionally nationalistic magazine as *Nihon oyobi Nihonjin* (Japan and the Japanese). Having noticed this kind of trend in Japan, Ch'ên Chio-shêng, a Nationalist diplomat, wrote a long article in protest:

Hitherto, we have understood that concerning the Manchurian-Mongolian problem the Japanese have referred to only a certain kind of limited rights and interests. But recently their opinion has changed drastically, and they seem to be talking about their broad territorial rights there. For us Chinese, such a tendency in Japanese public opinion is indeed surprising and regrettable. Even in the Diet where the most responsible opinions should be expressed, we hear such words as "our Empire's special position in Manchuria and Mongolia."

He noted that there was a great difference between "important interest" and "special position." He further asserted, "they should abandon the term which disregards Chinese sovereignty! Stop painting China's map arbitrarily! Look, a burning anti-Japanese feeling is rising everywhere in China!"[25] Nevertheless, the Japanese concern with these areas became even more acute, as Chiang's northern expedition advanced, and when Chang Hsüeh-liang joined the Nationalist Government in December 1928.

---

[25] *The Asahi Shimbun*, February 9 and 10, 1926.

Finally, as we have already seen, there was the problem of economic difficulty. Perhaps it is sufficient to point out here that between 1919 and 1924 Japan's total exports declined from 2,157 to 1,872 million yen and that Japan's share in the China market dropped from 40 per cent in 1917 to 23 per cent in 1924.[26] For several years after the war, Japan also suffered an unfavorable balance of trade. A representative appealed to the Diet:

> Last year we had a serious unfavorable balance of trade amounting to 300 million yen. It means that to that extent our fortune was taken away by other countries. If we lose 300 million or more annually, like we did in the last year, and this year and the next year, what will happen in the near future? We feel as if our flesh were torn and our bones were being shaved off year after year. How can we just calmly sit without doing anything about this problem?[27]

Conflicting Views on National Goals and Interests

In dealing with the foregoing problems, Shidehara Kijūrō and Tanaka Giichi demonstrated sharply contrasting approaches: "co-operative" versus "autonomous" diplomacy; "peaceful" versus "militant" diplomacy; the principle of non-intervention versus intervention in Chinese domestic affairs. Why were their policies so different? Partly it was due to the changing domestic and international environments. However, it was also, perhaps more dominantly, the product of their different personalities and national-cultural identities. Hence I would like to attempt to search for some deeper meanings beneath the contrasts in their policies hitherto observed.

What a diplomat considers his nation's ultimate goal becomes

---

[26]   Okazaki, Kajinishi, and Kuramochi (eds.), 409; Iriye, 26.
[27]   See note 23.

the general guideline for his policy.   Therefore, in order to understand Shidehara's and Tanaka's policies as a whole, we must first understand what they thought Japan's ultimate goals were.

Both Shidehara and Tanaka were seriously concerned about the question "What can Japan offer to the world?"   However, their answers differed greatly.   Shidehara hoped to make Japan a democratic and highly industrialized nation domestically and a peace-loving and co-operative member of the world internationally. As we have seen, his ideal of establishing world peace was clearly exemplified in the Shōwa Constitution.   Based upon these same principles, Shidehara during his foreign ministership constantly emphasized the necessity of creating "a world without war in co-operation with all mankind," echoing the spirit of the Geneva Protocol.   Tanaka, on the other hand, hoped to promote *kokutai* at home and to propagate its quintessence abroad.   He was convinced that Japan's *kokutai* was unsurpassed, and that therefore to exalt *kokutai* was the only way for Japan to claim her *raison d'être* in the world.   Nevertheless, he thought, it was being eroded by Western materialism and egoistic individualism.   Japan's first "urgent need" was to reconstruct the collapsing *kokutai*.   Otherwise, Japan would no longer be Japan.   However, Tanaka was not satisfied with just promoting *kokutai* within the nation.   His motto was *"sekkyoku shinshu"* (being positive and on the offensive), and in his strategic thinking offense was always the best defense. Consequently, Japan had to expand her own culture more positively against Western domination in the world.

Western individualism and materialism, Tanaka believed, would allow the individual to pursue his own egoism and material benefits indefinitely.   Such individualistic and egoistic attitudes of the West would lead both individuals and nations into endless wars.   On the other hand, if Japan's *kokutai* became dominant in the world, subjects would voluntarily sacrifice themselves to the Emperor, and the Emperor would be benevolent to the people. If Japan's traditional virtues, *jin* (love), *gi* (justice), *sei* (sincerity), and *shin* (trust) would prevail over the entire world, order and harmony would result and people could enjoy happiness. In short, the Imperial Way had to be spread over the world. In order to achieve this goal, Japan first had to become the "Lord" of Asia, and thus rid Asia of Western domination. On May 14, 1925, when Tanaka became chairman of the Seiyūkai, he declared to the party convention:

> The essence of politics is to promote the national fortune. We are not merely satisfied with the negative goal of obtaining security for our nation and people. But more positively, we aim to expand. We must make it our creed that Japan be able to act freely and firmly .... Politics are not discussion but action. By becoming the vanguard of the Imperial Way (*Ōdō Seiji*) which unites the Emperor and the subjects, we wish to revive the fresh air for the new age.[28]

On April 14, 1927, when Tanaka was newly elected to the chairmanship of the Seiyūkai, he asserted:

> Our Empire which is the Lord of East Asia must be prepared to renovate our policy toward China to protect the security of the whole area, and in order to achieve our self-defense and the maintenance of our rights and interests [in Manchuria].[29]

Another factor which exerts a great influence upon the diplomat's policy-making is his general concept of international relations. In this point, too, the "world" of Shidehara and that of Tanaka were different.

Shidehara held firm to his belief in egalitarian individualism. His correspondence with Ōhira Komazuchi during Japan's ultranationalistic period, and his courageous resistance against the totalitarian Imperial Rule Assistance Association are clear indications of this. These domestic aspirations of his were extended to his foreign policy. "Live and Let live," was his favorite slogan, and peaceful coexistence was his motto of diplomacy. He was convinced that, just as an individual is the sole sovereign of his

---

28 Quoted by Hosokawa, 121–122.
29 *Ibid.*, 135.

will and action in a democratic society, so in the international community each nation should be the sovereign of her activities. No country should intervene in another nation's affairs. As in a democratic society individual dignity and independence should be respected by government and society at large, simultaneously, public welfare should not be disturbed by the individual. Likewise, in the world community a nation's territorial integrity and independence must be observed by all powers, while, simultaneously, international welfare should be promoted by every member nation of the world community. His rich international experiences and universalistic perspective might also have influenced this view.

Tanaka, on the other hand, was a genuine traditionalist, wrapped with particularistic values and hierarchical human relations. Since he emphasized absolute loyalty to the Emperor and self-sacrificing devotion to one's superior in his domestic politics and private human relations, he expected the whole world to be constructed in this kind of hierarchical order. And as he himself endeavored to seek after power and glory, he hoped eventually to make Japan the "Lord" of the whole world. Tanaka's quixotic megalomaniac tendency further fostered such an ambition. Moreover, he cherished the samurai values. He believed that *bushidō* was the "essence" of all national virtues. As a man ought to have determination, unyielding spirit, and courage, so should the nation. Tanaka believed that "compromise" was "defeat"; and "conciliation" was "humiliation." This attitude has already been seen in his advocacy of war against Czarist Russia. Diplomacy was seen, in the final analysis, as a sword-fight. The ultimate purpose of diplomacy was to decide the question of who dominates whom. Unlike Shidehara, who considered diplomacy to be essentially composed of "compromise" and "negotiation," as in the case of a commercial transaction, Tanaka understood it to be an incessant contest among nations for power and glory. Japan ought not suffer any humiliation in this contest.[30]

---

[30] For theoretical aspects of this discussion, i. e. the inter-relationship

Keeping in mind these different concepts of international relations and Japan's ultimate goals held by Shidehara Kijūrō and Tanaka Giichi, let us now analyze the specific methods they used to solve problems which existed in Japan between 1924 and 1929.

For any diplomat, national security must be of primary importance. At this time Japan's position was rather precarious due to her international isolation. Shidehara tried to gain Japan's security by promoting general world peace in co-operation with the West by wholeheartedly supporting the Paris treaties, the Washington system, and the League of Nations. As late as December 1929, when Shidehara was Foreign Minister for the second time, he still emphasized peaceful co-operation with the Western powers. Referring to the London Naval Conference which was to be held soon, he stated in the Diet:

> Now the world is thirsty for happiness and security in individual life, and for peace and friendship in international relations. The London Conference will surely succeed, if the powers adhere to this world sentiment. All related powers [of course including Japan] should not disappoint such a demand by world public opinion. The Washington Conference has opened up a new epoch in history for the progress of all mankind. We hope that the same result will be brought about from the Conference at London.[31]

among personality, values and perception, see C. M. Kluckhohn, H. A. Murray, and D. M. Scheider, *Personality in Nature, Society and Culture* (New York, 1953); Harold and Margarett Sprout, *Man-Milieu Relationship in the Context of International Politics*, trans. W. R. Boyce Gibson (Princeton; 1956); Karl Zener, *et al* (eds.); C. Kluckhohn, "Values and Value-Orientations," *Toward a General Theory of Action*, ed. T. Parsons and E. A. Shils (Cambridge, 1951); Lasswell introduced a formula by which he attempted to explain how private motives are rationalized into public interest and how a private man is transformed into a "political man." Lasswell's formula is: $p]^d]r=P$ (p=private motives, d= displacement into a public object, r=rationalization in terms of public interest, P=political man), Harold D. Lasswell, *Psychopathology and Politics* (Chicago, 1930), 74–76. In the Japanese context, Maruyama Masao has shown how ultranationalists' paternalistic and hierarchical orientation influenced their views of international relations in *Thought and Behavior in Modern Japanese Politics;* with regard to actual thought and behavior of Shidehara and Tanaka, the biographical chapters and the following chapters on the analysis of their policies will reveal the relationships among their personalities, cultural-identities, and their private and public behavior.

Shidehara was well aware of the fact that Japan had to "co-operate" with leading Western nations, in order not to be driven into a major confrontation with them. Promotion of world peace and co-operation with the powers, he thought, would be the best means to obtain Japan's security and to save her from international isolation.

Tanaka, on the other hand, because of his long military life and his esteem for *bushidō*, was preoccupied with the defense problem. If to establish peace was Shidehara's primary concern, to win wars was Tanaka's. In this regard, Shidehara was rather optimistic, while Tanaka was pessimistic. Shidehara believed that there were more common elements among nations than differences and that the maintenance of peace was possible if nations would emphasize these common elements and try to compromise with one another. Tanaka's philosophy was more Hobbesian. Until the right order was established in the world by the Imperial Way, wars would continue indefinitely because each nation would seek her aggrandizement. Peace was only temporary and war was constant. International agreements were of no avail in maintaining peace. Besides, contemporary international laws and agreements were only tools for the Western domination. Indeed, Japan may have been isolated, but, he thought, in the final analysis the only recourse for a nation's security was her own military strength. Consequently, to defend herself Japan had to build up invincible military power. Hence Tanaka endeavored to establish a garrison-state by making the entire population into soldiers based upon his idea that "all-subjects-are-soldiers."

To Tanaka, however, winning a war had more meaning than just fulfilling the necessity of defending the nation. It gave him personal satisfaction as well. Just as samurai had hoped to gain their fame by winning a series of battles, so Tanaka hoped to raise

---

[31] Maezawa (ed.), II, 67.

Japan's prestige by winning war after war. For this purpose, making all subjects into soldiers was not enough. The nation had to cultivate her spiritual power, *bushidō* and *Yamato damashii*. A function of the Veterans Association and the Youth Association was to make Japan rich in the spirit of *bushidō*, ready to fight whenever necessary. Tanaka's readiness to resort to force was demonstrated by three different orders to dispatch troops to Shantung while he was Premier (in May 1927, April 1928, and May 1928), and by his advocacy for war against Czarist Russia and the Siberian expedition. Shidehara, on the contrary, was convinced that Japan's prestige would be increased in the world not by winning wars but by promoting world peace. As we shall see, he firmly opposed Japan's military intervention in Chinese affairs.

Shidehara and Tanaka likewise held contrasting views on the issue of "co-operative" versus "autonomous" diplomacy for a number of reasons. First of all, as we have just seen, their ideas about obtaining national security were different; Shidehara was an Anglo-Americanophile, whereas Tanaka was anti-Western; Shidehara had a more modern universalistic perception and Tanaka a traditionalistic, particularistic view. Therefore the former tended to identify himself with world public opinion, which favored international co-operation and democratic ways of solving conflicts among nations, while the latter was inclined to identify himself with his domestic colleagues who asserted anti-Westernism and an autonomous diplomacy; finally, international co-operation was the general principle of the Kenseikai which controlled the Katō and the Wakatsuki Administrations as opposed to Tanaka's Seiyūkai and the Army, which advocated an autonomous diplomacy.

However, there were more significant meanings to this issue. Traditionalists thought that Shidehara's so-called co-operative policy was "conciliatory" and even "subservient" to the West. They argued that Japan should take the initiative, instead of following the Western examples. Like Tokutomi Sohō, they contended that the West should "co-operate" with Japan, and not the opposite. For traditionalists who highly valued national "face" and "pride," the issue was partly a "face" problem. Ever since the opening of Japan by the Western powers, Japan had yielded to the West. Now that Japan had become a major power, it was about time she took the initiative. Furthermore, to co-operate with the West and to maintain the status quo meant to allow further Westernization of the world and conversely to lose Japan's significant role in world history. Consequently, Japan had to destroy these Westernizing trends and attempt to remold the world according to her own tradition under her own leadership. It was for this reason that the traditionalists obstinately refused to make Japan conform to the contemporary international "System," and advocated an autonomous policy instead. Tanaka's determination to challenge the Western domination was expressed in the Eastern Conference of 1927. To Commander Mutō of the Kwantung Army, Prime Minister Tanaka revealed his intention to fight the United States, Great Britain, and even his willingness to enter into a world war, in order to carry out the plans set forth at the Conference.[32]

At a minimum, autonomous diplomacy meant "independence" of the West, while more positively it meant Japan's will to pursue an "exclusive" *kokutai*, and her "challenge" to the West. The Western powers detected the real danger and aggressive nature of Tanaka's policy on this point. His policy was often called "militant," "aggressive," and "expansionistic," not simply because of his readiness to resort to force, but also because of this anti-Western tendency. Shidehara and other West-oriented democrats, on the other hand, felt that such a policy was extremely dangerous. Perhaps, it would eventually destroy Japan. From the viewpoint of Japan's security, they felt obliged to oppose such an exclusive policy. Besides, Shidehara and his colleagues were not especially

---

[32] Nakamura Kikuo, "Tanaka Naikaku no Taika Gaikō" (Tanaka Cabinet's Policy toward China), *Hōgaku Kenkyū* (September 1958), 37; Yamaura, 636–637.

interested in maintaining Japan's traditional politico-cultural identity.   They hoped to change both the self-image and the substance
of their nation.   They wished to modernize Japan and make her as
technologically advanced as the West.   Their co-operation with
the West ensued from these aspirations.

There is an important problem to be discussed briefly here:
there is always the interaction (or cycle) of influence between a
leader and his milieu.   Tanaka was one of the leaders who had
created an anti-Western sentiment and asserted an autonomous
diplomacy.   Yet, at the same time, he was affected by the milieu
which he himself had produced.   The same thing can be said of
Shidehara.   By 1929 the international mood for co-operation had
subsided considerably.   The increasing disco-ordination among
the powers was initiated partly by Japan's aggressive and unco-
operative policy during the Tanaka Administration.   Nevertheless,
Shidehara still stressed international co-operation with regard to
the London Naval Conference.   At the same time the leader is
also influenced by opposition forces.   Tanaka could not but give
some lip service to parliamentarism and to the Washington treaties
in his diplomatic speeches.   As traditionalism became stronger in
Japan, Shidehara's policy, too, changed in nuance though not in
principle during his second term.

Shidehara and Tanaka shared one common concern.   They
feared the spread of Bolshevism in Asia and in Japan.   However,
their approaches were again markedly different.   Since October
1917, diplomatic relations between Russia and Japan had been
severed.   Japan had sent troops to Siberia, which further strained
relations between the two countries.   In early 1921, the Hara
Cabinet undertook negotiations to settle their difficulties, but the
attempt had failed.   Even after that, fruitless negotiations had continued until May 1924.   When Shidehara became Foreign Minister, he was determined to solve this problem.   He ordered Japan's
Minister to China, Yoshizawa Kenkichi, to negotiate only the most

important problems and not to demand impossible things.[33] As a result, on January 20, 1925, the negotiations which had failed for so long were finally consummated in the Treaty of Peking. The treaty provided for the resumption of diplomatic relations; revision of the fisheries agreement of 1907; the most-favored-nation treatment; mutual prevention of propaganda or other inimical activities; and granted the citizens of each nation certain guarantees, such as those of travel and residence. Japan promised the withdrawal of her troops from northern Sakhalin by May 15 and received in return certain oil and coal concessions there. This solution suggested the typical procedure of Shidehara's policy. He hoped to terminate their mutual antagonism, to prevent Russian propaganda by international agreements, to relieve Japan's isolated position in Asia, and to obtain economic benefits from Russia.[34]

Tanaka was no less concerned with Bolshevism, yet his method was to rely upon Japan's military power. He was convinced that strategically Manchuria was vitally important for Japan in deterring the Russians' southward advance. The security of Manchuria, therefore, had to be preserved and "by all means." He further worried about the activities of Chinese communists, and hoped Chiang Kai-shek would eradicate the communists from his country. Hence, Prime Minister Tanaka promised Chiang that "if" Chiang's northern expeditionary troops were headed toward the final extermination of communists, then Japan should give him moral support and assist him in attaining his political goals.[35] At the same time, at home, Tanaka carried out the most ruthless anti-communist campaigns the nation had ever known. On March 15, 1928, more than a thousand Japanese communists (including 129 students) were arrested (March Fifteenth Incident). In the next month, the Labor-Farmer Party (Rōdō Nōmintō), the Japan Labor Council

[33] Shidehara Heiwa Zaidan (ed.), 324.

[34] *Shuyō Monjo*, II, 63–68; Chitoshi Yanaga, *Japan Since Perry* (New York, 1949), 459 ff.

[35] *Shuyō Monjo*, II, 34; Tanaka to Yoshizawa, May 20, 1927, JFMA PVM 41.

(Nihon Rōdōkumiai Hyōgikai) and the All Japan Proletarian Youth League (Zen Nihon Musan Seinen Dōmei) were banned in the so-called April Tenth Incident. A year later, the Tanaka Cabinet carried out the second anti-communist campaign. In between, Tanaka changed the peace regulations so that they now included a death penalty against those who tried to change the *kokutai* (June 1928). He also strengthened the Special Police Force (Tokubetsu Kōtō Keisatsu) to check "evil thoughts."

The best distinction between Shidehara's and Tanaka's policies may be discerned in their different ways of dealing with the economic, Chinese, and Manchurian problems. Because of his preoccupation with economic matters, Shidehara was extremely sensitive to Japan's economic difficulties. He believed that the most efficient way to save Japan from overpopulation and food shortage was to promote her commerce and industry. His "economic-oriented diplomacy" was based upon such an idea. Accordingly, as we have observed, he strove to expand Japan's trade by revising and concluding a number of commercial treaties with nations all over the world, and by sponsoring various trade conferences at home and abroad. For example, in January 1925, he sent a special goodwill mission to French Indo-China to cultivate Japan's market there. This later resulted in the establishment of a commercial agreement between the two countries.[36] Shidehara sponsored the Near Eastern Trade Conference (during April and May 1926) and the South Pacific Trade Conference (September 1926), in order to investigate what were Japan's promising products and

---

[36] There had been a great deficit in the balance of trade between Japan and Indo-China as the following table indicates. Shidehara strove to solve this unfavorable trade with Indo-China.

Table IV   Japanese Trade with Indo-China

	Japan's Import	Japan's Export
1894	6,204,147 yen	24,523 yen
1904	17,399,667	374,948
1914	15,052,211	803,545
1924	17,990,122	2,438,316

"Shidehara Keizai Gaikō Shiryō," 1–10.

industries as well as the best means to promote these interests in the said areas.

In his opening address to the South Pacific Trade Conference, Shidehara said:

> During World War I, Japan's foreign trade had achieved a remarkable development. After the war, however, a setback came, and finally the great earthquake and fire of the Kanto area in 1923 gave a serious blow to our financial circles. Our productive capacity was destroyed by the calamity, and Japan also had to rely upon foreign countries for materials to rehabilitate the nation. Hence we saw a great deficit in the balance of trade.... Thus the promotion of foreign trade and the encouragement of overseas investment became the most urgent business of our country. The aim of this conference is to study and discuss concrete methods to attain these purposes.

As usual, however, he did not forget to stress Japan's need for international co-operation even in her pursuit of economic interests.

> It goes without saying that international trade is carried out to seek mutual benefits. Its spirit is to benefit our country as well as others. This should also be our aim. The principle of our diplomacy is based upon co-existence and co-prosperity of all nations. In order to secure the real and eternal interests of our nation, there is no other way but this for us to pursue. To adhere to this principle is also the most efficient and sure policy even in our foreign trade.[37]

Shidehara was not as enthusiastic about sending immigrants abroad as about foreign trade. In the same speech he stated that Japan ought to avoid sending immigrants abroad recklessly without paying attention to the special situations of each foreign country. He was obviously referring to the cases of the United States and Manchuria.

Shidehara was especially concerned with the American and the Chinese markets. Having been Ambassador to the United States, he was well aware that the United States was an important customer to Japan.[38] In fact, during the 1920's the United States

---

[37] *Ibid.*, 14–15.
[38] See Appendix IV and V.

was Japan's biggest customer, annually taking at least 40 per cent
of her total exports.   Moreover, she bought 90 per cent of all the
silk thread which was the most important export commodity of
Japan[39].   Naturally, Shidehara could not become unfriendly toward the United States.   For example, he took pains to placate
the Japanese anti-American feeling caused by the discriminatory
Immigration Act.   In the Forty-ninth Diet, the Foreign Minister
said:

> In reviewing the development of this question, there are three
> points which engage our attention.
>
> First, no intimation has lately been made, even by the exclu-
> sionists, of any inferiority of the Japanese race.   Their contention is
> in effect that the Japanese are to the Americans what oil is to water.
> Neither oil nor water can be said to be superior or inferior to the
> other, but the fact is that in no case can oil dissolve and merge in
> water.   In other words, they say, Japanese are unassimilable to
> American life, and the introduction of such alien elements will prove
> a source of danger to the U. S....
>
> Secondly, it has always been consistently maintained by the
> United States that the liberty to limit and control immigration is
> one of the essential attributes of the inherent sovereign rights of each
> nation....
>
> Thirdly, it should be appreciated that the President and the
> Secretary of State of the United States have from the outset shown
> their opposition to the exclusion clause, and have made all possible
> efforts to have it eliminated from the Act.   Public opinion in the
> United States, as reflected by a great section of the American press,
> also appears to be sympathetically disposed to Japan's position in
> the matter.   It is a significant fact that the legislation in question
> has met with uniform disapproval by many influential newspapers
> of the United States.[40]

---

[39]   Ohara Keishi (ed.), *Nichi-Bei Bunka Kōshō-shi* (History of Japanese-
American Cultural Relations), II, *Tsūshō Sangyō-hen* (Commerce and trade;
Tokyo, 1954), Chaps. 1 (27–37) and 6; Matsui Kiyoshi, *Nihon Bōeki-ron* (Japanese
trade; Tokyo, 1950), 132.

[40]   The translation is taken from the telegram sent by the American

The same economic considerations were operating in his China policy. His principle of non-intervention in Chinese civil war and his initiative in recognizing the Chinese tariff autonomy in the Peking Tariff Conference were carried out partly in his hope to befriend China, a great potential market. So, for example, in the Second Fengtien-Chihli War of 1924, Shidehara refused to send troops to north China, though the majority of the Katō Cabinet was in favor of helping Chang Tso-lin against Wu P'ei-fu. In dealing with the Chinese civil war during Shidehara's leadership, Great Britain took the strongest position of all the powers. In January 1927 she proposed to Japan to send troops to Shanghai jointly to protect foreign residents' lives and property from anticipated danger. However, Japan's Foreign Minister again refused to accept this British invitation for military intervention. Hence, on January 25, 1927, Britain alone dispatched to Shanghai three brigades amounting to 20,000 soldiers. In February Shidehara, on the other hand, emphasized his principle of non-intervention in Chinese affairs in the Diet. In these ways throughout the period of civil war Shidehara tried not to antagonize the Chinese against Japan because of his economic interests in China.[41] The fact that Shidehara had some friends in the financial circle might have also influenced his economic-oriented policy. We must also take it into our consideration that "economic diplomacy" was a keynote among diplomats of capitalistic nations after World War I.

However, his economic interests were not the only reason Shidehara resolutely adhered to his principle of non-intervention in Chinese affairs. Being a pacifist and internationalist, he hoped to avoid Japan's involvement in the Chinese military confusions with the other powers, and to respect Chinese sovereignty. He believed that Japan had to be faithful to international laws once they had been signed. In the Fifty-first Diet, Shidehara said:

Chargé in Japan, Jefferson Caffery, to the Secretary of State, Charles E. Hughes, July 8, 1924, FRUS II.

[41] This theme will receive more detailed discussion in the next chapter.

Of course it is hopeful for both the Chinese people and the Japanese residents that The Three Eastern Provinces [Manchuria] will escape wars and maintain peaceful conditions. However, to do so is naturally the Chinese responsibility. And if we senselessly try to take their responsibility, we must disregard the fundamental concepts of international relations, the basic principles of the Washington treaties, and our government's previous resolutions. Once we make the mistake of disregarding them, we must be prepared to lose our national honor forever. Consequently, under no circumstances could I take such a thoughtless action.[42]

Shidehara emphasized Japan's adherence to maintaining China's sovereignty and international agreements, rather than to military adventures, as the policy for maintaining Japan's national honor. As the reader will recall, Shidehara was the first in Japan to ask for China's *agrément* in appointing ministers to China, expressing his wish to recognize China's equality and its sovereignty.[43]

His opponents violently criticized Shidehara's attitudes toward China as "weak-kneed," "negative," and "do-nothing," and Tanaka Giichi as their leader advocated a "positive" and "strong" policy instead. It was during the Tanaka Administration that Japan repeated the Shantung expeditions; that the rumor of the notorious "Tanaka Memorandum" was spread;[44] that the Japanese troops which had been sent to China collided with Chinese troops on May 3, 1928, in the Tsinan Incident; and that Chang Tso-lin was killed by a bomb probably placed by the Kwantung Army on June 4, 1928. Both China and the powers took these series of events as

---

[42] Maezawa (ed.), I, 700–701.

[43] "Shina Mondai Kankei," 58; Shidehara Heiwa Zaidan (ed.), 389.

[44] According to the rumor, Prime Minister Tanaka Giichi presented a memorial to the Throne in which he planned military conquest of China starting from Manchuria. Inau Tentarō made a thorough investigation on the validity of the rumor. Inau tends to hold a negative view, and I am inclined to agree with him. Tanaka might have entertained such an idea, but there was no such actual Memorandum written by Tanaka himself. Concerning various studies and Inau's judgement on this rumor, see Irau Tentarō, "Tanaka Jōsō-bun o meguru Ni-san no Mondai" (A few problems concerning the 'Tanaka Memorandum'), *Nihon Gaikō-shi no Shomondai*, I, ed. Nihon Kokusai Seiji Gakkai (Tokyo, 1964), 73–87.

clear evidence indicating that Japan's policy toward China had shifted remarkably from Shidehara to Tanaka, though Tanaka was not entirely responsible for all these events. Nevertheless, it is also true that Tanaka's aggressive tendency and his eloquent speeches emphasizing a "positive" policy fostered a societal atmosphere congenial to violence.

This change in Japan's diplomacy toward China essentially was the result of Tanaka's understanding of international relations and Japan's national interests, an understanding which was different from Shidehara's. Partly because of his paternalistic orientation and partly because of his feeling of racial affinity toward China and against the West, Tanaka, like many traditionalists, regarded the relationship between Japan and China as that of family members. Yet the proper order among the "Oriental" family members had to be regulated according to the Confucian rectification of names, i.e., superior-inferior relations. Consequently, he thought that Japan had an obligation to lead China to the "path of virtue" by guiding her toward anti-communism. Likewise he regarded Chang Tso-lin as his "younger brother." All of this indicates that Tanaka thought of China as Japan's younger brother.[45]

Thus Tanaka was vexed by China's taking advantage of Japan's "tolerance." Japan's national prestige should not be "humiliated" by a militarily "inferior" nation like China. In April 1927, Chairman Tanaka spoke at the Seiyūkai Convention, referring to the Nanking and Hankow Incidents of that spring:

> It is really deplorable that such incidents have occurred in south China because of the present government's senseless attitude. There has been no other time when our national prestige has been as seriously injured as it is today. In south China, our countrymen's lives and

---

[45] On May 15, 1927, before reporters, Tanaka expressed his view that the relationship between Japan and China could be understood as that of family members. See *The Asahi Shimbun*, May 15, 1927; Tanaka's concluding speech at the Eastern Conference. More discussion on this point will be made in Chapter 7. Ogata Sadako observes that Yamagata Aritomo, Tanaka's master, also had a sense of racial affinity toward the Chinese, see Ogata, 5.

property were illegally threatened, and they suffered extreme insults from the Chinese which is a fate more unbearable than death! These we can never forget. Moreover, businesses which had been carried out for thirty long years and with billions of yen in capital investments were rooted out, and thousands of our countrymen had to escape to Shanghai or to Nagasaki. We have never experienced such miserable humiliation in our history![46]

For Tanaka such "insults" thrust upon Japan by the Chinese were unbearable. He thought it a great shame and national defeat for the Japanese residents to have to "escape" from the dangerous area. These factors explain Tanaka's repeated dispatches of troops to China, his positive and strong policy, and his protection of the Japanese residents on the spot. Because of this kind of understanding of international relations, Tanaka also felt that China's demand for recovering its sovereign rights in tariff autonomy and control of industries in China was "outrageous."

Tanaka's way of thinking was not rational. If it had been, he would have thought twice about carrying out the first Shantung expedition. This costly military adventure was executed in the midst of a national financial crisis. The total number of Japanese residents in Tsinan was about 2,000. Therefore, from an economic point of view, it would have been much more sensible for Japan to evacuate her citizens temporarily from the dangerous area. In fact, both Shidehara and the United States Government had contemplated such a move.[47] Furthermore, Tanaka had to be prepared for the great sacrifice of the profitable China trade caused by such military adventures. Nevertheless, he was more concerned with such non-material benefits as military prestige and overcoming shame and humiliation. If Shidehara's policy was more rational and pragmatic, Tanaka's was more intuitive and emotional. Tanaka also worried about the declining prestige of

---

[46]   Hosokawa, 135.

[47]   MacMurray to Kellogg, March 28, 1927, FRUS II; Kellogg to Mac-Murray, March 31, 1927, *ibid*. For more discussion on this matter, see the following two chapters.

the Army.   Like the traditionalists who had advocated the Korean expedition to satisfy the frustrated ex-samurai in early Meiji, Tanaka hoped to raise the military spirit within the Army and society by sending troops to the Continent.

Finally there is the question of Tanaka's policy toward Manchuria and Mongolia.   In contrast to Shidehara's "China-First" policy, his was often called a "Manchuria-First" policy.[48]   Whereas Shidehara was primarily concerned with China trade, Tanaka was militarily preoccupied with Manchuria.   For Tanaka Manchuria was not only Japan's "life-line" against the Russian expansion toward the south but also — more "positively" — the key strategic position for Japan's eventual military hegemony over the entire East, and perhaps over the world.   Tanaka also regarded Manchuria and Mongolia as a buffer zone to protect Japan's *kokutai* from expanding world communism.   Simultaneously, these regions appeared to him to be the promised land where his utopia under the Imperial Way could be achieved.   Hence he tried to prevent Chinese Nationalist forces from coming into the area "by all means."   Because of their anti-communism — Shidehara being a supporter of bourgeois democracy and Tanaka being a believer in *kokutai* — they both supported Chiang Kai-shek's anti-communist campaign.   Shidehara also thought that the restoration of peace and national unification, including Manchuria, under the solid control of one responsible government in China would be advantageous for the promotion of Japan's China trade. Tanaka, on the other hand, supported Chiang except for his ambitions in The Three Eastern Provinces.   Tanaka was determined to "protect" Manchuria from Chinese communist and Russian infiltration even at the sacrifice of Japan's China trade and at the cost of international criticism.

---

[48]   The distinction between Shidehara's "China-First" and Tanaka's "Manchuria-First" policy has been made by Usui Katsumi and Ogata Sadako. See Usui's "Shidehara Gaikō Oboegaki," 62–68, "Tanaka Gaikō ni tsuite no Oboegaki," 26–35; and Ogata, 7–13.

   Another factor which produced their contrasting approaches
to Manchuria was their understanding of China's sovereignty
over the area.   As we have seen, Shidehara considered The Three
Eastern Provinces a part of China.   Tanaka, on the other hand,
called the area Japan's "special area" (*tokushu chiiki*).[49]   This
term is of great importance: it indicates that Tanaka had assumed
that Manchuria was a part of the Japanese Empire.   Just as in
his private life Tanaka's understanding of the realm of the individual was ambiguous because of his immersion in such traditional
relationships as *oyabun-kobun*, master-disciple, and superior-
inferior, so in his understanding of international relations the problem of national sovereignty and territorial integrity was blurred.
For example, Prime Minister Tanaka often stressed Japan's recognition of China's national sovereignty and territorial integrity
in his diplomatic speeches on the one hand, yet went ahead with
his aggressive plans to exploit Manchurian territory and resources
for Japan's own benefit on the other.   Perhaps Tanaka did not
or could not understand fully the real meaning of these international
terms based upon democratic principles.   Finally, because of his
physiocratic preference for farming instead of commerce and
industry, Tanaka thought that the cultivation of Manchurian land
by Japanese immigrants was the best remedy for Japan's economic
hardships.[50]   It was the Veterans Association and Youth Association under Tanaka's influence that sent many "Patriotic Corps"
to cultivate Manchuria and Mongolia.[51]

---

   [49]   For example, criticizing Shidehara's policy, Tanaka stated in the convention of Seiyūkai, April 15, 1927, "The government took the attitude of indifference even to the upheaval in Manchuria which is the 'special area' of our
Empire," quoted by Hosokawa, 135.
   [50]   The best sources on Tanaka's view on Manchuria and China are his
own articles on these matters, see "Taiman Shokan" (My views on Manchuria,
1915) and "Taishi Keiei Shiken" (My plan how to manage China, 1917).   The
reader will be shocked by Tanaka's aggressive plan for the "management" of
Manchuria and China.   Tanaka assumed that Manchuria was a part of Japan.
Complete texts of these articles are in Tanaka Giichi Denki Kankō-kai (ed.),
I, 547–584, 676–712.
   [51]   There were two distinct groups of people, one supporting Shidehara's

I have discussed Shidehara Kijūrō's and Tanaka Giichi's varying perceptions of Japan's national interests and international relations during the later 1920's mainly in terms of their different national-cultural identities. However, their personal idiosyncrasies might have also influenced their manner of pursuing these policies. Tanaka's aggressive and "quixotic" character, *oyabun* temperament, extraordinary pride, and propensity toward violence may have made his policies more militant, aggressive, and expansionistic. By contrast, Shidehara was a lone individual from childhood onward, and he was also a rather restrained person. It is also reported that, unlike Tanaka, Shidehara not only did not like martial sports but also actually disliked any kind of competitive game. This element in Shidehara's character may have been reflected in his "negative" or "restrained" policy toward China. Shidehara's rational and pragmatic disposition, on the one hand, and Tanaka's emotional and intuitive character on the other also

---

type of policy and the other holding Tanaka's type of view of the world. In the former group one can include Inoue Junnosuke (a democratic financier), Nagai Ryūtarō (a diplomatic councillor), Genrō Saionji Kimmochi, Yoshino Sakuzō, and Kiyosawa Kiyoshi (a liberal critic of foreign policy); whereas in the latter, such people as Yamamoto Jōtarō, Gotō Shimpei, Mori Kaku, Yamanashi Hanzō, and Fujimura Yoshio (a member of the Peers). For instance, Nagai Ryūtarō, fully supporting Shidehara's policy, stated:

"There have been two types of thoughts in our diplomacy. One is imperialism and the other, liberalism.... Most of our Foreign Ministers without strong determination and definite principles vacillated between the two types of policies.... However, a characteristic of Shidehara's policy is its consistent liberalism.

"Secondly, a change is also taking place in the relations between Japan and China. Since the Boxer Incident, there is no time when our relations with China is so good as it is today. This great change resulted from Shidehara's China policy, which has respected Chinese sovereignty and which hopes to achieve co-prosperity of Japan and China with fair and just attitudes toward China."

Fujimura Yoshio, on the other hand, bitterly criticized Shidehara's "weak-kneed" policy and upheld Tanaka's view that Manchuria was a part of Japan. The conflict between these two groups was not just on Shidehara's and Tanaka's China policies, but more fundamentally it was rooted in their different values, principles, and cultural-identities. See Nagai Ryūtarō's article, "Shidehara Gaikō no Honshitsu" (The essence of Shidehara Diplomacy), *Chūō Kōron*, Vol. XLII (March 1927), 91–95 and Fujimura's speech at the Fifty-first Diet in *Dai-Nihon Teikoku Gikai-shi*, January 22, 1927.

may have produced sharp contrasts in their approach to various problems. For example, Tanaka's assertion of "autonomous diplomacy" was emotional, disregarding Japan's need for co-operation with the United States and China in order to pursue her economic interests. His contention that Japan had to take the diplomatic "initiative" was more a matter of "face" than the result of any logical consideration of concrete national interests. Shidehara, on the other hand, thought that diplomacy was designed to seek the optimum national interests by the most effective and efficient means. Therefore, diplomacy could be co-operative sometimes and autonomous at other times, depending upon the situation. Thus, Shidehara's policy in the Special Tariff Conference (October 1925–July 1926) at Peking diverged greatly from his usual policy of co-operation with the West.

Shidehara, as a lawyer-bureaucrat, tended to emphasize established legal procedures. While he was Vice-Foreign Minister in 1918, for instance, he planned to send Nagai Matsuzō, a first-ranking secretary, to London without promoting him to the rank of councilor. Gotō Shimpei, then Foreign Minister, asked Shidehara why he would not promote Nagai. Shidehara answered:

"According to the regulations of the Ministry, Nagai has to wait another several months to be promoted."

"Never mind the regulation," said Gotō, "because Nagai will be pleased with his promotion."[52]

Such concern for due procedure as this may have produced Shidehara's strict adherence to international laws and regulations. Tanaka, like many traditionalists such as Gotō, tended to pay little attention to them.

We could observe many other contrasting attitudes between Shidehara Kijūrō and Tanaka Giichi in dealing with diplomatic problems. However, it seems now pertinent to study in detail how the foregoing points are reflected in a concrete international

---

[52] Nagai Matsuzō, "Shidehara Danshaku no Omoide," 92–93.

context. To do this I have chosen their policies toward China as a case study, inasmuch as the China problem was the most important issue for Japan during this period.

CHAPTER 6

SHIDEHARA KIJŪRŌ'S POLICY TOWARD CHINA JUNE 1924–APRIL 1927

THE SECOND FENGTIEN-CHIHLI WAR

On June 11, 1924, the Katō Coalition Government was established. Popular expectation for the long-awaited beginning
of party government was great, and hopes of democratization were
rising. Watanabe Tetsuzō, an influential journalist, wrote in the
Chūō Kōron:

> Especially since the Kenseikai advocated the need of universal
> suffrage, the number of young people and workers who support the
> party has increased. Young people's influence, supporting the Ken-
> seikai, already looked remarkable at the last election. But this time
> their zeal for the party seems to have increased even more because
> of the party's platform of defending constitutional government.
> Especially, the activities of newspapers in supporting the consti-
> tutional movement and in stimulating the general public were great.[1]

---

[1] *Chūō Kōron*, July 1924, 68.

Miyake Setsurei (1860–1945) gave another reason why the new Cabinet was popular:

> The reason why the new Cabinet is so popular is that the character of the three past Cabinets has been ambiguous. People have anxiously been waiting for a Cabinet with a distinct character. Therefore, when the party Cabinet based upon the House of Representatives was set up, it suddenly became popular.... The head of the leading party justly received the Imperial Mandate to organize the government, and the so-called three party-chiefs lined up in the Cabi-

ROUTES OF THE NORTHERN EXPEDITION*

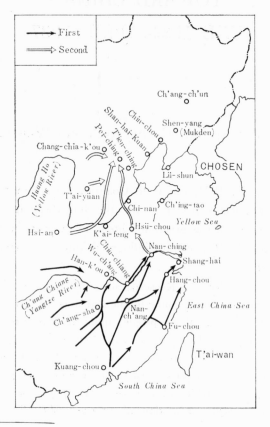

---

* Taken from Usui Katsumi's *Nitchū Gaikōshi* (A history of Sino-Japanese diplomatic relations; Tokyo, 1971), 207.

net. A Cabinet so structured gives us the impression that it is indeed the party government of the party governments.[2]

Abe Isoo (1865–1949) also remarked that the selection of ministers was "perhaps satisfactory for everybody."[3] In addition to this, internationalism was popular both at home and abroad. Hence the whole situation seemed congenial to Shidehara Kijūrō.

Supported by this social atmosphere, the new Foreign Minister made the following speech in the Forty-ninth Imperial Diet, convened on July 1.

> First, our government will protect and promote our just rights and interests but at the same time will respect other powers' just rights and interests as well. By doing so, we hope to secure peace in the Far East, the Pacific region, and thereby the peace of the whole world.... We do not intend to satisfy our unjust desires at the sacrifice of other nations. We will never be influenced by such an erroneous idea as an aggressive or expansionistic policy; such is not possible today.... That which we advocate is the coexistence and co-prosperity of all nations. The popular mind of the world is now awakening toward this direction. There is no doubt that the very foundation of the League of Nations is also based upon this enlightenment of the people. If the powers admit this basic principle, all international problems will find a basis for their own solutions.

Shidehara then stated his policy toward China as follows:

> It goes without saying that Japan and China have the closest relations in politics, economics, and culture. It is also self-evident that both countries must have mutual understanding.... Recently, because injuries to foreigners by the Chinese occurred frequently in various areas of China, foreigners tended to be more sensitive to the unsatisfactory political situation there. However, it is not an easy task for China to carry out improvements of all affairs at once. We must make allowance for this situation and pray for the success of the Chinese people with sympathy, patience, and hope. We must offer our friendly co-operation to China as much as possible, if she

---

[2] *Ibid.*, 79.

[3] *Ibid.*, 83.

seeks it. At the same time, however, we should never interfere in her domestic affairs.

We aim to establish a closer economic relationship between Japan and China under the principle of equal opportunities. In order to accomplish this, we shall take such methods as will bring equal benefits to both Japan and China. Our just and fair policy will surely be recognized by the Chinese people. As you all know, various treaties related to China were signed by the Washington Conference.... The policies prescribed in those treaties are exactly in accord with our policy. Consequently, our government is determined to pursue its policy thoroughly in the spirit of those treaties.[4]

The new Foreign Minister in the Katō Cabinet was especially popular in the United States. *The New York Times* of June 13, 1924, wrote:

Although the new Premier, Viscount Katō, is no especial friend of the United States, the fact that Baron Shidehara, formerly Ambassador in Washington, is to head the Foreign Office means that Americans will have a friend in court who thoroughly understands their point of view, and who knows that they have no dislike for the Japanese, nor wish them harm. There is further good news in the report that Viscount Ishii [Kikujirō] is to take the place of Ambassador Hanihara,... This makes it plain that the Japanese Government is determined to do all in its power to strengthen the ties between the two countries.

China was half suspicious and half expectant of the new Cabinet. The new Prime Minister was rather unpopular in China because of the fact that the notorious Twenty-One Demands had been thrust upon her while Katō was Foreign Minister in the Ōkuma Cabinet. However, Shidehara's emphasis on Japan's non-intervention in Chinese affairs, the coexistence and the co-prosperity of all nations, promotion of world peace, and a general friendly attitude toward China eased the Chinese fear of Katō. This mixed feeling of the Chinese was well expressed in the words of Chu Nien-tsu, a representative of the Peking regime:

---

[4] *Dai-Nihon Teikoku Gikai-shi*, XV, July 1, 1924.

Although the Chinese are afraid of the Twenty-One Demands as if it were a tiger, to me it is not alive, but a paper tiger. Those demands remain only in form and not in substance. I believe that the Katō Cabinet will make its best efforts to solve the remaining problems of those demands, in order to promote friendly relations between China and Japan.[5]

The first challenge to Shidehara came from the most unexpected place: the United States, with which he had the closest ties. On July 1, the very day when Shidehara was making his inaugural speech emphasizing the need for world co-operation and the welfare of the whole of mankind, the American Government put into effect the Immigration Act which included the exclusion provision. As we have seen, people like Tokutomi Sohō, Mori Kaku, and Tanaka Giichi were furious about this discriminatory law. Shidehara, as a well-known Anglo-Americanophile, could not but suffer from the growing anti-Americanism among the Japanese because of this incident. As an added aggravation, the American flag at the embassy was stolen by an angry mob. The Foreign Minister himself promptly visited the American *chargé d'affaires*, Jefferson Caffery, apologized for the diplomatic irregularity caused by the incident and promised to restore the Stars and Stripes as soon as possible. On the same day the American flag was found in Tokyo; the persons responsible were captured in Osaka. The State Department of the United States expressed deep appreciation for Japan's prompt action to redeem the incident and announced that the Japanese Government had done everything in its power and should not be held responsible by the United States. Shidehara at the same time, as we have seen, endeavored to iron out the tension created between the two nations by explaining the American situation behind the enactment of the Immigration Act to the Japanese Diet.

Not all Japanese were blinded by emotional anti-Americanism. Sugimori Kōjirō, for example, stated that the American enact-

---

[5]   Shidehara Heiwa Zaidan (ed.), 260–261.

ment of the Immigration Act indicated that both Japan and the
United States had failed to establish good diplomatic relations.
Therefore, before accusing the United States, Japan had to reflect upon herself to see whether there had been any fault on the
Japanese side. In the final analysis, Sugimori contended, Japan
had been too sycophantic to the West. And the fact that Japan
had lost her own self-respect made Westerners disrespectful of
Japan. He also cautioned the public not to engage in emotional
boycotts against American goods, for economic relations between
the two countries were mutually dependent and such deeds were
not appropriate for a "great" nation. Kikuchi Kan (Hiroshi, 1888–
1948), a famous novelist and columnist of the *Chūō Kōron*, said:

> Even if Japan tries to urge America to self-reflection by advocat-
> ing justice and humanity, Japan's "justice and humanity," too, like
> those of many other countries in the world, are essentially "political,"
> and therefore there would be no effect. It is nonsense for us to urge
> only the United States to adhere to justice and humanity, while we
> ourselves have been taking such an imperialistic approach to Korea
> and Manchuria.

Kikuchi Kan and many other people of common sense felt that
"sentimental" protests would make Japan's position look worse.
Therefore, they generally approved of Shidehara's policy on this
matter, namely to send an official protesting note but at the
same time not to aggravate Japanese-American relations in view
of Japan's future in international relations.[6]

A real challenge to Shidehara's principle of non-intervention
in Chinese affairs came in the early fall of 1924: the second Fengtien-Chihli War between Chang Tso-lin and Wu P'ei-fu.

Between September 1918 and June 1922 there had been
three major politico-military cliques in the north; the Anfu Club
led by Premier Tuan Ch'i-jui, the Fengtien clique headed by
Chang Tso-lin, and the Chihli clique controlled by Ts'ao Kun

---

[6] See articles by Sugimori Kōjirō, Kikuchi Kan, Abe Isoo, Horie Kiichi, and others in *Chūō Kōron*, August 1924, 79–105.

and Wu P'ei-fu.   Toward the end of 1920, the latter two cliques allied to oust the Anfu group and establish a Chihli-Fengtien Government.   The success of this scheme reportedly owed much to Wu's army and strategy.   Nevertheless, in the division of spoils by Ts'ao Kun and Chang Tso-lin, Wu was completely ignored.   Wu's enmity toward Chang on the one hand, and the latter's ambition to control the whole of north China on the other, led to a war in early 1922.   This was the first Fengtien-Chihli War.   Thanks to the aid of the Shensi General Feng Yü-hsiang, Wu's forces were victorious, and Chang retreated to Manchuria. Wu became more ambitious and set to work to unify the country by force.   By the summer of 1924, Wu was military overlord of most of China with the exception of the three southernmost provinces — Kwantung, Kwangsi, and Yunnan — and of Chekiang which was controlled by Lu Yung-hsiang, an ally of Chang Tso-lin.   In August 1924, war broke out between Lu of Chekiang and Wu's ally, Ch'i Hsieh-yüan of Kiangsu.   The war soon developed into a larger one between the belligerents' overlords, Chang Tso-lin and Wu P'ei-fu.[7]

Until Shidehara assumed control of the Foreign Ministry, the policies of both the Foreign Ministry and the military authorities towards the Fengtien-Chihli Wars were generally in favor of Chang Tso-lin, though there were differences of opinion not only between the two offices but also among various people connected with the policy-making.   Japan's support of Chang was due to her hope of maintaining her treaty rights and strategic concerns in Manchuria.   In December 1922, Foreign Minister Uchida Kōsai instructed the Consul General at Mukden that Japan should discourage Chang's attempt to mount an expedition to the center of China, in order for Chang to maintain peace and order in Manchuria; that it would also benefit Japan which had deep and complicated interest-relations with The Three Eastern

---

[7]   H. F. MacNair and D. F. Lach, 246–247; Tōa Dōbun-kai (ed.), I, 542–557.

Provinces; and that if Chang would do so, Japan should give as much aid to Chang as possible. Uchida, however, declined to give any military aid to Chang in view of Japan's relations with the other powers.[8] The General Staff, on the other hand, in response to Chang's request of July 1922 that Japan send officers specializing in railways, telegraphy and aviation, more openly supported Chang and conveyed to him its intention to strengthen Fengtien forces in Manchuria. But even the General Staff at this point hesitated to send officers on active duty lest various international problems arose.[9]

The above was the policy outline of the government headed by Admirals Katō Tomosaburō (June 1922-September 1923) and Yamamoto Gonnohyōe (September 1923-January 1924). During Kiyoura Keigo's Administration (January 1924-June 1924), a new development was evidenced in the "General Plan of Policy Toward China," established jointly by the Foreign Ministry, the War Ministry, the Naval Ministry, and the Finance Ministry. The "Plan" stated that Japan, instead of attaching too much importance to the central government alone, should also establish favorable relations with local powers (such as Chang Tso-lin) and by doing so had to attempt to expand her influence over various other areas of China. The Plan especially emphasized that Japan should plan not only to secure but also to expand her standing in Manchuria and Mongolia, for these regions bordered on Japan's territory and they had much deeper and even more special relations with Japan in view of her defense program than the rest of China. Accordingly, the Plan set up a more specific policy toward Chang Tso-lin. It stated:

> To Chang Tso-lin who is the real power in The Three Eastern Provinces, according to the already established plan, Japan will continue to give friendly support so as to let him secure his position in

---

[8] *Shuyō Monjo*, II, 25–31.

[9] Ikei Masaru, "Dai-niji Hō-Choku Sensō to Nihon" (The second Fengtien-Chihli war and Japan), in *Hōgaku Kenkyū*, XXXVII (March 1964), 51–52.

the area. However, Japan must be cautious not to bring ill effects upon her interest-relations with the rest of China by doing so.[10]

As we have observed, the Japanese Government had constantly striven to balance its "special interest" in Manchuria and Mongolia (and therefore in Chang's regime) on the one hand, and its international co-operation and its general interest in China as a whole on the other. Japan's Kwantung Army more openly stressed the need of helping a friendly regime so as to develop a closer tie with China. The plan of the Kwantung Army toward China reads (October 1923):

> To maintain the so-called principle of non-intervention in Chinese domestic affairs, which is the basis of our Empire's present policy toward China, will make China more dependent upon other powers while loosening ties between Japan and China. Therefore, to free China from international control and to develop a closer co-operation between Japan and China, Japan must open negotiations with influential politicians or warlords in China so that they can restrain the highhanded measures of the Chihli clique which is the great cause of the present confusion in China, solve the conflict between Chihli and Fengtien, and cultivate a situation in which a relatively just and fair generalissimo can unify China. Such a task is not necessarily difficult. In short, our Empire, because of its neighboring relation with China, must solve the conflicts of China today, even if such methods of solving this problem may look somewhat like Japan's interference in Chinese domestic affairs, though not to the extent that such methods look obvious. Otherwise the powers may take the initiative in adopting similar methods.[11]

We do not know whom the Kwantung Army considered "a fair and just generalissimo," but the fact was clear that it perceived the necessity for intervention.

As soon as the war broke out between Lu Yung-hsiang and Ch'i Hsieh-yüan, Chang repeatedly requested Japan's support. A request was sent directly to Foreign Minister Shidehara

---

[10]   *Shuyō Monjo*, II, 61.
[11]   Ikei, 52–54.

and another to Governor General Kodama of the Kwantung
Leased Territory. In these notes, Chang emphasized that,
although he had been prudent, the Chihli clique intended to take
over The Three Eastern Provinces, that the British and the Americans had expressed their desire to unify China, and that furthermore Soviet Russia was making approaches to both the Peking
regime and Sun Yat-sen. Against these international forces,
Chang stressed that Japan ought to support him, for he alone had
been friendly to Japan.[12] In Japan, too, there were persuasive
rumors that Great Britain and the United States were supporting
Wu P'ei-fu, for they too desired China's early unification. Funazu Tatsuichirō, the Consul General at Mukden, expressed his
opinion that if Chang's forces were defeated and the Chihli forces
should cross east of the Liao River, Japan would have to take
appropriate measures to prevent the Chihli forces from entering
Manchuria and might have to exercise force to defend her interests. This was exactly the same policy Tanaka pursued later
when Chiang Kai-shek's forces in the northern expedition were
about to collide with the Fengtien clique in Peking. The military
attaché to Japan's legation in Peking, on the other hand, advocated
that Japan side with the winning party, whether Chang or Wu,
so as to increase her overall influence upon China.[13]

Despite these various requests and suggestions, and despite
previous governments' general policies of supporting Chang, Shidehara adhered firmly to his principle of non-intervention. On
September 8, for example, he replied to Funazu that he would not
send either party even an "expostulation" to prevent the war
which Funazu forecasted, for three primary reasons: Japan had

---

[12]   Honjō to Shidehara, September 5, 1924, JFMA MT 161857 (the
original filing number at the Foreign Ministry is 161859); Kodama to Shidehara,
September 8, 1924, *ibid.* See more detailed report on the second Fengtien-
Chihli War and on the Japanese attitudes in JFMA MT 161857, I–VI. Volume
I deals with various attitudes within the Japanese Government and Volume II
with popular attitudes. See also Ikei, 54 ff.
[13]   Funazu to Shidehara, September 5, *ibid.*

to avoid any and every measure which might be interpreted as interfering in Chinese domestic affairs; the conflict between the Chihli and the Fengtien was "voluntary" and Japan had no legal right to impose any restraints on them; from a practical viewpoint, according to his past experience, such a warning would not bring any real result. He added in the telegram, "even if both parties come to a direct conflict, we will maintain a fair and just attitude and will not take any measure partial to one party or one faction."[14]

The next day, the Peking Government under Ts'ao Kun ordered an attack upon Lu Yung-hsiang, and the following day Chang declared for Lu. Thus, a full-scale war started between the two factions. Anxious about the situation, both the United States' acting Ambassador, Jefferson Caffery, and Britain's Ambassador, Sir Charles N. E. Eliot, visited the Foreign Ministry to sound out Japan on the war.[15] Consequently, the Foreign Minister ordered the Chief of the Asian Bureau, Debuchi Katsuji, to make a public announcement stressing Japan's policy of non-intervention and simultaneously sent the Governor General of the Kwantung Leased Territory instructions, headed, "to make sure of our government's position in this grave situation." The instructions to Governor General Kodama read:

> Considering not only Japan's special interests in Manchuria and Mongolia, but also our various interests in the whole of China, as well as the general trend of the international political situation, the best way for our government is to pursue a policy of non-intervention.... The conclusion of the Cabinet meeting was also the same. Therefore, both civilian and military authorities on the spot must strictly pursue this policy in concert. If at this moment our authorities are partial to one group, Japan's future relationship with China will be jeopardized, and furthermore Japan will lose her honor in the eyes of the world.[16]

---

[14] Shidehara to Funazu, September 8, *ibid.* Simultaneously, Shidehara in the same telegram ordered Funazu to consider the best possible means to protect the Japanese residents' lives and property there.

[15] Shidehara to Yoshizawa, September 12 and 13, *ibid.*

[16] Shidehara to Kodama, September 16; Shidehara to the Governor

On September 22, Debuchi, in line with Shidehara's instructions, announced before the press:

> In a speech delivered before the Imperial Diet in its last session, the Foreign Minister explicitly stated that Japan had adopted and would follow a policy of absolute non-interference in the internal affairs of China. It is therefore superflous to say that the Japanese Government will strictly adhere to this policy of non-intervention in the present civil war and will assume an attitude of impartiality toward any of the warring parties.
>
> Although reports to the effect that some of the powers are contemplating interfering in the domestic affairs of China at this juncture or that some are desiring to give help to the Chihli party are circulated from time to time, they are purely rumors deserving of no credence. The Japanese Government deeply regrets that the present disturbance has occurred in China and cannot help hoping that the Chinese authorities and people will fully realize the gravity of the situation and unite their best efforts to speedily put an end to the internecine war and to restore peace and order in their country.[17]

Meanwhile, in Japan, attacks upon Shidehara's policy of non-intervention increased. It was the dominant public opinion that because Japan and China had a "special relationship" unlike the relations between China and other nations, Japan need not adhere to non-intervention; moreover, Japan had to be prepared to use force to prevent disorder in Manchuria.[18] The Minister at Peking, Yoshizawa Kenkichi, noticing the Anglo-American support of Wu P'ei-fu, pointed out that Wu's entrance into Manchuria would surely destroy Japan's influence there and therefore Japan had to take decisive measures before the war should spread there. Funazu also sent a similar telegram to Shidehara.[19] Toward the end of September, the Japanese Committee of National Policy stressed the need of limiting the war as much as possible, while the

General of Korea, September 17, *ibid.*

[17] Gaimushō Kōhyō, No. 16, September 22, 1924, *ibid.*

[18] See for example the preface of *Gaikō Jihō*, October 15, 1924.

[19] Yoshizawa to Shidehara, September 23, JFMA MT 161857; Funazu to Shidehara, September 23, *ibid.*

Kenkyūkai of the House of Peers criticized Shidehara's non-intervention policy as a form of adulation to the United States and Great Britain.[20]   In October, as the war situation was developing unfavorably for the Fengtien clique, public accusations and agitations against Shidehara grew more furious.   On October 4, for instance, thousands of people attended a "National Convention Concerning China," sponsored by interventionists including Uesugi Shinkichi (1878–1929) of Tokyo University.   Rightists raided the Foreign Ministry, criticized Shidehara's "weak-kneed policy" and "incompetence," and distributed pamphlets urging "save our friends!"[21]

Under such circumstances, on October 23, Prime Minister Katō convened the Cabinet to reconsider Japan's policy toward the Chinese civil war.   The majority of ministers asserted that, because of the critical war condition, Japan was now obliged to help Chang in order to prevent war from spreading into Manchuria and to defend Japan's interests there.   Even the moderate Takahashi Korekiyo, the chairman of the Seiyūkai and Minister of Agriculture and Commerce, saw a need to support Chang Tso-lin.   Takahashi was obviously influenced by the dominant opinion of his own party, which was clearly pro-Chang.   The debate between Shidehara and other members of the Cabinet became so heated that the Prime Minister was obliged to declare a recess. At this time, the Prime Minister urged Shidehara to compromise with the rest of the members.   However, Shidehara answered, "There is no room for compromise.   I cannot curb my convictions.   If you, the Prime Minister, and the rest of the Cabinet members do not accept my assertions and still advocate the support of Chang Tso-lin, I will resign."   Facing such firm resolve on Shidehara's part, Katō replied, "If you are so determined, I do not have any objection to our adherence to the

---

[20]   *Jiji Shimpō*, September 22 and 27, 1924; *The Asahi Shimbun*, October 1924; Ikei, 58 ff.

[21]   *Jiji Shimpō*, October 5 and 8; Shidehara, *Gaikō Gojū-nen*, 98–99.

policy of non-intervention in Chinese affairs." The Cabinet meeting was adjourned without reaching any further agreement. A few hours later the report of Feng Yü-hsiang's revolt against Wu was conveyed to Japan. As a result, Wu was forced to flee southward by sea, eventually retreating to central China. Thanks to this turn of events, Japan got off without intervening in Chinese affairs, and Shidehara did not have to resign.[22]

In this process of policy-making, we find an interesting contrast between Tanaka Giichi and Shidehara Kijūrō resulting from their different personalities. Unlike Tanaka, Shidehara was not a "politician." He was by nature a lone individual. He lacked the traditional Japanese-type skills in political maneuvering, i.e., utilizing a complicated human nexus of bosses, subordinates, henchmen, or friends for his support. Furthermore, because of his principle of nonpartisan diplomacy, Shidehara did not belong to any political party. Consequently, he could not expect any partisan support in a Cabinet in which most members belonged to one of the three leading parties. Shidehara was his own brain trust. The only person upon whom he relied was Saburi Sadao, Chief of the Commerce Bureau under Shidehara's foreign ministership.[23] Shidehara, isolated in the Cabinet and unable to mobilize various influential people for his support, could only choose resignation in order to be faithful to his own principles.

Tanaka was entirely the opposite. Because of his *oyabun* temperament and skills, he could recruit many people to support him: General Shirakawa Yoshinori (1868–1932), General Yamanashi Hanzō, Yamamoto Jōtarō, Mori Kaku, Kuhara Fusanosuke (1869–1965), and Matsuoka Yōsuke, to name only a few. Tanaka's ability to maneuver politically, however, was both his strength and his weakness. He could rely upon many people to support him, but

---

[22] *Ibid.*, 100–101.

[23] Saburi Sadao specialized in law at Tokyo Imperial University and was a highly intelligent and rational diplomat. Both in philosophy and in personality Shidehara and Saburi were much alike. He became Minister to Peking in Shidehara's second term.

at the same time his policy tended to become "haphazard," "inconsistent," and even "chaotic," as many critics have pointed out, because he entrusted policy-making to so many different authorities. In fact, this chaos in various channels of his policy-making, some people claim, was the crucial factor which destroyed his government.[24] Shidehara's independence, on the other hand, was both his weakness and his strength. At the very least he could carry out his convictions consistently.

Among democrats and cosmopolitans at home, and especially among the Western powers, Shidehara's insistence upon Japan's non-intervention in the Fengtien-Chihli War won him great prestige as an international law-abiding and peace-loving man. Both the United States and the Peking Government, expressly conveyed their satisfaction with Japan's attitude. The Foreign Ministry of Japan also agreed that Shidehara's policy gave a good impression to the other powers.[25] Inoue Junnosuke, who attended the eighth convention of the League of Nations (June 27–July 3, 1924), reemphasized Japan's need for international co-operation and expressed his view that the high-handed policies of a few strong powers were gradually disappearing as international relations progressed. By stressing these points, Inoue indirectly supported Shidehara's policy. Ōta Unosuke also contributed an article in *The Gaikō Jihō* fully endorsing Shidehara's policy. Ōta, exactly in accordance with Shidehara's view, thought that the restoration of peace had to take place through co-operation with the Chinese people. He believed that all the powers could maximize their benefits by promoting Chinese trade without military interference.

Shidehara, on the other hand, made more enemies among traditionalists who had hoped to increase Japan's politico-military control in Manchuria by supporting Chang. Without paying much

---

[24] Authors of *Tanaka Giichi Denki* and of *After Imperialism* hold this kind of view.

[25] Debuchi memo, October 9, 1924, JFMA MT 161857.

attention to Chinese sovereignty, international law, or Japan's overall interests in China, they reproached him as though he had been
a traitor.[26]   Perhaps the most foreboding criticism not only for
Shidehara but also for Japan's future role in international
relations was the argument that Shidehara did not try to defend
Japan's special interests in Manchuria and Mongolia.   On December 24, for instance, Ogawa Heikichi of the Seiyūkai attacked
Shidehara in the Fiftieth Diet by asking, "Did you take any measures so that war would not occur in the Manchurian area?"   To
this and similar accusations, the Foreign Minister's answer was
always the same.   He reiterated that respect for national sovereignty was the basic principle of various international treaties and that
Japan had pledged her non-interference in Chinese affairs to the
world through treaties and government statements.   To violate
this pledge would ruin Japan's international honor and would be
detrimental to her overall international relations.   Above all he
emphasized that the maintenance of peace and order in The Three
Eastern Provinces was strictly China's responsibility and not
Japan's, because the area was under Chinese sovereignty.   Besides,
Shidehara added, although many people asserted Japan's "special
rights and interests" in Manchuria and Mongolia, "We do not
have any right or interest whatsoever in these areas except those
along the South Manchurian Railway" which had been guaranteed
by treaties.[26]

We must note three important points in connection with this
event: it sharply increased Japan's concern with the future status
of Manchuria and Mongolia.   In their emotional criticism of
Shidehara, traditionalists like Tanaka Giichi began to assume
that these regions were Japan's "special positions" or "special
areas."   In view of Shidehara's policies concerning the American
immigration issue and this event, those who advocated more high-
handed methods called his policy "weak-kneed," "non-resistant,"

---

[26]   *Dai-Nihon Teikoku Gikai-shi*, XV, February 1, 1925.

and "subservient to the West."[27]   A deep, irreconcilable gap was now evident between Shidehara and his supporters on the one hand and his opponents on the other.   This gap was concerned not merely with Japan's policy toward China on specific issues but also with the ultimate principles of overall national diplomacy. The irreconcilability of the two emanated fundamentally from the irreconcilability of two different Weltanschauungs.   Finally, Shidehara's policy stood in clear contrast to that of Tanaka Giichi, who, at the time of Chiang Kai-shek's northern expedition, not only dispatched many troops to Shantung but also declared that Japan would disarm both Chiang's and Chang Tso-lin's forces if the war extended to Manchuria.

From the May Thirtieth Movement to the Peking Tariff Conference

If Shidehara's policy of non-intervention in the Fengtien-Chihli War attested to his democratic and law-abiding principles of international relations, his dealings with the May Thirtieth movement and the Peking Tariff Conference demonstrated the essence of his "economic diplomacy" and his pragmatism.

The May Thirtieth movement of 1925 was by far the largest "anti-foreign" and "anti-imperialist" demonstration to occur in China since the Republican Revolution of 1911.   The smouldering nationalistic-revolutionary fire seemed to burst into flames and envelope the whole nation, from Shanghai up to Peking and all the way down to Hong Kong.   The movement broke out when British-officered police in Nanking Road shot thirteen demonstrators to death, most of them students, on May 30.   In Shanghai strikes and boycotts lasted several months.   On June 23 in Canton, demonstrators and the Anglo-French troops clashed at the consular

---

[27]   See various criticisms in *Gaikō Jihō*, October 15, 1924, 1–12, 19–32.

island of Shameen, and there were one hundred and fifty-nine
Chinese casualties (the so-called Shameen massacre). There
ensued a seventeen-month strike and boycott in the Hong Kong
and Canton areas, and among the 780,000 recorded participants
all social strata were represented: students, industrialists, workers,
merchants, and member's of both the Kuomintang and the Chinese
Communist Party.[28]

The Chinese anti-foreign boycotts and strikes were rooted in
several causes. The Japanese and British investments in the cotton
and spinning industries in China had increased rapidly since World
War I, just at the time when the Chinese economy and technology
had reached a level high enough to launch full industrialization,
especially in the textile industry which had a relatively low
financial and technological threshold. The Japanese and British
firms naturally had to meet strong opposition from the Chinese
merchants and industrialists. Furthermore, with the recru-
descence of feverish foreign competition, which was created partly
by the standstill of business at Lancashire and Osaka, the budding
Chinese firms tended to be either destroyed or absorbed by foreign
concerns. In addition, working conditions for Chinese laborers
in these foreign firms were very bad. Yü Kao-nin reports, "In the
case of Chinese factory girls [minors, twelve years old in average],
they had to work twelve hours a day and received only between 28
and 30 cents.... And yet their living expenses cost them 30 cents
a day." Finally, the foreign treaty-port establishment was closely
tied to the provincial military governors, which, to enlightened
Chinese nationalists, looked like an evil combination of "warlord-
ism" and "imperialism."[29]

In the beginning, the Chinese attack focused upon both Japan

---

[28]   Nakamura Ryūei (Takahide), "Go-sanjū Jiken to Zaikabō" (The May
Thirtieth Incident and the Japanese cotton industry in China), *Kindai Chūgoku
Kenkyū*, VI (Tokyo, 1964), 101; Dorothy Borg, *American Policy and the Chinese
Revolution, 1925–1928* (New York, 1968), 20–23; Fairbank, Reischauer and
Craig, 685.

[29]   Nakamura Ryūei, 103–120.

and Great Britain, but it gradually shifted to an exclusively anti-British movement. This change-of-course in Japan's favor was largely owed to the pragmatic insight of Shidehara's diplomatic leadership. As strikes, demonstrations, and boycotts spread all over China, the Japanese textile industry increasingly pressured the Foreign Ministry to put down the "riots" as soon as possible. Kita Matazō (1877-1932), the owner of Nihon Menka (Japan Cotton Company) and an important figure in the Japan-China Business Association, criticized Shidehara's policy of non-intervention as one which was in fact sycophantic toward China. He demanded the Foreign Minister's answer to the question: "If our factories were destroyed, or occupied, or set on fire by the Chinese mobs, what would you do?"[30]   Great Britain also proposed strong joint measures against the demonstrators and against the recurrence of similar incidents in the future. The Japanese Foreign Minister, however, thought that any forceful action would only incite further anti-foreign movements in China, and therefore he suggested to the British representative in Tokyo and to the Japanese industrialists that Japan temporarily withdraw her nationals from the interior of China to places of safety. The high-handed British policy, on the other hand, was soon to result in the Shameen massacre, as we have noted above.[31]

In the settlement of disputes, both parties, China and the foreign powers, made strong demands on each other. The Chinese demands on Japan consisted of four main points: condolence money; recognition of Chinese labor unions; wage increases of at least 20 percent; and indemnification of lost salary to the striking workers. The Japanese firms, on the other hand, not only refused to pay the condolence money — according to their own argument the Chinese were to be blamed since they had started the riots — but also demanded Chinese indemnification for damage of Japanese

---

[30]   *Ibid.*, 484.
[31]   Memo of conversation between Shidehara and Eliot, July 9, 1925, JFMA MT 532155.

factories. Shidehara, through Consul-General Yada at Shanghai and the Chief of Asian Bureau of the Foreign Office, Kimura Eiichi, persuaded the angry Japanese businessmen to pay the condolence money. He reasoned that the best solution for the Japanese cotton industry in China and for the overall economic interests of the nation was to settle the problem as soon as possible in order to restore the normal operation of Japan's China trade. As a result, the Japanese firms paid the condolence money of 10,000 dollars on June 20. However, strikes still continued, for the other demands had not yet been accepted. The dispute finally came to an end on July 23, when Japan promised the Chinese negotiators that the government would make the Japanese firms pay 100,000 yüan to the Chinese workers on strike (the equivalent of four days' wages per person) and that it would approve the establishment of unions when the Chinese Government introduced proper labor laws.[32]

In contrast to Japan's attitude of conciliation toward China, the oppressive measures of the British invited the Chinese anti-imperialist attacks. As early as June 10, Yüan Liang, an important leader of the National Anti-Imperialist Convention, indicated to Minister Yoshizawa his intention to separate the anti-Japanese and the anti-British movements. On June 22, the head of Chinese General Chamber of Commerce, Yü Hsia-ch'ing, conveyed his opinion to the Japanese Chamber of Commerce that China hoped to solve the disputes with Japan as soon as possible but that she could never forgive the "savage act" of the British at Nanking Road. The Shameen Incident which occurred on the following day aggravated Chinese-British relations even further. Strikes in British factories and boycotts against British goods continued until the end of September. Settlement of the prolonged dispute came rather abruptly because of the complicated domestic affairs of

---

[32] Usui Katsumi, "Go-sanjū Jiken to Nihon" (The May Thirtieth Incident and Japan), *Aziya Kenkyū*, IV (Oct. 1957), 54–60; Nakamura Ryūei, 151–167.

China: as the anti-imperialist movement increasingly inclined toward the left due to communist penetration, the co-operation between the KMT and the CCP as well as the industrialists and workers collapsed; as Sun Ch'uan-fang in Chekiang raised the standard of revolt against the Fengtien group and Chiang Kai-shek began to contemplate his northern expedition, China was about to fall again into the abyss of civil war; and the Peking Government felt obliged to terminate the dispute by executing important labor leaders in order to successfully implement the Peking Tariff Conference which was placed on the agenda in October.[33]

Shidehara was hesitant to adopt a strong policy against the May Thirtieth movement because of his concern for Japan's overall China trade. His view is best represented by the following words of Ishii Itarō, who worked as Shidehara's secretary in Washington:

> Mr. Shidehara was convinced that there was no other way for Japan to stabilize her people's livelihood in the future except by devoting herself to promoting industry, commerce and trade. Above all, China was most important for Japan. China had a population of 450 million. This was regarded as the best potential market for Japanese goods. Japan ought to secure these 450 million consumers.[34]

From this view point, Japan first had to win popularity among the Chinese people. To send troops in defense of Japan's interests in Manchuria, to intervene in the Fengtien-Chihli War, or to suppress the May Thirtieth movement by force would be fatal to Japan's overall interests. Furthermore, there was a distinct difference between Shidehara's and Tanaka's understanding of

---

[33] Nakamura Ryūei, *ibid.*; Usui, 60–64; See the Chinese anti-British activities and the American policy toward the May Thirtieth movement in Borg, 23–46, and Harold R. Isaacs, *The Tragedy of the Chinese Revolution* (Stanford, 1951), 70–73.

[34] Ishii Itarō, "Shidehara-dan no Keizai Gaikō ni tsuite" (Baron Shidehara's economic diplomacy), "Shoka no Shidehara-kan," 276.

contemporary Chinese affairs. Shidehara saw rising Chinese nationalism as the fundamental cause of her anti-imperialist and rights-recovery movements. If this was the new social trend in China, he believed, Japan had to go along with it. Tanaka, on the other hand, held the view of old China, as he did of old Japan. He regarded the Chinese rights-recovery movement as "outrageous" and believed that Japan could and should suppress it by force. He also thought that Japan could promote her own interests by manipulating various factions in China.[35]

Shidehara's extraordinary interest in the China trade and his view of "modern China" in contrast to Tanaka's view of "old China" were clearly observed in his policy toward the Peking Tariff Conference. In the Conference, Shidehara instructed the Japanese delegation to take the initiative among the powers in admitting the principle of China's tariff autonomy. Hence, at the beginning of the Conference the Japanese delegation, having expressed various difficulties which Japan had also experienced in the process of abolishing unequal treaties, stated, "China is still following the same paths that we once pursued. The difficulties, the embarrassments, and the perplexit es that confront China today have once been ours. The Japanese delegation will approach the problems before this conference with sympathy and understanding and with intimate apprehension of the Chinese position. I am happy to state at the outset that the Japanese delegation is fully prepared to consider in the friendliest way the question of tariff autonomy which appears in the agenda presented by the Chinese delegation."[36] Shidehara explained the reason for Japan's doing this in the Fifty-first Diet:

> I would like to explain [our policy] toward the special conference

---

[35]   Nakamura Ryūei and Usui Katsumi view Shidehara's pragmatic solution of the May Thirtieth Incident as a clever method to switch the originally revolutionary anti-imperialist movement to a mere labor dispute. Usui, 54; Nakamura, 132–133, 167–169.

[36]   *Shuyō Monjo*, II, 76–78; MacMurray to Kellogg, October 26, 1925, FRUS I.

on the Chinese tariff. Those who watch the development of the Chinese situation carefully cannot but admit various symptoms which indicate that the Chinese people are gradually awakening to political affairs. New China is replacing old China.... It is a grave mistake for us to disregard this remarkable change in recent Chinese sentiments. Some military powers will rise and some others will fall depending upon vicissitudes of civil wars in China. But as to popular enlightenment, once it springs up, it will never become extinct. If some external oppression is inflicted upon it, it will become more serious. The Chinese desire for recovering their tariff autonomy is a part of their expression of this enlightenment among them. Judging by this trend in China, we have decided on our policy toward the tariff conference.[37]

How did Shidehara reach this decision? To investigate his way of decision-making will enable us to understand this diplomat and his policy further. But first let us see briefly the background leading up to the opening of the Conference.

In the Washington Conference the United States and Great Britain argued that to achieve the rehabilitation and political security of China some measures to raise the revenues of the Chinese Government had to be considered and that the increase of tariff rates would be an effective measure. Consequently, it had been decided in the Conference that, as soon as all the powers had ratified the Washington customs treaty, a conference on the Chinese tariff would be held. Meanwhile, in China, due to the defeat of Wu P'ei-fu in the Second Fengtien-Chihli War, the government which had been supported by the Chihli clique fell and the provisional government under Tuan Ch'i-jui was established in Peking, backed by Chang Tso-lin and Feng Yü-hsiang. As for the Chinese nationalists, the abrogation of extraterritoriality and the recovery of tariff autonomy had been their long-time aspirations. On June 24, 1925, the Tuan regime taking advantage of the May Thirtieth Incident sent two notes to the Washington powers

---

[37] *Dai-Nihon Teikoku Gikai-shi*, XVI, January 21, 1926.

stressing the need of abolishing all unequal treaties, which were the fundamental cause for Chinese anti-foreign sentiments. The notes asserted that this was necessary "in order to definitely assure friendly relations between China and the foreign powers and a permanent peace," "in line with the generally accepted conceptions of international justice and equity."[38] By doing this, Peking hoped to win popularity among the Chinese nationalists and to strengthen its financial power. In the meantime, the French ratification of the Washington customs treaty obliged the Washington powers to agree to the convening of a tariff conference. Hence, on August 19 the Peking Government conveyed notes to the powers expressing its hope of convening a special conference on the Chinese tariff to be opened on October 26, 1925, at Peking.

Shidehara was a quiet, rather restrained, but highly efficient bureaucrat. As we have seen, to establish any policy he made a thorough investigation of the question, and his thinking was always rational, practical, and calculated. This was another respect in which Shidehara differed from Tanaka. Tanaka was intuitive or emotional and liked extravagance. Under such circumstances, Tanaka might have had another big conference as he did when he convened the Eastern Conference summoning all the diplomatic and military authorities. Shidehara, on the other hand, tried to solve his problems in a businesslike manner. He first would find out the American, British, French, and Italian attitudes toward this problem. Then he would order the Information Bureau of the Foreign Ministry to do research on the Japanese public reaction to this problem. He would listen to the various opinions of interested groups and having gathered all the necessary information, he would then order a few reliable subordinates — in this particular case such people as Chief of the Commerce Bureau Saburi and Horiuchi Tateki (1889–1951), a diplomatic secretary — to extend their investigation further and prepare

---

[38]   Mayer to Kellogg, June 24, 1925, FRUS I.

tentative plans. However, Shidehara was hardly influenced by subordinates. He took various suggestions and requests into consideration, but the final decision was always his alone. He was firm in his own decisions to the point of stubbornness and inflexibility on occasion.

According to the research of the Information Bureau, two major metropolitan newspapers, *The Asahi Shimbun* and *The Tokyo Nichinichi*, were generally in favor of the eventual acceptance of China's tariff autonomy, provided that China tried to achieve it by proper diplomatic means. *The Mainichi Shimbun*, another major paper almost equal in its influence to *The Asahi Shimbun* but having more clients in rural areas and therefore more conservative, asserted that China had to settle its own internal disorders before she could legitimately demand the recovery of her tariff autonomy. *The Jiji Shimpō*, on the other hand, contended that China's assertion was "outrageous," because she never met such international demands as the abolition of Likin and the protection of foreign nationals.[39] Various Chinese merchant associations in Japan approached Shidehara and argued that Japan ought to accept China's tariff autonomy. The All Chinese Merchants Association in Osaka, for example, stated that Japan's support of China in the conference would mitigate Chinese popular sentiments and would lead to harmonious Japanese trade with China eternally.[40] The Japanese industries which did business with China, such as the Japan Trading Association, were strongly opposed to China's tariff autonomy. The Chamber of Commerce and Industry in Osaka and Kyoto expressed the more moderate view that Japan would eventually be obliged to admit China's tariff autonomy but that she ought to endeavor to limit the increase of tariff as much as possible. They felt that even an

---

[39] Memo of the Information Bureau, September 7, 1925, JFMA MT 291013.

[40] The All-Chinese Merchants Association's appeal to Wakatsuki and Shidehara, September 5, 1925, *ibid.*

increase of 2.5 percent according to the provision of the Washington customs treaty was too much.[41]

Having exchanged views with the representatives of the great powers, Shidehara came to the conclusion that neither Great Britain nor the United States was inclined to accept China's tariff autonomy immediately. Moreover, Shidehara feared, "by urging the Chinese to recover order, the British may intervene in Chinese affairs without hesitation."[42] Shidehara's worries were not groundless. Among the powers, the British were taking the most rigid attitude toward the Chinese rights-recovery movement during this period. To the Chinese notes of June 24, for example, which expressed the hope of abolishing all unequal treaties, the British Government answered that "the powers should indicate an unwillingness to discuss particular reforms or to review treaty relations until order has been restored and the Chinese Government has evidenced its determination to repress anti-foreign agitations and to enforce protection of foreigners."[43] The United States, on the other hand, was more willing to accept China's tariff autonomy. Secretary of State Frank B. Kellogg believed, like Shidehara, that it was necessary to placate China by making some concessions and to revise the treaties eventually, looking toward ultimate tariff autonomy.[44] Nevertheless, at the same time, Kellogg agreed with the British:

> The reply of the Diplomatic Body at Peking should embody an emphatic statement that there can be no discussion of particular reforms, much less a review by the Powers of their treaty relations with China until the Chinese Government has given evidence of its ability and willingness to suppress disorders and to enforce respect for the safety of foreign lives and property and put an end to strikes

---

[41] See appeals to Wakatsuki and Shidehara by Nihon Yushutsu Dōgyō Kumiai and the Secretary of Osaka Chamber of Commerce, September 5, 1925, *ibid.*

[42] Shidehara to Yoshizawa, September 10, 1925, *ibid.*

[43] The British *Chargé*, H. G. Chilton to Kellogg, July 3, 1925, FRUS I.

[44] Kellogg to Chilton, July 23, *ibid.*

and agitations which are harmful to 'Chinese and foreign commercial interests.'[45]

Hence, Shidehara correctly judged that, although the United States was more willing to accept China's tariff autonomy than Great Britain, "she does not have any concrete plan except some temporary expediencies to placate the Chinese antagonism (toward the powers)."[46]   Under such circumstances, he instructed Minister Yoshizawa in Peking that "a larger [measure of] co-operation between the United States, British, and Japanese Governments, with respect to China than merely co-operation regarding the Shanghai Incident...had to be sought."   Shidehara, with the co-operation of the United States, hoped to mediate the two extreme positions taken by the British and the Chinese not only on the May Thirtieth Incident but also on the problem of the Chinese tariff.[47] In September Shidehara reemphasized this attitude and wrote to Yoshizawa, "Japan must make considerable effort to maintain the co-operation of these countries.   However, she has to refuse strictly any measure involving intervention in Chinese domestic affairs [that Great Britain might propose in the conference] and at the same time must endeavor to harmonize the ideal and the practical to bring about some kind of compromise to the extent that the result would not be too much out of step with the real situation in China."[48]

His policy toward China, between the May Thirtieth Incident and the opening of the tariff conference, is a typical example of Shidehara's way of thinking.   Being an Anglo-Americanophile himself, he wanted to co-operate with these nations as much as possible, even though the positions of the Big Three on this problem differed widely.   In view of both Japan's international security and her economic interests, Shidehara believed, she should

---

45   *Ibid.*
46   Shidehara to Yoshizawa, September 10, JFMA MT 291013.
47   Mayer to Kellogg, July 5, 1925, FRUS I; Shidehara to Murakami, July 22, 1925, JFMA MT 532155.
48   Shidehara to Yoshizawa, September 10, JFMA MT 291013.

not alienate these powerful Western nations. At the same time, Japan had to remain sympathetic to legitimate Chinese claims as much as possible. The best solution, therefore, would be a compromise among all the nations involved or a balance between the "ideal" and the "practical." The ideal would be to abolish unequal treaties immediately. In reality, however, the insecurity of foreign nationals due to continuous civil wars and anti-foreign demonstrations as well as the powers' real desire to limit a tariff increase and to abolish the Likin system would make it impossible to satisfy China's demands immediately. No party should hold out for extreme demands. Instead, all parties should compromise for only by doing so might fruitful results be obtained from the conference. Hence Shidehara's principles of co-óperation, compromise, and practicality were all equally emphasized in this policy.

What were Japan's real interests? What compromises should Japan make with China and other powers? When Japan and the United States had stressed that some kind of measures to placate China had to be sought, the British Government expressed its preference for a tariff conference rather than a meeting of the extraterritoriality commission. Britain further indicated that the government was willing to increase the tariff up to 12.5 percent, and the United States announced that she would do the same.[49] In Japan, Saburi Sadao, Horiuchi Tateki, and others in the Foreign Ministry argued that if Great Britain and the United States really carried out a uniform tariff increase of 12.5 percent, it would be greatly disadvantageous to Japan. Because most of Japanese commodities exported to China were articles of daily use and half of those goods were cotton materials which China was also producing, the Japanese goods could not compete with Chinese products at the higher rate. British and American commodities exported to China, on the other hand, were mostly luxury articles or things which China did not produce. At the same time, they argued that,

---

[49]   Grew to Mayer, July 6, 1925, FRUS I; Perkins to Kellogg, July 29, 1925, SDA 500A4e/297.

because the abrogation of unequal treaties was one of China's national aspirations, Japan ought to be sympathetic to this demand as much as possible, in order to promote the China trade. Thus they concluded that Japan first had to admit the principle of China's tariff autonomy, and by winning China's good will toward Japan she had to obtain either a graduated tariff system or some kind of reciprocal agreement. Shidehara agreed to their proposal.[50]

When the Special Tariff Conference was opened in Peking on October 26, the conference developed exactly as Shidehara had assumed. The Chinese Government — the Chief Executive of the provisional government, Tuan Ch'i-jui in his opening address, Shen Jui-lin, Minister for Foreign Affairs and Chairman of the Chinese delegation, and C. T. Wang of the delegation — repeatedly advocated China's recovery of tariff autonomy. Wang on behalf of the Chinese Government offered the following proposals:

> The customs participating powers formally declare to the government of the Republic of China their respect for its tariff autonomy and agree to the removal of all the tariff restrictions contained in existing treaties.

> The government of the Republic of China agrees to the abolition of Likin simultaneously with the enforcement of the Chinese national tariff law which shall take effect not later than the 1st day of January, 1929.[51]

The Japanese delegation, according to the plan developed in Tokyo, immediately expressed its sympathy with the Chinese demand, but Great Britain and the United States reserved their decision on China's tariff autonomy "until further examination of China's plan for abolition of Likin and internal taxes." The British delegation even contended:

> One of the essential aims of the Conference as laid down in the Washington treaty is the elaboration of measures leading to the abolition of Likin and other internal levies on trade and in the view

---

[50]   Shidehara Heiwa Zaidan (ed.), 301–302.
[51]   MacMurray to Kellogg, October 26, 1925, FRUS I.

PART THREE

of His Majesty's Government this must necessarily entail some read-justment of the fiscal relations between the Central Government and the provinces.[52]

These opening statements by the British and American delegations greatly disappointed the Chinese, for the British stressed that the major aim of the conference was to take "measures leading to the abolition of Likin," and even the United States expressed her unwillingness to grant China tariff autonomy until after the abolition of Likin.

The situation was much the same in the first session of the committee on tariff autonomy, which was held on October 30. Wang reiterated China's need to recover tariff autonomy, and the British and American delegations made the abolition of Likin a condition for realization of the Chinese demand.[53] In the second session of November 3, however, a new development appeared. To placate China, the United States proposed to "authorize at once the levying of the surtax of 2.5 percent and, as soon as the requisite schedules can be prepared, to authorize the levying of a surtax of 5 percent on luxuries."[54] Such a proposal, however, did not please the Chinese delegation. The real issue for China was the restoration of her national "face" and sovereignty. She was interested only in the matter of principle, not in an actual raise of tariff rates, to say nothing of such a small increase as 2.5 percent. In contrast to the British and American attitude, the Japanese delegation throughout the period stressed the need for China's tariff autonomy. In the second session, they reemphasized this point:

> The contracting powers, other than China, [should] hereby sol-emnly declare their recognition of the principle that, as an inherent right of a sovereign state, China is to enjoy full autonomy with respect to customs tariff.[55]

---

[52] *Ibid.*
    [53] The American delegation to Kellogg, October 30, 1925, *ibid.*
    [54] MacMurray to Kellogg, November 4, 1925, *ibid.*
    [55] *Ibid.*

Thus, Japan skillfully won the gratitude of the Chinese delegation. Sometimes Shidehara's policy toward China — as illustrated in his adherence to the principle of non-intervention and his recognition of the principle of Chinese tariff autonomy — has been regarded as "friendly" in contrast to Tanaka's "aggressive" policy.[56] However, Shidehara's "friendly" attitude toward China was not entirely based upon altruistic motives. Both Tanaka and Shidehara were primarily concerned with Japan's national interests. They differed greatly, however, in their understanding of the nature of Japan's interests and the means to secure these interests. Hence, the Japanese delegation, while admitting the principle of China's tariff autonomy, proposed:

First. That a statutory tariff on a fair and reasonable basis be established for general application subject to the provisions of a special conventional tariff on certain specified articles to be agreed upon separately between China and each of the powers directly interested; or

Second. That a graduated tariff so devised as to be acceptable to the powers concerned be established at an average rate of not more than 12.5 per centum ad valorem and generally in a manner consistent

---

[56] Nezu Masashi and Imai Seiichi for some time have been engaged in a major debate as to whether Shidehara's policy toward China was "friendly." Imai from a Marxist point of view argued that it was not "friendly." Instead, Imai emphasized, his was just as imperialistic as Tanaka's. The only difference between the two was that Shidehara sought economic aggression whereas Tanaka's was militaristic. Nezu opposed this view and supported the traditional and dominant view that Shidehara was "friendly" and "peaceful" in contrast to Tanaka. Both Nezu and Imai are right in one sense and wrong in another. The debate on Shidehara's policy toward China should not be focused upon the question of whether it was altruistic and friendly or imperialistic and aggressive. As Imai points out, Shidehara, like Tanaka, was primarily interested in promoting Japan's national interests. However, he was certainly not aggressive. He was more understanding and conciliatory toward the Chinese demands than Tanaka, and hoped to solve various diplomatic problems between the two nations by peaceful means as much as possible. See Imai Seiichi, "Seitō Seiji to Shidehara Gaikō" (Party politics and Shidehara diplomacy), in *Rekishigaku Kenkyū*, No. 219 (May 1958), 20–26; Nezu Masashi, "Shidehara Gaikō no Sai-hyōka" (Reappraisal of Shidehara diplomacy), in his *Hihan Nihon Gendai Shi* (A critical modern Japanese history; Tokyo, 1958), and Nezu Masashi, "Shidehara Gaikō no Hyōka ni tsuite Imai-shi ni Kotaeru" (A reply to Imai's criticism of Shidehara's policy), in *Rekishigaku Kenkyū*, No. 227 (January 1959), 41–43.

with the provisions of Article II of the Washington treaty.[57]
Furthermore, in the first session of the committee on tariff autonomy of October 30, the Japanese delegation argued that, "While the
[Chinese] statutory tariff is to be made by China freely as it pleases,
such a tariff should be so devised as not to hurt trade relations
between China and other countries."[58] Again one finds Shidehara's balance between the "ideal" and "practical," i.e., his respect for China's free will hand in glove with promotion of Japan's
China trade. Shidehara, by admitting the principle of China's
autonomy, hoped to obtain some advantageous positions for Japan
in either the statutory tariff or the graduated tariff.[59]

Nevertheless, Shidehara's policy was not exclusively based
upon economic "calculation." He genuinely wished to accede
to China's demands as much as possible by bringing some fruitful
results out of the conference. Britain often argued that the conference should be postponed, sometimes suggesting the impossibili-
ty of reaching any satisfactory agreement among China, Japan,
Britain, and the United States, with their widely differing proposals,
and at other times taking advantage of the precarious position of
the Peking Government in the continuing civil wars. Shidehara,
on the other hand, argued that the conference had to be brought
to a conclusion which would improve China's tariff system. He
once told the British Ambassador in Tokyo that this had to be done
because the recovery of tariff autonomy was the popular hope of
China; not to meet this demand would cause more political instability in China, which would be harmful both to China and to the
powers; and because it was his conviction that the powers could
reach an agreement if they would "sincerely" work for it.[60]
With this conviction, Shidehara, through the Japanese delegation,

---

57   *Shuyō Monjo*, 76–81; MacMurray to Kellogg, October 26, 1925,
FRUS I.
58   MacMurray to Kellogg, October 31, 1925, *ibid.*
59   See the Japanese delegation's statements on October 26, 30, and November 4, 1925, in *Shuyō Monjo*, II, 76–81.
60   *Ibid.*, 81–82.

suggested that the Chinese delegation declare "voluntarily" — instead of being coerced by the powers — the abolition of Likin, which Wang did on October 30. Thus, finally on November 19 the delegates resolved:

> The contracting powers other than China hereby recognize China's right to enjoy tariff autonomy, agree to remove the tariff restrictions which are contained in existing treaties between themselves respectively and China, and consent to the going into effect of the Chinese national tariff law on January 1st, 1929.[61]

The main discussion in the conference then shifted to specific measures which China should take during the interim period. Japan now had to stand on the defensive, for both the United States and Great Britain were willing to increase surtaxes up to 12.5 percent, which went beyond the Washington treaty provisions of 2.5 percent on ordinary imports and 5 percent on luxury items. Shidehara hoped to conclude with China either a reciprocal agreement independent of the other powers or a graduated tariff agreement together with the powers. Of the two plans, Shidehara and the Japanese delegation preferred the former. The Chinese delegation, on the other hand, proposed another interim plan. According to this, all export goods to China were roughly classified into three categories: 30 percent surtax for first-class luxuries including tobacco and liquor, 20 percent for second-class luxuries, and 5 percent for general goods. From this China could expect a 102.4 million yüan increase of revenues. The Chinese plan was too ambitious, and all the powers were opposed to it. Hence, the United States drafted an amended plan. According to this plan, commodities were divided into eight classes and the tariff rates ranged from 8.5 percent to 20 percent at the maximum. Chinese income was to increase 96 million yüan.

Toward the end of January, C. T. Wang promised the Japanese

---

[61] The Chinese Foreign Ministry (ed.), *Special Tariff Conference on the Chinese Customs Treaty* (*October 1925–April 1926*) (Peking: Chinese Foreign Ministry, 1928), 197.

delegation that China would conclude a bilateral agreement of new tariff rates on Japanese goods. This was a great success for Shidehara. His method of winning China's good will by taking the initiative among the powers in admitting the principle of China's tariff autonomy appeared to have paid off. However, such an agreement was to be negotiated after the interim period and the enactment of a statutory tariff. In other words, the settlement of the surtax during the interim had to come first. According to Japan's original adherence to the Washington treaty provisions, China was to gain only about 30 million yüan, which was far short of the American plan, to say nothing of the Chinese. Consequently, the Foreign, Finance, and Commerce and Industry Ministries discussed various amended plans, and in February Japan proposed a graduated tariff system with seven categories. According to this plan, the rates were to be increased from 2.5 percent — therefore the lowest rate would be 7.5 percent — to 22.5 percent at the maximum. About 60 percent of Japanese commodities including cotton materials, toys and ceramic wares were to have a minimum increase of rate, 2.5 percent, whereas the Western luxuries were to be levied at a higher rate. The American and British delegations were not willing to accede to such a proposal. In addition, China naturally hoped to increase the number of items classified as luxuries. Originally, China enumerated 152 items as luxuries.

In addition to these conflicts of interests among Japan, the Western nations, and China, there were many other disagreements. The United States and Britain asserted that the increased revenues by raising tariff rates had to be used for replacing Likin. Japan, on the other hand, contended that the revenues had to be used for the payment of Chinese debts to the powers. Japan had about 3 million yüan worth of credit with China, either with uncertain security or without any security, including the Nishihara Loans. Over the issue of how to use the increased revenues, Japan and Great Britain especially came to a headlong clash. Britain was also China's creditor, but she enjoyed the security of the railroads.

However, the British had also suffered a great decrease in revenue from the Chinese railroads because of the continuous civil war. Therefore, they stressed that at least 10 million yüan had to be saved as a reserve for the repayment of railroad loans and another 10 million to 23 million yüan had to be paid for their railroad loans. Moreover, the two countries disagreed over the question of where the revenues from tariffs were to be kept. Traditionally, most of the tariff revenues were held in trust by the British banks in China, and the British banks obtained an annual profit of over 13 million yüan. Japan proposed a plan whereby the increased revenues had to be held in trust in various foreign banks according to the amount of each nation's export to China.[62]

Besides these disagreements among the powers, the internal situation of China made the continuation of the conference increasingly difficult. From the outset, the Chihli clique was opposed to the conference lest the success of the conference strengthen the Tuan regime. Already in October 1925, Wu P'ei-fu and Sun Ch'uan-fang had revolted against the Peking Government and the Fengtien clique in opposition to the conference. In November, Kuo Sung-ling rebelled against his Manchurian overlord, Chang Tso-lin. In concert with Kuo, Feng Yü-hsiang's forces under Li Ching-lin attacked Peking, forcing the people in the Tuan regime to flee from the capital. In late December, under the influence of Feng, a new Cabinet was set up in Peking. Wu P'ei-fu then rose up once again, this time in alliance with Chang Tso-lin against Feng Yü-hsiang. Wu's forces began a march toward Honan, and Chang's forces pushed toward Peking. Ac-

---

[62] Concerning detailed reports of the Customs Tariff Conference, see Taiwan Sōtoku Kambō Chōsa-ka, *Shina Kanzei Tokubetsu Kaigi no Keika* (The procedure of the special conference on the Chinese tariff; Taiwan, 1927); the American delegation's report to the Secretary of State on the official proceedings of the Special Conference on the Chinese Customs Tariff, July 8, 1926, FRUS I; and the *Special Conference on the Chinese Customs Tariff, October 1925–April 1926* (Peking, 1928). A copy of this publication is available in the Library of Congress and another in the Department of State filed as No. 500A4e Minutes Special Conference/ 18.

cordingly the Cabinet was changed once again to favor Chang and Wu. Then, on April 10, 1926, Lu Chung-lin, an ally of Feng Yü-hsiang, carried out a successful coup d'État in Peking. As a result, the provisional government of Tuan Ch'i-jui collapsed on April 20. Taking advantage of these continuous civil wars, Britain argued that the conference be postponed.[63] This was partly because the British anticipated that if the tariff conference ended successfully and tariff autonomy were granted to China, they would be obliged to give up their control of the Maritime Customs Administration.[64]

In May, representatives of the Fengtien and Chihli cliques entered Peking and organized a temporary Cabinet, which collapsed within a month. Thus, in June, Peking was left without a government. Even toward the end of May, however, Shidehara still stressed the need to continue the conference. He told Mac-Veagh, the American Ambassador to Japan, that "reports to the effect that he expected the suspension of the Customs Conference at Peking had no truth to them, and that he had every reason to believe that the Conference would continue until the conferees reached some plan that was definite, at least sufficiently definite to submit it to the Government of China when one was established."[65] With no government to negotiate with in Peking, the delegates of the foreign powers to the Tariff Conference met and agreed upon the following press statement: "the Delegates expressed a unanimous and earnest desire to proceed with the work of the Conference at the earliest possible moment when the Delegates of the Chinese Government are in a position to resume discussion with the foreign Delegates of the problems before the Conference." At the close of the meeting on July 3, however, it was generally understood among the delegates that "no further progress could be

---

63   See for example the American delegation to the Secretary of State, April 26, 1926, FRUS I.

64   Borg, 117–121.

65   MacVeagh to Kellogg, May 26, 1926, FRUS I.

made until the formation of a new government and that recognition of such a government would, in all probability, be a condition requisite to resuming negotiations."[66]

Shidehara's management of the Chinese Customs Conference clearly illustrated the nature of his policies. First of all, in reality he was not so subservient to the West as his opponents contended. On the contrary, it was Shidehara who took the initiative in admitting the principle of China's tariff autonomy. His plan for a graduated tariff was radically different from both the American and the British drafts. The policy was also practical and rational. Shidehara was not so much concerned with the "face" issue as was Tanaka. He thought it nonsensical to argue whether the "principle" of diplomacy was "autonomous" or "co-operative." The essence of diplomacy was the attempt to promote the nation's best interests. "In short," he stressed, "diplomatic policy should be decided according to cool judgment of advantages and disadvantages. If a nation's diplomacy is controlled by such a vacant and emotional opinion as to judge whether it is weak or strong, the nation will ruin its fortune."[67] Shidehara demonstrated this conviction in the Customs Conference. Finally, his dealing with the Chinese tariff problems in the midst of civil war was a good example of his "economic-oriented diplomacy." When Feng Yü-hsiang and Kuo Sung-ling revolted against Chang Tso-lin in December 1925 and their forces were temporarily victorious over Chang's, Shidehara again strictly adhered to the policy of noninterference. He did so because he hoped to realize Japan's proposal of reciprocal arrangements and consolidation of unsecured debts at the Conference.

---

[66]   The American delegation's report to the Secretary of State on the official proceedings of the *Special Conference on the Chinese Customs Tariff*, 839–840.

[67]   Shidehara Heiwa Zaidan (ed.), 270, 320.

THE NANKING INCIDENT

Abroad, Shidehara's policy was popular. His faithful adherence to the principle of non-intervention in Chinese domestic affairs and his "friendly" attitude toward China's aspirations for recovering tariff autonomy greatly improved diplomatic relations between the two nations, which had been tense ever since Japan's Twenty-One Demands of 1915. Horiuchi Tateki, Shidehara's subordinate, writes of Sino-Japanese relations under Shidehara's leadership:

> At the Special Customs Conference held in Peking during 1925 and 1926, Japan took the initiative among the powers in proposing the acceptance of China's tariff autonomy. By doing so, she initiated the abrogation of China's unequal treaties which was the main aspiration of the Chinese people. Because of this perceptive measure, in the conference Japan always led the powers and won the wholehearted trust of the Chinese people, especially of the so-called "Young China" centering around the Kuomintang which was advancing northward from Canton. Thanks to this great diplomatic measure, the anti-Japanese feeling among the Chinese which had continued for seven years disappeared, and instead a friendly atmosphere toward Japan gradually developed in China.[68]

Shidehara's internationalism and peace-loving attitude also won the trust of the Western powers. Observing this pleasant turn of events, Genrō Saionji contentedly said that just then the British Ambassador seemed to consult more with Japan than with his own Foreign Minister and that even the American Ambassador approached Shidehara frequently to discuss international affairs. Saionji also wrote to the Ministry of the Imperial Household that "Japanese-American relations have become very good." Shide-

---

[68] Horiuchi, 62.

hara was on especially good terms with the American Secretary of State, Frank B. Kellogg.

Shidehara succeeded not only in recovering Japan's international credit and prestige but also in improving trade. Thanks in part to his industry in concluding or revising so many commercial treaties, in convening various trade conferences, and in mitigating anti-Japanese sentiment among the Chinese, Japan's overall exports increased from 1,948 million yen in 1920 to 2,306 million yen in 1925. The increase was particularly great in the China trade. The latter advanced from 287.2 million yen in 1921 to 468.4 million yen in 1925. After Shidehara, under Tanaka's aggressive policy, Japan's China trade abruptly declined to 373.1 million yen in 1928, due to the Chinese boycotts.[69]

At home, however, criticism of his policy increased. There was a general rise of more exclusionist nationalism which was opposed to Shidehara's type of peace-loving internationalism. The traditionalists, as we have noted, called for a radical reform of Japan's diplomacy in the Shōwa Restoration and attacked his policy as "weak-kneed," "non-resistant," and "subservient to the West." In fact, to some extent, Shidehara himself stimulated this trend by his unyielding attitude to opposition groups. His and the Japanese delegation's efforts notwithstanding, the Japanese industrialists and trading firms in China were not happy about Japan's conciliatory policy toward China in the May Thirtieth movement and in the Tariff Conference. In April 1925, Tanaka Giichi replaced Takahashi Korekiyo and became the Chairman of the Seiyūkai. Soon the coalition between the Kenseikai and the Seiyūkai turned into a mud-slinging power struggle. The Seiyūkai under Tanaka, supported by such militant members as

---

[69] Naikaku Kambō (ed.), 552; Uchida Naosaku, "Sensō Boppatsu to Chūgoku no Tainichi Boikotto Mondai" (The outbreak of the Pacific War and the problem of China's anti-Japanese boycotts), *Taiheiyō Sensō Gen'in-ron* (Causes for the Pacific War), ed. Nihon Gaikō Gakkai (Tokyo, 1953), 582-583; C. F. Remer, *A Study of Chinese Boycotts, with Special Reference to Their Economic Effectiveness* (Baltimore, 1933), Appendix I-III, 253-267.

Mori Kaku, Hatoyama Ichirō, and Yamamoto Jōtarō, began to attack the Kenseikai Cabinet in concert. Shidehara was their special target. Furthermore, Japanese popular sentiment toward China was becoming increasingly "unfriendly," because of the frequent dangers caused to the lives and property of Japanese nationals created by the Chinese civil wars and anti-foreign movements. According to Etō Shinkichi's statistical analysis of public opinion toward China during this time, the popularity curves declined and tension increased between the two nations.[70] The Nanking Incident occurred at this juncture and gave the final blow to Shidehara's leadership in Japan's diplomacy.

In March 1925, Sun Yat-sen died without accomplishing his long harbored hope of national unification. Chiang Kai-shek took over the leadership of the Kuomintang and was determined to carry out the northern expedition to unite all China under his personal control. By October 1926, Chiang's forces, in alliance with the troops of T'ang Sheng-chih, controlled Kwantung and Kwangsi and advanced along the Yangtze capturing Hankow, Hanyang, and Wuchang. Wu P'ei-fu, in the face of the rapidly advancing Nationalist forces, made a quick *rapprochement* with his traditional enemy, Chang Tso-lin, in Peking near the end of the Tariff Conference, but he was soon defeated by Chiang's forces. By mid-November Kiangsi had fallen to the Nationalists, and early in January Nationalist forces from Fukien and Kiangsi advanced into Chekiang. In March, Anhwei, Shanghai, and Nanking fell into the hands of the Nationalist revolutionaries in quick succession. At the same time the nationalistic rights-recovery movement and general anti-foreign sentiment among the Chinese people were becoming stronger. The victories of the Kuomintang seemed to enhance these popular sentiments. On November 19, 1926, for example, Chiang expressed his determination to abolish immediately extraterritoriality, foreign

---

70 Etō, *Chūgoku o meguru Kokusai Seiji*, 183–236.

concessions, and all foreign special rights and privileges.[71]   The
British, quick to perceive this new turn of events in China, began to
alter their oppressive policy of military intervention in order to
placate the Kuomintang's anti-British sentiments. A major change
to a more conciliatory policy was observed in the notes which
the British Government communicated to representatives of the
Washington Treaty powers in Peking on December 18, 1926.
The notes said,

> The political disintegration in China has, however, been accom-
> panied by the growth of a powerful nationalist movement which aimed
> at gaining for China an equal place among the nations, and any failure
> to meet this movement with sympathy and understanding would not
> respond to the real intentions of the powers toward China.
>
> His Majesty's Government, after carefully reviewing the posi-
> tion, desire to submit their considered opinion as to the course which
> the Washington Treaty powers should now adopt. His Majesty's
> Government propose that these governments shall issue a statement
> setting forth the essential facts of the situation; declaring their readi-
> ness to negotiate on treaty revision and all other outstanding questions
> as soon as the Chinese themselves have constituted a government
> with authority to negotiate;... They should abandon the idea that
> the economic and political development of China can only be se-
> cured under foreign tutelage, and declare their readiness to recognize
> her right to the enjoyment of tariff autonomy as soon as she herself
> has settled and promulgated a new national tariff [sic].[72]

The notes also strongly urged that "the Powers should now authorize the immediate levy of the Washington surtaxes uncondi-
tionally throughout China." The notes went even so far as to
suggest that the funds collected from the surtaxes need not be
deposited in foreign banks but might be deposited wherever the
proper authorities indicated.

---

[71]   Morse and MacNair, 734.
[72]   The British Secretary of State (Chamberlain) to the British Minister
in China (Lampson), transmitted by the British Ambassador to the Secretary
of State, December 23, 1926, FRUS I.

In spite of the British efforts to mitigate the Chinese anti-British sentiments, the anti-British movement still continued in China. On January 3–5, 1927, before the powers could reply to the British memorandum, a Chinese mob attacked the British concession in Hankow. In keeping with the policy change, the British authorities refrained from firing. No attack was made upon either the French or the Japanese concession. On January 6 similar onslaughts were made upon the British concession in Kiukiang, and looting was carried out by Nationalist soldiers. Soon the British Government was obliged to surrender its concessions in Hankow and Kiukiang. Then the Nationalist revolutionary forces marched along the Yangtze toward Shanghai. The British, no longer able to adhere to their policy of conciliation, urged Japan to join the British in dispatching troops to Shanghai as a precautionary measure. In London, the Foreign Secretary, Sir J. Austen Chamberlain, requested the Japanese Ambassador, Matsui Keishirō, to comply with the British proposal. In Tokyo, the British Ambassador, Sir John Tilley, visited the Foreign Ministry of Japan almost every day for the same purpose. According to the original plan of the British Government, Japan was to send one brigade, while Britain was to dispatch another from India.[73] Nevertheless, the Japanese Foreign Minister, Shidehara, consistently declined to join the British. Shidehara pointed out that it would be a grave misapprehension of the Chinese situation for Britain to take such steps and expressed his preference for evacuating Japanese nationals from dangerous areas.

The negotiation with Japan being to no avail, on January 24 the British Government unilaterally announced that it would reinforce the troops in Shanghai by sending three additional brigades. In Japan at about the same time, in the Fifty-second session of the Diet, Shidehara reemphasized the need for Japan

[73] Yoshizawa to Shidehara, January 19, 1927, JFMA S 16154. See also Isaacs, 130–141 on the Shanghai insurrection.

"to respect China's sovereignty and territorial integrity," in order
"to observe the principle of non-intervention strictly," so as "to
promote economic co-operation for co-existence and co-prosperity
of the two nations" and "to express Japan's fullest sympathy and
good will toward Chinese national aspirations." In the same
speech he once again reminded those who were advocating a
"positive" policy toward China of the fact that Japan's "most
urgent and important need in her policy toward China is to increase her foreign trade as much as possible" and that "Japan's
aim is not to procure territory but markets."[74] Meanwhile, the
Nationalist forces having occupied Shanghai entered Nanking on
March 24 and once more carried out looting and onslaughts upon
foreign nationals, this time indiscriminately assaulting Japanese,
Americans, French, and Britons. The attack continued overnight, resulting in the deaths of six foreign civilians (three Britons,
two French, and one American) and many injuries. Japanese,
British and American soldiers on guard also suffered casualties.[75]

Upon receiving the report of the incident, Shidehara immediately sent a telegraph to Yada, the Japanese Consul General in
Shanghai:

It is a great surprise for both our government and people that
violence was done by those Southern forces which stand for national
revolution and are proud of their observance of discipline. Because
of this unfortunate incident, there are indications of great change in
Japanese public opinion which had been growing sympathetic toward
the Southern forces. In addition, more than a hundred British and
American residents were detained, and some were shot on their way
to refuge by the Southern forces, and finally the American and British
warships fired to rescue their nationals. However, the confusion
is such that they cannot complete relief work. And yet the Chinese
local authorities avoid their responsibilities and their arrogant attitude
is causing great indignation among the British and the Americans.

---

[74] See Shidehara's speech in the Fifty-second Diet on December 26,
1926, in Maezawa (ed.), I, 711–718.
[75] For a more detailed account of the incident, see JFMA PVM 26.

It is not difficult for us to conjecture that under such circumstances the United States and Great Britain might make a grave decision as a measure of emergency, and the situation may become very serious. At this moment, some responsible and influential people like Chiang Kai-shek should go to Nanking as soon as possible to settle the disorder in such a way as to satisfy the powers. Otherwise, it might have a grave influence upon the Nationalist forces and the Nationalist Government.[76]

The telegram raises several important points. The tone is unusually strong for a restrained man like Shidehara. He was indignant over the incident in spite of his adherence to a policy of nonintervention and of sympathy toward China's aspirations for abrogating the unequal treaties. He also hoped for China's national unification, if possible under the Kuomintang, not under the warlords in the north. He was sympathetic to Chiang and hoped to offer Japan's good offices between China and the United States and Great Britain, since only the Japanese warships had not fired upon the Chinese troops.

Shidehara's fears proved to be correct. This time even the American Minister in China, MacMurray, who had been pursuing a much more moderate policy than the British authorities, repeatedly urged Washington to take strong measures. On March 28, for example, he wrote to the Secretary of State:

As I am absolutely convinced this campaign of terrorism and insult to foreigners was not only officially countenanced and directed but even prearranged, the incident could hardly have been more outrageous. But for the timely bombardment the worst incidents could have been multiplied manifold. The significance of this is enormous and I respectfully suggest the immediate withdrawal of all Americans in Nationalist territory and the taking of some sufficiently strong action to deter the perpetration of similar incidents elsewhere.[77]

---

[76]   Shidehara to Yada, March 26, 1927, JFMA PVM 27.
[77]   MacMurray to Kellogg, March 28, 1927, FRUS II; MacMurray to Kellogg, March 27, 1927, *ibid.*

The following day MacMurray wrote to Kellogg that the American policy of conciliation toward the Nationalist Government had failed and that unless a strong attitude was taken promptly all foreign lives and property in China would be in increasing jeopardy. Under such circumstances Shidehara wrote to Yada that he should meet Chiang Kai-shek immediately and suggest to Chiang that he work out remedial measures before the whole situation deteriorated. He added that Chiang should promptly conclude a pact with Japan, the United States, and Britain. Yada, having noted that the powers would be satisfied only with an apology, reparations, punishment of those responsible for the incident, and future guarantees of lives and property of foreign residents in China, recommended to Chiang that he take the initiative in making such a voluntary statement before the powers forced him to do so.[78]

The British Government took the strongest attitude on the incident. The government conveyed its intention to the Japanese and American Ministers in China to activate the British fleet at Shanghai and suggested that Japan, Great Britain, and the United States jointly bombard the Chinese military installations if the Chinese authorities would not admit their responsibility and agree upon apologies and reparations within a fixed time. The American Ambassador in Tokyo consulted the Japanese Foreign Minister concerning the British proposal. In the interview with Ambassador MacVeagh, Shidehara stressed that "the occurrences at Nanking had not caused the Japanese Government to change its Chinese policy and the Japanese Government did not at this time consider it necessary or advisable to send troops to China." Shidehara was also convinced that "Chiang Kai-shek was strongly opposed to these outrages upon foreigners and would exert his utmost efforts to suppress them and maintain order." Hence, Japan and the United States declined to join in the drastic measures

---

[78] MacMurray to Kellogg, March 29, 1927, *ibid.*; Shidehara to Yada, March 26, 1927, JFMA PVM 27; Yada to Shidehara, March 26, 1927, *ibid.*

suggested by the British Government which might have led to a new Boxer incident. However, the American Minister in China, together with the naval authorities, was still contemplating the possibility of destroying the forts at Kiangyin near Nanking, which could be done without unduly endangering noncombatants. Another measure which the American Minister proposed to Washington was blockading all Chinese ports from Shanghai south. These measures were to be carried out as last resorts, in order "to avoid an unfortunate new Boxer movement, organized and encouraged with the audacity and adroitness which has been introduced into the Chinese anti-foreign movement by the Russians."[79]

In the meantime, on March 27, Ministers of the three powers in China, Japan, the United States, and Great Britain, agreed upon a recommendation which they could offer to their respective governments. According to the recommendation, each government was:

A. To take the matter up at once with Chiang Kai-shek through our consul general at Shanghai and present to him the following terms: (1) Adequate punishment of the commander of the troops responsible for the murders, personal injuries and indirect and material damage done; as also of all persons found to be implicated. (2) Apology in writing by the commander in chief of the Nationalist army including an express written undertaking to refrain from all forms of violence and agitation against foreign lives and property. (3) Complete reparation for personal injuries and material damage done.

B. Simultaneously to inform Chiang Kai-shek through our consuls general that unless he demonstrates to our satisfaction his intention to comply promptly with these terms the interested powers will find themselves compelled to specify a time limit for compliance, failing which they reserve to themselves the right to take such measures as they consider appropriate.[80]

The Ministers agreed that such demands had to be presented to

---

[79] Yoshizawa to Shidehara, March 29, 1927, *ibid.*; MacVeagh to Kellogg, March 28, 1927, FRUS II; MacMurray to Kellogg, March 29, 1927, *ibid.*
[80] *Ibid.*

Chiang immediately. The British Minister felt that if negotiations with Chiang failed, the powers at least ought to blockade the Yangtze River and Canton. The Japanese Minister in Peking, Yoshizawa, also thought that if Chiang failed to comply with the demands the powers were obliged to take some sort of military action such as that advocated by the American Minister and the British Government. Subsequently, on March 29, the French and Italian Ministers also joined in the same proposal to their governments.[81]

Shidehara rejected this plan of thrusting the ultimatum upon Chiang Kai-shek for the following reason; through the information given to him by the consul general in Shanghai, he was convinced that the outrages had been caused by the forces of the communist-controlled Wuhan regime in order to discredit Chiang.[82] Therefore he wrote to Yoshizawa and told the American Ambassador in Tokyo that, since "Chiang Kai-shek would be both willing and able to maintain order, it would be a mistake for any of the powers to take oppressive measures at the present time, as this would merely assist the enemies of Chiang Kai-shek and enable the radicals amongst the Cantonese to get control of the Cantonese Government and army." Furthermore, if Chiang was ousted due to the powers' oppressive measures, China — especially south of the Yangtze — would be once again thrown into chaos, which would not be at all beneficial either for the Chinese people or for the powers. Consequently the best conceivable policy for the powers would be to let the Chinese people voluntarily iron out their own difficulties and maintain peace and order by themselves. Shidehara was opposed not only to the idea of the ultimatum itself but also to its content. He instructed Yoshizawa to suggest to other representatives of the powers in Peking that they change the wording of the original recommendation from "when he [Chiang]" to "the Nationalist Army" and to delete the entire phrase

[81] Yoshizawa to Shidehara, March 29, 1927, JFMA PVM 27.
[82] Yada to Shidehara, March 26 and 29, 1927, *ibid*.

on the time limit. By making the first change, Shidehara hoped
to make the Wuhan regime as well as Chiang responsible for the
incident, and by suggesting the second change he hoped to alter
the nature of demands from an "ultimatum" to a request so that
the powers were not forced to take some drastic measures if Chiang
failed to meet the demands within the time limit.[83]

Simultaneously, Shidehara sent two instructions to Yoshizawa
in Peking: "If Japan is to join the negotiations with Chiang
together with other powers, she must strive to mediate between
the powers and China, so that the former will not make excessive
demands," and that Yoshizawa was "to prepare for the withdrawal
of all Japanese residents north of Hankow." Shidehara ordered
Yada, the Japanese consul general in Shanghai, to recommend to
Chiang that he make a statement voluntarily expressing his basic
agreement to those demands, before he was forced to agree to them
when the demands were actually thrust upon him. Chiang told
Yada that he would admit his responsibility and would carry out
punishment and reparation as soon as he finished his investigation
of the situation.   In the interview with Yada, Chiang also expressed
his gratitude that Japan did not join the bombardments by the
American and British warships. Chiang stated, "this fact will
prove to the Nationalist Revolutionary Army and the Chinese
people in general that Japan's policy toward China is different
from and independent of the oppressive policies of the United
States and Great Britain and that it will have a good influence, to a
great extent, upon Sino-Japanese relations." The Japanese naval
authorities agreed to Shidehara's suggestion to delete the phrase
of the "time limit" but for a different reason: as they saw it, it
would take at least two or three weeks for them to prepare for any
military action in China.[84]

---

[83]   Shidehara to Yoshizawa, March 30, 1927, *ibid*.
[84]   Shidehara to Yoshizawa, March 29; Yada to Shidehara, March 30;
the agreement between Kimura and the Bureau Chief of Naval Affairs, March
31, *ibid*.

On March 29 the meeting of the Japanese, American, British, French, and Italian Ministers in Peking resulted in concurrence with the Japanese Government's suggestion that a time limit for compliance be deleted and that demands be presented simultaneously to both Eugene Ch'en of the Wuhan regime and Chiang Kai-shek. But the British Minister, Sir Miles Lampson, told the other representatives that "the British Government was reconsidering the whole problem of China in the light of the Nanking Incident and was drawing up certain proposals in consultation with British military and naval experts to be referred to the other four powers chiefly concerned." Lampson presumed that these proposals dealt with sanctions. Furthermore, the five interested Ministers were in agreement that "time is essential for the success of any demands but that it would be worse than useless to make such demands if the interested powers were not definitely resolved to follow them up by any necessary means to secure satisfaction." This implied that some sort of sanctions should be applied if China failed to comply with the powers' demands. In the meantime, the American Minister in Peking received a telegram from Secretary of State Kellogg disapproving of the ultimatum for reasons similar to those of Shidehara. Kellogg's telegram was dispatched on March 31, two days before Shidehara's view had been conveyed to Kellogg through the American Ambassador in Tokyo. Kellogg's telegram indicates that there was a conflict between Kellogg and MacMurray, the American Minister in Peking, for the latter was in favor of stronger measures than was Kellogg.[85]

On April 2 the British Government simultaneously approached Tokyo and Washington. The British Embassy in Washington conveyed a note to Kellogg which said, "His Majesty's Government assumes that the United States Government does not contemplate allowing this outrageous affair to pass without insisting on a prop-

---

[85]   MacMurray to Kellogg, April 1 (8 p.m.), 1927, FRUS II; MacMurray to Kellogg, April 1 (9 p.m.), 1927, ibid.; Kellogg to MacMurray, March 31, 1927, ibid.

er apology and reparation, and that they will be ready to co-operate with the other Powers concerned in opposing and doing what they can to prevent for the future so flagrant a manifestation of the present wave of violence and disorder which prevails throughout the south of China, accompanied as it has been by deliberate outrages and insults to peaceful and law-abiding American and other foreigners." The note expressed the British Government's hope that "the American Government would co-operate wholeheartedly in defending common interests in China." The British Ambassador in Tokyo visited Shidehara and expressed the same view. He emphasized that Japan and Great Britain had to come to a "concord not only with regard to the Nanking Incident but also to their China policies in general." Sir John Tilley, the British Ambassador, also indicated the possibility of applying sanctions against China such as had been advocated by his government.[86]

In the interview, Shidehara reiterated his opposition to any ultimatum which would leave Chiang with only two choices, either to refuse or to yield to the demands, for either way such an ultimatum would destroy his position in the Kuomintang. With regard to the proposed sanctions, he was adamant in his refusal. As to the blockade of the Yangtze River and Canton, he thought that such a measure would cause more trouble to foreign residents and traders than to the Chinese. The measure would make the powers themselves suffer. As to the suggested bombardment, he stated that such bombardments should probably be aimed at strategic positions of the southern forces, but since there was no one "heart," such an attack would not be fatal to them. Instead, there were many small strategic "points," and to attack all of them would not only be very difficult for the powers but would also eventually corner the powers, not China. The military occupation of these strategically important points which were spread all over

---

[86] The British Embassy to the Department of State, April 2, 1927, *ibid.*; the British Ambassador's interview with Shidehara, April 2, 1927, JFMA PVM 27.

China would be more difficult. To accomplish the task, the powers would have to send a great number of troops and spend much of their resources. Even if the powers could have done so, still it would be they who would be exhausted without attaining their original purpose, and they would disgrace themselves. Hence it would be impossible for the powers to take any effective measure to implement sanctions. And even if they could do so, the result would only be to destroy the responsible Nationalist Government, to foster anarchism, and to stimulate more violent anti-foreign sentiment among the Chinese, resulting in more harm for foreign residents in China. "Therefore," Shidehara stated, "I am convinced that there is no other way but a peaceful, diplomatic measures to settle the present problem."[87]

The British Ambassador further asked Shidehara what he would do if the Chinese people could not settle the problem by themselves and if violent communist influences should spread over the whole of China. Shidehara replied that, first of all, it would be very unlikely that such a situation would occur in China, and that, secondly, should China become a communistic country, within two or three years it would become possible for foreigners to reside and trade in China. In fact, although the Western powers had been afraid of the Bolshevik Revolution, Japan had restored normal diplomatic relations with the U. S. S. R., and the Japanese were residing in Russia and trading with Russians without any difficulty. "Consequently," he stated, "even if China should become a communist nation, we do not have to be too afraid of it."

He concluded the interview by saying, "In short, no matter how the present situation in China develops, the powers should leave China to its own course and wait for the result with patience. There is no other way but this. Being anxious about the present Chinese situation and making impossible demands upon her without

---

[87] *Ibid.*

carefully deliberating the consequences are not measures for statesmen to take."[88]

In the meantime, Chiang Kai-shek found it difficult to comply
with Shidehara's recommendation, i.e., to make a voluntary statement expressing his apology and granting future guarantees of the
lives and property of foreign residents, for to do so would make him
a direct target for nationalists and communists alike. On April 1
and 2, he surrounded the so-called "Nationalist" forces which had
committed outrages in Nanking and disarmed more than 500
soldiers, thereby demonstrating his willingness to punish those
Chinese soldiers who were responsible for the incident. Consequently, Shidehara hoped, the severe demands which had been
prepared by the powers would not have to be thrust upon Chiang
Kai-shek. Shidehara instructed Yoshizawa to urge the other
powers to hold up any presentation of their demands until
Chiang could voluntarily make an offer to meet them. The irri-
tation of the American Minister at Japan's request to delay the demands — to say nothing of the British who had been taking an
even stronger position against China — is evident in his telegram
to the Secretary of State in Washington:

> Yoshizawa then read an instruction from his government instruct-
> ing him to request several days' delay to allow time for an effort,
> through Japan's consul general at Shanghai, to induce Chiang to take
> the initiative in making an offer to meet the views of the powers.
> All of us, Yoshizawa included, regretted the delay, especially as a
> message had already been received from the Japanese consul general
> at Shanghai saying that he could see no prospect that Chiang would
> agree. We could not, however, take action until Yoshizawa received
> new instructions. He said he would request those at once.[89]

On April 3, outrages similar to those of the Nanking Incident
broke out in Hankow. As a consequence, Shidehara could no

---

[88] *Ibid.*
[89] MacMurray to Kellogg, April 5, 1927, FRUS II; Yoshizawa to Shidehara, April 4, 1927, JFMA PVM 27.

longer prevent the other powers from presenting their demands. On the next day, Shidehara conveyed to Yoshizawa the Japanese Government's decision to join the prepared demands of the powers. However, Shidehara re-emphasized that the demands should be presented simultaneously both to Shanghai (Chiang Kai-shek) and to Hankow (the left-wing of the Nationalist Government). On the same day, the British Ambassador in Tokyo visited Shidehara to sound out the latter's attitude should Chiang and Eugene Ch'en not accept the demands. The British Ambassador once again alluded to joint military sanctions, and the Japanese Foreign Minister once again declined such ventures. Shidehara told Tilley:

> The amount of trade between Japan and China comprises an important portion of the total amount of Japan's foreign trade. Although the British trade with China must also be important, there would be no comparison between the ratio of Japan's China trade to its total trade and the ratio of the British China trade to its total trade. Consequently, Japan could hardly take such measures as to disturb this important China trade for any length of time.[90]

Shidehara also expressed the view that, even from a political point of view, due to Japan's geographical proximity, she ought to keep friendly relations with China in order to maintain eternal peace in Asia, and that it would be unbearable for the Japanese to suffer the deep enmity of the Chinese people for a long time.[91]

On the next day, April 5, Frank B. Kellogg expressed an attitude similar to Shidehara's. He was opposed to the time limit, the ultimatum, and the sanctions. Through exchanges of telegrams between Kellogg and John V. A. MacMurray, the American Minister in Peking, one can observe the former's efforts to restrain the latter. MacMurray was advocating more oppressive measures against China than was his government in Washington. On April 5 the British *Chargé*, Chilton, presented a note from the British

---

[90] Shidehara to Yoshizawa, April 4, 1927, JFMA PVM 27; the memo of the British Ambassador's interview with Shidehara, April 4, 1927, *ibid.*

[91] *Ibid.*

Government saying that "His Majesty's Government had agreed to the formula to be presented to Chiang Kai-shek on the understanding that the other Powers accepted in principle the application of sanctions in the event of the Nationalist Government refusing to give satisfaction to their demands." Kellogg told Chilton, "we were under no obligation at all to endorse, in principle, sanctions." On the next day, in the interview with Kellogg and Joseph C. Grew, the American Under Secretary of State, Japanese Ambassador Matsudaira told them that Shidehara had been opposed to three kinds of sanctions suggested by the British Government: (1) blockade, (2) bombardment, and (3) occupation of certain areas in China. Matsudaira then conveyed his view that the Japanese Government was entirely in accord with the American position that "no sanctions should be agreed to or applied at the present time." Matsudaira reported the result of this interview to Shidehara, saying that, when he had made his statement, "the Secretary of State's face brightened with joy and Kellogg said that that was the same view as that of the American Government."[92]

Because all five powers — Japan, the United States, Great Britain, France, and Italy — at least agreed upon sending protest notes over the Nanking Incident, on April 11 identical notes were handed to Chiang Kai-shek in Shanghai and Eugene Ch'en in Hankow. The American note handed to Ch'en — the same notes were transmitted to Chiang and Ch'en by the other powers — read:

> Sir: Under instructions of the American Government I am directed by the American Minister to present to you the following terms [which are simultaneously being communicated to General Chiang Kai-shek, Commander-in-Chief of the Nationalist Armies] for the prompt settlement of the situation created by the outrages against American nationals committed by Nationalist troops at Nanking on 24th of March last:

---

[92] The British Ambassador, Esme Howard, to Kellogg, April 5, 1927, FRUS II; memorandum by the Secretary of State, Kellogg, April 6, 1927, *ibid.*; memorandum by the Under Secretary of State, Grew, April 6, 1927, *ibid.*; Matsudaira to Shidehara, April 6, 1927, JFMA PVM 27.

1. Adequate punishment of Commanders of the troops responsible for the murders, the personal injuries and indignities and the
material damage done as also of all persons found to be implicated.

2. Apology in writing by the Commander-in-Chief of the Nationalist Army including an express written undertaking to refrain
from all forms of violence and agitation against foreign lives and
property.

3. Complete reparation for the personal injuries and material
damage done.

Unless the Nationalist Authorities demonstrate to the satisfaction
of the interested governments their intention to comply promptly
with these terms the said governments will find themselves compelled
to take such measures as they consider appropriate.

F. P. Lockhart[93]

(Consul General at Hankow)

However, at this point it seemed most unlikely that in reality any
form of sanctions would be taken jointly by the powers against
China, because of the joint Japanese and American opposition to
such measures.   As we have observed, throughout the negotiation
of this settlement Shidehara Kijūrō took the initiative.   His opposition to an ultimatum with the condition of a time limit and
his original suggestion to communicate the note to both Chiang
and Ch'en were accepted by the powers.   And thanks to his and
Kellogg's refusal of military intervention as proposed by the British
Government, the powers and China were spared the recurrence
of another Boxer Incident.

Shidehara's handling of the Nanking Incident best demonstrated the gist of his policy: his rationality, pragmatism, peace-loving
attitude, and orientation toward economic interests.   It is particularly interesting to note that he was opposed to any form of
military intervention, even if China should have become a communist nation, for he was convinced that he could establish normal

---

[93]   The American Consul General at Hankow (Lockhart) to the Minister
for Foreign Affairs of the Nationalist Government (Ch'en), April 11, 1927,
FRUS II.

diplomatic and trade relations with a communist China just as he had succeeded in doing with Soviet Russia. It was also significant that Shidehara believed that anti-foreign sentiments among the Chinese could not be suppressed and that any oppressive measure taken by the powers would only aggravate Chinese anti-foreignism. Shidehara expressed his conviction to the British Ambassador that mutual understanding and perseverence between China and Japan, which would increase friendly feelings between the two nations, would be the only method of maintaining peace in Asia.[94] His policy with respect to the incident also revealed the fact that he was an anti-communist and that he therefore tried to support Chiang Kai-shek by mitigating the powers' pressure against him as much as possible. As we shall see, Tanaka's understanding was entirely different from Shidehara's. Tanaka was equally an anti-communist. However, he hoped to defend Japan and China against Russian influence by establishing an invincible strategic position in Manchuria and Mongolia. Against the Chinese anti-foreign movement he took the "initiative" among the powers, not in restraining but rather in advocating military pressure.

In Japan, the public attack on Shidehara's conciliatory policy toward China came to a peak during the Nanking and Hankow Incidents. On March 30, First Lieutenant Araki Sadao (1877–1966), who had been ordered by the naval authorities to go to Nanking to protect the Japanese nationals there, attempted suicide because of his failure to carry out his assigned duty. Araki had ordered his subordinates to observe strict non-resistance against the Chinese outrages, because of pleas from Japanese residents and diplomatic representatives who feared that any attempt at counter-assault upon the Chinese soldiers would further endanger them. Araki's attempted suicide generated a wave of bitter public criticism against Shidehara's "weak-kneed" policy toward China. The military

---

[94] The memo of the British Ambassador's interview with Shidehara, April 4, 1927, JFMA PVM 27; the British Ambassador's interview with Shidehara, April 2, 1927, *ibid.*

authorities stated publicly that the government, for the sake of "national prestige," had to make China accept responsibility for the outrages. The Privy Council blamed Shidehara's "do-nothing" policy as the basic cause for Japan's humiliation. The Japan-China Trade Association (Nikka Jitsugyō Kyōkai) repeatedly urged the Foreign Ministry to give them an absolute guarantee of protection in future. And even the liberal *Asahi Shimbun* warned Shidehara editorially not to confuse "non-intervention" and "non-resistance" and suggested that he take more decisive measures against Chinese assaults upon Japanese residents.[95]

When the Hankow Incident broke out on April 3, public criticism of Shidehara became more intense. Day after day newspapers reported Japanese casualties sensationally: "The Chinese soldiers' atrocities beggar all description!" "Rioters swarmed at Hankow; The city became a hell on earth!" The Japanese cotton industries in China announced that they could no longer trust the Foreign Ministry and that they would protect themselves by requesting firm support from the Army and the Navy. On April 7, the Ministry of Naval Affairs, held an extraordinary meeting, requesting the Minister of the Navy, Takarabe, to approve its decision to send a fleet to north China. The Seiyūkai also held an extraordinary convention under Tanaka Giichi's leadership, denounced Shidehara's "negative" policy, and instituted a nationwide movement to overthrow the Cabinet. The party simultaneously decided to send Yamamoto Jōtarō, the Chairman of the Executive Board, to Genrō Saionji in order to urge a change of Ministry. Members of the House of Peers became equally vociferous against Shidehara's policy. For instance, the Kōseikai, invited Yamamoto Jōtarō and Matsuoka Yōsuke, on the 12th, to discuss the matter and proposed that the government carry out more "positive" measures. The severest attack on Shidehara came from the Privy Council, which asserted that his non-resistance had caused great humiliation

---

[95] *The Asahi Shimbun*, March 30–April 3, 1927; *The Mainichi Shimbun*, March 30–April 3, 1927.

to the Emperor and the nation. Itō Miyoji (1857–1934) in the general meeting of the Privy Council bitterly decried Shidehara in the presence of the Emperor.[96]

The Wakatsuki Cabinet (because of Katō's death in January 1926, Wakatsuki Reijirō, who had been Katō's Minister of Internal Affairs, had organized the Kenseikai Cabinet) simultaneously had to cope with the financial crisis. The government tried to rescue those banks which were floundering, without collateral through an Imperial Edict. However, the Privy Council, which had the official right to approve or disapprove the governmental appeal to the Emperor, rejected Wakatsuki's plea. The Seiyūkai did not miss this golden opportunity to destroy the Kenseikai Administration. It disclosed the financial panic of the government in the Diet, which immediately led to a nationwide run on the banks. Many banks were either bankrupted or obliged to close indefinitely. As a result, having aggravated the financial crisis and being unable to obtain the Imperial Edict which was the only possible remedy, the Wakatsuki Cabinet was forced to resign *en masse* on April 17, 1927. Although the financial crisis was the direct cause for the fall of the Kenseikai Administration, the increasing public criticism of Shidehara's "weak-kneed" policy was in fact the fatal wound. Shidehara's fundamental difficulty was how to offset the rapidly developing Chinese nationalism and anti-imperialism on the one hand and the equally pressing Japanese public demands for "tougher" or "stronger" measures (*kyōkō-saku*) against the Chinese "outrages" on the other. When the Wakatsuki Cabinet fell, the majority of the Japanese public expected a strong personality to pursue a "positive" policy (*sekkyoku seisaku*) toward China.

---

[96] *The Asahi Shimbun*, April 4–17, 1927; *The Mainichi Shimbun*, April 4–17, 1927; Shidehara, *Gaikō Gojūnen*, 257–260.

CHAPTER 7

TANAKA GIICHI'S POLICY
TOWARD CHINA
APRIL 1927–JULY 1929

When the Wakatsuki Kenseikai Cabinet fell, Vice-Grand Chamberlain Kawai, acting on Imperial orders, paid a visit to Prince Saionji to receive the Genrō's advice about the next head of the Cabinet.   Saionji, according to his own principle of maintaining party government, had to choose Tanaka Giichi, who was chairman of the second largest party, the Seiyūkai, although he himself favored Shidehara's type of diplomacy.[1]   Hence, on April 20, 1927, the Tanaka Cabinet was formed.   A few days earlier, at the Seiyūkai Convention, Chairman Tanaka had already emphasized the need for pursuing a "positive" policy in order to break through Japan's national "crisis" both at home and abroad. Referring to foreign affairs, he had said:

> The Katō Cabinet had disregarded even the turmoil in Manchuria, which is our Empire's *special region*.... The incidents in south China humiliated our nation, and our officials and residents were put

---

[1] Saionji, when the Seiyūkai had approached him to urge a change of Ministry in early April, had still firmly supported Shidehara. *The Asahi Shimbun*, April 13, 1927.

to extreme humiliation. Our *national prestige* was lost. Nevertheless, the government does not worry about the situation and exalts
the principle of non-resistance! Obviously, the government aban-
doned our Empire's position in East Asia, and disregarded the collapse
of the security of the Orient. Our Empire which is the *Lord of
East Asia* ought to be determined to renovate our China policy, in
order to defend our Empire and to protect its rights and interests
there, and also to maintain the security of the whole of East Asia.
(Italics mine)[2]

At the same convention, the party declared its determination to
assist the rule of the new Shōwa Emperor through sincere devotion
and loyalty to the Imperial Household.

Tanaka, in order to carry this out, decided to hold concurrently
the portfolio for Foreign Affairs and the Premiership. He chose
General Shirakawa Yoshinori as War Minister and Mori Kaku
as Vice-Minister of Foreign and Political Affairs. Mori's appoint-
ment was noteworthy, for he was even more aggressive than
Tanaka. With regard to the Washington treaties, Mori was of the
opinion:

If you study the Nine Power Treaty carefully, you will soon
realize that the treaty intends to put Japan into a cage; it puts the
yoke, handcuffs, and fetters on Japan.... So long as those treaties
exist, the Japanese people cannot act freely in the world. Such
treaties make us hesitant in our action and Japan cannot expand
herself. We inevitably suffer insecurity.

Mori, therefore, suggested that in order to free herself from
Western domination and promote her national fortune Japan would
have to overturn the Washington System.[3] Thus the tough
combination of Tanaka-Mori-Shirakawa was formed to pursue
Japan's "positive" diplomacy.

On April 22 the new Cabinet announced its foreign policy:

We have deep sympathy with China's just demands. We intend
to give considerable aid to the realization of those demands according

---

[2] Quoted by Kawai, 493.
[3] Yamaura, preface 18–21.

to our own judgment of domestic and foreign situations. However, we believe there is a proper way of realizing such demands. We do not believe it the real intention of the Chinese people to accelerate the turmoil of China more violently. Neither do we believe it is their real wish to endanger relations between China and other powers, for if they restrain themselves from doing so, their just demands will be realized.... On this point, we cannot but hope that the Chinese people will prudently reflect upon themselves.

[However], we cannot remain indifferent to the communist activities in China, for we receive their direct influence and we bear a grave responsibility for the maintenance of security throughout East Asia.[4]

In this announcement, Tanaka expressed both a soft and a hard line. He made a gesture toward maintaining a sympathetic attitude to the Chinese rights-recovery movement. Simultaneously, however, he suggested that Japan would not tolerate communist activities or the civil war, and he warned of possible intervention.[5] Tanaka's soft attitude was partly due to democratic sentiment at home and partly due to the still prevailing anti-imperialism throughout the world. More importantly, however, the Emperor — concerned about Tanaka's aggressive tendencies — had restrained his high-handed policy by warning, "You must be especially cautious about foreign affairs."[6]

Many who had been frustrated by Shidehara's conciliatory policy toward China welcomed the change in Japan's diplomatic leadership. At the same time, however, they felt anxious about the future development of Sino-Japanese relations should Tanaka determinedly carried out his "strong" policy. *The Asahi Shimbun* wrote:

---

[4] Tanaka Naikaku (ed.), *Tanaka Naikaku* (Tanaka Cabinet; Tokyo, 1928), 15.

[5] As we have noted in Chapter 5, the Soviet infiltration into the Chinese labor movements and anti-imperialism was known to many Japanese, and Tanaka was especially sensitive to this problem. Yamamoto Jōtarō who had come back to Japan from his investigation tour in China a few days before, had also warned Tanaka of this danger.

[6] Hosokawa, 141.

We were not satisfied with the former Cabinet's foreign policy. However, we are simultaneously afraid whether Japan might be endangered by the new Cabinet, which might suddenly change our policy from a negative to a positive one in reaction to the former Cabinet.

Nobody has any objection to Shidehara's principle of non-intervention, which is not prejudicial to any party or faction in China. We wonder, however, whether Shidehara's foreign policy was not too faithful to this principle, perhaps too negative, obscuring the danger to Japanese residents through bland reports. On the other hand, it showed extreme toleration and generosity to China. We had considerable regrets about Shidehara's judgment about Chinese affairs and his means of protecting our residents there....

China must be especially watchful of every activity of Prime Minister Tanaka. Consequently, we hope the Premier will be particularly careful in executing his policy. It is of course our wish that the Premier make a greater effort to protect Japanese residents in China. The Premier's announcement gave us some satisfaction, but at the same time we cannot but anticipate danger in the future.[7]

The American reaction to this change in Japan's foreign policy was quick. On April 25, the acting Ambassador, Norman Armour, visited the Ministry of Foreign Affairs to present a note expressing his government's disapproval of Japan's strong China policy by referring to the spirit of the Washington treaties. On the same day, at the twentieth anniversary dinner of the United Press Association, President Coolidge also urged restraint on Japan's part, saying:

The friendship of America for China has become proverbial. We feel for her the deepest sympathy in these times of her distress. We have no disposition to do otherwise than to assist and encourage every legitimate aspiration of a national spirit and the realization of a republican form of government....

The civilization of the world has been accomplished by the acceptance and general observance of definite rules of human conduct. Our duty demands that it be clearly understood at home and abroad,

[7] *The Asahi Shimbun*, April 23, 1927.

that we are unwavering in our faith to those principles. Those who violate them cannot hope for our approbation.... Toward those who are yet struggling to improve the conditions of their people and achieve a larger liberty it is especially one of forebearance....[8]

The change in Japan's diplomacy was also noted by the U. S. State Department. During Shidehara's Administration Japan had been the most moderate of the powers concerning the "punishment" of Chiang Kai-shek, who was considered responsible for the Nanking Incident. Shidehara had always been opposed to sanctions against Chiang. But, as soon as Japan's diplomatic leadership passed to Tanaka, she emerged as the prime advocate of strong sanctions. The change was so drastic that Secretary of State Kellogg remarked, "I fail to understand such action taken by Japan."[9]

A real test of Tanaka's "positive" policy came in May, as Chiang Kai-shek's forces, having defeated the Fengtien forces in Honan, continued to advance northward to control the Peking-Tientsin region. On April 14, as a sense of renewed danger spread among foreigners in the area, the British Ambassador, Esme Howard, sounded out the American Secretary on the possibility of organizing international forces to protect their nationals. At that time, Howard gave Kellogg his government's estimate that 25,000 men would be needed to defend both Peking and Tientsin. The British Ambassador also informed Kellogg, "Unless effective international co-operation can be secured, he must make arrangements, in case of necessity, for the evacuation by the British of both Peking and Tientsin."[10] Kellogg, on April 26, replied to the British Ambassador, "In event of grave danger, evacuation of Peking and Tientsin would be preferable to the expense and loss of life necessary to maintain Legation and nationals by force." The American Secretary had already ordered Minister MacMurray

---

[8] *New York Times*, April 26, 1927.
[9] Kellogg to J. V. A. MacMurray, April 28, 1927, FRUS II.
[10] The British Ambassador, Esme Howard, to the Secretary of State, April 14, 1927, FRUS II.

to prepare for removing the Legation, not to "repeat the events of 1900."[11]   Shidehara, as we have noted, had already expressed to the British Ambassador in Tokyo his intention to remove the Japanese residents to places of safety.   Hence by early May the British and the American Governments had come to the conclusion that should an emergency arise they would evacuate their Legations and nationals from the troubled area.

In Japan, on the other hand, there was a widely believed rumor that the Tanaka Cabinet, in accordance with its proclaimed "positive" policy, would send a large body of troops to Shantung, to protect the Japanese residents in north China.   On May 27 it was reported that about 4,000 or 5,000 troops were to be sent to Tsinan from Manchuria and more troops would follow from Japan if necessary.[12]   On the next day, the Tanaka Cabinet announced its decision to send 2,000 troops to Tsinan:

> In the recent disturbances in China, particularly on the occasion of the unfortunate incidents which transpired in Hankow, Nanking, and elsewhere, serious injuries have been inflicted upon the lives and property of the Japanese residents in these localities, and in some cases violence prejudicial to Japan's honor has been committed, owing to the insufficiency of means of protection provided by the Chinese authorities.   In the imminence, therefore, of a military situation developing in North China, a recurrence of such unfortunate incidents is feared.   In fact, at the present moment when Chinese civil strife appears to be extended toward Tsinan, the safety of the lives and property of Japanese residents there is greatly apprehended....   In these circumstances, the Japanese Government has been forced to adopt the measure of protecting the lives and property of Japanese residents there by land forces in order to prevent the repetition of unfortunate events.   Considerable time, however, is required to send troops there for such a purpose, and in view of the constantly changing military situation it has been decided to dispatch immediately

---

[11]   The Secretary of State, Kellogg, to MacMurray, April 12, 1927, FRUS II.

[12]   *The Asahi Shimbun*, April 27, 1927.

about 2,000 troops from Manchuria to Tsingtao as a precaution.[13]
The troops arrived at Tsingtao on June 1.

Japan's first Shantung expedition was an abrupt departure from Shidehara's policy, which had opposed the use of force. On March 30, 1927, when Shidehara was still Foreign Minister, he had instructed Yoshizawa in Peking to make all necessary preparations for the evacuation of Japanese residents and the Legation from the Peking-Tientsin area.[14] This shift in Japan's China policy not only surprised the other powers, but it also caught the Japanese residents in north China totally unaware. Tani Masayuki, a diplomatic secretary who was sent to Tsinan, wrote to the Foreign Ministry in Tokyo:

> Influential people here have reported that in the light of the former policy of our country they had never expected the dispatch of troops. And yet, our government this time quite readily decided to send troops. Having noticed this fact, the Japanese residents here have understood that a sudden change arose in the national policy.[15]

The Shantung expedition was not based upon any treaty agreement with China. Great Britain and the United States had already expressed their preference for evacuation to the protecting their nationals by force. Even from an economic point of view — especially at a time of financial crisis — it was much more sensible to evacuate the residents at Tsinan than to send troops there, since the total number of Japanese residents there was only about 2,000.

The decision to carry out the Shantung expedition raises some interesting points. In terms of the decision-making process within the Tanaka Administration, the proposal was first put forward by the War Minister, Shirakawa. Tanaka and Mori responded

13 *Shuyō Monjo*, II, 96.
14 Shidehara to Yoshizawa, March 30, 1927, JFMA PVM 27.
15 Baba Akira, "Dai Ichiji Santō Shuppei to Tanaka Gaikō" (The first dispatch of troops to Shantung and Tanaka diplomacy), *Ajiya Kenkyū* (Oct., 1963), 60.

favorably to it, and Cabinet meetings and discussions among the Army, the Navy, and the Foreign Ministry were held. The Shantung expedition also demonstrated Tanaka's long-claimed "positive" and "autonomous" policy. Nevertheless, there was a considerable gap between the number of troops which had been forecast by the mass media and the actual number of troops which Tanaka sent to Shantung. This gap between public expectations and reality may be explained as follows: Over the question whether Japan should dispatch troops to Shantung, the Seiyūkai was split in two, but the majority was of the opinion that if Japan could not avoid sending troops, she should limit their numbers as much as possible, "for there was no difference between the present situation and several military upheavals which had taken place previously;"[16] the Kenseikai, democrats, and the officials of the Foreign Ministry also acted as a restraining force upon Tanaka; at the same time, his aggressive character led the public to exaggerated expectations.

Tanaka's hope that Japan would take an initiative in international relations was realized by this action. Encouraged by the Japanese action, the powers which had given up the protection of their nationals by force now decided to reinforce their troops at Peking and Tientsin. The British Counselor — in the absence of the British Minister — expressed his gratitude, saying, "in view of the new position taken now by the Japanese, his government no longer has the abandonment of Peking by its Legation under consideration, and will participate if necessary in defending this area with such forces as his government could make available." And the American Minister MacMurray who, in contrast to Kellogg, had been in favor of military protection, sent a cable to Kellogg on May 31:

> Although the number of troops [the reinforcements of powers encouraged by Japan's dispatch of troops] involved is comparatively small, it seems to me that the Japanese Government's long-delayed

16   *The Asahi Shimbun,* May 26, 1927.

avowal of its determination to take military measures of a precautionary character to protect Japanese interests in North China puts a wholly new light upon the various questions which relate to the situation of Legations and foreign interests in this area.[17]

Accordingly, the American Government also decided to send troops to Tientsin. On June 2 the American Legation sent the following notification to the Chinese Ministry of Foreign Affairs:

> The American Legation presents its compliments to the Ministry of Foreign Affairs, and has the honor to inform the Ministry that a reinforcement to the American forces maintained at Tientsin under the authorization of the Boxer Protocol, consisting of one regiment of Marines, has been dispatched to Tientsin and will arrive at Taku Bar on or about June 4, 1927.[18]

Thus, due to Japan's initiative, the whole situation in north China abruptly changed to military intervention by the powers. Tanaka's dispatch of troops became the best means to carry out the "sanctions" which the powers had contemplated against the "outrageous" Chinese. It should be remembered that the forces at Tientsin entered under the authorization of the Boxer Protocol, but Japan's troops at Tsinan did not.

Within Japan various leaders noted the pros and cons of Tanaka's expedition. Both Gotō Shimpei and Yamamoto Jōtarō thought that Tanaka's decision was "the most appropriate means." Yamamoto stated, "especially when we think about our Empire's position in China, north of Tsinan, this decision is very significant." Ozaki Yukio, a prime advocate of party government, emphasized that the dispatched troops had to be strictly instructed that their function was only to protect Japanese residents. At the same time he expressed his fears: "historically our Army has had a close connection with Chang Tso-lin and tended to support him. Therefore I worry very much whether the present Cabinet, which it headed by the powerful leader of the military clique, can really

---

[17]   MacMurray to Kellogg, May 31, 1927, FRUS II.
[18]   The American Legation to the Chinese Ministry of Foreign Affairs, June 2, 1927, *ibid.*

maintain its neutral position."[19]   Yoshino Sakuzō, more straightforward in his opposition, wrote in *Chūō Kōron* that "to dispatch
troops to another nation against that nation's will is obviously a
violation of her sovereignty" and that those who support Japan's
dispatch of troops under the pretext of protecting the Japanese in
China logically must accept American and Chinese troops coming
into Japan to protect their nationals, should an upheaval occur in
Japan.[20]

> Tanaka gave his own views on the dispatch to reporters:
>
> In short, the present dispatch of troops is to insure that an
> incident similar to the Nanking Incident will never be repeated.   My
> first principle is to protect Japanese lives and property.   Therefore,
> even if some anti-Japanese movements arise in response to the present
> action, I will not pay any attention to them.   Some anti-Japanese
> campaigners may make noises, but it cannot be helped.   If the
> Japanese residents who have made such hard efforts for many years
> to build their economic foundation there are forced to evacuate
> completely, Japan's "position" which has just been planted in China,
> will be rooted out.[21]

In this statement one finds a remarkable contrast with Shidehara's
views.   One of the reasons Shidehara was opposed to sending
troops was his fear that such military ventures would increase
anti-Japanese sentiment among the Chinese, which would bring
more danger to the Japanese residents there as well as ruin Japan's
China trade.   Tanaka, however, clearly asserted that he would
ignore all such consequences.   This conviction came from his
belief that he could protect his nationals on the spot by sending
troops.   He also believed that it should be done to maintain Japan's
national "honor and prestige."   Tanaka thought Shidehara's
policy of evacuating the Japanese nationals from dangerous areas
to places of safety was a humiliating and defeatist attitude.[22]

---

19   *The Asahi Shimbun*, May 29, 1927.
20   Yoshino Sakuzō, in *Chūō Kōron*, July 1927.
21   *The Asahi Shimbun*, May 29, 1927.
22   See Tanaka's speech of September 14, 1927, at the branch convention
of the Seiyūkai at Nagoya, quoted by Kawai, 594–595; see also Shigemitsu, 32.

Shidehara, on the other hand, thought that to send troops to a foreign country arbitrarily would harm Japan's international honor and prestige.

China's reaction to Japan's dispatch of troops was swift and bitter. The three governments of China, one at Peking, another at Nanking, and the third at Wuhan, all sent protest notes to the Japanese Government on June 1. They all pointed out that Japan's military "invasion" without procuring a previous agreement from the Chinese Government was a violation of Chinese sovereignty and international treaties. *The Tientsin Ta Kung Pao* wrote that Sino-Japanese friendship was destroyed at a stroke by this action of Japan. *The Hankow Tribune* stated that, in spite of various diplomatic pretexts, Japan's action was clearly an intervention in Chinese domestic affairs and that Chinese public resentment would rise to such an extent that even the Chinese Government could no longer control it. Quite soon this proved to be the case. As the news of Japan's Shantung expedition spread throughout the country, violent anti-Japanese movements arose in a chain reaction from Shanghai to Amoy and Canton. In Shanghai a huge mass rally was held, and economic relations with Japan were formally severed. Boycotts of Japanese goods followed in many cities.[23]   Hence the friendly relationship between China and Japan cultivated by Shidehara was shattered; thus began Japan's troubles with China which were to increase steadily during the Tanaka Administration.

The Eastern Conference

Prime Minister Tanaka, hoping to set up a China policy different from that of his predecessor, convened a conference in

---

[23]   Baba Akira, 64–65.

Tokyo from June 27 to July 7. Had he been Shidehara, he might have gone about it in a more business-like manner with less publicity. However, Tanaka, always grandiose, summoned all the key men who dealt with Japan's China policy both at home and abroad, such as Vice-Minister of Political Affairs Mori Kaku, Chief of the Asian Bureau of the Foreign Ministry Kimura Etsuji, Vice-Minister of State for War Hata Eitarō, Vice-Chief of the General Staff Minami Jirō, Commander of the Kwantung Army Mutō Nobuyoshi, Governor of the Kwantung Territory Kodama Hideo, Minister Yoshizawa Kenkichi, Consuls General Yoshida Shigeru of Mukden, Yada Shichitarō of Shanghai — twenty-two key figures in all. Tanaka called this meeting the Eastern Conference (Tōhō Kaigi). Several weeks before the Conference, it had already been touted as a great convention. Such large-scale publicity for the meeting naturally attracted Chinese attention and was interpreted as a disclosure of the Tanaka Cabinet's nakedly aggressive nature. It was under such circumstances that a rumour spread among the Chinese that Prime Minister Tanaka had presented a memorandum (the so-called Tanaka Memorandum dated July 25, 1927) to the Emperor, in which Tanaka had said that Japan ought to occupy Manchuria and advance upon the rest of China.[24]

Underlying the Conference was the fact that ever since childhood Tanaka had a special interest in China and now was very much concerned that China's traditional virtues were being destroyed by "communists" — he tended to associate all Chinese radicals and nationalists who disturbed the traditional order with the "communists." In February 1927, because of his special interest in China, Chairman Tanaka had sent Mori Kaku, Yamamoto Jōtarō, and Matsuoka Yōsuke, his most trusted protégés and influential members of the Seiyūkai, to China in order to investigate the situation. Upon his return from China in March, Mori

---

[24] See Inau, n. 45 of Chap. 5.

reported to Tanaka that Chiang Kai-shek was an honest and reliable man who was truly an anti-communist, that communist influence was so deeply rooted in China that even Chiang was having difficulty in controlling leftist members of his own party, and that behind these communist activities in China there was strong Russian support. Mori concluded that if Japan did nothing about this dangerous situation, within a few years the communist forces would grow into a menacing power.[25]   Yamamoto, returning about a month after the Mori group, confirmed this opinion. He added, however, that Chinese boycotts and insults to Japan occured, because they were "contemptuous" of the Japanese who were promoting Sino-Japanese friendship for the sake of economic benefits, and that Japan therefore might have to put more military pressure upon the Chinese. Yamamoto also stressed that Japan which had taken over Manchuria from Russia by shedding the blood of 100,000 soldiers and spending 2 billion yen naturally had a greater right to determine Manchuria's future than the Chinese.[26]

Thus Tanaka's major concerns in the Eastern Conference were to find ways to deal with the "rampant communists" who were responsible for the revolutionary atmosphere in China and at the same time to establish a defense for Japan's "position" in Manchuria. At the outset of the Conference, Tanaka distributed copies of his own speeches made at the Seiyūkai extraordinary convention (April 16), at the Seiyūkai Kantō convention (June 12), and at the inauguration of his Cabinet, to serve as guidelines for the deliberations.

With regard to the present and future situation in China proper and Manchuria, Consul General Yoshida stated that, regardless of the question of who controlled The Three Eastern Provinces, Japan's position in Manchuria had already been firmly

---

[25]   Baba Akira, 54.

[26]   Nakamura Kikuo, "Tanaka Naikaku no Taika Gaikō" (Tanaka Cabinet's policy toward China), *Hōgaku Kenkyū* (Tokyo; April 1958), 12; Yamamoto Jōtarō-ō Denki Hensan-kai (ed.), 510–513.

established. All Japan had to do was to defend her investments in China. He added that Japan ought to take a strictly just and neutral position toward China and should avoid abusing her military power. Consul General Yada, who had worked closely with Shidehara, held that Chiang's Nationalist forces had gained powerful popular support and that they were very different from conventional warlords' forces. Therefore, whether Japan liked it or not, Chiang's forces would eventually control the whole of China. "In any event," he emphasized, "now that popular power has become so great in China, foreign material support to one faction, such as funds and ammunition, will be of no avail. Foreign intervention is not only outmoded but also harmful to the solution of the problem." He concluded that Japan's major diplomatic goal toward China should be to maintain trade and investment and that to ensure this goal she had to find a government that would have a certain durability and would maintain peace and order.[27]

In contrast to these diplomats, General Matsui of the General Staff expressed the utmost concern with the military situation in China. He thought that among the various forces in China, Chiang's Army seemed to be the strongest, judging from its organization, morale, and finance but that the Nanking, the Wuhan, and Feng Yü-hsiang forces might collide soon. In any event, the position of the Fengtien clique in the north would be secure for the time being. He hinted that he would support Chang Tsolin in the north, should Chiang Kai-shek try to occupy areas north of Shantung. Commander Mutō of the Kwantung Army contended that the Russian force of world revolution would eventually reach Japan and that the most important aim of Japan's China policy was to meet this force. Hence the natural resources and the transportation system in Manchuria ought to be more developed. He pointed out that the major reason these developments had been delayed was that Japan had not had any coherent

---

[27]   JFMA PVM 41, 295–356.

policy toward Manchuria. Mori Kaku took a position similar to
those of Tanaka, Yamamoto, and Mutō. He was of the opinion
that, from the historical, economic, and strategic points of view,
Manchuria and Mongolia were Japan's "life-line" and that Japan
ought therefore to make her position secure in Manchuria. Then,
with political influence in Manchuria and Mongolia strengthened
— implying Ōdō Seiji (politics in the Imperial Way) — Japan
together with China would get rid of the Bolshevik influence on
the Asiatic continent.[28]

On the fourth day of the Conference, in the absence of the
Premier, Vice-Minister of Foreign Affairs Mori presided over the
session which dealt exclusively with the Manchurian-Mongolian
problem. The day's conclusion may be summarized as follows:
a "special relationship" between Japan and Manchuria was recognized. Nevertheless, Japan's policy toward Manchuria had
come to a dead end. The major causes for its failure were that
Japan did not have a right to land ownership, except for the land
attached to the South Manchurian Railway and the leased territory;
that the transportation system was not yet well equipped; that political stability in Manchuria had not been achieved; that political
change and civil war in China proper caused uneasiness in Manchuria; and that above all, Japan had not pursued a coherent policy
toward Manchuria and Mongolia. As to practical solutions to
these problems, it was argued that Japan had to make the Chinese
officials admit Japan's right to own land and that industrialization
of Manchuria and Mongolia should be facilitated — the Japanese
industries which had been concentrated only in Talien should be
expanded — by constructing more railways.[29]

Three conflicting opinions were expressed concerning the
increasing anti-Japanese sentiment and boycotts of Japanese goods
in China. Some unhesitatingly spoke out that the fundamental
cause of the anti-Japanese movement was Japan's Shantung ex-

---

[28]   *Ibid.*; Tanaka Giichi Denki Kankō-kai (ed.), II, 655–657.
[29]   Yamaura, 595.

pedition. To avoid further harm to Japan's China trade, troops
had to be withdrawn immediately from Shantung; by so doing
anti-Japanese sentiment in China would probably diminish.
Others held that the purpose of sending troops to Shantung had
been to protect the Japanese residents there. Therefore, the government should not withdraw troops now, for the situation was
even more dangerous than when the troops were sent a month
previously. A third group stressed that the anti-Japanese movement stemmed largely from agitation by the Southern Government
and that the movement had not necessarily been caused by Japan's
dispatch of troops. To evacuate the forces because of fears of
China's anti-Japanese movement might invite increased presump-
tuousness on the part of the Chinese. Instead of withdrawing the
troops, therefore, Japan should apply further military pressure
to China, if necessary striking the Southern forces a blow.[30]

Although Tanaka embellished the Conference with much publicity, the meeting was actually an unnecessary event, since he did
not seem to be very much influenced by opinions contrary to his
own. On the last day of the meeting he gave these instructions
to the military and diplomatic leaders at the Conference:

> The fundamental principle of our policy toward China is to
> secure peace in the Far East and to attain the co-prosperity of Japan
> and China. However, in view of Japan's special position in the Far
> East, the means to achieve these goals in China proper naturally
> ought to be different from those toward Manchuria and Mongolia.

Having thus made a clear policy distinction between China and
Manchuria-Mongolia, he read an eight-point outline of his policy.
Because his statement was to be announced publicly, Tanaka ad-
mitted "in principle" his government's "respect for the popular
will" of China and "non-intervention" in the Chinese civil war.
However, his Shantung expedition had already violated these prin-

---

[30] JFMA PVM 41, 367–370.

ciples.   At the same time, his hard line was expressed very clearly in the statement.

(5)   During this period [until China proper is united under one government] taking advantage of political insecurity in China, recalcitrant elements will become rampant, resulting in increased disorder and international incidents.   The Government of the Empire expects the Chinese Government in co-operation with its people to suppress these recalcitrant elements and to maintain order.   However, should a danger arise in which the Empire's rights and interests and our residents' lives and property are unjustly violated, the Empire cannot but take some determined measures to protect them in self-defense and according to necessity.   Especially our Empire will make those who carry out unjust anti-Japanese movements and boycotts, agitated by false rumors, forsake such misdeeds.   But at the same time, we will take more positively some precautionary measures to protect our rights against them.

With regard to the policy toward Manchuria and Mongolia, the Prime Minister announced:

(6)   Manchuria and Mongolia, especially The Three Eastern Provinces, have vital relations with Japan from the viewpoint of our national defense and national existence.   Our country not only must be especially concerned with the area but also has a *duty and responsibility*, as a neighboring country, to make the area a happy tranquil land for natives and foreigners alike by maintaining peace and developing the economy.

(7)   If an influential leader of The Three Eastern Provinces respects our *special position* in Manchuria and Mongolia and sincerely makes efforts to stabilize the same area, our government should support him with appropriate means.   (This section not to be made public).

(8)   If it is anticipated that the upheaval will spread to Manchuria and Mongolia, public peace and order will be disturbed, and our *special position* as well as our rights and interests will be violated, we must be prepared to take immediate and appropriate means to

---

[31]   *Shuyō Monjo*, II, 101-102.

protect the area and to maintain it as a peaceful land for development by both natives and foreigners. (Italics mine)[31]

Following the Prime Minister's instruction, Mori Kaku explained the real intention of Tanaka's China policy. Some of the points he made are noteworthy. Concerning Tanaka's dispatch of troops to Shantung, Mori explained:

Today the Chinese harbor "contempt" toward us Japanese. We believe that because they despise us they felt free to carry out without scruple such outrages toward us as recently occurred. They seem to think that Japan cannot do anything about even their boycotts. Thus we must now beat the idea into the heads of the Chinese that Japan will never tolerate such infringements of Japan's national prestige and interests by them. As Minister Yoshizawa mentioned recently, whether Japan should dispatch troops or withdraw them must be decided solely according to Japan's own judgment. Japan should never be afraid of their boycotts. Taking a broad view of things, we must decide on our own attitudes and make the Chinese authorities thoroughly recognize our determination.

With regard to Tanaka's term "recalcitrant elements," Mori explained that Tanaka meant communists and others (nationalists) who agitated for anti-foreign, especially anti-Japanese, movements. Mori said, "We can never pass over them and their activities in silence." As to the middle-of-the road group — those between anti-communists and communists — it was Japan's responsibility to "lead them into the right path."[32] As Tanaka himself later admitted in the Diet, the decisions reached at this Conference became the basic policy of the Tanaka Administration toward China.[33]

Perhaps the most important point in the statement is that Tanaka clearly separated his policy toward China proper from that toward Manchuria and Mongolia. Unlike Shidehara, who thought that Japan had "no rights nor interests whatsoever in Manchuria except those which belonged to the South Manchurian Railway,"

---

[32]   Tanaka Giichi Denki Kankō-kai (ed.), II, 655-657.
[33]   *The Asahi Shimbun*, January 26, 1929.

Tanaka not only considered Manchuria-Mongolia as separate entity from China proper but also thought that Japan had a "special position" there. As a result, he assumed that Japan had a special "duty and responsibility," as "Lord of East Asia," to maintain peace and order in the region. He hoped to turn this region into a "peaceful land" for both nationals and foreigners. From this one can understand that Tanaka entertained a similar idea to that of Ishiwara Kanji, who hoped to establish "Paradise under the Imperial Way (Ōdō Rakudo) in Manchuria." In this conjunction one must pay special attention to section seven of Tanaka's instruction which he ordered not to be made public. One must also note Mori's explanation of Tanaka's statement that his government would make contact with moderate local regimes. Mori said that this meant that when such regimes were firmly established, Japan would send authorized diplomats to them so that other powers would also recognize them as official governments.[34] Against China's national aspirations for unity, Tanaka and Mori hoped to take advantage of the divisive situation in China for Japan's own benefit. Their method was very similar to the old diplomatic maxim of "divide-and-conquer."

Tanaka's instructions disclosed the real nature of his "positive" policy. His dispatch of troops to Shantung was not intended merely to "protect the Japanese nationals on the spot." He also hoped to intimidate the disdainful Chinese by demonstrating Japan's military power. To overlook hostile Chinese attitudes would hurt Japan's national prestige. To use Tanaka's own words, "such insults were more unbearable than death!"[35] Therefore, even at the sacrifice of Japan's trade, he felt compelled to carry out the Shantung expedition. Tanaka anticipated, as he suggested to reporters right after the first Shantung expedition, that more boycotts of Japanese goods might result. Nevertheless,

[34] Tanaka Giichi Denki Kankō-kai (ed.), II, 655–657.
[35] Tanaka's speech at the Seiyūkai extraordinary convention on April 16, 1927, quoted by Kawai, 492.

he was convinced that eventually the Chinese anti-Japanese movements could be suppressed by a strong policy backed by military
power, for such movements were essentially caused by the Chinese
scorn for the Japanese. Following this reasoning, on the same
day that the Conference ended, Tanaka successfully pleaded with
the Emperor to grant His Majesty's approval of reinforcing the
troops in Shantung. The next day, he dispatched another 2,200
troops to China. On April 20, 1928, a third dispatch of troops
led to the Tsinan Incident. At that time the total number of
Japanese troops in Shantung amounted to 15,000. Moreover, on
May 9, Tanaka carried out a fourth dispatch of troops.

Another noteworthy aspect of Tanaka's statement is that he
used the term *futei bunshi* for all the Chinese who participated in
patriotic movements. The term *futei* means "recalcitrants,"
lawless people and rascals. Tanaka applied the same term to all
Japanese communists, socialists, and anarchists who disturbed
the order of Japanese society. For Tanaka, the Chinese nationalists
who were carrying out anti-Japanese movements were all "communists" and "rascals."

Tanaka's path to these conclusions was more intuitive and
emotional than logical. On the one hand, he stated that Japan
would respect "the Chinese people's will," but on the other he
openly carried out Japanese military intervention, not once but
four times. He said that he would observe the principles of an
"open door" and "equal opportunity of trade" in Manchuria, and
yet he simultaneously fought for Japan's "special position" and
special "responsibility" in Manchuria. It was because of these
self-contradictions that many people labeled his policy "haphazard," "incoherent," and "irrational." Indeed, in reading this
and other statements by Tanaka, one tends to feel unsure of his
meaning. Some even criticized him by saying that what he did
was beyond the comprehension of a normal mind. "Tanaka must

have his blood examined. It would be interesting to analyze his brain!"[36]

It has been argued that the incoherence of Tanaka's policy derives from the fact that he was easily influenced by other people. I do not think that this view is quite true. Tanaka had a strong and determined personality. His *oyabun* temperament, his leadership in the Army, and his determination to construct a garrison-state all suggest that he was a man of strong will. When criticized by his opponents in the Diet, he roared, "I will assert what I think I should assert. I am Prime Minister and Minister of Foreign Affairs. I am also Chairman of the party. Nobody can order me to do this and that." Perhaps a more plausible reason for his self-contradictions, in addition to his intuitive thinking, is that, when he stated that he would respect the "people's will," "international co-operation," and the "open door," he did not fully comprehend what these terms meant in an international context. Being wrapped up in a hierarchical traditional milieu, he lacked any understanding of democratic principles. But because these terms were still fashionable both at home and abroad, he had to pay lip service to them.

MANCHURIA AS JAPAN'S PROTECTORATE

Both in his inaugural speech and at the Eastern Conference, as we have seen, Prime Minister Tanaka had expressed his extraordinary concern with the future status of Manchuria and Mongolia, and his administration was to give this problem priority over all other issues. It is for this reason that his policy is often called a "Manchuria-First" policy as opposed to Shidehara's "China-First" policy, by which is meant that Shidehara considered

---

[36] Baba Tsunego, "Tanaka Giichi-ron," 38–39; Nakamura Kikuo, "Tanaka Naikaku no Taika Gaikō, II," *Hōgaku Kenkyū* (Tokyo; September 1958), 33.

Japan's China trade more important than the Manchurian problem.
Let us first survey the background of this issue.[37]

There were certain events around Tanaka which caused him
to worry about Japan's "special position" in Manchuria and
Mongolia more than before. He and his colleagues thought that
a Bolshevik take over of Asia was imminent. They believed that
the sporadic strikes and labor disputes in Manchuria were instigated by Russian and Chinese communists. The Wuhan regime —
the government of the Wuchang, Hankow, and Hanyang area —
was obviously controlled by the Comintern and its Chinese allies.
Chiang Kai-shek's Nationalist forces were rapidly advancing north
to unite China. Furthermore, although the split between Chiang
and the Wuhan group had been clear to Shidehara by the time of
the Nanking Incident, Tanaka and his subordinates tended to
consider all Chinese patriots "communists" and "rascals" and still
had a deep suspicion of the southerners. Yamamoto Jōtarō and
Mori Kaku, having returned from China, reported to Tanaka that
half of China was in the grip of Borodin and a small number of

---

[37] I have a very different view of Tanaka and of his policy from that of
Iriye, especially on the significance of the Eastern Conference. Iriye thinks
that the Conference "was more a meeting of officials to exchange information
than to define a new policy" (Iriye 152), which is actually the view expressed by
Tanaka Giichi Denki, an apologetic biography of Tanaka written by a group of
Chōshū compatriots and Tanaka's protégés. However, I tend to agree with Usui
Katsumi's and Nakamura Kikuo's views that the Conference was very important,
for it became the basis of Tanaka's China policy which was to be developed
subsequently. Tanaka himself admitted this in public both in the Diet and
before reporters. This point will soon be proved, as we shall follow the development of Tanaka's China policy. Iriye is also inclined to overevaluate Tanaka's
eloquence stressing "the principles of the open door and equal opportunity,"
while neglecting to see his real intention of the hard line. A careful consideration of the record of JFMA PVM 41 and Tanaka's instructions — especially from section (5) to (8)—will lead most readers to disagree with Iriye's view
that Tanaka's instructions "contained nothing suggestive of a new departure
in Japanese policy" (Iriye 171). Iriye takes the position that although Tanaka
"faithfully followed his predecessor's [Shidehara's] China policy" and they both
"shared an image of a new era based on solid understanding between Japan
and China," "even Tanaka" had to "depart in certain respects from the
policies formulated by Shidehara" due to the rapidly changing developments in
China and to Tanaka's tendency to be easily swayed by men around him (Iriye
125, 144–145, 147).

Russians and Chinese communists.[38]   Chiang Kai-shek himself declared, on March 7, that he would co-operate with the Soviet Union insofar as the latter would pursue the spirit of equality in dealing with China and anti-imperialist movements.[39]

Under these circumstances, at home the popular cry of conventional slogans, "Defend Japan's life line" or "Don't abandon Manchuria for which Japan has shed the blood of 100,000 soldiers" grew ever more commonplace. The mass media were reporting rapid population increases and probable future food shortages. Accordingly, the Ministry of Agriculture and Forestry advocated that it was necessary for Japan to procure more "new territory" for increased food production. Gotō Shimpei, perhaps the most important opinion leader during this time, made a "mysterious" statement that Japan should not aim at self-sufficiency within the nation as it had hoped to do.   Instead, she had to work at self-sufficiency by expansion.   "I wonder," Gotō said, "whether the lesson of our fairytale about how Momotarō went to the demons' land to conquer the demons would not be the best solution of this problem."[40]   The general tone of these arguments — the need for new territory and the conquest of the demons' land — sounded to the populace as if Japan had her eye on Manchuria.   Major General Saitō (1858–1936), the chief of staff of the Kwantung Army, more openly put forward Japan's need to strengthen her position in Manchuria and eastern inner Mongolia by saying that Japan could establish new agreements on railway construction and increase agricultural productivity in these regions.   In order to achieve these goals, Saitō suggested that an autonomous region under a Chinese governor might have to be established in these areas.[41]

---

[38]   Yamaura Kan'ichi (ed.), 535–539; Yamamoto Jōtarō-ō Denki Hensan-kai (ed.), 507–508; *The Asahi Shimbun*, April 7 and 9, 1927.

[39]   *Chiang Chieh-shih hsien-sheng Yenshuo-chi* (Collection of Chiang Kai-shek's speeches; Canton, 1927), 641–648.

[40]   *The Asahi Shimbun*, May 20, 1927.

[41]   Saitō's memorandum, June 1, 1927, JMA T 635; Iriye, 163.

It should be noted, however, that this situation did not occur
suddenly just as Tanaka replaced Shidehara. The population
increase and accompanying food shortages had been a major domestic issue since 1925 after the national issue of universal suffrage was
settled. The Comintern activities in China had been known to
Shidehara throughout the period when he was in the head office
of the Foreign Ministry. Manchuria had been in danger of being
occupied by many warlords, such as Wu P'ei-fu and Feng Yü-
hsiang, who attempted to oust Chang Tso-lin. Chiang Kai-shek
had already launched his northern expedition in July 1926. The
Wuhan regime had been firmly established by the end of 1926
and in February 1927 it had publicly announced its split from
Chiang's Canton Government. Consequently, the important
motivation which made Tanaka carry out his "Manchuria-First"
policy came not so much from external circumstances as from
within his own mind.

In diplomacy there are always many problems to be dealt with
simultaneously. The question is which one to choose first and
how to interpret various events in international relations. This
question is largely determined by what one might call "selective
permeability," to use De Vos' term,[42] and by the diplomat's
reference group — in Tanaka's case people like Yamamoto Jōtarō,
Mori Kaku, Matsuoka Yōsuke, the Army, and the Kwantung Army,
and in Shidehara's case his colleagues in the Foreign Ministry,
such as Saburi Sadao and Kimura Etsuji, democratic critics like
Yoshino Sakuzō and Kiyosawa Kiyoshi, and businessmen. Interpretation of events depends upon one's values, ideology, and what
one thinks is the most important national interest. Shidehara
did not think that the Manchurian problem was the most important
question for Japan, for it was under Chinese sovereignty. For
Tanaka it was Japan's "special position" and therefore it was
vitally important. Shidehara welcomed Chiang's northern ex-

---

[42] See Introduction, n. 22.

pedition to unite China, for Chiang's Government seemed to be orderly, durable, and dependable and Chinese national unification under such a government would be beneficial to Japan's China trade. This line of thinking has exemplified in his response to the Nanking and the Hankow Incidents. To aggravate Chinese anti-imperialist and anti-Japanese sentiments by intervention or by sending troops, Shidehara thought, was more dangerous than China's becoming communist, because the former would make Japan China's eternal enemy. Tanaka believed, on the other hand, that he had to prevent China from becoming communist by all means in order to preserve China's traditional virtues and to defend Japan's *kokutai*.[43]

Tanaka had long had an interest in Manchuria and Mongolia. As early as 1913, while in Manchuria, he had established a "General Plan for the Management of the Continent and Manchuria," distributing it to influential figures in political and military circles.

> We can never forget the historical fact that our country spent 2 billion yen and shed the blood of 230,000 people for south Manchuria. We must also constantly keep in mind that the very reason why we dared to stake our national destiny in the two great wars of the past twenty years was that we believed that the first condition for the continued prosperity of our race was continental expansion. Yet, what happened to us? Within less than ten years since the end of the war most of our people have lost the spirit of that time, have deteriorated, have given up [our continental expansion], and worst of all, some people even openly suggest giving up Manchuria....[44]

> There are only two courses for Japan to take — either to advance or to retreat. Unless we aim at constant advancement, history proves,

---

[43] The memo of the British Ambassador's interview with Shidehara, April 4, 1927, JFMA PVM 27; Shidehara to Yoshizawa, April 4, 1927, *ibid*.; the memo of the British Ambassador's interview with Shidehara, April 2, 1927, *ibid*.

[44] Tanaka's "General Plan for the Management of the Continent and Manchuria" is printed in Tanaka Giichi Denki Kankō-kai (ed.), I, 547–584. The original title is "Taiman Shokan" (literally, My Views on Manchuria). See also Tanaka's article, "Taishi Keiei Shiken" (My plan for the management of China), *ibid*., 676–712.

there is no other way for the nation to choose but her own retro-
gression and destruction. Our nation has acquired land on the
continent. But if we only hope to defend it and do not take the
positive step of expansion, we shall soon be doomed to retreat across
the ocean and to defend desperately our solitary islands. Our [suc-
cessful] management of the continent is *sine qua non* for the survival
of our nation and for the advancement of our race....

There is a limit to natural resources at home. There is not
much left to increase our production except by industry. In contrast to this, the value of south Manchuria, as I mentioned in the
former chapter, is [tremendous]. Even in its present state of development it is showing promising figures. It is obvious that if we
cultivate it more progressively in the future it will bring immense
benefit to our Empire. It is regrettable that many people idly take
a pessimistic view of Japan being a poor country without making
any positive plan to make poor Japan into a rich Japan. The only
way to make Japan rich and strong is to utilize Chinese resources.
Above all, there is no better way than to develop Manchuria and
Mongolia, the unopened treasures, which are already under the
sphere of Japanese influence. What a foolish thing it is for people
to call their own country poor without noticing this opportunity,
and to lose their nation's prestige, because by calling their country
poor they invite the other powers' contempt for themselves!

Therefore, the government must establish a grand plan of
managing Manchuria and Mongolia, and think out methods of how
to increase our countrymen's advances there.[45]

Tanaka then proposed various practical means to realize this
plan. First of all, he advocated, Japan had to establish a consistent
policy toward Manchuria and Mongolia. Second, by combining
the Governor-Generalships of Korea and of the Kwantung Leased
Territory, a unified organ to control both Korea and Manchuria
should be established. Third, all consulates in Manchuria should
be placed under the jurisdiction of this unified organ. Fourth,
the Korean Railway and the South Manchurian Railway Companies

---

[45] *Ibid.*, 554–556.

should be amalgamated to operate a "Korean-Manchurian Railway." Fifth, Japan must obtain from China the right of land ownership and residence in the entire area of Manchuria and Mongolia. Sixth, Japan ought to "own" the five new railways in these region's which were originally to be loaned to Japan. Then, Tanaka contended, Manchuria and Mongolia would become the "healthiest colony" in the world because of her clean air and beautiful nature. The acquisition of the area would bring enormous benefit to Japan for her further military advancement on the continent, especially against Russia, and for her to secure land and food for a rapidly increasing population at home. Tanaka especially emphasized the need for agricultural development. His agrarian ideal was observed in the same "Plan":

> Above all, we must improve rice cultivation in Manchuria, and must extend it to the uncultivated area of Mongolia....Because the rice cultivation in these areas is still too negative, we must take more positive steps to increase resources there.

However, he warned that the Chinese were a people who valued "face" above all, so Japan had to satisfy them by giving them nominal sovereignty over these areas.[46]

Tanaka's extraordinary interest in Manchuria and Mongolia was a product of three major concerns: his hope to protect Japan's *kokutai* from communism; his concern with Japan's strategy throughout East Asia against Russia and the West; and his interest in acquiring national resources there for Japan. So he had formulated this plan as early as 1913 and hoped to realize it at an opportune time. During the World War, for example, as Vice-Chief of the General Staff under the Ōkuma Cabinet, he plotted to make Manchuria and Mongolia independent of China proper by supporting a puppet regime.[47] After that attempt failed, Tanaka as the

---

[46] *Ibid.*, 559–561.

[47] Ishigami, 289–290; Tai Tien-ch'ou, *Nihon-ron* (Treatise on Japan; Tokyo, 1946), trans. Fujita Kenji, 104; Taishi Kōrō-sha Denki Hensan-kai (ed.), II, 1337.

chairman of the Seiyūkai repeatedly emphasized the same idea. His persistent interest in these regions is further indicated in the speech he made in 1927 at the branch convention of the Seiyūkai in Nagano Prefecture:

> I pray for the healthy development of China, for our country has a direct and great interest in this neighboring country. I do not like to see the spread of destructive movements accompanied by radical thought in China. We must by all means prevent disturbances from spreading into Manchuria and Mongolia especially, because our country has the most important political and economic relations with those regions.[48]

In this speech, Tanaka clearly indicated his determination to protect Manchuria and Mongolia from the undesirable influence of radical thoughts and movements "by all means." In other words, those regions were to become Japan's special protectorates.

Manchuria and Mongolia were above all to serve Japan's military interests. Therefore, in his "General Plan" of 1913 he had stressed the need for establishing more railways for the swift transportation of soldiers and munitions as well as of natural resources. Railways should be so constructed as to best serve strategic purposes. At the same time, the development of Manchuria and Mongolia should be supported by Japan's military power. For this purpose, even during peace time, at least two army divisions and two cavalry brigades ought to be stationed there, and to support them he recommended the stationing of four divisions in Korea. From a strategic point of view, the Japanese army ought to occupy at least Kirin, Chiangch'un, and Chengchia-tun. In conclusion he stated:

> From ancient times, Japan's national principle (*kokuze*) has been to seek military prestige, values, and ethics (*bu*). The harmony of the Army and the Navy is the foundation of nation-building.

---

[48] His speech at Nagano is printed in Kawai, 586–589; Tanaka also emphasized his determination to protect Manchuria and Mongolia from disturbances in his speech at the Kantō branch convention of the Seiyūkai, June 1927, see *ibid.*, 575.

If the Army and the Navy without mutual co-operation wish to realize independent aims, they will fail. If they hope to achieve their respective purposes, they must co-operate sincerely and with justice. If men are so determined, they can even conquer the heavens.[49] For Tanaka, the development of Manchuria and Mongolia was ultimately aimed at the strengthening of Japan's military power and the spread of her military prestige, which was what he called Japan's "*kokuze*," the foundation of national policy.

To conclude: Tanaka's extraordinary interest in Manchuria and Mongolia was, in the final analysis, related to his ultimate concern with Japan's defense. His "Manchuria-First" policy was to be carried out in line with this perception of Japan's ultimate national interest. The time was ripe. He controlled the Japanese Government both as Prime Minister and Minister of Foreign Affairs. Popular interest in Manchuria and Mongolia was increasing at home, and Chang Tso-lin, who owed him a great debt of gratitude because Tanaka had saved his life during the Russo-Japanese War, was in control of Manchuria.[50] Now he was to put the plan into practice. The policy outlined at the Eastern Conference was the first step toward its execution. Even Tanaka, however, did not believe that the whole scheme could be realized at once. Therefore, according to the decision reached at the Eastern Conference, he stressed three major objectives to be achieved first: to establish a consistent policy toward Manchuria and Mongolia; to construct more railroads along which the Japanese sphere of influence could be expanded and resources and troops could be transported; and to urge and to help Chang Tso-lin consolidate his power more firmly in Manchuria.

---

[49] Tanaka's "General Plan," in Tanaka Giichi Denki Kankō-kai (ed.), I, 582.

[50] During the Russo-Japanese War, some Chinese bandits who were suspected as Russian spies were caught by the Japanese Army in Manchuria, Chang Tso-lin was among them. Chang, though he was only thirty years old at that time, looked more distinguished than the others. Tanaka thought that Chang was more reliable and could be used for Japan in the future. So Tanaka

As a second step, Prime Minister Tanaka established the Bureau of Resources (Shigen Kyoku) and the Inquiry Commission of Resources (Shigen Shingi Kai) immediately after the Conference. These commissions were to investigate not only domestic but also foreign resources and to establish plans to exploit them for primarily defense purposes. By doing so, they were to serve Tanaka's Total National Mobilization Plan (Kokka Sōdōin Keikaku). The following speech by Tanaka at the inauguration of the Inquiry Commission of Resources in July 1927 indicates his real intentions:

> In order to break through these national difficulties and to develop our national economy, there is no other way but to make our utmost efforts to best utilize all of our resources.... At the same time, we must carry out a careful investigation of both our domestic and our foreign resources and must exert ourselves to cultivate and promote those resources according to a coherent and systematic plan....
>
> In essence, control and development of resources is to increase our national defense power.... If we can prepare a thoroughly reliable plan of controlling and utilizing resources for national emergencies, we can swiftly establish the most orderly war structure to meet all demands of this military nation, to secure our national life, and fully demonstrate the greatest ability of national defense.[51]

His plan of exploiting resources of Manchuria and Mongolia was to become a part of this Total National Mobilization plan.

As expressed in his "General Plan" on the management of Manchuria and Mongolia and in his instructions at the end of the Eastern Conference, Tanaka thought the railway problem in those areas was the key to Japan's further expansion and to her establishment of Ōdō Rakudo (paradise in the Imperial Way) on the continent. This intention of Tanaka is clearly seen in his telegram to Yoshizawa dated November 7, 1927:

> From the beginning the policy of this government toward Man-

---

asked the Commander-in-Chief to pardon Chang's life. Chang was reported to have said that he owed his life to Tanaka. See Ishigami, 265.

[51] This speech is printed in Kawai, 582–583.

churia and Mongolia has been to maintain peace and order in these areas without failure and to make the region a peaceful and secure land for both natives and foreigners. At the same time, this government aims at full economic development of the region for the benefit of us, Japanese, as well as for the natives. As I made it clear to the participants, the major objective of the policy outlined at the Eastern Conference was to solve various pending problems in Manchuria and Mongolia. And in order to carry out this objective, we are to make Chang Tso-lin understand the important position of The Three Eastern Provinces [to Japan] in the past, present, and future, and to bring Chang to agree to our objective. By doing so, we hope to establish ties of cordial friendship with Chang Tso-lin....[52]

Tanaka added in the telegram that the construction of more railways in Manchuria and Mongolia was a concrete measure to carry out the "Empire's Grand Plan," namely, to establish a peaceful and secure land for the natives and foreigners, and that it was also the principal aim of the conclusion reached at the Eastern Conference. Tanaka finished the telegram by saying, "I am sure that you know very well all what I have said above, but I just wanted to make sure." The telegram indicated that the Eastern Conference was not just a meeting for exchanging views, that the major concern at the Eastern Conference was the Manchurian and Mongolian problem, and that the railway problem was crucial.

Nevertheless, the railway problem in Manchuria under Chang Tso-lin was not developing favoiably for Japan. Her management of the South Manchurian Railway was based upon the Portsmouth Agreement between Japan and Russia (signed September 5, 1905) and the Peking Agreement between Japan and Ch'ing China (December 22, 1905). Thereafter, Japan made several additional loan agreements with China in order to construct both branch and independent lines of the main line of the South Manchurian Railway. From the outset, the railway had two important functions, military and economic. Manchuria being located at the

---

[52]   Tanaka to Yoshizawa, November 7, 1927, JFMA PVM 24.

center of the triangle connecting Japan, China, and Russia, the network of railways was so constructed as to best serve military purposes. For example, the line connecting Kirin and Kainei was the shortest direct route between Japan and Ch'angch'un through Korea. In this way, according to traditional military ideas, if Manchuria was Japan's "life line," the railways were the "veins" of that life line. But China had not faithfully observed the railway agreements with Japan, partly because of rising nationalism even in Manchuria, partly because of continuing civil wars, and partly because of the increasing ambition of Chang Tso-lin who had controlled not only Manchuria but also north China as the Generalissimo of the Peking Government since June 1927.[53]

Japan's expansion of its military as well as economic power along the railways in Manchuria could not but antagonize local patriots. Even Chang Tso-lin said that he felt as if another person's blood veins were running through his own body.[54] Consequently, Chang, with the strong support of the natives, decided to build his own railways, one between Tahushan and Tungliao and another between Fengtien and Hailung. Both violated former agreements with Japan. The former line was to run parallel to the South Manchurian Railway, which violated the secret protocols attached to the Peking Agreement. The third section of the protocols read:

> The Chinese Government engage, for the purpose of protecting the interest of the South Manchurian Railway, not to construct, prior to the recovery by them of the said railway, any main line in the neighborhood of and parallel to that railway, or any branch line which might be prejudicial to the interest of the above-mentioned railway.[55]

---

[53] Nakamura Kikuo, II, 27–30.

[54] *Ibid.*, 27.

[55] "Secret Protocols to Treaty of December 22, 1905, relating to Manchuria," in *Treaties and Agreements with and Concerning China: 1894–1919*, compiled by MacMurray (Washington, D. C.: Carnegie Endowment for International Peace Division of International Law 1921), I, 554.

The latter line not only violated the same agreement, but also was a part of the line which Japan intended to build according to the agreement of 1918.

It was against this background that Tanaka, on July 20, 1927, appointed Yamamoto Jōtarō, a strong personality with similar ideas about the future status of Manchuria and Mongolia, as President of the South Manchurian Railway. Matsuoka Yōsuke, Tanaka's compatriot and protégé, was made Vice-President. While Mori and Shirakawa were to assist Tanaka's hard line of diplomacy, these two were to support his Manchurian policy. He hoped to solve various pending problems related to this matter at once by utilizing these men of strong personality. At the special committee meeting of the Seiyūkai, expressing his full trust in Yamamoto, Tanaka said:

> I believe that Mr. Yamamoto Jōtarō is the best person for the Presidency of the South Manchurian Railway. This government regards the China problem as one of the most important.... The base of all economic establishments in Manchuria is the South Manchurian Railway. Therefore, in the selection of this post I have considered it most carefully and have come to the conclusion that Mr. Yamamoto, whom I consider a part of myself, would be the best. At my urging, Mr. Yamamoto has accepted this responsibility .... Because I believe that nobody is better than Mr. Yamamoto for this position, I have urged him to accept the post in order to fulfill the policy of our government.[56]

Yamamoto's mission was to settle the conflicts with Chang and also to obtain rights for Japan to construct seven more lines. Even Yamamoto knew that this was a very difficult task which would require great determination on Japan's part. Tanaka, however, gave Yamamoto a firm answer when the latter asked him whether he was prepared to take on all of the anticipated difficulties.

He said, "We must do it at all costs. If Chang refuses this

---

[56] Hosokawa, 155.

proposal, we must put it to the test of the sword. I mean our national military power!"[57]

Tanaka decided to carry out this scheme by secret and direct negotiations between Yamamoto and Chang without using normal diplomatic organs. There were several reasons for this: he first of all hoped to avoid diplomatic entanglements with the other powers in realizing this scheme; he also hoped to do away with opposition within the Ministry of Foreign Affairs where there were still many moderate career diplomats; above all it was his belief that laws and international treaties were not effective, even useless unless the contracting parties really intended to observe those agreements. Unlike Shidehara who always emphasized regularity and international laws, Tanaka disregarded the importance of laws and treaties. He further lacked faith in the idea of "contract." Instead, he thought that the most important thing was "sincerity" and mutual understanding within *hara*, as between two samurai who committed themselves to carry out a secret plot. It was this tendency of Tanaka to neglect the importance of international laws that enabled him to openly violate Japan's commitments in the Washington treaties and other international agreements.[58]

The negotiations between Chang Tso-lin and Yamamoto Jōtarō were also conducted in a typically traditional Oriental manner. First of all, contrary to the contemporary emphasis on "open diplomacy" in international affairs, the negotiations were conducted secretly. Second, Chang and Yamamoto continually maneuvered and countermaneuvered. For example, Yamamoto sent his wife and other women to "spy" on Chang under the pretext of taking a sightseeing tour to Peking. Chang, on the other hand, said to Yamamoto's aides that because he had received great favors from Tanaka, he would like to return *on*, thanks, if possible. Throughout the negotiations, "go-betweens" constantly ran back and forth between Chang and Yamamoto, and between Yamamoto

---

[57] Yamamoto Jōtarō-ō Denki Hensan-kai (ed.), 561.
[58] Tanaka to Yoshizawa, November 7, 1927, JFMA PVM 24.

and Tanaka. Despite this superficially friendly atmosphere, both parties were extremely tense. As soon as Chang saw the proposal, he realized that those seven lines were directly aimed at Russia. It was as if he were to hold a bomb to his chest. Besides, he also had to worry about patriotic protests by his people against such a proposal. It was reported that the Generalissimo often shivered in wrath. The Japanese negotiators, on the other hand, were so firmly determined to succeed in the negotiations that Yamamoto himself had to warn his aides "not to commit suicide" if they failed.[59]

On November 12, 1927, the negotiations were finally concluded, not as an official agreement between Tokyo and Peking but as a private "understanding" between Chang and Yamamoto, since the other members of the governing board of Peking refused to accept Japan's proposal.[60] In this private understanding Japan obtained from Chang a recognition that she could build five railway lines between Tunhwa and Tumên, between Yenki and Hailin, between Kirin and Wuch'ang, between Chiangch'un and Talai, and between T'aonan and Solun. Chang was forced to agree to this proposal, because he was worried about the Nationalists' continuing northern expedition, the Russian threat, and the already known "strong" policy of the Tanaka Administration toward Manchuria. The Japanese negotiators, according to Tanaka's original promise, even suggested that Japan might have to fight Chang, if he would not agree to the proposal. In exchange, Yamamoto proposed to Chang an offensive and defensive alliance against Russia, together with the promise of economic co-operation between Japan and Manchuria. According to this scheme, Chang was to be made the Emperor of Manchuria supported by Japan. Chang was reported to be pleased with this reward from Japan. Very much satisfied with these results, Yamamoto remarked, "If this scheme really materializes, it will be as if Japan buys up the

---

[59] Yamamoto Jōtarō-ō Denki Hensan-kai (ed.), 559-588.
[60] Yoshizawa to Tanaka, October 13, 1927, JFMA PVM 24.

whole of Manchuria!" The General Staff equally expressed its
satisfaction with this settlement since it would greatly promote
Japan's defense program on the continent. In this way, by tight-
ening the military, political, and economic relationships between
Japan and Manchuria, the foundation of Manchukuo was laid
under the Tanaka Administration.[61]

Tanaka's maneuver in negotiating with Chang Tso-lin without going through proper diplomatic channels offended Japanese
career diplomats. Minister Yoshizawa, who was supposed to
represent Japan in China, was never informed of the negotiations.
He must have been extremely offended, for he not only wrote
protesting letters to Tanaka but also in his memoirs he recalled it
as one of the most unpleasant experiences of his career.[62] Arita
Hachirō, Chief of the Asian Bureau, and other officials of the
Foreign Ministry resolved to demand the resignation of Yamamoto
from the Presidency of the South Manchurian Railway.[63] Tanaka was also attacked by these officials. However, he not only
succeeded in patching up bad feelings created in the Ministry
but also reconfirmed Yamamoto's full authority in all further
negotiations with Chang about matters related to railway construction based upon the agreement.[64] On November 7, 1927,
the Prime Minister instructed Yoshizawa to accept the Chang-

---

    61   See details of negotiations in JFMA PVM 24, "Mammō Mondai ni
kansuru Kōshō Ikken: Yamamoto Mantetsu Shachō to Chō Saku-rin to no
Kōshō Kankei" (Documents relating to negotiations concerning Manchurian
and Mongolian problems: Documents relating to the negotiations between
Yamamoto Jōtarō, President of the South Manchurian Railway Company, and
Chang Tso-lin); with regard to the contents of actual agreement, see Yoshizawa
to Tanaka, October 14 and 19, 1927, *ibid.*, and the memo of Tanaka's explanation of the agreement to the Privy Council, December 19, 1927, *ibid.*; The Vice-
Chief of the General Staff to Lieutenant-General Honjō in Peking, toward the
end of October, 1927, *ibid.*; see also Yamamoto Jōtarō-ō Denki Hensan-kai
(ed.), 562–588.
    62   Yoshizawa to Tanaka, October 13 and 17, 1927, JFMA PVM 24;
Yoshizawa Kenkichi, *Gaikō Rokujū-nen* (Sixty years of diplomacy; Tokyo,
1958), 85–88.
    63   Yamamoto Jōtarō-ō Denki Hensan-kai (ed.), 583–584.
    64   Yamamoto apologized to Arita on October 29 according to the memo of
October 31, JFMA PVM 24; and Tanaka did the same to Yoshizawa, Tanaka
to Yoshizawa, November 7, 1927, *ibid.*

Yamamoto agreement as the basis for a new Sino-Japanese understanding on railway construction in Manchuria. In the same
telegram, Tanaka congratulated himself and Yamamoto by saying
that the agreement carried one step further the negotiation of
Manchurian and Mongolian problems, which had been initially
discussed at the Eastern Conference. Tanaka avoided concluding an official treaty, since "other powers might suspect Japan's
real intention," and instead decided to take the form of exchanging
letters between Chang Tso-lin and Yoshizawa, as the official representative of Japan to China. He once again emphasized to
Yoshizawa that the important thing was *hara*, sincerity and mutual
understanding, and not the form of agreement such as a treaty.
Tanaka himself wrote those letters to both Chang and Yoshizawa,
and he ordered Yoshizawa to ask Chang to sign the letter as if
Chang himself had written it. Thus, on December 9, Chang
and Yoshizawa exchanged signatures on those letters to conclude
the long and bitter negotiations as a "cordial" and "friendly"
understanding between Chang Tso-lin and Japan.[65]

TANAKA AND CHIANG AND CHANG

Tanaka's dealings with Chiang Kai-shek were complicated.
Every time Chiang pushed his forces further north, Tanaka dispatched more troops. These Japanese troops in north China were
widely recognized, both at home and abroad, as Japan's attempt
to oppose Chiang's northern expedition. For instance, *The
Asahi Shimbun*, under the heading of "The Government Dispatched Troops, Chang's Collapse Disadvantageous to the Empire,"
wrote that the protection of nationals was not the only purpose of
the Tanaka Administration. By sending troops to north China,

---

[65] *Ibid.*

Japan hoped indirectly to protect the Fengtien forces from attack by the Nationalists.[66] Nevertheless, at the same time Tanaka made a gesture of support for Chiang. On May 20, 1927, the Prime Minister instructed Minister Yoshizawa and Consul General Yada that if Chiang Kai-shek and his group continued to suppress communists and insured China's internal stability, the Japanese Government would give him moral support.[67] Moreover, on the same day he ordered Yoshizawa and Consul General Yoshida at Mukden to induce Chang Tso-lin in Peking to return to Manchuria so as to concentrate on problems inside Manchuria and stabilize conditions there.[68] What was the real intention of Tanaka in these apparently contradictory policies toward Chiang and Chang? Did Tanaka sincerely hope to see China united under Chiang's leadership and therefore was his policy essentially the same as his predecessor's?[69]

To understand Tanaka's policies toward Chiang and Chang, we must first survey the entangled politico-military relations not only between the above two contestants but also among them and the Wuhan group as well as Feng Yü-hsiang, who became a powerful warlord after Wu P'ei-fu's defeat by Chang Tso-lin in the autumn of 1926.

Toward the end of 1926, Chang organized a united front of various minor warlords in the north in opposition to the Nationalist Army, calling this allied force the National Anti-Revolutionary League Army. He had himself appointed Commander-in-Chief of the Ankuo-chun. On December 27, he declared that, because

[66] *The Asahi Shimbun*, May 27, 1927.

[67] Tanaka to Yoshizawa, May 20, 1927, JFMA PVM 41.

[68] *Ibid.*; Tanaka to Yoshida, May 20, 1927, JFMA PVM 41.

[69] Akira Iriye contends that Tanaka's policy was essentially the same as Shidehara's, because they both supported Chiang Kai-shek (Iriye, 144–145). However, he overlooks an important fact that Tanaka's support to Chiang was not unconditional. Tanaka, unlike Shidehara, had two qualifications in doing so: "If" Chiang tried to suppress communists and to insure China's internal stability; and in so far as Chiang hoped to unite China without Manchuria. We shall see this point soon.

communism was the enemy of the world, he would subjugate the "Reds" in cooperation with the powers. On April 6, 1927, he successfully raided the Russian Embassy in Peking and disclosed the Comintern's subversive activities in China to the world. Finally, on June 18, taking advantage of his growing fame as a result of this incident, Chang became Generalissimo of the Peking Government and expressed his ambition to control the whole of China.[70]   Chiang Kai-shek had believed that the Nanking and Hankow Incidents were communist plots to make him face the direct accusation of the powers. The result of Chang's raid upon the Russian Embassy further convinced him of the communists' plan to overthrow him and revolutionize China. Hence he was determined to start ruthless suppression of the communists. Between April 11 and 13, Chiang's troops, under the command of Pai Ch'ung-hsi and assisted by underground gangs, attacked the headquarters of the General Labor Union and other labor organizations scattered throughout Shanghai. Their quarters were occupied, pickets and labor leaders were disarmed and arrested, and many were shot to death. Similar coups were carried out in Kwangtung, Fukien, Szechwan, Kiangsu, and Chekiang. On April 18, Chiang established his own government at Nanking.[71]

On the same day, Chiang Kai-shek declared that he would fight communists as well as imperialists and warlords, and the central executive committee of his government announced that the legitimate regime of the Nationalist Government was transfered to Nanking and that it would dissolve the Wuhan Government. The Wuhan group, on the other hand, as a countermeasure, declared that it would not only dismiss Chiang from the membership of the Kuomintang but also arrest him as a "traitor." Thus open antagonism between the government at Nanking and that at Hankow ensued.[72]   It was under such cir-

[70]   Taishi Kōrō-sha Denki Hensan-kai (ed.), 572.

[71]   Borg, 373–378; Isaacs, 175–185.

[72]   KMWH XVI, 2810–2820; *Chiang Chieh-shih hsien-sheng Yenshuo-chi,* 677–686; Iriye, 135–138; Isaacs, 183–185.

cumstances that Tanaka instructed Yoshizawa to give Chiang moral support, "if" the latter would continue to suppress communists. About the same time Chang Tso-lin, encouraged by the split within the Nationalist Army, attacked the Hankow armies and caused them severe casualties of 13,000. In the end, however, he was defeated being sandwiched by the Nationalist Army and Feng Yü-hsiang's troops from the west. Just prior to this war, the Tanaka Administration carried out its first Shantung expedition. In June, having failed in making an alliance with Hankow, Marshal Feng approached Chiang Kai-shek. They had two common goals to pursue, namely, to capture Peking, now under the control of Chang Tso-lin, and to suppress communists in the Wuhan area.[73]

Since Chang's disclosure of the Russian plot, a schism had been taking place at Hankow between the communists and the anti-communist faction, headed by Sun Fo and Wang Ching-wei, who had returned to Hankow from his European tour (April 1, 1927). The conflicting issues were how to deal with Moscow, with Japan which had just carried out the Shantung expedition, and with the other powers concerning the settlement of the Nanking and Hankow Incidents. Finally in July, the anti-communist group revolted against the communists, which, coupled with attacks by neighboring warlords, led Borodin, his Russian colleagues, and their Chinese followers — including Eugene Ch'en and Madame Sun Yat-sen — to flee to Russia. It was reported that in the coup more than 4000 Chinese communists and labor leaders were put to death. On August 12, 1927, Chiang Kai-shek abruptly retired from the Nanking Government. This was partly because of his failure to complete the northern expedition and partly because of his hope to unite the Kuomintang under one government. Chiang thought that he was the stumbling block to party unity. After many conferences between the representatives of the Han-

---

[73]   Borg, 376.

kow and Nanking groups, a united Kuomintang Government was established in September 1927, and Chiang left for Japan. The major purpose of his visit was to meet Tanaka and to acquire the latter's support for his northern expedition, since Chiang's failure in this task was partly due to Japan's intervention at Tsinan against the passage north of the Nanking forces.[74]

Having enjoyed his vacation at Beppu and Unzen hot spring resorts in Kyushu, Chiang visited Tanaka at the latter's private residence in Tokyo on November 5. In the conference, the Japanese Prime Minister once again promised his strong support of Chiang. In August, he had already sent Minister Yoshizawa to Nanking. Yoshizawa was the first foreign minister to visit Nanking after its takeover by the Nationalists. His visit was recognized by the Nationalists as a Japanese gesture of moral support. And yet, in the Eastern Conference Tanaka had stressed that he would support Chang Tso-lin, if the latter would endeavor to maintain peace and order in Manchuria. In fact, Tanaka had sent military advisers headed by Colonel Doihara Kenji to Chang to strengthen the Fengtien Army.[75] The Shantung expedition also, though indirectly, thwarted Chiang's northern expedition. Many students of Tanaka's policy, therefore, have held that this apparent contradiction was another example of his haphazard tendencies. However, as far as Tanaka's policy toward Chiang and Chang was concerned, he was always consistent. For Tanaka Manchuria was important, but the spread of communism in China was even more menacing to Japan's *kokutai*. He was convinced that Chiang, because of his prestige and the relatively sound organization of his army, was the only reliable person among the Chinese leaders who could accomplish this difficult task for Japan. Therefore already in May, when Chang Tso-lin was preparing for a direct showdown against the Nationalist forces both at Nanking

---

[74] *Ibid.*, 376–377.
[75] Tanaka Giichi Denki Kankō-kai (ed.), II, 739; Kazama Atsushi, *Kinsei Chūgoku-shi* (A history of modern China; Tokyo, 1937), 251.

and at Wuhan, Tanaka had strongly urged Chang through Consul General Yoshizawa at Mukden to return to Manchuria.

Hence Tanaka had to walk a tightrope between his interest in anti-communism and his interest in Manchuria. He would back Chiang so long as Chiang carried out his anti-communist campaign and confined himself to consolidating his power in the south. This point became clear in the conference between Tanaka and Chiang. The Japanese Prime Minister stated:

> Among the powers, Japan has the closest relations with China. Japan will never interfere with your domestic strife. However, it cannot allow the spread of communism in your country. In this regard, Japan strongly desires that you, being an anti-communist, consolidate your strength in the south. Japan will not spare efforts to give her full support to your task, so long as international considerations permit it and her own interests are not sacrificed.

Tanaka also said:

> Japan has consistently opposed the spread of communism in your country because of her own defense. For this reason, we are expressing our sympathy toward you, Mr. Chiang. If you were a communist sympathizer, we would not trust you. However, I am convinced that your attitude toward communism is the same as mine.[76]

With regard to anti-communism, Tanaka and Chiang were of one mind. Tanaka expressed his warm friendship toward Chiang, and the latter asked the former's "instructions" as his esteemed "*sempai*," senior. However, both leaders carefully avoided discussion of Manchuria or China's total unification.[77] Chiang's real hope was, of course, to unite the whole of China, and after the decline of Russian influence in China his chief enemy was Chang Tso-lin. Tanaka's true interest, on the other hand, was to partition off Manchuria and Mongolia from China proper and not let the Nationalist forces come into Manchuria. Because Tanaka

---

[76] *Shuyō Monjo*, II, 104–105.
[77] The outline of the discussion in the conference, *ibid.*, 102–106.

could not express this idea openly to Chiang, he insistently advised Chiang to devote himself to consolidating his position only in the south, at least for the time being. The conflict of interest between the two was soon to be brought out into the open.

On December 1, soon after Chiang Kai-shek returned to Shanghai from Japan, he married Soong Mayling. While Chiang was still on his Chekiang honeymoon, he was made the Commander-in-Chief of the Nationalist armies at the fourth plenary session of the central executive committee of the Kuomintang. The swift reappointment of Chiang was mainly due to two reasons. During Chiang's retirement, Li Tsung-jen and Pai Ch'ung-hsi of the Kwangsi clique increased their power and clashed with Ho Ying-ch'ing, who was a direct subordinate of Chiang. Furthermore, T'ang Sheng-chih of the Wuhan clique also aimed to take over the military power of the Nationalist armies. As a consequence, while Chiang was in Japan, the internal schisms of the Kuomintang were aggravated, and the committee at the fourth plenary session concluded that Chiang was the only person who could control the various factions and carry out the northern expedition. It was also said that Chiang's marriage to Mayling, a sister of Madame Sun, Madame H. H. Kung, and T. V. Soong, enhanced Chiang's position through the support of the powerful Soongs. Thus, on December 10, the central executive committee of the Kuomintang decided to renew the northern expedition under Generalissimo Chiang's command. Warlords Feng Yü-hsiang and Yen Hsi-shan had already joined the Nationalist armies in the early summer of 1927. With this organization, the northern expedition started afresh in January. Feng and Yen's forces were to advance along the Peking-Hankow and Peking-Suiyuan railways respectively, while Chiang's forces were to follow the Tientsin-Pukow line.[78]

On the other hand in Japan after the new year, because the

[78] Hollington K. Tong, *Chiang Kai-shek: Soldier and Statesman* (Shanghai, 1937), I, 196–200; Kazama, 251–252.

Seiyūkai was a minority party, the first general election was held according to the universal manhood suffrage bill.[79]   For the election campaign, the Seiyūkai established the following policy platform toward China:

> If Japanese subjects' lives and property are endangered, the Empire will warn the government authorities of that country.   If this warning is still not effective, we will naturally have recourse to appropriate means of self-defense, in order to maintain our rights and to protect our nationals' lives and property.   Although this Cabinet has no intention of interfering with the domestic strife and administration of China, we have firmly established it as our policy to protect our nationals' lives and property [on the spot].   Therefore, when the southern revolutionary force took over Hsuchow and were about to reach Tsinan last May, the government dispatched about 4,000 troops to Tsinan and Tsingtao, and by doing so protected our nationals' lives and property in those areas.   Furthermore, the present government, in order to secure mutual economic development of the Japanese and Chinese people, protected our rights and interests based upon treaties and our residents' lives and property throughout China [saying this meant that by taking such a precautionary measure as to send troops to these areas, by demonstrating Japan's determination, Japan could intimidate the Chinese so as not to endanger the said interests of Japan in China].   With regard to Manchuria and Mongolia, because they are the areas which have special relations with our country, under no circumstances do we plan to let the military disorders of China proper spread in these areas.   And by doing so, we are planning to make those areas a peaceful and happy land for both natives and foreigners and to stimulate economic development of these said areas under the principles of the open door and equal opportunity.[80]

The election was held on February 20, 1928.   The Seiyūkai barely defeated its rival party, the Minseitō (formerly the Kenseikai). Two hundred and eighteen members of the Seiyūkai were elected,

---

[79]   At the time of dissolution, the Minseitō — formerly the Kenseikai — had 219 seats, while the Seiyūkai held 190 seats.

[80]   The Seiyūkai's policy platform is printed in Kawai, 650.

while the Minseitō obtained two hundred seventeen seats. Having won the election, Tanaka was determined to execute more decisively his promise of a positive policy both at home and abroad. At the convening of the Fifty-fifth Diet, the Prime Minister reemphasized his determination to break up the ubiquitous sense of deadlock through his positive policy. With regard to his foreign policy, he hinted at his resolution to protect Japanese residents by force, should a danger similar to that of May and June arise in China. As to his domestic policy, he appealed to the need for a "general mobilization of the national spirit" and "absolute loyalty to the Imperial Household and zealous patriotism." He then swore to eradicate all elements which might endanger Japan's *kokutai*.[81] According to this promise, during 1928, Tanaka carried out purges of communists and anarchists, changed the peace-preservation law so as to include the death penalty for those who attempted to threaten the *kokutai*, and strengthened the special police force. He was to carry out the same positive policy toward China.

From an overall point of view, the Tanaka Administration appeared to be successful until early 1928. Tanaka's hope to take the initiative among the powers had been realized in his first Shantung expedition — the other powers soon sent troops following the Japanese example — although it led to a Chinese anti-Japanese campaign. He had formulated the outline of a "positive" policy toward China at the Eastern Conference. He had established friendly relations with Chiang Kai-shek in their mutual co-operation to fight communism in China. His scheme to exploit Manchuria's natural resources for Japan's benefit and to build a stronger

---

[81]   Tanaka's speech is printed in Maezawa (ed.), I, 763–764. In connection with this election campaign, there is a famous anecdote told of Tanaka which may indicate the carefree aspect or *oyabun* temperament of his personality. When the campaign was about to start, Chairman Tanaka invited each of his members to his office one by one, grabbed bundles of hundred-yen notes which had been piled up on his desk, wrapped them in a piece of old newspaper, and gave it out to each without counting the exact amount. See Hosokawa, 162.

military position for Japan in Manchuria seemed to be realized in the Chang-Yamamoto agreement. Thanks to Chang's raid upon the Russian Embassy in Peking, the Comintern's subversive activities had been disclosed in April 1927, which led to the flight of Russian revolutionaries and the Chinese communist leaders to Moscow. As a consequence, Soviet influence had declined in the once powerful revolutionary center in China. The financial crisis had been resolved by Finace Minister Takahashi Korekiyo's drastic methods — the Seiyūkai called it "positive" measures — of issuing a moratorium on all banks. And, finally, Tanaka's "positiveness" apparently had given some satisfaction to the Japanese public, which had been frustrated by Shidehara's "weak-kneed" policy toward China and the sense of deadlock concerning many domestic problems.

However, as Tanaka boldly attempted to pursue his positive policy further in China, Chinese nationalists reacted ever more violently to the Tanaka Administration. Other powers also began to react against Japan's overly aggressive attitude toward China. A remarkable change in international relations was taking place as a result of the shift from Shidehara's leadership to Tanaka's. Toward the end of Shidehara's leadership China felt that Japan was the most friendly nation to her and hoped to mitigate the strong position of the British Government through Japan's good offices. The United States co-operated with Japan in restraining Great Britain and other European powers in their dealings with Chinese nationalism. During the early Tanaka Administration, all the powers in China followed Japan's lead. The British especially welcomed Japan's stronger stand against China. However, there was a certain limit to the powers' willingness to allow Japan to take "autonomous" — to them unco-operative and exclusive — action. During the latter half of the Tanaka Administration, both the United States and Great Britain strongly criticized Japan. As a result, relations between America and Britain became closer, while Japan was more and more isolated by the other powers. At the same time, Chinese antagonism also swung from Great Britain toward Japan.

THE FAILURE of TANAKA'S POSITIVE POLICY

By mid-April 1928, Chiang Kai-shek's advance forces had reached the vicinity of the Tsinan-Tsingtao line. Judging from Tanaka's first Shantung expedition and his repeated statements of "protecting the Japanese nationals on the spot," Chiang was fully aware of the danger to his task of China's unification, should an incident occur between his soldiers and Japanese residents in Shantung. Consequently, he took all possible precautions to avoid such a risk. In February he appointed Huang Fu as Foreign Minister to replace for C. C. Wu, who was anti-Japanese. Huang had studied in Japan and knew the Japanese situation well. Huang Fu, on assuming office, announced that the Nationalists would protect "to their fullest ability the lives and property of foreigners in China in accordance with international law and usage." Chiang himself made several statements guaranteeing the Nationalists' respect for the lives and property of foreigners. He also declared that he would never tolerate anti-foreign outbursts by his troops. In March, Chiang appealed to Japanese correspondents that Japan not interfere with the revolution since, he said, Japan was China's best friend.[82]

Nevertheless, the Tanaka Cabinet, on April 20, once again announced the dispatch of troops to Shantung. This time about 5,500 soldiers were sent from the sixth Army division, which

---

[82]   KMWH XVIII, 3191–3194, 3199–3201; Iriye, 193–194; State Department Archives, Dispatch No. 793, SDA 893,00 P. R. Nanking /2; Dispatches Nos. 5322 and 5440, SDA 893,00 P. R. Shanghai/ 2; William E. Morton, "Sainan Jiken" (Tsinan Incident), *Nihon Gaikō-shi Kenkyū: Nitchū Kankei no Tenkai* (A study of Japanese diplomatic history: the development of Sino-Japanese relations; Tokyo, 1961), 103–104.

resulted in the Tsinan Incident of May 3. The fight soon spread
over the entire city involving both the Japanese and the Chinese
residents there. A truce was not reached until May 5. Commander Fukuda Hikosuke of the sixth division thrust four demands
upon Chiang and ordered him to answer within 12 hours. Those
demands were: an end to all anti-Japanese propaganda; punishment for all Chinese officers who were responsible for the incident;
disarming of all Chinese forces now stationed outside of Tsinan;
and an evacuation of all Chinese troops within 20 Chinese-li of
Tsinan and along the Tsinan-Tsintao line. Chiang Kai-shek
refused to disarm his forces and said that the Japanese officers responsible for the fight had to be punished too. Contending that
Chiang's answer "lacked sincerity," Commander Fukuda resumed
fighting on May 8. As a result, 16 Japanese residents and 230
soldiers were killed, while Chiang's troops suffered 2,000 casualties.
It was ironic that the Japanese troops which had been sent to
"protect" their residents only brought more danger to them.
And yet, on May 8, to support the sixth division in the incident,
Tanaka sent 15,000 more troops to Shantung. On the ninth, further reinforcements for Shantung were announced.[83]

Tanaka's real intention in carrying out his Shantung expedition is clarified in the following documents. His memorandum
(May 16, 1928) on the dispatch of troops read:

> The life of the population in China is characterized by extreme
> unrest and distress owing to the constant disturbances there, which
> have now extended over many years; and foreign residents enjoy
> there no assurance of safety in the pursuit of their occupations. It
> is, accordingly, the earnest desire of Chinese and foreigners alike
> that the disturbances should terminate, as soon as possible, in such
> a manner as may lead to the emergence of a united and peaceful
> China. Especially is this keenly hoped for by Japan, whose interests

---

[83] *Ibid.*, 103–118; Tatsuji Takeuchi discusses on the Tsinan Incident in
Chap. 22;   Concerning the details of military negotiations, see JFMA S 1. 1. 1.
0–4 and PVM 25.

are specially and deeply involved, on account of her being China's nearest neighbour.

The disturbances, however, now threaten to spread to the Peking and Tientsin districts, and it is feared that Manchuria may also be affected. The Japanese Government attaches the utmost importance to the maintenance of peace and order in Manchuria, and is prepared to do all it can in order to prevent the occurrence of any such state of affairs as may disturb that peace and order, or constitute a probable cause of such disturbance. In these circumstances, should the disturbances develop further in the direction of Peking and Tientsin and the situation become so menacing as to threaten the peace and order of Manchuria, the Japanese Government, on its part, may possibly be constrained to take appropriate and effective steps for the maintenance of peace and order in Manchuria.[84]

The second paragraph is especially significant in showing Tanaka's determination to "protect" Manchuria. On May 18, the Memorandum was sent to both Foreign Minister Huang Fu of the Nationalist Government and Generalissimo Chang Tso-lin of the Ankuo-chun in Peking. Following this, 13 companies of Japanese troops were stationed in Tientsin, and in addition the third division was hurriedly sent to the same area via Tsingtao from Japan.[85]

The real purpose of these actions taken by Tanaka became crystal clear in his interview with Hayashi Gonsuke, a diplomatic elder with views similar to Tanaka's, who was sent as Tanaka's emissary to Manchuria in July. The Prime Minister told Hayashi that the sole reason why Japan had supported Chiang in his northern expedition was that by doing so Japan wished to receive a free hand from Chiang in dealing with Manchuria. Tanaka con-

---

[84] The translation of the Memorandum by the Ministry of Foreign Affairs, May 16, 1928, JFMA S 1.6.1.5.31; Tanaka to Yoshizawa, May 16, 1928, *ibid.*; *Shuyō Monjo*, II, 116.

[85] The memo of Tanaka's interview with French, British, and Italian Ambassadors, and the American *chargé d'affaires*, May 17, 1928, JFMA S 1. 6. 1. 5. 31. In this interview, Tanaka told the foreign representatives in Tokyo that if the war expanded beyond Shanhaikwan, Japan would take appropriate measures independently, without consultation with China and the other powers.

tinued, "the Memorandum of May 18 was issued in order to fulfill this purpose, and the dispatch of the third division was to strengthen the Memorandum by real force." In the interview Tanaka and Hayashi agreed that they would endeavor to establish a "buffer zone" and a peaceful and tranquil land in Manchuria against communist infiltration from Russia and China.[86] This intention of Tanaka was further revealed in his instruction (August 9) to Plenipotentiary Uchida Kōsai who left for Paris to sign the Kellogg-Briand Pact:

> We must by all means prevent the communist elements from coming into The Three Eastern Provinces, in order to maintain order there. Once they enter, disorder will occur, our economic foundation will be destroyed, and the entire Three Eastern Provinces will collapse. Furthermore, this will have no little effect upon our rule of Korea and will eventually have an ill effect on our relations with Russia.
>
> Under these circumstances, I am convinced that it is not desirable for Japan to see Chang Hsüeh-liang [Chang Tso-lin had been assassinated on June 4] come to terms with the southern forces.... It is fortunate for Japan that Chang refused to do so. If he continues to take the same policy voluntarily, Japan will help him as much as possible from behind the scenes.[87]

Perhaps it is self-evident from these documents that by sending troops to Shantung Tanaka demonstrated his determination to prevent the Nationalist forces from coming into Manchuria. Moreover, according to the secret section of the Memorandum of May 18 specified, "not to be made public," Tanaka even ordered the Commander-in-Chief of the Kwantung Army together with the Japanese troops stationed in the area of Peking-Tientsin to make sure that any armed forces — regardless whether they were Chiang's or Chang's — would never enter Manchuria, once the war

---

[86]   Memo of the Tanaka-Hayashi conference, July 31, 1928, JFMA PVM 53; Vice-Minister of Foreign Affairs Yoshida to Minister Hayashi in Mukden, July, 31, *ibid.*

[87]   *Shuyō Monjo*, II, 118.

had spread over the Peking-Tientsin region.[88]   Tanaka's real
intention was to separate Manchuria eventually from China proper
and to control it through a local — and if possible a puppet —
government. This idea had been established in his "General
Plan" of 1913, reiterated in his instructions at the end of the Eastern Conference, and further stressed in his instructions to Hayashi
Gonsuke and Uchida Kōsai. His intention to ignore the Chinese
anti-Japanese sentiments and boycotts in order to carry out this
scheme and to pursue his positive policy of "protecting the Japanese
nationals on the spot" had been emphasized in his interview with
reporters at the time of his first Shantung expedition and was reconfirmed in the "Plan of China Policy" of the Tanaka Administration. According to this plan established on July 9, 1928, it was
stated that regardless of Chinese political conditions, Japan ought to
make Manchuria and Mongolia her "special position," that she
ought to set up various facilities so that no country could interfere
in the area, and that for this purpose, even if anti-Japanese feelings
and boycotts among the Chinese were temporarily precipitated,
Japan had to disregard them.[89]

As the real nature of Tanaka's "positive-aggressive" policy
was gradually disclosed, protests to the Tanaka Administration
came from all over. On May 19, the American Secretary of State
said that the United States could not approve Tanaka's Memorandum, for the United States considered Manchuria a part of Chinese
territory. On the same day the British Ambassador in Tokyo
expressed his government's hope that from now on Japan would
obtain British understanding beforehand with regard to any Japanese action toward China. The British Minister in China made
a similar protest to Japan's Minister Yoshizawa.[90] The criticism

[88] The secret section of the Memorandum in the memo of May 16,
1928, JFMA S 1. 6. 1. 5. 31; Tanaka to Yoshizawa, May 16, 1928, *ibid.*
[89] See the unclassified document entitled *Taishi Hōsaku An*, drafted on
July 9, 1928, in the archives of the Japanese Foreign Ministry.
[90] The British Minister in China to Yoshizawa, May 20, 1928, JFMA
S 1. 6. 1. 5. 31; The memo by the Assistant Secretary of State (Johnson)

of *The New York Times* (May 19) was more straightforward than
these official notes from the American and the British Governments.   Under the headline, "Chinese Get Tokio Warning against
War in Manchuria; Protectorate Move Seen," it was stated that
"the note is regarded as a virtual declaration by Japan of her intention to establish a protectorate over Manchuria," that "Tokio
desires impartially to advise China as a whole of her intentions not
to be rooted out of Manchuria, no matter what the cost of Premier
Tanaka's 'positive policy' there and elsewhere China evokes,"
and that "the possibility of Tokio's desiring to establish an Oriental
'Monroe Doctrine' in Northern Asia is gaining credence."[91]   *The
Manchester Guardian* wrote (May 19):

> One might suppose from the terms of the Note that Manchuria
> was a Japanese province instead of being, nominally at least, a Chinese
> dependency.   Japan has certain treaty rights there, largely obtained
> in virtue of the ultimatum which in 1915 accompanied her iniquitous
> "Twenty-one demands," but these do not entitle her to act as a su-
> zerain power even in Manchuria, and still less to intervene in China
> proper, as she threatens, in order to prevent a situation arising which
> might have indirect reactions upon Manchuria.[92]

Several days later, *The Pravda* joined the American and the British
press in the protest against Japan.

As Japan's repeated Shantung expeditions, the Tsinan Incident, and now the Memorandum followed one after another, it
was a matter of course that the Chinese anti-Japanese movements

read: "The Japanese Ambassador called on the Secretary today and stated
that he had received a telegram from his government saying that it was reported
in the Japanese press that the advice which had been addressed by the Japanese
Government to the Nationalist and Northern authorities in China had been
looked upon with suspicion in the United States where it was interpreted as
indicating a desire on the part of the Japanese to declare Manchuria as being a
protectorate of Japan and it was reported that the Secretary of State during
press conferences had indicated by the tone of his replies to questions that he
was somewhat disturbed by this action on the part of Japan."   May 22, 1928,
FRUS II; *The Asahi Shimbun, The Mainichi Shimbun*, and *The Jiji Shimpō*,
May 17-21, 1928.

    [91]   *The New York Times*, May 19, 1928.
    [92]   *The Manchester Guardian*, May 19, 1928.

became more violent and boycotts of Japanese goods spread throughout China.[93] Moreover, now even the overseas Chinese in San Francisco, New York, Panama, and elsewhere started boycotts of Japanese goods. *The Peking Reader* of May 20, under the heading of "Japan's Open Intimidation to China," wrote that Japan intended to establish a protectorate not only in Manchuria but also possibly in the Peking-Tientsin area and that China would urge the other powers to prevent this bold aggression of Japan. The same newspaper, in concert with Chinese public opinion, attacked the Tanaka Administration, saying that it was attempting to make Manchuria a second Korea, Shantung Province a second Manchuria.[94] The government at Peking sent a protesting note to Tokyo on May 25, and the government at Nanking did the same on May 29. Both notes declared that Japan's Shantung expeditions and the Memorandum were "obviously" an intervention in Chinese domestic affairs. The note from the Nationalist Government read:

> The Government of Japan frequently dispatched troops to Shantung, caused the unfortunate Incident, and violated the sovereignty of our nation. It is our infinite regret that the above said actions of Japan have aroused a wave of popular indignation throughout the country. Nevertheless, the Nationalist Government, in its hope to maintain friendly relations between the two countries, has led the Chinese people so as to settle the Incident by diplomatic means. This was all because we believed that such a solution would be beneficial for both countries. And yet, now when our troops have advanced toward the Peking-Tientsin area, your country proposed the Memorandum that Japan would "take appropriate and effective steps for the maintenance of peace and order in Manchuria." We can never approve the Memorandum, which clearly intends to destroy international laws and to intervene in our domestic affairs by force.[95]

---

[93] See the report of anti-Japanese movements and boycotts of Japanese goods, JFMA S 1. 1. 1. 0–13.

[94] Consul Yada in Shanghai to Tanaka, May 23 and 24, JFMA S 1. 6. 1. 5. 31; *The Peking Reader*, May 20, 1928.

[95] Consul Okamoto in Nanking to Tanaka, May 28, 1928, *ibid.*; Yada to Tanaka, May 29 and 30, 1928, *ibid.*

We must recall that it was Tanaka's intention to let Chiang Kai-shek control China proper against the spread of communism and to let Chang Tso-lin govern Manchuria. Therefore, he put strong pressures not only upon Chiang but also upon Chang: for the former not to advance further north-east of Shanhaikwan and enter Manchuria and simultaneously for the latter to evacuate his forces from Peking and swiftly return to his home territory.[96] Already in the early summer of 1927, Tanaka, through Consul-General Yoshida at Mukden and General Yamanashi Hanzō, Tanaka's close friend from the Military Academy, had strongly urged Chang to go back to Manchuria and devote himself to administering the region. It was reported that Chang refused to accept Yamanashi's expostulation and said, "I have advanced as far as to Peking in order to fight communists. My war is Japan's war. And yet, Japan now orders me to return to Manchuria while aiding Chiang Kai-shek who is tainted with 'Red.' I don't understand Japan's real intention in doing this to me."[97] In late autumn of the same year, Yamamoto Jōtarō, who had been appointed President of the South Manchurian Railway by Tanaka, also tried to persuade Chang during the negotiations to permit more railway construction in Manchuria. In the spring of 1928, Kuhara Fusanosuke — another close friend of Tanaka and his financier — was sent to Peking as Tanaka's secret emissary. Kuhara proposed to Chang the establishment of a buffer zone combining a part of Manchuria, northern Korea, and a part of eastern Siberia. The combined area was to be governed by a committee system. Chang, having a morbid fear of communism, adamantly rejected Tanaka's idea of establishing a "committee system," which reminded him of the Soviet regime.[98]

On May 16, 1928, as the direct confrontation between the Southern forces and the Northern forces drew near, the Japanese

[96]   Tanaka to Yoshizawa, May 16, 1928, JFMA S 1. 6. 1. 5. 31.
[97]   Shigemitsu, I, 34.
[98]   Yoshizawa Kenkichi, 86–88.

Prime Minister dispatched the following instructions to Minister Yoshizawa: (1) if the Southern forces would continue attacking the Manchurian troops after the latter had already evacuated themselves from Peking, Japan would check the former in their further advance north of Shanhaikwan; (2) if the two forces would engage in a war in the Peking-Tientsin area and Chang's troops would escape into Manchuria in defeat, and if the Southern forces would attack the routed troops of Chang, Japan would disarm both forces before they could enter Manchuria in order to prevent the war disturbances from spreading over Manchuria; (3) Yoshizawa and all available agents of Japan in China would contact Chang Tso-lin and his aides and would order Chang to return to Manchuria immediately. In the same instruction Tanaka once again emphasized that to maintain peace and order in Manchuria was Japan's "duty" and "responsibility."[99] In a Cabinet meeting, two days later, the Premier said that although Japan had to be neutral to both forces at least for the sake of appearances, the commanders on the spot had to use their discretion to help the Northern forces so that they would not be destroyed completely by the Southern forces.[100]

Career diplomats in the Foreign Ministry like Arita Hachirō, chief of the Asian Bureau, were opposed to Tanaka's policy. Arita reasoned that if Japan should forcefully separate The Three Eastern Provinces from China proper and violate her previous diplomatic statements and the Nine Power Treaty, she would have to suffer verbal attack from the other powers as well as from China. He also knew that these results would be crucial to Japan's future.[101] This was the same view that Shidehara had taken time and again while he had been in office. Even the Navy disagreed with Tanaka's plan. Sakonji Seizō, chief of the Naval Affairs Bureau, said:

The defense of Japan's rights and interests in Manchuria must

---

[99] Tanaka to Yoshizawa, May 16, 1928, JFMA S 1. 6. 1. 5. 31.
[100] The memo of the Cabinet meeting, May 18, 1928, *ibid.*
[101] Arita's memo, July 21, 1928, *ibid.*

be based upon international treaties. Japan should restrain herself from carrying out such a radical policy of expansion as to invite the other powers' criticisms and to bring about a great confusion in international relations.... If the government dares to put military pressures [upon Chiang and Chang] in order to maintain peace and order in Manchuria by using the Emperor's prerogative of supreme command, it will give a third power a good reason for intervention. And if the government recalls the prerogative of supreme command after the third power's intervention, our Empire's international position will be greatly impaired and we shall also lose our prestige in China...., then our China policy will meet with difficulties in every respect. If, on the other hand, the government still carries out its initial plan even against the third power's intervention, it must be prepared to stake its national destiny. The German violation of neutrality upon the pretext of her own defense, invited the war with Great Britain, and it also gave the United States an opportunity to join the war against Germany. Hence, Germany lost world sympathy, and this was a cause for the fall of the German Empire. Japan must not repeat the mistake of Germany. In view of the international situation, domestic affairs, and of our war preparation, we must be most cautious when we use our forces. I must warn the government strongly that it should never act rashly.[102]

Tanaka overruled all of these objections and carried out his initial plan.

In spite of Chang's defiance of Tanaka's repeated recommendations to return to Manchuria, Chang was still Tanaka's favorite. Tanaka believed that Japanese interests in Manchuria could be best preserved under the rule of Chang, who had expressed his willingness to pay back *on*, his debts, to Tanaka. He also hoped to realize the advantageous Chang-Yamamoto agreement under Chang's leadership in the region. Consequently, according to Tanaka's instruction, Yoshizawa met Chang on May 19 and strongly urged him to withdraw beyond the Great Wall immediately.

---

[102] A warning note to Arita, chief of the Asian Bureau, written by Sakonji, chief of the Naval Affairs Bureau, May 19, 1928, *ibid.*

Otherwise, Yoshizawa threatened Chang, Japan would disarm his forces as they escaped into Manchuria. Chang, shivering in wrath, replied that he could never accept Japan's recommendation even if he had to stake his own life to do so, should his troops evacuate themselves from Peking and should Feng Yü-hsiang happen to control the capital. Chang pleaded with Yoshizawa to let him fight at least one battle with the Southern forces, for he had as many as 600,000 troops under his command. Yoshizawa spent four hours, but the negotiation ended in vain.[103]   Major General Tatekawa Yoshitsugu, the military attaché at Peking, also ordered Chang Hsüeh-liang to persuade his father to return to his own home territory. Doihara, military adviser to the Ankuo-chun, and Consul-General Hayashi at Mukden did the same to Chang through various channels. War Minister Shirakawa at the same time instructed the commander of the Kwantung Army to check the passage of the Northern as well as the Southern forces beyond the Great Wall by all means.[104]

Finally, at the military council of the Ankuo-chun all generals except Chang Tso-lin agreed that there was no choice left for them but to return to Manchuria.[105]   In the meantime, Chiang Kai-shek's forces, having changed course to avoid Tsinan where the Japanese troops were now stationed, pushed forward directly to Peking. The tide of war was obviously turning against Chang Tso-lin. Generalissimo Chang, unable to find any recourse, left Peking at dawn on June 3. *The Asahi Shimbun* dramatically reported the scene of Chang's departure:

> The moon was shedding her weird rays upon the city wrapped with fresh verdure. Standing at the main gate of the residence

[103]   Yoshizawa to Tanaka, May 19, 1928, *ibid.*; Yoshizawa to Tanaka, May 20, 1928, *ibid.*; Yoshizawa to Tanaka, May 21, 1928, *ibid.*

[104]   Consul-General Hayashi to Tanaka, May 19, 1928, *ibid.*; Yoshizawa to Tanaka, May 19, 1928, *ibid.*; Yoshizawa to Tanaka, May 21, *ibid.*

[105]   The information acquired by Doihara through Yang Yü-t'ing, an influential leader of Chang's Army. See also the memo of "The Outline of Conference between Military Attaché Tatekawa and Chang Hsüeh-liang and Yang Yü-t'ing," May 22, 1928, *ibid.*

where the Generalissimo had lived for the past two years, Mr. Chang
wistfully turned his head to gaze at the deep forest. In his eyes,
unusual for this man, tears gleamed.... At 1:15 A. M., leaving
only the echo of a steam whistle behind, his train left the station
silently.[106]

Early the next morning, Chang died when his train was blown up.
Later it was proved that Colonel Kōmoto Daisaku of the Kwantung
Army planned the act and that the Korean engineer corps set the
bomb by his order. However, this was not an "official" decision
made by the Kwantung Army, nor by Prime Minister Tanaka
Giichi. It was reported that Tanaka was shocked by the news;
his next letter to Yamamoto dated June 6 indicates that he was
innocent of the plot.

> Having been informed of Chang Tso-lin's accident, I am ex-
> tremely anxious as to whether our previous plan which we have dis-
> cussed might be brought to a standstill. However, Chang is a child
> of fortune. Perhaps he will recover this time too. And we must
> hope so in order to carry out our previous plan successfully. Now I
> only pray for this. Although I am sure you know this, I believe it
> is important for you to take scrupulous care to express our public
> sympathy for his accident.[107]

Yamamoto Jōtarō, a robust man, was also disheartened and remarked, "What I have planned and hoped for the future since I came
to Manchuria has today ended in vain. The Tanaka Cabinet will
also soon crumble."[108]

A question remains: why did Kōmoto carry out such a bold
scheme? For the answer, we must probe the environment in
which he lived. Both the Army at home and the Kwantung Army
had been very much concerned with the future status of Manchuria
because of Chiang's northern expedition. Japanese public concern
with Manchuria and Mongolia was also deepening rapidly. Prime

---

[106] *The Asahi Shimbun*, June 4, 1928.
[107] Nakamura Kikuo (September, 1958), 40.
[108] Yamamoto Jōtarō-ō Denki Hensan-kai (ed.), 617.

Minister Tanaka, too, said that Japan had to defend Manchuria by all means, and he further argued that Manchuria had to be made into Japan's "special region," for it was her "life-line." Influenced by these opinions, Kōmoto became extremely worried about Manchuria. In March 1926, he was transferred to the Kwantung Army commanded by General Shirakawa Yoshinori, now War Minister of the Tanaka Cabinet. Having been affected by Shirakawa, Kōmoto's concern with Manchuria further increased. In Manchuria he saw an increase of anti-Japanese feeling among the natives. Then he attended the Eastern Conference. He understood that both Mutō Nobuyoshi, the new commander of the Kwantung Army, and Prime Minister Tanaka in the Conference were in favor of a military solution of pending difficulties in Manchuria, especially the railway problem. In the Conference, Mutō asked Tanaka whether the latter was prepared to fight a world war against the United States and Great Britain in order to carry out the great plan reached in the Conference. Tanaka emphatically answered in the affirmative. Kōmoto, irritated by Chang's refusal to follow Japan's repeated "recommendations," came to the hasty conclusion that the best and quickest solution would be to kill Chang and let Japan herself set up a puppet regime.[109]

The specific means which Kōmoto took differed from those of Tanaka or Shirakawa. Kōmoto was both more extreme and less cautious than his superiors. However, their ideas were basically the same. Furthermore, a violent atmosphere conducive to Kōmoto's action was created by people like Tanaka, Shirakawa, and Mutō. This was a case similar to the notorious "Tanaka Memorandum." Tanaka was not responsible for either, but

---

[109] Concerning the assassination of Chang Tso-lin and Kōmoto Daisaku, see Nakamura Kikuo II, 35–40; Usui Katsumi, "Chō Sakurin Bakushi no Shinsō" (Truth of the assassination of Chang Tso-lin), in *Himeraretaru Shōwa-shi* (Secret stories of Shōwa history, a special issue of *Chisei*: Tokyo, 1956), 26–28; Kōmoto Daisaku, "Watakushi ga Chō Sakurin o Koroshita" (I killed Chang Tso-lin), *Bungei Shunjū* (December 1954), 194–201; Baba Akira, "Tanaka Gaikō to Chō Sakurin Bakusatsu Jiken" (Tanaka diplomacy and the assassination of Chang Tso-lin), *Rekishi Kyōiku* (February 1960), 41–48.

he was responsible for having created a milieu in which they were likely. This milieu also helps to explain the nature of the "defiance of authority" which was often repeated by the subordinate officers. The atmosphere which was congenial to such actions was created by their leaders. The "rebels" actually did not feel that they were "defying" authorities. On the contrary, they felt that eventually their deeds would be sanctioned by their superiors. This is also the reason the *fait accompli* became a common practice in Japanese decision-making.[110]

Four days after the assassination of Chang Tso-lin, the advance force of the Nationalist Army entered Peking, and by the middle of 1928 the Nationalist unification of China, except for The Three Eastern Provinces, was accomplished. In the region of The Three Eastern Provinces, on the other hand, a new leadership was established under Chang Hsüeh-liang, the son of Chang Tso-lin, who was appointed Commander-in-Chief of The Three Eastern Provinces on July 3. The Young Marshal had three immediate problems to face: the Nationalist Government; Japan; and the great confusion created by the death of the powerful leader, especially the increasing anti-Japanese movements and bandit activities which often took place in co-ordination.[111] At the outset, Chang's policy

---

[110] See Maruyama Masao's interesting comments on the practice of *fait accompli* by the Japanese leaders of World War II, *Thought and Behavior of Modern Japanese Politics*, Chap. 3.

[111] Even in The Three Eastern Provinces patriotic movements were rising. On September 4, 1927, for example, the Tanaka-Yamamoto plan to construct more railways in the region by force incited native anger, and about 20,000 people gathered at Mukden and chanted, "Down with the Tanaka Cabinet." As Chang Hsüeh-liang was coerced to yield to Japan's pressure, the patriotic anti-Japanese movements by the natives simultaneously became anti-Chang movements. On August 4, 1928, for instance, the All Student League of Kirin Province criticized the Tanaka Administration and at the same time attacked Chang Hsüeh-liang as Japan's puppet. The League held a public convention and declared that it would fight both the Japanese Government and the government at Mukden headed by Chang Hsüeh-liang. As we shall see, when this tendency — the combination of the anti-Japan and anti-Chang movements — increased, Chang realized the danger of his conciliatory policy toward Japan. Hence, from about the end of July, Chang began to turn against Japan, and by doing so he attempted to shift the anti-Chang movements among the populace to a movement which would support Chang who now showed clearly his anti-Japanese posture. Consul-General Suzuki to Tanaka, August 4, 1928, JFMA PVM 53.

was to play off the Nationalist Government against Japan. He relied upon the Kwantung Army to suppress bandit and other activities against his regime, but he tried at the same time to use the patriotic anti-Japanese movements in Manchuria as his own bargaining tool against Japan's pressure.[112] The Tanaka Administration in its hope to pursue the same initial scheme decided to support Chang by keeping the dispatched troops in Shantung even after the need of "protecting the nationals on the spot" ended, and by concentrating more troops of the Kwantung Army in the Mukden area, in order to back up the newly established regime against various opposition forces.

Let us now follow up more closely the development of the Manchurian situation after the assassination of Chang Tso-lin, an event which eventually led to a complete failure of Tanaka's widely advertised "Manchuria-First" policy. On June 25, 1928, Prime Minister Tanaka "advised" Chang Hsüeh-liang through Consul-General Hayashi Syūjirō at Mukden that Chang should not take such an hasty attitude as to compromise with the Nationalist Government, but should maintain the status quo by defending Manchuria against external enemies and by promoting internal security (*hokyō anmin*).[113] Since then the Tanaka Administration lost no opportunity to put constant pressures upon Chang through various diplomatic and military channels like Doihara Kenji, the Military advise to the Ankuo-chun, and the military attaché, Tatekawa Yoshitsugu. Tatekawa even asserted that, if necessary, Japan would "force" the Manchurian Government not to submit to the Southern regime.[114]

Finally on July 18, because Chang was still wavering, Tanaka

---

[112] The report of political situation in The Three Eastern Provinces from June to September, 1928, JFMA PVM 52; Consul-General Hayashi at Mukden to Tanaka, June 26, 1928, *ibid.*; Consul-General Hayashi to Tanaka, July 17, 1928, JFMA PVM 52.

[113] Tanaka to Consul-General Hayashi, June 25, 1928, *ibid.*

[114] Tatekawa to Hata, June 25 and July 6, 1928, JMA T 864, T 845; The record of the General Staff dated September 6, 1928, JFMA PVM 52.

instructed Consul-General Hayashi to deliver an official note demanding Chang to adhere to his father's principle of *hokyō anmin* and not to adopt the Three People's Principles of the Nationalist Government. In the same instruction Tanaka clearly indicated that "the entrance of the Southern influence — here Tanaka meant not just actual troops but also more general political influence — into Manchuria was unacceptable" to Japan, and that the Young Marshal "had to be so determined as to declare even martial law so as to prevent its happening in Manchuria." Tanaka at the same time conveyed his intention that:

> If the Southern forces will advance further toward Manchuria..., Japan, according to the policy established in the Memorandum of May 18, will definitely defend the peace and order of The Three Eastern Provinces against them. If Chang makes up his mind, he can, with Japan's military support, surely reject the invasion of the Southern influence into Manchuria.[115]

At the end of the instruction Tanaka added that because Japan's attitude toward Chang Hsüeh-liang had been "too friendly," Chang tended to "think light of Japan" and thought that he could handle Japan easily. Consequently, Tanaka said, Japan might have to crack down upon Chang, depending on how he would reply to this demand.[116]

As Japan's pressure upon Chang increased, to that extent Chang approached the Nationalist Government more closely. In late June, Chang still expressed his hope to make The Three Eastern Provinces an autonomous region independent of China proper by making an alliance with Japan. Toward late July, however, there appeared clear indications that the Young Marshal began to take sides with his father's enemy. On July 20, for instance, Chang confessed to the Nationalist representatives for

---

[115] Tanaka to Consul-General Hayashi, July 18, 1928, JFMA PVM 53; The record of the General Staff dated September 6, 1928, JFMA PVM 52.

[116] Tanaka to Consul-General Hayashi, July 18, 1928, JFMA PVM 53; The Commander-in-Chief of the Kwantung Army also criticized Chang Hsüeh-liang's "weak-kneed" policy toward the Nationalists, July 21, 1928, *ibid.*

peace negotiation with the Manchurian Government that although he, trusting Chiang Kai-shek, was willing to make terms with the Nationalist Government, he then did not know how to evade Japan's direct threat. A week later, the Young Marshal even sent a secret telegram to Generalissimo Chiang requesting the latter's mediation to curb Japan's pressure. In the telegram he addressed to Chiang as "his best and sole friend" and begged Chiang's eternal guidance.[117]   Various factors other than Japan's threat also operated to push Chang toward Chiang: the majority of the executive committee at Mukden led by Yang Yü-t'ing, Chang's rival ever since his father's death, began to lean toward the Nationalist Government, and therefore if Chang continued his attempt to make a deal with Japan, he would have become alienated from the rest of his government; the populace in Manchuria was demanding that he make peace with the Nationalists, and therefore by doing so Chang could switch various anti-government movements to an exclusive anti-Japanese movement; the Nationalist military superiority over the Manchurian forces was obvious.[118]

Having noticed Chang Hsüeh-liang's changing attitude, Minister Yoshizawa and Consul-General Hayashi frequently warned Tanaka of the danger that even seemingly possible agreements with Chang might become impossible in the end, if Tanaka ventured to execute "too tough" a policy toward Chang. They suggested to Tanaka that some kind of compromise with Chang might be necessary for example, to allow him to raise the Nationalist

---

[117] Consul-General Hayashi to Tanaka, June 26 and July 16, 1928, JFMA PVM 52; The record of the General Staff dated September 6, 1928, JFMA PVM 52.

[118] The report of the political situation in The Three Eastern Provinces from June to September, 1928, JFMA PVM 52; Consul-General Hayashi to Tanaka, July 4, 16, and 18, *ibid.*; Some members of the executive committee charged that Tanaka's demand of July 18 was a clear intervention in Manchurian domestic affairs; an information obtained through the Japanese intelligence service which was communicated to Tanaka by Consul-General Hayashi, July 20, 1928, JFMA PVM 53.

flag. They worried that Tanaka's naked intervention to separate Manchuria from China proper would cause more violent anti-Japanese movements and boycotts of Japanese goods both in China and Manchuria, would invite bitter criticisms from the other powers, and would bring about great injury to Japan's economic interests and international position.[119]   Tanaka did not seem to be set back by these warnings. On the contrary, he became even "tougher." He was more determined to prevent the Man-churian Government from coming to terms with the Nationalists. He decided to send Baron Hayashi Gonsuke as his secret emissary to Chang. On the surface, Baron Hayashi as Japan's diplomatic elder was to attend Chang Tso-lin's funeral, which was to be held from August 4 to 7. But the real purpose of his visit was, as Yoshida Shigeru — now Vice-Foreign Minister of the Tanaka Administration — communicated with Consul-General Hayashi at Mukden, "to convey Tanaka's hidden intention — what he would do if Chang would not obey his order — to Chang." Yoshida informed Hayashi that the Prime Minister and the Baron had had a long intimate talk on the Manchurian problem.[120]   Fur-thermore, on August 7, Tanaka established new "Measures to Counter the Sudden Change of the Manchurian Situation."

Although we have already seen a part of the Tanaka-Hayashi conference, in his briefing of Baron Hayashi, Tanaka said:

> There is no reason why we should sacrifice Manchuria in order to promote China's unification. We have co-operated with China for her unification for many years, simply because we hoped that Japan could direct Manchuria at her own will, in return. Some people say that the adoption of the Three People's Principles and the Nationalist flag means nothing. But I am convinced that "a fallen leaf will suggest the coming of autumn" and that once we start to negotiate with the Nanking Governemnt about the management

---

[119] Yoshizawa to Tanaka, July 17, 1928 and Hayashi to Tanaka, July 17, 1928, *ibid*.; Yoshizawa to Tanaka, July 26, 1928, *ibid*.

[120] Yoshida to Consul-General Hayashi at Mukden, July 31, 1928, *ibid*.

of Manchuria, the problem will be internationalized and [the scheme] would never work. Therefore, we must avoid such a thing by all means.[121]

Tanaka also stressed to Hayashi that "Japan dares to sacrifice [certain other national interests] in order to maintain security in Manchuria" and that "she is willing to help Chang in various needs such as financial readjustment and military buildup in order for Chang to defend Manchuria against external enemies and to promote internal security."[122] Tanaka's new "Measures to Counter the Sudden Change of the Manchurian Situation" were: (1) Japan would warn Chang once again not to compromise with the Nationalists and if he did, Japan would definitely take appropriate means to defend Manchuria and would cut off all friendly relations which she had maintained with Chang; (2) If Chang would take Japan's warning and decide to co-operate with Japan, then as the next step Japan would demand that Chang execute various pending agreements with Japan, and at the same time Japan would promise to help Chang as much as possible; (3) If otherwise, and if Japan's rights and interests in Manchuria were violated by Chang in co-operation with the Nationalists, Japan would, of course, use force in self-defense; (4) If (3) was the case, Japan would also destroy Chang and his group, would maneuver to help the establishment of a new friendly regime behind the scenes, and would attempt to establish facilities in Manchuria in active co-operation with that government.[123]

Along these lines Baron Hayashi, a powerful figure and former samurai, met Chang Hsüeh-liang not once but three times, pressing him hard to yield to Tanaka's demands. Consul-General Hayashi simultaneously negotiated with Chang on August 8 and 9.

---

[121] The memo of the Tanaka-Hayashi conference, July 31, 1928, JFMA PVM 53.

[122] *Ibid.*

[123] Tanaka's "Measures to Counter the Sudden Change of the Manchurian Situation," addressed to the General Staff, August 7, 1928, JFMA PVM 52; Hayashi to Tanaka, August 8 and 9, 1928, *ibid.*

For Chang there seemed no way out but to submit to Japan's virtual military threat. He finally decided to postpone the peace negotiations with the Nationalist Government for three months. Upon receipt of this news on August 13, Tanaka sent a telegram to Consul-General Hayashi congratulating him and other agents for their efforts and said, "I, the Prime Minister, am greatly satisfied with the news." Tanaka reemphasized in the same telegram that he would "never" alter the already established policy toward Manchuria under any circumstances.[124]

Since the Tsinan Incident, Chiang Kai-shek's conciliatory attitude toward Japan changed abruptly. Replacing the pro-Japanese Huang Fu, Chiang appointed Wang Chêng-t'ing, a Yale graduate and pro-American, anti-Japanese diplomat, as Foreign Minister. Having at least nominally achieved national unification, Chiang now hoped to accomplish two more things before he could finally incorporate The Three Eastern Provinces, namely the abrogation of the unequal treaties and the recognition of his regime by the world powers. Wang depended on American good will to solve these problems, while taking a strong policy toward Japan. On May 28, he presented Tanaka's Memorandum of May 18 to the League of Nations as a violation of Chinese sovereignty. In early June, he also refused to negotiate with the Kwantung Army concerning the solution of the Tsinan Incident. As a solution to the Tsinan Incident, Tanaka had made four demands upon Chiang Kai-shek, namely Chiang's apology, reparations, punishment of responsible officers, and a guarantee of future security for the lives and property of the Japanese residents in Shantung. Foreign Minister Wang was unyielding, and the negotiations became prolonged. For Tanaka, General Matsui Iwane, Tanaka's envoy for the negotiation, as well as for Chiang, the most important issue was Tanaka's demands for Chiang's "apology," for the problem was related to "face."

---

[124]   *Ibid.*; Tanaka to Consul-General Hayashi, August 13, 1928, *ibid.*

Tanaka also ordered Minister Yoshizawa to give Chiang a firm warning:

> If further danger is offered to the lives and property of the Japanese residents due to insufficient control of their own people by the Chinese authorities, the Japanese Government will no longer admit the sincerity of the Chinese authorities. Accordingly, it will have to take necessary and proper means for the protection of its residents on its own accord. The Chinese authorities should be prepared to understand that such an action taken by Japan may have extremely serious consequences.[125]

While the Tsinan Incident was still unsettled, Sino-Japanese relations became even more tense with regard to the abrogation of China's unequal treaties. By the end of 1928, following the American initiative, Great Britain, France, Italy, and Germany all accepted China's tariff autonomy. Japan alone failed to do so. On July 19 when the Nationalists communicated to Japan the abrogation of the Sino-Japanese commercial treaties of 1896 and 1903, Tanaka was reported to have remarked that the Chinese demands were "*gongo dōdan*," (outrageous or preposterous). This negotiation remained unsettled until Shidehara replaced Tanaka in Japan's diplomatic leadership (July 2, 1929).[126]

For Chiang Kai-shek and the Nationalists the bitterest issue with the Tanaka Administration was still the problem of incorporating The Three Eastern Provinces. Because Chang Hsüeh-liang was forced to give up the peace negotiations with the Nationalists due to Tanaka's threat, the Nationalist Government sent emissaries to Mukden as sight-seeing tour groups on several occasions. Perhaps, the most important mission among them was the group headed by Yeh Ch'i which visited Chang in the autumn of 1928. On two occasions Yeh Ch'i made public statements unhesitatingly denouncing Japan:

---

[125] Consul-General Okamoto to Tanaka, May 28, 1928, JFMA S 1.6.1.5.31; the memo of the Cabinet meeting of July 10, JFMA PVM 25; Tanaka to Yoshizawa, July 13, *ibid.*; *Shuyō Monjo*, II, 42.

[126] Usui, "Tanaka Gaikō ni tsuite no Oboegaki," 29–32; Morton, 109.

China's endless civil wars are due to Japanese instigation. Since Chang Tso-lin's death, Japanese machinations have become increasingly knavish and unscrupulous. From now on we must endeavor to defend ourselves [in co-operation] against Japan, watching carefully every move of Japan.... In this regard, the South and The Three Eastern Provinces have the same trouble (or enemy). Japan plots to monopolize The Three Eastern Provinces by establishing various political and military facilities there. Seriously reflecting upon themselves, both the Southern and the Northern authorities must take counter measures against Japan's ambitious and aggressive policy. The reason why Japan wants The Three Eastern Provinces is because she knows that she can hardly match the United States in a future war between the two countries, and therefore she plans to utilize the resources of the region. Thus, our military and political authorities must be awakened, must end civil wars, and must save ourselves from the ravages of national destruction [by the Japanese intrigue].[127]

Chang Hsüeh-liang gave Yeh Ch'i and his group unusually warm receptions. He reported to Yeh his extreme difficulties in dealing with Japan, and requested him to become the official representative of the Nationalist Government at Mukden.[128]

The greatest mistake of all for the Tanaka Administration was that it accelerated Chinese nationalism and intensified anti-Japanese feeling by its aggressive policy and naked intervention. Contrary to Tanaka's expectations, based upon his old image of the Chinese, once they were enlightened the Chinese people could never be subdued by force. As Tanaka increased Japanese military pressure upon the "scornful" Chinese, their national consciousness and patriotism increased all the more. This was a grave miscalculation on Tanaka's part — perhaps the crucial element in his failure. In July 1928, as the truth of Chang Tso-lin's assassination became gradually known, the anti-Japanese movement in China burst into flame. A great convention of anti-

---

[127]   Consul-General Hayashi to Tanaka, October 31, 1928, JFMA PVM 52.
[128]   *Ibid.*

Japanese groups was held in Shanghai, and its spirit soon spread all over the country, resulting in the organization of the National Anti-Japanese League. In January 1929, anti-Japanese strikes spread in Hankow.[129] Backed by these powerful anti-Japanese movements of the populace, Foreign Minister C. T. Wang also staged a strong anti-Japanese campaign. He encouraged the boycott of Japanese goods. He ordered commercial concerns to register all goods imported from Japan and banned the sale of Japanese goods.

Both government-sponsored and voluntary boycotts menaced the Japanese economy. According to the "Report of the Commission of Enquiry of the League of Nations," Japanese exports to China in 1925 — during Shidehara's leadership — were valued at 468.5 million yen. The amount declined to 334.2 million yen in 1927 and 373.1 million yen in 1928. This meant that Japan lost more than 100 million yen worth of China trade. During the same period, Japan's share in Chinese trade declined from 27.91 per cent in 1925 to 25.74 per cent in 1927 and 24.89 per cent in 1928. In addition to these losses, Japan also had to suffer overseas Chinese boycotts in South East Asia, the United States, and Latin America.[130]

Tanaka's long-term scheme to separate The Three Eastern Provinces from China proper and to turn the region into Japan's "place in the sun" also failed in the end. As soon as the three-month period of postponement was over, Chang Hsüeh-liang resumed negotiations with the Nationalists. By this time because Chang had learned that his father was actually killed by Japanese soldiers, his determination to co-operate with Chiang Kai-shek against Japan was firm. At the same time Tanaka's forceful

---

[129] In late July, 1928, Shanghai newspapers publicized that Chang Tso-lin was actually killed by the Japanese soldiers. This news more excited the Chinese patriots who had already been furious at the Tanaka Administration. Shimizu *chargé d'affaires* to Tanaka, August 21, JFMA PVM 53; Consul-General Okamoto at Nanking to Tanaka, September 7, 1928, JFMA PVM 52; *Shuyō Monjo*, II, 43, 46.

[130] Uchida Naosaku, 575–604.

intervention in the attempt of *rapprochement* between Chang and Chiang ended up precipitating mutual concessions. Hence, in spite of — or rather because of — Tanaka's continuing pressure, the Young Marshal decided to bring The Three Eastern Provinces into political union with the rest of China under the Nationalist regime. This was accomplished by the end of December 1928.[131]

Tanaka not only antagonized the Nationalist Government, the Chinese patriots, and failed in his well-advertised "Manchuria-First" policy, but he also isolated Japan from the other powers in China. While American popularity was rapidly ascending among the Chinese people, the British Government also made efforts to shift Chinese anti-British feeling to anti-Japanese by adopting a co-operative policy with the Nationalists. Japan being isolated, Tanaka desperately sought British collaboration with Japan on such problems as recognition of the Nanking Government and tariff. Tanaka entrusted this task to Uchida Kōsai, the plenipotentiary to Paris for signing the Kellogg-Briand Pact. In the autumn of 1928, however, the Uchida mission proved to be a complete failure. The British flatly refused to co-operate with Japan. Against the Tanaka Administration's maneuver to delay the recognition of the Nationalist Government and China's tariff autonomy, the British, following the United States, preceded Japan in opening official diplomatic relations with the Nationalist Government (December 20, 1928). It was ironic that Tanaka, who had

---

[131] The terms reached in the final settlement between the Southern and the Northern regimes were: (1) The Three Eastern Provinces were to be placed nominally under Nationalist sovereignty; the political system of the region was to be modeled after that of the Kuomintang; and it would become a branch of the Nationalist Government; (2) However, in reality the region was to enjoy virtual autonomy, all members of the executive committee of The Three Eastern Provinces were to be elected from among the natives headed by Chang Tso-hsiang in Kirin, Wan Fu-lin in Heilungkiang, and by Chang Hsüeh-liang in Fengtien Province; (3) Jehol was to be governed by a committee composed of three members from the Fengtien group, two from Jehol, and three from the Nationalist Government, and the committee was to be headed by a representative of the Fengtien group. The above was the information obtained by Consul-General Hayashi at Mukden. Hayashi to Tanaka, December 8, 1928, JFMA PVM 52.

stressed an "autonomous diplomacy," in the end was obliged to plead for British "co-operation."[132]

Criticism against the Tanaka Administration was also sharply increasing in Japan. Business circles, in alliance with students and leftists, strongly attacked the Tanaka Administration, although for different reasons: the former because of the rapid decline of Japan's China trade and the latter because of their principle of anti-imperialism. On February 17, 1929, several thousand people gathered at Aoyama Hall in Tokyo and declared:

> The unification of our neighboring country, China, will bring a good opportunity for a fundamental alliance of two great nations, Japan and China. Nevertheless, what the Tanaka Administration is doing is harmful not only to our own national interests but also to the general welfare of East Asia.... For the sake of "popular diplomacy" we are determined to destroy the Cabinet.[133]

The Minseitō, the opposition party to Tanaka's Seiyūkai, bitterly criticized Tanaka's failure in his policy toward China and Manchuria. Shidehara Kijūrō in the House of Peers also attacked the Prime Minister. Shidehara was a quiet person and never was an orator. At this time, however, he made a long impressive speech which lasted one hour and a half. He reemphasized Japan's primary economic interest in China, Manchuria as a part of China, internationalism and a diplomacy seeking practical interests rather

---

[132]   From about the end of July, 1928, as Japan was more and more isolated, she desperately began to seek the other powers', especially Britain's, "co-operation." Japan requested the British Government to pursue a "tough" policy in co-operation with Japan toward the Nationalist Government which, having succeeded in the northern expedition, became, as Tanaka put it, all the more "arrogant" and "audacious" (*bōjaku mujin*). The British, however, having observed Japan's aggressive policy in her frequent Shantung expeditions, the Tsinan Incident, and in her naked intervention to separate The Three Eastern Provinces from China proper, kept declining Japan's repeated pleas. Britain, on the contrary, rather approached the United States and took measures to aid the Nationalist Government against Japanese pressure. See this process of Japan's increasing isolation and her desperate efforts to seek for the other powers' co-operation in *Shōwa Sannen-matsu ni okeru Taishi Rekkoku Kyōchō Mondai no Ikken* (Problems relating to the co-operation of the powers' concerning their China policies toward the end of 1928), JFMA PVM 29.

[133]   Usui Katsumi, "Tanaka Gaikō ni tsuite no Oboegaki," 33.

than "face saving." To give some excerpts from his long speech:

A "strong" or "positive" policy might please some people, but most people will not feel comfortable in listening to this kind of assertion. Suppose other powers should assert this against Japan, what do we feel? The government should reflect upon itself....

If a "strong" policy means to protect our interests by coercive power and to go hell-bent for this, are you confident that you can deal with such complicated international relations as those of today by such a simple method? Did you ever bring any actual benefit to our Sino-Japanese relations by your "positive" policy? Isn't it true that because you raised your fist, the other party became more aggressive in response? Was the relationship betweem Japan and China bettered by your Shantung expeditions? To be "positive" in a real sense means to progress from the status quo.... The political purpose [of Japan's China policy] must be economic advancement. Nevertheless, did the government make any effort to promote Japan's economic development in the policy toward China?...

Secondly, I would like to ask one question about our country's "position" in The Three Eastern Provinces. The other day, Prime Minister Tanaka stated in this Diet that he would get rid of those who would disturb peace in those regions, in order to make Manchuria a peaceful and happy land for the natives and foreigners. Do you mean by saying this, for example, that the Japanese Government even intends to suppress bandits when they threaten people other than the Japanese? Do you mean that you intend to use force in Chinese territory in order to protect even those interests which are not our own? Prime Minister Tanaka's statement causes international suspicion that Japan will violate other countries' territorial sovereignty. I would like to urge the Prime Minister to withdraw his statement immediately....

Thirdly [a criticism of Tanaka's attempt to prevent the *rapprochement* between the South and the North in China].

Fourthly, I would like to ask the Prime Minister about the Shantung expeditions. Casualties of Japanese residents in Shantung are still frequently taking place even after the dispatch of troops. Does the government think the "protection of Japanese residents on the spot" has really been successful? Wasn't there any other method to protect them without sending troops? If the government thought that the Nationalist Government was not trustworthy, why didn't it evacuate Japanese residents from Tsinan? When we compare the Nanking Incident and the Tsinan Incident, in the former case not a single person was either killed or humiliated because troops were not sent from Japan. Whereas in the latter, to which troops were sent, several tens of Japanese residents were killed. Isn't this an irony?[134]

Having pointed out these mistakes, Shidehara concluded by asking, "Isn't the government ashamed of its present China policy in the light of our country's position and honor in international circles?"

From early 1929 on, various attempts to overthrow the Tanaka Cabinet were gradually concentrated into the attack upon its mismanagement of the Chang Tso-lin Incident. Nakano Seigō of the Minseitō, for example, in the Fifty-sixth Diet (December 1928-March 1929), pressed the Prime Minister hard on his responsibility for Chang Tso-lin's assassination. Many other representatives, such as Nagai Ryūtarō and Kudō Tetsuo, also attacked the Tanaka Administration on the same issue.[135] The Prime Minister, the War Minister, Army leaders, and some members of the Seiyūkai were of the opinion that the government should not take any strong measures against Kōmoto Daisaku and others who had committed the crime of Chang's assassination, in order not to disclose the truth to the world and thereby injure the prestige of the Army and the nation. Finally, Genrō Saionji, who had usually restrained himself from intervention in the decision-making of the government so as to promote party government, reprimanded Tanaka for his indecisiveness in not punishing the assassins. The Genrō demanded that if Japanese soldiers were the assassins they had to be punished immediately, "in order to maintain Japan's international prestige."

---

134   Maezawa Hiroaki (ed.), II, 44–46.
135   *The Asahi Shimbun* and *The Mainichi Shimbun*, January 25–30, 1929.

Saionji also recommended that Tanaka report swiftly on the truth of the incident, at least to the Emperor.

Tanaka, at first, vaguely reported to the Emperor, "Some suspicious points about the Army have come to light. Therefore, I have ordered the War Minister to investigate the matter." Having heard of this report, Saionji was very angry. He said, "What the Cabinet members say is contrary to reason. They say, 'If it has been proven that the assassins are Japanese soldiers, it will be detrimental to Japan's international trust and the Imperial prestige.' But that is entirely wrong. Only when they punish them justly according to strict military discipline can Japan maintain her international trust and the Imperial prestige!" On December 24, in a meeting with the Emperor, Tanaka did express his intention "to punish those assassins, if they were indeed Japanese soldiers." Nevertheless, on June 26, 1929, pressed by the Army, Tanaka changed his mind. He officially announced that after the investigation of the incident there was no evidence that the Japanese were involved in it. Two days later Tanaka made the same report to the Emperor. This false report, as we have seen, offended the Emperor, which was the final blow to the already seriously ailing Cabinet.[136]

On July 2, 1929, the Tanaka Cabinet fell and in the Hamaguchi Osachi (Yūkō)'s Minseitō Cabinet Shidehara's leadership in Japan's diplomacy was once again restored. Hence, another switch came about in Japan's policy toward China. In the Fifty-seventh Diet, Foreign Minister Shidehara Kijūrō made the following speech:

> For many years wars have continued in China, and the Chinese people have suffered extreme hardships. The wars in China have also brought serious disadvantageous effects upon Japan in our political and economic relations with China. However, thanks to great efforts of the Nationalist Government, the great task of national unification was at least nominally achieved. We are pleased

---

[136] Tanaka Giichi Denki Kankō-kai (ed.), II, 1027–1043, Harada Kumao, I, 9–11.

at this accomplishment more than anything else. Of course, the complete unification of China cannot be achieved in a day, because of historical, geographic and other difficulties in China.... In the future, some stormy situations might recur. However, we cannot but pray for the success of those who take it upon themselves to save the situation, and extend our sympathy and patience to their hardships and efforts....

Because Sino-Japanese relations are especially close in various aspects, naturally we cannot avoid the occurrence of many diplomatic negotiations. Among those problems, some may often get on our nerves, while also getting on Chinese nerves as well. Nevertheless, in considering our mutual development of national fortunes, there is no other way for us but to co-operate even in politics (to say nothing of economics)....

With regard to the problem of unequal treaties in China,... if we put ourselves in their place, we can understand very well that the continuation of unequal treaties will give unendurable hardships to their life. It is also obvious that the fact that many nations in the East outside China which had been bound by the same treaties freed themselves from those restraints and thus gave further painful affront to the feelings of the Chinese people. It is not a constructive policy of ours to disregard their frustrations for a long time. Particularly, our country which had experienced the same hardships must be determined to co-operate with China as much as possible so as to abrogate those unilateral restraints upon her sovereignty. As a friendly neighboring nation, too, it is a natural course for Japan to take toward China.[137]

On July 9, 1929, in the ten principles of policy announced by the Hamaguchi Cabinet, Shidehara stressed:

To mobilize troops carelessly will never raise Japan's national prestige. That which the government seeks is co-existence and co-prosperity. Especially in economic relations between Japan and China, we expect free and unbound development.... Simultaneously, Japan will co-operate with the activities of the League of Nations,

---

[137] This speech is printed in Shidehara Kijūrō Heiwa Zaidan (ed.), 389–392.

and understand in its lofty ideals a duty to contribute to world peace
and the welfare of mankind.[138]
Based upon these principles, Shidehara exerted himself to placate
the Chinese anti-Japanese sentiments. Due to the efforts of
his and his subordinates in the Foreign Ministry, the boycott
of Japanese goods and the anti-Japanese movements in China
subsided almost completely by the end of the summer of 1929.[139]
As we have seen, because Shidehara was firmly convinced that
Chiang Kai-shek's regime was most trustworthy and durable,
he fully supported the Nationalist unification of China which
would also be beneficial for Japan's China trade. Furthermore,
in September 1929, he proposed to conclude a non-aggression
pact with the Nationalist Government. In January 1930, he
ordered Shigemitsu Mamoru, the *chargé d'affaires* in China, to
resume the negotiation on various terms leading to China's
tariff autonomy. On May 6, 1930, the negotiations finally
succeeded. However, the Army and the Kwantung Army were
strongly dissatisfied with Shidehara's "conciliatory" policy toward
China, especially his full support of the Nationalist unification
of China incorporating The Three Eastern Provinces. Japan
was also hit severely by the world depression, and the economic
hardships of Japan made Manchuria look all the more attractive
for many Japanese. Finally, on September 18, 1931, the Manchurian Incident broke out by the instigation of the Kwantung
Army. Several months later, Manchukuo — Japan's puppet
regime — was established in The Three Eastern Provinces.

---

[138] *Ibid.*, 383–384.
[139] Toward the end of July, 1929, Consul-General Shigemitsu Mamoru
sent this report to Tokyo, *Shuyō Monjo*, II, 50.

CONCLUSION

THE MEANING
OF
"DOUBLE DIPLOMACY"

Japan in the 1920's and the 1930's was frequently criticized abroad for carrying out "double diplomacy." This criticism meant two things. First, it sometimes refered to the competition between civilians and military leaders for control of diplomacy, the former being thought of as peaceful and the latter as aggressive. Second, it sometimes suggested that Japan is "two-faced" and therefore untrustworthy. The contrast between Shidehara's and Tanaka's policies clearly illustrates both points. The former represented peaceful civilian diplomacy; the latter, the aggressive military. It is also true that Japan carried out considerably different policies toward China during the Shidehara and Tanaka Administrations, thereby creating the impression among the powers that Japan was two-faced. The change from one to the other was so drastic that the American Secretary of State, Kellogg, remarked that he "failed to understand" the situation.[1] The conventional distinction between a military foreign policy and a civilian policy, however, does not suffice to indicate the more pro-

---

[1] Kellogg to MacMurray, May 9, 1927, FRUS II.

found differences in personal style and diplomatic philosophy between Tanaka Giichi and Shidehara Kijūrō. Note, too, that some civilian leaders, such as Kita Ikki and Ōkawa Shūmei, were considered to be more aggressive than some military men like Ugaki Kazushige,[2] while certain civilian politicians, such as Mori Kaku and Gotō Shimpei, enthusiastically supported Prime Minister Tanaka Giichi's foreign policies. Tanaka's Kogetsu-kai, which had advocated war against Czarist Russia, included among its members many officials from the Foreign Ministry. The real source of Japan's "double diplomacy," therefore, should be sought in her "split" national identity. Japan's inconsistent diplomatic conduct — therefore often "incomprehensible" to the other powers — was a result of what might be termed national schizophrenia.

SHIDEHARA AND KASUMIGASEKI DIPLOMACY

Shidehara Kijūrō is often considered the implementer of the orthodox "Kasumigaseki Diplomacy," and many of his successors believe that Shidehara's was a good example of "modern" diplomacy. In this regard, his rise to power was a turning point in Japan's diplomatic history. What is, then, the so-called "Kasumigaseki Diplomacy"? Since Shidehara himself thought that he was the founder of "Kasumigaseki Diplomacy," and since many people consider his policy itself as its orthodoxy, let us look at his own understanding of the question. When he assumed the office of Foreign Minister, he stated:

> We must dissolve all factional struggles such as Komura Jutarō
> (1855–1911) versus Katō Takaaki, hitherto existing within the Foreign

---

[2] Ugaki as War Minister under the Hamaguchi Cabinet (July 1929–November 1930) carried out a reduction of armaments which caused great anger within the Army. Because of this incident, when the Imperial order fell upon Ugaki to form a new Cabinet on January 25, 1937, the Army was adamantly opposed to him. As a result, he failed to form a government.

Ministry, I am not a successor of Katō. As a legitimate successor of the whole Kasumigaseki tradition, I hope to promote Japan's diplomacy in much broader perspective.

Then, what is Japan's new diplomacy? Imperialistic and nationalistic ways and means which the Western powers have pursued are already out-of-date. According to the new international trends, we must alter such old ways, and promote the spirit of peaceful co-operation and co-prosperity of the world. This must be the very "new" diplomacy which Japan has to pursue from now on. Those who have said that the essence of diplomacy is to promote military power might think that I attach only secondary importance to national prosperity. But this is not true. Diplomacy also must make great progress in order to promote the welfare of mankind and the development of culture by maintaining world peace.

To attain this goal, I am resolved to maintain a fair and just attitude. Although I am a relative of Katō, I shall never be partial to one particular party or faction. I intend to take a nonpartisan, or beyond partisan, attitude, and to lead Japan's diplomacy in peace and justice.[3]

This statement provides us with a feeling for "Shidehara Diplomacy," and consequently that of the orthodox "Kasumigaseki Diplomacy." In addition to internationalism, pacifism, and nonpartisan diplomacy, some have included among its attributes an economic orientation, non-interventionism, rationalism, pragmatism, and a Western (especially Anglo-American) oriented diplomacy. However, these principles were not established overnight by Shidehara on his own.

First we must recognize the historical and international setting of Japan's diplomacy. Since the Meiji Restoration Japan, as an "underdeveloped" country, hoped to become advanced and modernized like the Western nations. In order to win trust from the West and become a full member of the international community as a "civilized" nation, Japan had to emulate and co-operate with

---

[3] Ujita, 8.

the West. In terms of national survival, Japan was obliged to do so. The Foreign Ministry, more exposed to international contacts than other agencies, was naturally most aware of this necessity. Hence there was a general tendency of *"datsua nyūō"* (getting rid of Oriental or backward aspects and accepting Western or modern elements) in the Foreign Office. This was the source of the internationalism and pro-Western attitude of Japan's Foreign Ministry. For this reason many career diplomats tended to pursue rational, co-operative policies as opposed to those who more emotionally advocated exclusive and militant policies. The former were more pragmatic, while the latter aimed at more "spiritual" or psychological satisfactions. Furthermore, to make Japan advanced, the Foreign Ministry tended to emphasize the policy of *fukoku* (enrich the nation). The military, on the other hand, due to its preoccupation with defense, stressed *kyōhei* (strengthen the army).

In the beginning, in order to maintain national security and abolish the unequal treaties, the Foreign Ministry was a sycophant to all Western nations. From about the time of the Triple Intervention, however, Japan began to reconsider its attitude. In a letter to Yamagata Aritomo (May 16, 1895), Aoki Shūzō cynically and critically revealed Japan's foreign policy.

> Japan's policy reminds us of the attitude of a geisha who has a smile for everybody. As a result, Japan has never gained a true friend.... If we perpetuate this kind of condition,... in case of emergency we must suffer great disadvantages.[4]

This recognition, together with the contemporary international situation and the fact that Great Britain alone earned Japan's appreciation by staying out of the intervention, drove Japan into alliance with Great Britain. Kasumigaseki now took a clearer line, i.e., pro-Anglo-American, instead of being indiscriminately subservient to all the Western powers. There was another important factor which contributed to this trend. Kasumigaseki had

---

[4] Uchiyama, 11.

had two influential advisers, Sir Harry Parkes and Henry W. Denison. The former was the British diplomat who contributed greatly to the establishment of the Foreign Ministry in its initial stage, and the latter was the American adviser who had served Japan for more than thirty years from 1880 to 1914. Most prewar career diplomats received instructions from Denison. Indeed, Shidehara was his best disciple. Nor should the influence of Katō Takaaki, an enthusiastic Anglophile who had become Foreign Minister four times before Shidehara, be neglected, either.

However, it was in fact Mutsu Munemitsu (Foreign Minister, 1892–95) and Komura Jutarō (Foreign Minister, 1901–05 and 1908–11) who contributed greatly to the establishment of "Kasumigaseki Diplomacy" in its early period. Mutsu succeeded in altering the unequal treaties and Komura concluded the Anglo-Japanese Alliance. Both were "friendly" to the West. They held to policies, however, quite different from those of Shidehara Diplomacy, namely oppression of weaker Asian nations as well as utilizing political maneuvers and machinations. Furthermore, in competition with the military, they took the initiative on war policy. Both Mutsu and Komura were born to *bushi* families in the late Tokugawa and had strong samurai temperaments. This is another indication of the superficiality of the usual distinction between the peaceful civilian (or Foreign Ministry) and the aggressive military. International imperialism also dictated their militant attitudes. At the same time, like Shidehara, they were skillful negotiators, rational planners, and strict adherents to international precedent and Western etiquette. Their cultural identity was not clear, somewhat modern and somewhat traditional like Japan itself in the Meiji period.

The people in the next generation who furthered "Kasumigaseki Diplomacy" were Katō Takaaki and Hara Kei. Katō, in some aspects, was like his predecessors, in his samurai origin and temperament, aggressive policies against militarily weaker nations, and a pro-Western attitude. These points lead us to suggest that pro-Western does not necessarily entail internationalism in a real sense. Mutsu, Komura, and Katō all were extremely oppressive to other Asian nations. In fact, *"datsua nyūō"* inherently implies an attitude of subservience to the West and arrogance toward Asia. Their samurai values, such as unyielding spirit and extreme sensitivity to humiliation, and the hierarchical orientation with which they viewed international relations, may have led them to transfer their sense of humiliation arising from inferiority to the West to being overbearing to militarily inferior nations. The psychology of "transferring oppression" which Maruyama Masao found among the wartime leaders was also observable among these diplomats. In this regard, Miyakezaka (the Army) as well as Kasumigaseki were equally aggressive to lesser nations, at least up to the early Taishō period. Katō's special contributions to the "Kasumigaseki Diplomacy" were his efforts to establish the independence of the Foreign Ministry's policy from military and Genrō interference, and to promote an economic-oriented diplomacy. This last aspect of his policy was largely influenced by his personal connection with the Mitsubishi Zaibatsu. This point also indicates that economic-oriented diplomacy and strong business backing did not necessarily result in peaceful diplomacy. In reality, as we have seen, Japanese industrialists dealing with China were opposed to Shidehara's "weak" policy.

Hara Kei as Vice-Foreign Minister (1895–96) and as Prime Minister played an important role in promoting the "Kasumigaseki Diplomacy." It is reported that Hara was the person who really drafted the new examination system for the diplomatic service during Mutsu's foreign ministry, hence contributing to the creation of a career diplomatic corps. As Prime Minister he supported the Paris Peace Treaty and the Washington Conference. He also advocated the policy of non-intervention in Chinese affairs and the promotion of Japan-China trade.

As we have seen, there had been some vague guidelines for so-called "Kasumigaseki Diplomacy" before Shidehara. However, it contained various elements, some, in fact, in conflict with others. It was Shidehara, therefore, who clearly established "Kasumigaseki Diplomacy." His followers, in turn, have regarded "Shidehara Diplomacy" itself as the "orthodox" Kasumigaseki Diplomacy.

A number of factors came into play in these diplomatic developments. Unlike some of his predecessors who had had both traditionalistic and modernistic aspects, Shidehara's cultural identity was clear. This was partly due to the fact that Japan's cultural identity in Taishō, unlike Meiji, was fairly clearly divided. In contrast to most previous diplomats, Shidehara was not of *shizoku* (samurai) status, and he had been born in Meiji instead of in late Tokugawa. Japan's domestic and international situation had also changed greatly. Aspirations for internationalism and democracy were strong at home and abroad. Western diplomats like Woodrow Wilson and Lloyd George also sought a "new" diplomacy, forsaking the "old." Thanks to great national progress, both economically and militarily, Japan no longer had to be subservient to the West. Japan could enjoy her own realm of diplomacy and seek her place in world history. She could also take the diplomatic initiative, as Shidehara did in the Special Tariff Conference. Hence, to a diplomat like Shidehara with a broad international frame of mind, the "transfer of oppression" was not necessary. Furthermore, because of the war boom, Japan had become a capitalistic and highly industrialized nation. Shidehara, to further economic progress and to overcome the recession after the Kantō earthquake, recognized the need for economic-oriented diplomacy. The fact that he had some friends in the business circle also might have influenced him in pursuing such a policy.

Indeed, as many people noted, Shidehara Kijūrō was the first "new" diplomat in the "new" age. He was convinced that Japan's "unique" contribution to world history was to promote international co-operation, justice, and peace, in contrast to the "old" Western diplomacy of statism and imperialism. He hoped to make this the "orthodox" Kasumigaseki Diplomacy. Shidehara was also the first Foreign Minister to emerge from those who came up under the new examination system for career diplomats. After him, Yoshida Shigeru, Ashida Hitoshi, and Shigemitsu Mamoru followed the same course. Shidehara's influence upon these diplomats as well as their followers was profound. These new diplomats were all college graduates, mostly from Tokyo Imperial University, well educated in international law and precedent. In office, they diligently studied specialized problems. They also had a good command of foreign languages. They stood in sharp contrast to the diplomats of the old type, such as Gotō Shimpei, Hayashi Gonsuke, and Ijūin Hikokichi on the other. Both in philosophy and predispositions they were more like Tanaka than Shidehara. All of them were born in late Tokugawa and of *bushi* origin. They all possessed gallant samurai qualities — in this sense, I assume, their childhood socialization in a *bushi* family must have been important — intuitive leadership, and were strongly motivated to politico-military domination. Gotō Shimpei advocated Greater Asianism, and Hayashi Gonsuke through his skillful machinations and power manipulation made Korea Japan's protectorate.[5]

THE WORLD OF THE TRADITIONALISTS

A common question among students of Japanese diplomatic history has been, as David Lu puts it, "Why did Japan enter into the Pacific War?" "Was it a national hara-kiri?"[6]

---

[5]   The discussion of this section is based upon the following sources: Gaimushō Hyakunen-shi Hensan Iinkai (ed.); Uchiyama; Ujita, *passim*; Matsumoto Shigeharu, *et al.*, *Kindai Nihon no Gaikō* (Modern Japanese diplomacy; Tokyo and Osaka, 1962), *passim*; Nichi-Bei Tsūshin-sha (ed.), *Nihon Gaikō Hyakunen Shōshi* (One-hundred-year history of Japanese diplomacy; Tokyo, 1956), *passim*.

[6]   David J. Lu, *From the Marco Polo Bridge to Pearl Harbor* (Washington,

One cannot solve this historical riddle until one understands the mentality of the ultranationalists in Shōwa. And yet one finds a remarkable line of continuity in attitudes, values, and principles from Tokugawa Nariaki (1800–60), who advocated the *jōi* (expel the barbarians), in order to protect the "Divine Country" (Shin Koku) at the end of the Tokugawa period, through traditionalists like Tanaka Giichi and Gotō Shimpei in the Taishō era, to the wartime leaders of the Shōwa period. Furthermore, being one of the few leaders of the 1920's who had been born in the Tokugawa period, Tanaka served as the vital "link" between the Meiji traditionalists and the Shōwa ultranationalists. In fact, he was the protégé of Genrō Yamagata Aritomo and General Nogi Maresuke, the latter of whom demonstrated his absolute loyalty to the Meiji Emperor by committing *junshi* (loyal suicide) after the Emperor's death. Tanaka was simultaneously a teacher of the young ultranationalistic officers who emerged in the 1930's. In this regard, to understand Tanaka's thought and behavior may provide us with a key to unlock the riddle.

Just as Nariaki was dependent upon a form of "spiritual" power such as determination, both Tanaka and the wartime leaders relied upon "will power," like that of *bushidō* and *Yamato damashii*, or upon "extra-material power" like the *kamikaze* (divine wind). In this sense, all of them were irrational. At the International Military Tribunal in Tokyo, the Prosecuting Attorney, Golunsky, remarked:

> There are very many intelligent people who are astonished, and not without reason, at Japan daring to attack both the United States and Great Britain, having the unfinished war with China on her hands, and preparing an attack on the Soviet Union.[7]

D. C., 1961), Preface, vii.

[7] Maruyama Masao has provided an excellent analysis of the psychology of wartime leaders. Many of the following quotations are taken from his book, *Thought and Behavior in Modern Japanese Politics*. The immediate quotation is taken from page 85 of the same book. See also International Military Tribunal for the Far East (IMTFE), No. 85, 7275, Oct. 8, 1946.

And Blewett, an American member of the defense counsel, agreed to this observation and used it as the basis of his argument. He stated:

> To American counsel who represent a nation which produced fifty thousand planes or more in one year it is an allegation which is not ludicrous but downright tragic in a case where the lives of conscientious public officials are at stake. No one but a Don Quixote would start to conquer the world with a handful of aircraft — not in this day and age.[8]

Tanaka Giichi also demonstrated this "quixotic" character.

The ultranationalists shared Tanaka's "sink or swim" attitude, expressed in his advocacy of war against powerful Czarist Russia, and Gotō Shimpei's direct-action mentality, which was shown in the debate on the Siberian expedition. A member of Ketsumeidan (the Blood Pledge Corps), which produced the May 15 Incident of 1932, declared in court:

> We thought about destruction first. We never considered taking on the duty of construction. We foresaw, however, that, once the destruction was accomplished, someone would take charge of the construction for us. We had no guiding principle, but thought to set up a military government after first proclaiming martial law.[9]

Above all, the wartime leaders who made Japan plunge into World War II most remarkably but tragically demonstrated this direct-action approach. Maruyama is quite right in stating:

> During the war Allied observers generally assumed that, since Japan had deliberately embarked on a large-scale war against the two most powerful countries in the world, she must have set up an organization and formulated plans based on a reasonably clear forecast of the future. It is no wonder, then, that the Allies should have been more and more amazed as the truth of the matter dawned on them. The real nature of the Japanese decision was a riddle even to members of the Prosecution.[10]

---

[8] IMTFE, No. 391, 43240, March 11, 1948; Maruyama, *Thought and Behavior in Modern Japanese Politics*, 86.

[9] *Ibid.*, 53–54.

Nevertheless, it was also the behavior of samurai who, wielding swords, fought their way into large and powerful enemy camps. Just as these samurai risked their lives on one spectacular charge against the enemy, so Japan staked her whole national destiny on a single war. They prepared themselves for death, instead of what they perceived as a shameful escape from and surrender to the Western domination in the world.

The direct-action attitude has another facet, namely nonrecognition of discussion and compromise. This was the natural disposition of many samurai. *"Mondō muyō!"* (no need for discussion) was a common phrase among samurai who quickly drew swords against persons who displeased them. Tanaka's desire for war against Czarist Russia and his repeated military expeditions in China indicate the same point. The young officers who came to assassinate Prime Minister Inukai Tsuyoshi also shouted *"Mondō muyō!"* when the aged Premier tried to stop them by saying, "Let's talk. Then we will come to an understanding." The officers tried to kill parliamentary government itself by killing the last party government headed by Inukai. Likewise, Tanaka had no intention of adhering to democratic principles. either at home or abroad. Instead, both Tanaka and the ultranationalists hoped to propagate the Imperial Way (Tanaka called it *ōdō seiji*), which was to be operated by entirely non-democratic principles, such as loyalty and total obedience.

As Shidehara Kijūrō emphasized, rational diplomacy depended upon making a "compromise" at a timely point in negotiation. Due to their adherence to hierarchical values, however, all traditionalists fostered the psychology of superior-inferior and pride-humiliation consciousness. They felt that "compromise" was "submission" and "concession," "defeat." In negotiations with the United States prior to World War II, the basic American condition was Japan's withdrawal of troops from China. The wartime

---

[10] *Ibid.*, 85.

leaders felt this to be an extremely "shameful" thing, which Japan could never do. Prime Minister and General Tōjō Hideki thought that, if Japan had to compromise on that point, "he would never be able to sleep facing the Yasukuni Shrine." And General Matsui Iwane said:

> If we were now to settle the China Incident by compromising with England and America and co-operating with the Anglo-Saxons, how would we be able to face the myriad spirits of our war dead?[11]

This was the same mentality as Tanaka's. His policy of protecting Japanese residents on the spot by dispatching troops rather than by withdrawing them from dangerous areas, even in the midst of financial crisis and at the sacrifice of Japan's international prestige and China trade, was based upon the same pride-humiliation consciousness. And for him to see the Japanese nationals bullied by the militarily inferior Chinese without resorting to any "positive" measure was a national humiliation which was "more unbearable than death!"

Wartime leaders, like Tanaka, held to a hierarchical view of international relations. Such a belief was caused by their daily environment wrapped in paternalism, *oyabun-kobun*, and master-disciple relationships. At the same time, they also shared the sense of "racial-affinity" toward the Chinese with Tanaka Giichi, Tokutomi Sohō, and Yamagata Aritomo. Hence, General Matsui Iwane asserted:

> The struggle between Japan and China was always a fight between brothers within the "Asian family".... It has been my belief during all these years that we must regard this struggle as a method of making the Chinese undergo self-reflection. We do not do this because we hate them, but on the contrary because we love them too much. It is just the same as in a family when an elder brother has taken all that he can stand from his ill-behaved younger brother and has to chastise him in order to make him behave properly.[12]

---

[11] *Ibid.*, 112–113.
[12] *Ibid.*, 95. IMTFE, No. 310, Nov. 7, 1947.

The above remark of Matsui reminds us of Tanaka's conviction that Japan had to lead China to "the path of virtue" and that Chang Tso-lin was his "younger brother." Conversely, because of their hierarchical orientation, the wartime leaders as well as Tanaka never fully understood egalitarian principles of international relations or the modern international convention that international treaties had to be observed faithfully. Just as Tanaka unhesitatingly violated China's sovereignty, her territorial integrity, and the Washington treaties, while proclaiming his "intention" to observe them, so the wartime leaders broke the Kellogg Pact, the Nine Power Treaty, and the Covenant of the League one after another. Joseph Grew, the American Ambassador to Japan, was right to doubt whether they seriously thought that they did wrong. He remarked, "such a mentality is a great deal harder to deal with than a mentality which, however, brazen, knows that it is in the wrong."[13]

One of the distinctive characteristics of Japanese ultranationalism, as Maruyama points out, was its extreme fantasy and lack of planning. The movement was always governed by some kind of "mythological optimism." Japan's venture in the Pacific War clearly indicated this point. As Inoue Nisshō, the leader of the Blood Pledge Corps Incident, explained his motivation: "It is more correct to say that I have no systematized ideas. I transcend reason and act completely upon intuition."[14] We could also find ample evidence of this "intuitive" nature in Tanaka's leadership. His assertion of "autonomous diplomacy" was more intuitive than logical or practical. Many people criticized his policy as "chaotic" and "haphazard." Nagai Matsuzō, who observed a contrast between Shidehara Kijūrō and Gotō Shimpei, also found the same inclination in the latter. As opposed to Shidehara's rationality, practicality, and careful planning, one outstanding characteristic of Gotō was his "intuitive" leadership which was demonstrated in the Siberian expedition. The American

---

[13] Joseph C. Grew, *Ten Years in Japan* (New York, 1942), 84.
[14] Maruyama, *Thought and Behavior in Modern Japanese Politics*, 53.

Ambassador could never understand Foreign Minister Gotō's puzzling answer, "Force is spirit!"[15] The assertion of Tokugawa *jōi* people "to cut down the canvas ropes of the Black Ships with Japanese swords like they cut noodles," or "to set fire to them by sending small boats loaded with fired dry grasses" was nothing but a "fantasy."

The various characteristics which we have observed such as irrationality, intuitive leadership, pride-shame consciousness, hierarchical orientation, naïveté, and exclusivity, were not "peculiar" to ultranationalists alone. On the contrary, they were common to all the traditionalistic leaders of Japan. In fact, they were characteristics of Japanese tradition itself, especially that of the samurai. To rational, enlightened, and modern people, their thought and behavior may look "ludicrous" and even "abnormal." Their abnormality, however, does not come — as Maruyama contends — from an abnormal "psychology." Rather, it originates from their different principles and standards of judgment. As Blewett had to admit, their standards were not those of "this day and age."[16] They lived in a traditionalistic world. In their frame of mind, however, their way of thinking was totally understandable. In other words, their "perception" of this world was different from that of the modernizers, as we have seen in the differences between Tanaka Giichi and Shidehara Kijūrō. They lived in the same "objective" world, and yet in an entirely different "subjective" world.[17] When values and beliefs are different, there exists a clear "discontinuity of communication" between two groups of people. This was the very source of the "apparent" abnormality of the traditionalists' thought and behavior.

Seppuku (or *hara-kiri* in a more vulgar rendering) was common

---

[15] Nagai, 132–135. See more discussion about this incident on page 39.

[16] IMTFE, No. 391, 43240, March 11, 1948. Maruyama, *Thought and Behavior in Modern Japanese Politics*, 86.

[17] See the Introduction, Chapter 5, and their notes.

among the samurai. It had been so common as to be institution-alized. But when values and ideas are institutionalized, they reinforce people in thinking and acting in that way. They are habitualized.[18] Even after the end of the Tokugawa regime, the traditional world still remained strong in Japan. This tra-ditional world had to come to an end in the Pacific War, but in the manner suitable to the traditional institution, a national *seppuku*. Japan's — or more precisely the traditionalists' — plunge into the Pacific War was, indeed, a "myth of the twentieth century" to many modern people. But when a "myth" was boldly put to the reality, it could not avoid ending in tragic disillusionment.

THE DEVELOPMENT OF *KOKUTAI*
AND *KŌDŌ* SINCE TANAKA

All traditionalists were opposed to Westernization and mod-ernization in their hope to preserve *kokutai*. Let us survey, therefore, the development of *kokutai* since Tanaka.

The "traditional" mentality that I have discussed was not the only cause for Japan's showdown with the West. More funda-mentally, the showdown occurred because the traditionalists' belief in Japan's ultimate goal diametrically contradicted the aspirations of the West. They were convinced that the guiding principle of Japan's diplomacy should be the Imperial Way, the external expression of *kokutai*. This recognition also gave psycho-logical satisfaction to Japanese who had long perceived Western oppression and domination. They thought the propagation of the Imperial Way could tear the West-dominated world order

---

[18]   Myths and beliefs, institutions, and customs and manners are all inter-related in influencing people's thought and behavior. See Miki Kiyoshi, *Kōsōryoku no Ronri* (Mechanism of thought) in *Miki Kiyoshi Zenshū* (Complete works of Miki Kiyoshi; Tokyo, 1967), VIII; see also his bibliography on related themes; Wilhelm Arnold, *Kultur und Rechtsleben*, 1865; and Ruth Benedict, *Patterns of Culture* (Boston and New York, 1934).

into pieces and Japan could make a spectacular leap into the world. In this regard, too, Tanaka's role was significant.

Tanaka was one of the first to advocate Japan's "autonomous diplomacy," independent of and something entirely different from modern Western diplomacy. Autonomous diplomacy, for him, meant a "challenge" to the West. Japan was to replace the existing world order, which reflected the Western world view, and build a new order based upon Japan's tradition such as absolute loyalty to the Emperor, paternalism, obedience, frugality, and other traditional values. His diplomacy was "aggressive" not simply because it was militant but also because it directly opposed the Western-dominated status quo. Japan's "initiative" which he advocated in the international community was a result of his intuition of these national goals.

Tanaka's reverence for the Emperor was especially strong. He was also thoroughly convinced that the beauty of Japanese tradition was *bansei ikkei*, eternal rule by the unbroken line of Emperors. Nevertheless, he was neither a lawyer nor a philosopher. He never had a systematized idea of *kōdō*. For him, samurai temperament rather than ideas always came first. He used the term *ōdō*, like Ishiwara Kanji who dreamed of establishing a utopia in Manchuria based upon *ōdō*. Like Ishiwara and other traditionalists, Tanaka was convinced that Japan had to become the *meishu*, the lord, of Asia. This was thought to be the "mission" of Japan. Putting all of these characteristics of Tanaka together — his samurai temperament, his emphasis on *kokutai*, autonomous diplomacy, anti-Western attitudes, and Japan's sense of mission — Tanaka resembled the ultranationalistic wartime leaders. He was a transitional figure on the road toward ultranationalism. After him, the ideas of *kokutai* and *kōdō* were more solidly conceptualized.

In 1933, Tazaki Jingi combined and clarified various ideas related to the Imperial Way and asserted that the term *kōdō* was the most suitable. He pointed out that *ōdō* had a more Chinese connotation, while *kōdō* was specifically "Japanese." Both terms imply a paternalistic political system as opposed to a democratic system based upon individualism. The political system under *kōdō* and *ōdō* could be understood as the relationship between parents and children, and the basic principles of this system were benevolence and obedience. The difference between *kōdō* and *ōdō* was that the latter was a fictitious form of the father-son relationship and implied the possibility of revolution. *Kōdō*, on the other hand, meant the "real" father-son relationship based upon the unbroken line of the Imperial Rule.[19] By the end of the decade *kōdō* had become the fixed term. Tokutomi Soho wrote a very influential book in 1938 entitled *Kōdō Nihon no Sekaika* (to propagate Japan's *kōdō* throughout the world), and Doihara Kenji's *Kōdō no Shinseishin* (the true spirit of *kōdō*) was published in the next year.

The most important development in the idea of *kokutai* and *kōdō* was the reappearance of the notion of *saisei itchi*, the unity of politics and religion, which had been revived but soon abolished at the beginning of the Meiji period. But in the late 1930's the Emperor became once more not only the political head but also the religious head of the state. It was the resurgence of the ancient concept of the priestly ruler. The significant point of this development in the light of diplomacy is that *bushido* and Shintō myths were amalgamated into a basis for Japanese diplomacy. According to the ancient belief of *saisei itchi*, Shintō Kami were influential only in the realm which the Emperor controlled politically. Delmer M. Brown best explains this characteristic of Shintō as "Shintō particularism."[20] Furthermore, the gradual expansion of the realm controlled by the Imperial Clan within Japan was achieved through military expansion. In other words, the spread of Kami power was dependent upon the spread of the Imperial Clan's

---

[19] Tazaki Jingi, *Kōdō Nihon to Ōdō Manshū* (Kōdō Japan and ōdō Manchuria; Tokyo, 1933).

political power, which in turn was possible because of its military power.

During the Second Sino-Japanese War (July 1937–August 1945), this idea was adopted in the diplomatic sphere. On November 3, 1938, Prime Minister Konoe Fumimaro (1891–1945) announced to the world:

> What Our Empire ultimately seeks is to establish a New Order in East Asia by which the Empire is to secure an eternal stability in that region. Here lies the ultimate goal of the present expeditionary war....
>
> Our Empire wholly trusts the powers to adapt themselves to this new situation in East Asia by accurately recognizing the real intention of Our Empire.... [Note that Konoe followed Tanaka's and Sohō's contention that Japan, not the West, should take the diplomatic initiative — the author's note.][21]

The expansion of the Imperial Way was not only the expansion of Japan's political system but also the spread of Shintō beliefs. Military power was the best means for carrying this out. The samurai posture of military strength demonstrated by people like Tanaka Giichi was now endowed with ideological significance. A trinity of the Imperial Way was organized: military power, political power, and Kami power. When Japanese troops invaded Southeast Asian countries, they hurriedly built *torii*, Shintō gates, as the Imperial Clan had done in ancient times. Those *torii* were symbols indicating that Japan's Kami power was now influential in those areas. Thus the ideological backbone of *hakkō ichiu*, to spread the Imperial Way to the eight corners of the world, was formulated. And the establishment of the New Order in East Asia (*Tōa no Shin Chitsujo Kensetsu*) was its first step. Thus, Tanaka's intention to make Japan the "Lord" of East Asia was faithfully carried out by the Shōwa ultranationalists.

---

[20] Delmer M. Brown, *The Nature of Shintō*, presented at the Colloquium of the Center for Japanese and Korean Studies, University of California, Berkeley, May 18, 1966.

[21] *Shuyō Monjo*, II, 401.

In the meantime, at home, the movement to articulate *kokutai* had reached its apogee with the publication by the Ministry of Education of *Fundamentals of Our National Polity* (Kokutai no Hongi) in 1937. In this text all concepts of *kokutai* hitherto developed — the Imperial Rule, loyalty and patriotism, filial piety, paternalism, and *bushidō* — were integrated.[22] The fundamental goal of consolidating the foundation of Japan's *kokutai* was to save "the entire human race which is struggling to find a way out of the deadlock which Western individualism faces." Since both democracy and communism were based upon Western individualism, only Japan's Imperial Way would save mankind.

On July 26, 1940, the second Konoe Cabinet reached a decision on the "Fundamental National Plan" (Kihon Kokusaku Yōkō). The Plan stated:

> Now, the world has come to a great turning point in history. New formations of politics, economics and culture have begun to emerge, based upon the development of several groups of nations. The Imperial Nation (*Kōkoku*), facing the unprecedented ordeal, is determined to accomplish this national principle.... It is of the most urgent importance that the Imperial Nation strive for the establishment of a national defense system by conquering every difficulty and by making fundamental renovations in all aspects of our government. [Tanaka's original idea of the garrison-state reappears here — the author's note.]

The Fundamental Plan

> The fundamental principle of the Imperial Nation is to bring about world peace based upon the founding spirit of this nation, namely, to unite the eight corners of the world under the one roof of the Imperial Way. To begin with, by making the Imperial Nation the core, a new order of the Great East Asia based upon the firm unity of Japan-Manchuria-China is to be established. For this purpose, the Imperial Nation, mobilizing its whole energy, pushes forward

---

[22] See Japan Ministry of Education, *Kokutai no Hongi*, trans. John O. Gauntlett, ed. with an intro. Robert K. Hall (Cambridge, Mass., 1949).

on the establishment of the best national system which meets this new situation.[23]

Accordingly, in September 1940, all political parties were dissolved into the Imperial Rule Assistance Association (Taisei Yokusan-kai), to unify the whole nation for the achievement of this mission.

Two months later, a grand national ceremony was carried out celebrating the 2,600th year (Kigen 2,600-nen) of the founding of Japan by the Emperor Jimmu. Thus Japan plunged herself into the "mission" of constructing the Greater East Asia Co-Prosperity Sphere (Dai Tōa Kyōei Ken) and A New World Order (Sekai Shin Chitsujo Kensetsu). *The Imperial Rescript Declaring War on the United States and British Empire* asserted:

> Now that we have risen up in arms, we must accomplish our ultimate end. Herein lies the core of our theory. In Nippon resides a destiny to become the Light of Greater East Asia and to become ultimately the Light of the World.[24]

And the *Draft of Basic Plan for Establishment of Greater East Asia Co-Prosperity Sphere* declared:

> The Japanese empire is a manifestation of morality and its special characteristic is the propagation of the Imperial Way. It strives but for the achievement of *Hakkō Ichiu....* It is necessary to foster the increased power of the empire, to cause East Asia to return to its original form of independence and co-prosperity by shaking off the yoke of Europe and America, and to let its countries and peoples develop their respective abilities in peaceful co-operation and secure livelihood....
>
> The ultimate aim in thought construction in East Asia is to make East Asiatic people revere the Imperial influence by propagating the Imperial Way based on the spirit of construction, and to establish the belief that uniting solely under this influence is the one and only way to the eternal growth and development of East Asia.[25]

As we look back upon the course Japan took to the Pacific War, we realize that the period between 1924 and 1931 when Shidehara

---

[23]   *Shuyō Monjo*, II, 436.
[24]   Tsunoda, de Bary, and Keene (comps.), II, 293.

Kijūrō and Tanaka Giichi alternated in the Ministry of Foreign Affairs was crucial in modern Japanese diplomatic history. This period was a watershed in the rise and fall of the Japanese Empire. From this time on, the "Rising Sun" began to decline, though it looked as if it were rising continuously as its power overshadowed the Continent. In the midst of national devastation at the end of World War II, Ishii Itarō, a veteran diplomat, lamented: "If only the 'Shidehara Diplomacy' had been strong enough to survive, Japan would not have been subjected to national ruin."[26] Since then until recently, with the resurgence of popular aspirations for democracy, Westernization, and modernization, Shidehara's type of "economic-oriented" diplomacy and internationalism with emphasis on the United Nations and the co-operation with the West — especially with the United States — have revived in Japan. However, more than two decades have elapsed since the end of World War II, and some Japanese are already disenchanted with the results of the rapid postwar modernization. Hopes for a Japanese military build-up are also beginning to appear in some segements of society. Traditionalistic nationalism and anti-Americanism are rising once again. The international environment is also changing rapidly from the bipolar to ever more complicated multiple relations. Many people have begun to search for the nation's new identity: democracy, traditionalism, communism, or something else? I do not know. We will see whether Japan finds a new course with respect to the historical alternatives between which she has hitherto vacillated.

---

[25]   *Ibid.*, 294–298.
[26]   Ishii, 460.

APPENDIX I.

JAPANESE TRADE DURING THE TAISHŌ AND
THE EARLY SHŌWA PERIODS* (¥ 1,000)

year	export	import	balance
1916	1, 199, 614	808, 642	(+) 391, 052
17	1, 701, 158	1, 106, 017	(+) 595, 141
18	2, 074, 031	1, 778, 091	(+) 295, 940
19	2, 238, 168	2, 387, 757	(−) 149, 589
20	2, 102, 972	2, 545, 530	(−) 442, 558
21	1, 353, 023	1, 793, 539	(−) 440, 516
22	1, 736, 040	2, 066, 145	(−) 330, 105
23	1, 542, 106	2, 154, 997	(−) 612, 891
24	1, 923, 103	2, 653, 179	(−) 730, 076
25	2, 305, 590	2, 572, 658	(−) 269, 068
26	2, 044, 726	2, 377, 484	(−) 332, 758
27	1, 992, 317	2, 179, 154	(−) 186, 837
28	1, 971, 955	2, 196, 315	(−) 224, 360

* Kodama Kōta et al. (eds.), *Zusetsu Nihon Bunkashi Taikei*: *Taishō-Shōwa Jidai* (Illustrated Japanese cultural history: Taishō and Shōwa periods; Tokyo, 1956), XII, 150.

APPENDIX II.
CHINESE IMPORTS BY COUNTRIES,*
Showing percentage of total imports into China from each of the important countries, 1904–32.

	From Japan	From Hong Kong	From United States	From Great Britain
1904	14. 6	41. 0	8. 5	16. 6
1905	13. 7	33. 1	17. 2	19. 3
1906	14. 9	35. 3	10. 8	19. 2
1907	13. 8	37. 4	8. 9	18. 6
1908	13. 3	38. 1	10. 5	18. 4
1909	14. 3	36. 0	7. 8	16. 3
1910	16. 6	37. 0	5. 4	17. 6
1911	16. 9	31. 4	8. 7	19. 1
1912	19. 2	31. 2	7. 7	15. 8
1913	20. 9	30. 1	6. 2	17. 0
1914	22. 3	29. 5	7. 2	18. 5
1915	26. 5	32. 7	8. 2	15. 7
1916	31. 1	29. 7	10. 4	13. 6
1917	40. 3	28. 9	11. 1	9. 5
1918	43. 0	29. 2	10. 6	9. 0
1919	38. 2	23. 7	17. 0	9. 9
1920	30. 1	20. 9	18. 8	17. 3
1921	23. 2	25. 5	19. 4	16. 5
1922	24. 5	25. 3	17. 9	15. 4
1923	22. 9	26. 9	16. 7	13. 0
1924	23. 1	24. 0	18. 8	12. 4
1925	31. 6	18. 6	15. 0	9. 8
1926	30. 0	11. 1	16. 7	10. 3
1927	29. 0	21. 0	16. 5	7. 4
1928	26. 7	18. 9	17. 2	9. 5
1929**	25. 5	16. 9	18. 2	9. 4
1930**	25. 0	16. 7	17. 7	8. 3

* C. F. Remer, *A Study of Chinese Boycotts, with Special Reference to Their Economic Effectiveness* (Baltimore, 1933), Appendix II.
** The world depression and the Manchurian Incident

APPENDIX III.
CHINESE BOYCOTTS AND THEIR EFFECT UPON JAPANESE TRADE*

year	Lytton Report Japan's China trade (except Kwantung Province and Hong Kong) (Yen)	Lytton Report Balance with the previous year (Yen)	Chinese Customs Report Imported from Japan (HK. Taels)	Chinese Customs Report Balance with the previous year (HK. Taels)	Chinese Customs Report Exported to Japan (HK. Taels)	Chinese Customs Report Balance with the previous year (HK. Taels)	Causes for boycotts
1915	141,125,000	− 21,000,000	120,249,514	− 6,870,478	77,676,817	+13,060,758	The Twenty-One Demands
1916	192,712,000	—	160,490,720	—	112,922,258	—	
1917	318,380,000	—	221,666,891	—	105,773,819	—	
1918	359,150,000	—	238,858,578	—	163,394,092	+31,611,940	The Shantung Problem
1919	447,049,000	+ 88,000,000	246,940,997	+ 8,082,419	195,006,032	—	
1920	410,270,000	—	229,135,866	—	141,927,902	—	
1921	287,227,000	—	210,359,237	—	172,110,728	—	
1922	333,520,000	—	231,428,885	—	157,754,351	—	
1923	272,190,000	− 61,000,000	220,242,970	−11,185,915	198,517,346	+40,762,995	The Port Arthur and Dairen Problem
1924	348,398,000	—	234,761,863	—	201,175,926	—	
1925	468,438,000	+120,000,000	299,755,611	+64,993,748	186,337,037	−14,838,889	The May Thirtieth Incident
1926	421,861,000	—	399,909,441	—	211,740,889	—	
1927	334,183,000	− 87,000,000	293,793,760	−46,115,681	208,838,810	− 2,902,079	The Shantung Expeditions
1928	373,141,000	+ 39,000,000	319,293,439	+25,499,179	228,642,453	+19,803,643	The Tsinan Incident
1929	346,825,000	—	323,141,662	—	256,428,320	—	
1930	260,825,000	—	327,165,000	—	216,555,000	—	
1931	155,751,000	−105,000,000	295,727,119	−31,457,881	264,956,013	+48,401,013	The Manchurian Incident

* Uchida Naosaku, "Sensō Boppatsu to Chūgoku no Tainichi Boikotto Mondai" (The outbreak of the Pacific War and the problem of China's anti-Japanese boycotts), Taiheiyō Sensō Gen'in-ron (Causes for the Pacific War), ed. Nihon Gaikō Gakkai (Tokyo, 1953), 582–583.

APPENDIX IV.
JAPANESE EXPORTS BY COUNTRIES,*
Showing percentage of total exports from Japan to each of the
important countries, 1907–32.

	To China	To United States	To British India
1907	30. 2	30. 3	3. 0
1908	25. 5	32. 3	3. 6
1909	26. 9	31. 8	3. 5
1910	28. 9	31. 3	4. 1
1911	30. 3	31. 9	4. 5
1912	32. 5	32. 0	4. 5
1913	34. 5	29. 2	4. 7
1914	36. 9	33. 0	4. 4
1915	26. 9	28. 8	6. 0
1916	23. 5	30. 2	6. 3
1917	27. 5	29. 9	6. 3
1918	27. 5	27. 0	10. 3
1919	31. 3	39. 5	5. 6
1920	30. 7	29. 0	9. 9
1921	33. 9	39. 6	6. 7
1922	28. 8	44. 7	5. 9
1923	27. 3	41. 8	6. 9
1924	27. 7	41. 2	7. 5
1925	27. 9	43. 6	7. 5
1926	28. 1	42. 1	7. 6
1927	24. 7	41. 8	8. 4
1928	27. 4	41. 9	7. 4
1929**	24. 8	42. 5	9. 2
1930**	27. 4	34. 4	8. 8

* C. F. Remer, *A Study of Chinese Boycotts, with Special Reference to Their Economic Effectiveness* (Baltimore, 1933), Appendix III.

** The world depression and the Manchurian Incident

APPENDIX V.

VALUE OF JAPANESE MERCHANDISE EXPORTED TO ITS MAJOR TRADING PARTNERS

country / year	Asia			Europe				North America	
	Kwantung Province	China	Hong Kong	Great Britain	France	Germany	Russia	United States	Canada
	Yen	Yen	Yen	Yen	Yen	Yen	Yen	Yen	Yen
1912	27,544,858	114,823,721	28,712,905	29,791,898	43,871,410	13,487,589	2,540,737	168,708,896	4,808,263
13	29,836,345	154,660,428	33,621,978	32,869,657	60,229,619	13,131,709	4,897,420	184,473,382	5,090,018
14	22,270,379	162,370,924	33,277,071	33,086,274	31,209,330	9,962,093	1,967,802	196,539,008	4,994,125
15	22,200,802	141,125,586	27,401,346	68,494,011	42,293,232	5	11,239,224	204,141,844	7,024,068
16	37,059,910	192,712,626	34,980,507	101,657,565	64,006,603	…	33,421,097	340,244,817	11,301,990
17	95,724,838	318,380,530	57,176,210	202,646,125	97,820,708	…	13,514,547	478,536,845	16,158,202
18	116,373,972	259,150,814	63,699,799	142,866,369	142,199,063	…	162,268	530,129,393	27,334,805
19	150,129,187	447,049,267	59,155,766	111,452,780	66,844,652	63,643	464,390	828,097,621	24,839,228
20	113,685,671	410,270,499	74,066,243	97,797,246	71,652,639	1,064,632	209,475	565,017,126	21,669,786
21	77,569,443	287,227,081	59,304,076	32,772,308	35,166,991	2,216,871	50	496,283,879	13,415,987
22	71,858,804	333,520,262	65,421,815	54,437,542	78,686,296	3,724,051	1,658	732,376,607	13,687,282
23	67,871,337	272,190,662	55,317,955	40,409,806	25,656,317	3,391,109	130	605,619,436	14,349,310
24	72,601,146	348,398,787	79,010,627	61,044,019	85,789,951	8,564,196	642	744,925,600	15,450,706
25	101,647,368	468,438,956	73,629,010	59,716,478	58,854,954	11,844,213	528,194	1,006,252,759	20,838,296
26	99,606,771	421,861,235	52,973,011	59,493,735	42,415,882	8,131,002	4,646	860,880,579	24,753,778
27	91,270,539	334,183,608	66,528,996	64,929,713	54,045,068	10,612,162	869,307	833,804,256	27,401,680
28	110,190,388	373,141,911	56,204,353	58,904,459	63,408,931	12,582,099	1,197,621	826,141,097	27,047,237
29	124,476,203	346,652,450	61,065,164	63,183,354	44,494,959	13,446,619	2,303,819	914,084,452	27,096,148
30	86,814,090	260,825,838	55,646,381	60,682,453	26,302,071	11,106,454	1,345,245	506,112,145	17,884,784

* *Foreign Trade of Japan, A Statistical Survey*, ed. Tōyō Keizai Shimpō-sha (Tokyo, 1935), 349–354

APPENDIX VI.
VALUE OF MERCHANDISE IMPORTED FROM JAPAN'S MAJOR TRADING PARTNERS*

Country / year	Asia			Europe				North America	
	Kwantung Province	China	Hong Kong	Great Britain	France	Germany	Russia	United States	Canada
	Yen	Yen	Yen	Yen	Yen	Yen	Yen	Yen	Yen
1912	25,707,353	54,807,116	881,550	116,146,973	5,421,103	61,075,924	73,619	127,015,757	664,463
13	30,877,894	61,223,038	1,294,749	122,736,970	5,828,992	68,394,798	40,943	122,408,361	1,839,426
14	31,277,019	58,305,783	876,022	92,302,307	4,371,217	44,922,005	39,909	96,771,077	1,073,023
15	27,819,092	85,847,735	1,594,113	58,084,368	3,890,983	5,919,464	607,245	102,531,279	1,063,009
16	33,953,897	108,638,636	1,015,293	81,732,097	4,467,653	4,139,447	1,104,323	204,078,950	1,666,230
17	53,180,199	133,271,036	1,803,803	63,304,384	4,364,619	2,520,241	1,309,438	359,707,853	2,557,108
18	100,517,806	281,707,333	833,766	66,067,257	3,730,147	3,430,393	685,583	626,025,530	7,775,180
19	162,394,349	322,100,628	1,536,891	127,541,962	8,831,291	258,584	389,476	766,381,438	6,126,416
20	196,861,271	218,090,911	2,231,586	235,352,505	14,481,820	11,974,686	386,254	873,182,251	5,051,478
21	111,931,580	191,678,314	1,017,171	184,306,793	11,691,319	47,713,086	437,835	574,400,915	8,946,591
22	130,574,264	186,343,719	690,035	232,310,383	18,462,691	110,622,311	877,363	596,169,490	16,559,153
23	148,806,406	204,678,551	1,654,020	237,135,942	22,201,635	120,242,681	261,624	511,977,136	24,358,332
24	175,744,318	237,544,093	1,099,252	312,751,429	32,771,209	144,643,248	481,256	670,993,130	40,024,779
25	176,596,197	214,657,519	475,903	227,292,002	33,377,407	123,819,262	291,414	664,992,279	37,132,413
26	157,033,706	239,410,462	1,426,286	170,274,500	24,545,101	145,220,980	793,635	680,185,761	63,929,190
27	132,447,855	226,034,359	1,598,590	153,271,946	27,309,700	131,390,530	1,606,312	673,685,906	55,669,652
28	150,439,022	234,556,683	1,117,763	164,830,419	24,002,571	133,537,490	2,141,551	625,536,409	66,464,953
29	166,322,386	209,975,360	607,745	153,045,820	26,185,050	157,273,913	3,080,902	654,058,260	68,729,648
30	121,405,498	161,666,652	538,201	92,561,422	16,635,566	106,183,336	2,582,908	442,881,606	46,164,489

* Tōyō Keizai Shimpō-sha (ed.), *Foreign Trade of Japan, A Statistical Survey* (Tokyo, 1935), 359–364.

APPENDIX VII.
JAPAN'S VITAL STATISTICS*

year	birth	death	stillbirth	marriage	divorce	rate/1000 (stillbirth rate/1000 births)				
						birth	death	stillbirth	marriage	divorce
1872	569,034	405,404	...	...	...	17.1	12.2	...	...	...
1875	869,126	654,562	...	...	...	25.3	19.1	...	...	...
1885	1,024,574	886,824	...	259,497	113,565	26.9	23.2	...	6.8	3.0
1895	1,246,427	852,422	117,215	365,633	110,838	29.5	20.2	86.0	8.6	2.6
1905	1,442,004	997,065	142,092	347,518	59,460	30.6	21.1	89.7	7.4	1.3
1915	1,788,521	1,084,274	141,300	438,708	59,050	33.2	20.1	73.2	8.1	1.1
1925	2,071,560	1,199,936	124,394	516,639	50,741	35.0	20.3	56.6	8.7	0.9
1930	2,070,765	1,161,504	117,729	501,831	50,516	32.4	18.2	53.8	7.9	0.8
1935	2,174,291	1,152,371	115,592	551,032	47,721	31.7	16.8	50.5	8.0	0.7
1940	2,100,161	1,176,517	102,033	660,184	47,804	29.4	16.4	46.3	9.2	0.7
1943	2,235,431	1,204,802	92,882	736,183	48,832	30.2	16.3	39.9	10.0	0.7
1947	2,678,792	1,138,238	123,837	934,170	79,551	34.3	14.6	44.2	12.0	1.0
1948	2,681,624	950,610	143,963	953,999	79,032	33.5	11.9	50.9	11.9	1.0
1949	2,696,638	945,444	192,677	842,170	82,575	33.0	11.6	66.7	10.3	1.0
1950	2,337,507	904,876	216,974	715,081	83,689	28.1	10.9	84.9	8.6	1.0
1951	2,137,689	838,998	217,231	671,905	82,331	25.3	9.9	92.2	7.9	1.0
1952	2,005,162	765,068	203,824	676,995	79,021	23.4	8.9	92.3	7.9	0.9
1953	1,868,040	772,547	193,274	682,077	75,255	21.5	8.9	93.8	7.8	0.9
1954	1,765,126	720,813	187,023	697,792	76,479	20.0	8.2	95.8	7.9	0.9

* Naikaku Kambō, Japan (ed.), *Naikaku Seido Shichijūnen-shi* (Seventy-year history of the Cabinet; Tokyo, 1955), Table VIII.

APPENDIX VIII.
JAPAN'S MILITARY EXPENDITURE*

(unit = ¥ 1 million)

year	Administrative Expenditure		Military Expenditure		National Bonds and Loans	
1915	240	41.1%	182	31.2%	123	21.0%
1920	555	40.8	650	47.8	95	7.0
1925	725	47.5	444	29.1	221	14.5
1926	774	49.0	434	27.5	233	14.8
1927	848	48.0	492	27.8	282	16.0
1928	865	47.7	517	28.5	286	15.7
1929	811	46.7	495	28.5	230	16.1
1930	689	44.2	443	28.4	273	17.5
1931	650	44.0	455	30.8	214	14.5
1932	858	44.0	686	35.2	241	12.4
1933	879	39.0	873	38.7	335	14.8
1934	685	31.7	942	43.5	361	16.7
1935	623	28.2	1033	46.8	372	16.9

* Naikaku Kambō, Japan (ed.), *Naikaku Seido Shichijūnen-shi*, Table XXXII.

APPENDIX IX.

INTEREST RATES OF JAPANESE INDUSTRIES

DURING WORLD WAR I* (In Terms of the Paid Capital)

	1915 1st half	1916 1st half	1916 2nd half	1917 2nd half
cotton spinning	251%	452%	772%	922%
textile	212	401	425	458
hemp	153	294	368	300
silk reeling	212	465	493	489
milling	184	212	288	312
mining	201	508	381	388
brewing	182	183	300	244
fertilizer	184	351	389	626
ceramics	90	224	421	648
chemical	380	1035	747	1567
privately owned railway	81	93	107	112
electric power	108	129	129	130
gas	83	98	96	118
marine transportation	368	897	1147	1127
machine and shipping	164	351	546	861
exchange	158	197	315	190
warehouse	83	102	152	118
property	71	76	80	774
miscellaneous	142	183	214	290

* Ōshima Kiyoshi, *Nihon Kyōkōshi-ron* (A treatise on the history of Japan's panics; Tokyo, 1952–1955), II, 31.

APPENDIX X.   DEVELOPMENT OF SCHOOLS IN JAPAN*

year	1875	1885	1895	1905	1915	1925	1930
Primary Schools							
number	24,303	28,283	26,631	27,407	25,578	25,459	25,673
teachers	44,565	99,510	73,182	109,975	162,992	209,894	234,799
pupils	1,926,126	3,097,235	3,670,345	5,348,213	7,454,652	9,188,560	10,112,226
Junior High Schools							
number	116	106	87	259	321	502	557
teachers	265	1,005	1,324	5,113	6,575	11,748	13,843
pupils	5,620	14,084	30,871	104,968	141,954	296,791	345,691
Girls' High Schools							
number	—	9	15	100	366	805	975
teachers	—	72	186	1,561	3,590	12,043	15,223
pupils	—	616	2,897	31,918	95,949	301,447	368,999
Vocational High Schools							
number	1	26	54	270	547	797	976
teachers	1	102	397	2,633	4,962	10,643	14,592
pupils	15	990	2,459	39,182	93,736	212,867	288,681
Senior High Schools							
number	—	1	7	8	8	29	32
teachers	—	45	275	284	365	1,163	1,418
students	—	964	4,289	4,904	6,259	158	20,551

Blind & Dumb Schools							
number	—	3	4	26	71	113	125
teachers	—	24	24	138	455	718	1,027
pupils	—	198	229	1,433	3,073	5,716	8,137
Teachers' Colleges							
number	16	57	50	77	100	158	155
teachers	588	753	717	1,283	1,936	3,047	3,461
students	7,696	7,764	7,586	20,574	29,196	50,180	49,119
Technical Schools							
number	110	75	52	63	88	135	162
teachers	489	541	746	2,113	2,864	5,213	7,087
pupils	7,686	8,820	9,798	29,495	38,666	67,277	90,043
Colleges & Universities							
number	—	2	1	2	4	34	46
teachers	—	176	161	404	895	4,219	5,941
students	—	1,720	1,620	5,821	9,696	46,690	69,605
Miscellaneous Schools							
number	—	1,448	1,250	2,018	2,479	1,763	1,932
teachers	—	2,488	3,250	6,754	8,275	13,116	16,401
students	—	62,966	64,948	133,292	169,136	235,939	217,257

* Naikaku Kambō, Japan (ed.), *Naikaku Seido Shichijūnen-shi*, Table XLI.

APPENDIX XI.

TOKYO WHOLESALE PRICE INDEXES*

(annual average of 1934—1936=100)

year	Total-average	Staple goods					
		rice	silk	cotton	lumber	steel	coal
1915	62. 5	45. 7	133. 7	59. 2	53. 4	138. 7	43. 7
1920	167. 8	154. 7	334. 9	232. 1	205. 3	233. 3	139. 7
1925	130. 5	145. 3	303. 6	173. 5	120. 1	110. 8	100. 0
1926	115. 7	131. 3	249. 4	124. 5	107. 4	95. 5	96. 0
1927	109. 9	122. 6	210. 8	117. 3	103. 2	91. 0	103. 0
1928	110. 6	107. 8	202. 4	125. 5	100. 5	97. 3	99. 0
1929	107. 5	101. 2	201. 2	123. 0	94. 2	99. 1	96. 0
1930	88. 5	88. 5	132. 5	78. 1	72. 5	73. 0	86. 3

* Naikaku Kambō, Japan (ed.), *Naikaku Seido Shichijūnen-shi*, Table XXVI.

APPENDIX XII.

EMPLOYMENT RATES OF COLLEGE
GRADUATES IN JAPAN**

	1923	1924	1925	1926	1927	1928	1929
law, economics	72%	62	55	52	65	46. 7	38. 1
science	88%	86	80	69	76	73. 3	76
agriculture	71%	70	58	63	61	49. 5	58. 8
medicine	92%	85	76	59	73	69. 2	70. 5
education	100%	100	97	80	89	86	70. 9
art	—%	—	49	39	31	53	40. 2
girls' colleges	55%	42	33	48	37	36	31
average	82%	75	66	59	64	54	54

** Abe Isoo, *Shitsugyō Mondai* (Problems of unemployment; Tokyo, 1929), 195.

APPENDIX XIII.
UNEMPLOYMENT RECORDED AT TOKYO
EMPLOYMENT OFFICES*

| year, month | job open- ings | jobs wanted | | employed | unem- ployed | unem- ploy- ment rate | number of em- ployment offices |
		registered	re-regis- tered				
1927 Jan.	14, 621	19, 043	5, 435	3, 658	15, 385	81%	24
Feb.	15, 005	16, 828	5, 507	4, 004	12, 824	76	24
Mar.	20, 234	20, 355	7, 331	5, 123	15, 232	75	24
Apr.	18, 562	21, 982	8, 892	5, 064	16, 918	77	24
May	16, 685	23, 098	9, 747	5, 191	17, 907	78	24
June	16, 280	20, 991	8, 625	5, 001	15, 990	76	24
July	15, 456	17, 465	6, 691	4, 631	12, 834	73	24
Aug.	17, 439	17, 218	7, 093	4, 472	12, 746	74	24
Sept.	17, 378	21, 953	9, 013	4, 887	17, 066	78	24
Oct.	18, 264	21, 074	8, 927	4, 672	16, 402	78	24
Nov.	16, 858	19, 711	8, 354	4, 091	15, 620	79	24
Dec.	11, 298	13, 691	4, 998	3, 746	9, 945	73	24
Total	198, 180	233, 409	90, 613	54, 540	178, 869	77	24
1928 Jan.	17, 472	17, 680	6, 159	4, 084	13, 596	77%	23
Feb.	19, 001	20, 470	8, 467	4, 661	15, 809	77	23
Mar.	24, 983	21, 303	8, 175	6, 216	15, 087	71	23
Apr.	20, 513	21, 100	9, 176	4, 724	16, 376	78	23
May	21, 285	21, 733	9, 395	5, 344	16, 388	75	23
June	16, 511	17, 696	8, 435	4, 239	13, 457	76	22
July	15, 691	15, 650	6, 487	3, 937	11, 713	75	22
Aug.	18, 316	14, 920	5, 967	3, 626	11, 294	76	22
Sept.	18, 922	17, 630	6, 854	4, 352	13, 278	75	22
Oct.	20, 063	19, 070	6, 753	5, 033	14, 037	74	22
Nov.	15, 126	16, 157	5, 728	3, 991	12, 166	75	22
Dec.	11, 035	14, 048	4, 734	3, 523	10, 525	75	22
Total	218, 917	217, 456	86, 330	53, 730	163, 726	75	22

* Abe Isoo, Shitsugyō Mondai, 178–179.

APPENDIX XIV.
LABOR DISPUTES, NUMBER OF PARTICIPANTS AND UNIONS*

year	Total Labor unions	Union members	Total labor disputes number	Total labor disputes participants
1917	40	...	...	...
18	107	...	...	...
19	187	...	2, 388	335, 225
20	273	...	1, 069	127, 491
21	300	...	896	170, 889
22	389	103, 000	584	85, 909
23	432	137, 000	647	68, 814
24	469	126, 000	933	94, 047
25	457	228, 000	816	87, 117
1926	488	285, 000	1, 260	127, 267
27	505	309, 000	1, 202	103, 350
28	501	309, 000	1, 013	98, 278
29	630	331, 000	1, 408	171, 688
30	712	354, 000	2, 284	190, 300
31	818	369, 000	2, 415	152, 161

* Okazaki Jirō, Kajinishi Mitsuhaya, and Kuramochi Hiroshi (eds.), *Nihon Shihonshugi Hattatsu-shi Nempyō* (The chronological table of the development of Japanese capitalism; Tokyo, 1949), Table LXI and LXII.

APPENDIX XV.
TOTAL AGRICULTURAL PRODUCTION PER FAMILY, AND ITS INDEX**
(the average of 1921−1924=100)

	1925	1926	1927	1928	1929	1930
Niigata actual number	720 Yen	580	600	567	553	364
Niigata index	114	91	94	89	87	57
Nagano	916 Yen	729	518	568	684	358
	126	100	71	78	94	49
Ibaragi	838 Yen	713	685	636	548	426
	124	106	102	94	81	63
Wakayama	651 Yen	523	526	499	535	371
	122	100	99	94	101	70
average	772 Yen	667	616	604	606	415
	117	101	93	91	92	63

** Kimura Seiji, *Nihon Nōgyō Kyōkō no Bunseki* (An analysis of agrarian panic in Japan; Tokyo, 1948), Table VI.

APPENDIX XVI.
TENANT DISPUTES, NUMBER OF TENANT UNIONS, LANDLORD UNIONS, AND CO-OPERATIVES*

year	tenant disputes	participants		tenant unions		landlord unions		co-operatives	
		landlords	tenants	number of unions	number of members	number of unions	number of members	number of unions	number of members
1921	1,680	33,985	145,898	681	—	192	—	85	—
22	1,578	29,077	125,750	—	—	—	—	—	—
23	1,917	32,712	134,503	—	—	—	—	—	—
24	1,532	27,223	110,920	2,337	232,100	414	31,900	524	70,400
25	2,206	33,001	134,646	—	—	—	—	—	—
26	2,751	39,705	151,061	3,926	346,700	605	41,400	1,491	164,600
27	2,052	24,136	91,336	4,582	365,300	734	57,100	1,703	174,200
28	1,866	19,474	75,136	4,353	330,400	695	55,700	1,909	190,400
29	2,424	23,505	81,998	4,156	315,800	655	55,100	1,986	224,900
30	2,478	14,159	58,565	4,208	301,400	640	53,300	1,980	247,900

* Okazaki Jirō, Kajinishi Mitsuhaya, and Kuramochi Hiroshi, *Nihon Shihonshugi Hattatsu-shi Nempyō*, Table LXIII.

APPENDIX XVII.
NUMBER OF MAJOR CRIMES*

year	persons convicted (at the first trial)	murder	robbery	theft	gambling
1920	91, 927	810	343	13, 121	50, 596
21	80, 466	842	326	10, 720	44, 947
22	80, 332	767	341	10, 088	45, 778
23	83, 883	1, 015	323	9, 517	49, 107
24	88, 650	914	397	11, 164	51, 823
25	101, 636	944	596	12, 320	60, 386
26	104, 374	930	490	11, 686	62, 318
27	105, 780	961	630	13, 802	62, 104
28	87, 348	816	642	12, 775	47, 221
29	96, 282	573	676	13, 959	53, 121
30	97, 426	754	748	16, 508	49, 692

* Ōuchi Hyōe (comp.), *Nihon Keizai Tōkei-shū* (Japanese economic statistical tables; Tokyo, 1958), 328. Note general increase of crimes during 1925–1927.

APPENDIX XVIII.
NUMBER OF SUICIDES AND CAUSES*

reason	1925		1926		1927		1928		1929	
	M	F	M	F	M	F	M	F	M	F
delirium	2,004	1,153	1,956	1,186	1,887	1,139	1,812	1,139	1,745	1,036
suffering from illness	2,129	1,369	2,091	1,421	2,279	1,471	2,202	1,475	2,240	1,417
poverty	464	160	463	134	477	154	439	170	490	159
love suicides	194	224	214	230	252	266	245	257	250	265
amorous passion	84	115	70	112	60	106	62	106	54	85
guilt complex	125	44	131	46	159	54	133	49	113	38
family problems	177	320	221	293	220	305	214	354	261	305
fear of incrimination	133	19	126	14	116	22	124	14	123	19
fear of the future	179	109	238	149	311	183	258	178	271	159
debts	224	17	177	15	219	14	220	25	211	20
divorce	34	61	27	72	25	86	32	75	28	58
pregnancy by illicit intercourse	6	47	7	74	1	56	3	81	5	57
marriage	6	35	14	36	10	41	5	31	5	46
disappointed love	120	137	125	160	156	161	132	165	131	149
disability	49	38	57	40	63	37	52	53	64	34
deaths in family	54	60	59	51	52	48	68	58	60	76
illness in family	31	20	24	28	20	31	22	22	22	26
dissipation	130	18	126	18	139	18	136	18	141	23
fear of senility	160	112	162	111	172	146	184	143	174	142
taedium vitae	1,666	1,085	1,638	1,101	1,863	1,148	1,970	1,040	1,845	1,029
superstition	4	8	10	12	17	17	3	7	10	7
disqualification from conscription	1	—	6	—	4	—	4	—	3	—
avoidance of conscription	4	—	6	—	6	—	9	—	10	—
miscellaneous reasons	309	259	336	252	246	220	247	191	223	167
unknown reasons	925	308	890	269	931	230	680	207	834	213
sub-total	9,220	5,712	9,174	5,824	9,686	5,953	9,258	5,858	9,313	5,517
total	14,932		14,998		15,639		15,114		14,830	

* *The Asahi Nenkan* (Tokyo, 1932), 362–363.

APPENDIX XIX.
POPULATION INCREASE IN JAPAN PROPER*

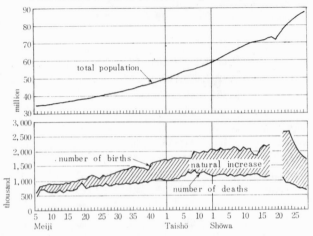

* Naikaku Kambō, Japan (ed.), *Naikaku Seido Shichijūnen-shi*, Graph I.

APPENDIX XX.
RAILROAD DEVELOPMENT** End of 1927

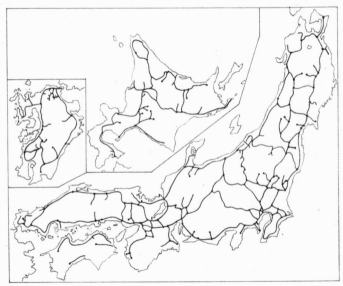

compared to the development of 1955.

** Naikaku Kambō, Japan (ed.), *Naikaku Seido Shichijūnen-shi*, 580.

APPENDIX XXI.
INVISIBLE BALANCE OF TRADE DURING WORLD WAR I*

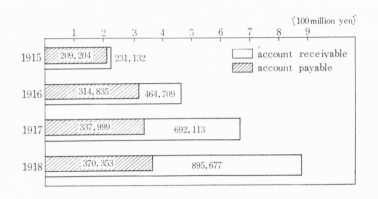

APPENDIX XXII.
JAPAN'S TRADE INCREASE DURING WORLD WAR I**

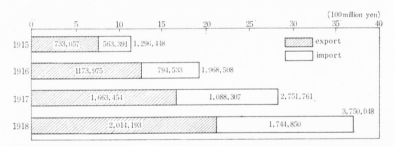

** Kodama Kōta, et al. (eds.), *Zusetsu Nihon Bunkashi Taikei: Taishō Shōwa Jidai* (Illustrated Japanese cultural history: Taishō and Shōwa periods; Tokyo, 1956), XII, 94.

APPENDIX XXI

INVISIBLE BALANCE OF TRADE DURING WORLD WAR II

BIBLIOGRAPHY

The following list is a select bibliography and it is by no means a comprehensive one. Many books and articles that are included in the footnotes, especially those related to methodology, are omitted from the list. Because Akira Iriye's work, *After Imperialism*, provides the readers with a good coverage of international documents, I put more emphasis on the investigation of domestic documents such as records of the Diet, important Japanese magazines and newspapers, and published as well as unpublished documents on Shidehara Kijūrō's and Tanaka Giichi's biographies and personalities, which Iriye neglected. This different emphasis of research materials is mutually justified, for Iriye's major aim is to "search for a new order in the Far East" of the 1920's by adopting the international system approach, whereas this study is primarily an investigation of domestic milieu vis-à-vis diplomatic leaderships which created different kinds of foreign policies between Shidehara and Tanaka. The British archives of the period of this study were not available at the time of this research — except *Documents on British Foreign Policy* which has nothing pertinent to the subject matter of this study —, though the British government changed its policy this year and its archives up to 1940 are now available for the public usage.

OFFICIAL DOCUMENTS

Chinese Foreign Ministry Archives. Academia Sinica, Taiwan.

Dai-Nihon Teikoku Gikai-shi 大日本帝国議会誌 (The Diet record of Great Japanese Empire), ed. Dai-Nihon Teikoku Gikai-shi Kankō-kai 大日本帝国議会誌刊行会, XIV-XVIII. Tokyo, 1930.

Documents on British Foreign Policy, ed. E. L. Woodward, Rohan Butler, and J. P. T. Bury. London, 1956.

FRUS: Papers Relating to the Foreign Relations of the United States. Washington, D. C.

Gaimushō Kōhyō-shū 外務省公表集 (A collection of official statements by the Foreign Ministry of Japan). Tokyo.

JFMA: Japanese Foreign Ministry Archives. Tokyo.

JMA: Japanese Military Archives. Tokyo.

KMWH: *Ko-ming Wen-hsien* 革命文献 (Documents of the revolution), ed. Lo Chia-lun 羅家論. Taipei, 1953.

Saikin Shina: *Saikin Shina Kankei Shomondai Tekiyō* 最近支那諸問題摘要 (Summaries of recent problems relating to China), ed. Gaimushō 外務省. Tokyo.

SDA: United States, State Department Archives. National Archives; Washington, D. C.

Shina Kankei Jōyaku-shū 支那関係条約集 (The collection of treaties and agreements related to China), ed. Gaikō Jihō-sha 外交時報社. Tokyo, 1930.

Shina Kanzei Tokubetsu Kaigi no Keika 支那関税特別会議の経過 (The progress of the special conference on the Chinese customs tariff). Taiwan Sōtoku Kambō Chōsa-ka 台湾総督官房調査課. Taiwan, 1927.

Shuyō Monjo: *Nihon Gaikō Nempyō narabini Shuyō Monjo* 日本外交年表並主要文書 (Chronological tables and documents of Japanese diplomacy), ed. Gaimushō; 2 vols. Tokyo, 1965–1966.

Special Tariff Conference on the Chinese Customs Treaty, October 1925–April 1926, ed. the Chinese Foreign Ministry. Peking, 1928.

Treaties and Agreements with and concerning China, 1894–1919, ed. John V. A. MacMurray; 2 vols. Washington, D. C., 1921.

MAGAZINES AND NEWSPAPERS

Akahata 赤旗 (The red flag). Kyoto.
The Asahi Nenkan 朝日年鑑 (The Asahi annual). Tokyo.
The Asahi Shimbun 朝日新聞. Tokyo.
Bungei Shunjū 文芸春秋 (Literary miscellany). Tokyo.
China Weekly Review. Sanghai.
China Year Book. London and Tientsin.
Chūō Kōron 中央公論 (Central review). Tokyo.
Gaikō Jihō 外交時報 (Current report of diplomacy). Tokyo.
The Jiji Sjimpō 時事新報. Tokyo.
The London Times. London.
The Mainichi Nenkan 毎日年鑑 (The Mainichi annual). Osaka.
The Mainichi Shimbun 毎日新聞. Osaka.
The Manchester Guardian. Manchester.
The New York Times. New York.
Nihon oyobi Nihonjin 日本及日本人 (Japan and the Japanese). Tokyo.
Nihon Rōdō Nenkan 日本労働年鑑 (Japan labor yearbook). Tokyo.
North China Herald. Shanghai.

PUBLISHED AND UNPUBLISHED BOOKS AND ARTICLES

Abe Isoo 安部磯雄. *Shitsugyō Mondai* 失業問題 (Problems of unemployment). Tokyo, 1929.
Abend, Hallett. *My Life in China, 1926–1941.* New York, 1943.
Alcock, Sir Rutherford, K. C. B. *The Capital of the Tycoon.* New York, 1868.
Almond, Gabriel A., and Coleman, James S. *The Politics of the Developing Areas.* Princeton, 1960.
Almond, Gabriel A., and Verba, Sidney. *The Civic Culture.* Princeton, 1963.
Amakusa Rintarō 天草麟太郎. *Nihon Kyōsantō Dai-kenkyo-shi* 日本共産

党大検挙史　(A history of great arrests of Japanese communists). Tokyo, 1929.

Aoki Keiichirō (Keiichi) 青木恵一郎 (恵一). *Nihon Nōmin Kumiai Undō-shi* 日本農民組合運動史 (A history of the Japanese farmers' union movement). Tokyo, 1931.

Aoki Tokuzō 青木得三. *Wakatsuki Reijirō, Hamaguchi Osachi* 若槻礼次郎, 浜口雄幸. Tokyo, 1958.

Arahara Bokusui 荒原朴水. *Dai-Uyoku-shi* 大右翼史 (The great history of the right wing). Tokyo, 1966.

——. *Nihon Kokka-shugi-dantai Meikan* 日本国家主義団体名鑑 (A dictionary of Japanese nationalist associations). Tokyo, 1963.

Arai Tatsuo 新井達夫. *Katō Tomosaburō* 加藤友三郎. Tokyo, 1958.

Araki Sadao 荒木貞夫, ed. *Gensui Uyehara Yūsaku-den* 元帥 上厚勇作伝 (General Uyehara Yūsaku's biography). Tokyo, 1937.

Arendt, Hannah. *The Origins of Totalitarianism*. New York, 1951.

Arita Hachirō 有田八郎. *Bakahachi to Hito wa yū* 馬鹿八と人はいう (They call me foolish Hachi). Tokyo, 1959.

Asahi Journal 朝日ジャーナル ed. *Shōwa-shi no Shunkan* 昭和史の瞬間 (Great moments of Shōwa history); 2 vols. Tokyo, 1966.

Asahi Shimbun 朝日新聞, ed. *Kindai Nihon no Gaikō* 近代日本の外交 (Diplomacy of modern Japan). Tokyo, 1962.

Asahi Shimbun Seiji Keizai-bu 朝日新聞政治経済部, ed. *Manmō no Shomondai* 満蒙の諸問題 (Problems in Manchuria and Mongolia). Tokyo, 1931.

Ashida Hitoshi 芦田均. *Dainiji Sekai Taisen Gaikōshi* 第二次世界大戦外交史 (A diplomatic history toward World War II). Tokyo, 1959.

Baba Akira 馬場明. "Dai Ichiji Santō Shuppei to Tanaka Gaikō" 第一次山東出兵と田中外交 (The first dispatch of troops to Shantung and Tanaka diplomacy), *Ajia Kenkyū* アジア研究 (Asiatic studies). October 1963, pp. 50–77.

——. "Tanaka Gaikō to Chō Sakurin Bakusatsu Jiken" 田中外交と張作霖爆殺事件 (Tanaka diplomacy and the assassination of Chang Tso-lin), *Rekishi Kyōiku* 歴史教育 (History and education), VIII, No. 2 (February 1960), pp. 41–48.

Baba Tsunego 馬場恒吾. *Gendai Jimbutsu Hyōron* 現代人物評論 (Comments on contemporary figures). Tokyo, 1930.

——. *Seikai Jimbutsu Fūkei* 政界人物風景 (A sketch of political figures). Tokyo, 1931.

Baker, P. J. Noel. *The Geneva Protocol.* London, 1925.

Banno Masataka 坂野正高. "Dai-ichiji Taisen kara Go-sanjū made: Kokken Kaifuku Undōshi Oboegaki" 第一次大戦から五・卅まで：国権回復運動覚書 (From World War I to the May 30th Incident: A study of the Rights Recovery Movement). *Gendai Chūgoku o meguru Sekai no Gaikō* 現代中国を繞る世界の外交 (World diplomacy and China), ed. Ueda Toshio 植田捷雄. Tokyo, 1951, pp. 1–67.

Banno Masataka 坂野正高 and Etō Shinkichi 衛藤瀋吉. *Chūgoku o meguru Kokusai Seiji* 中国をめぐる国際政治 (International politics and China). Tokyo, 1968.

Beasley, W. G. *The Modern History of Japan.* New York, 1964.

Beckmann, George M., and Ōkubo, Genji. *The Japanese Communist Party: 1922–1945.* Stanford, 1969.

Bellah, Robert N. "Ienaga Saburō and the Search for Meaning in Modern Japan," *Changing Japanese Attitudes toward Modernization,* ed. Marius B. Jansen, Princeton, 1965, pp. 369–423.

——. "Japan's Cultural Identity: Some Reflections on the Work of Watsuji Tetsurō," *Journal of Asian Studies,* XXXIV, No. 4 (August 1965), pp. 573–594.

——. *Tokugawa Religion; The Values of Pre-Industrial Japan.* Glencoe, Ill. 1957.

Benedict, Ruth. *The Chrysanthemum and the Sword; Patterns of Japanese Culture.* Boston, 1946.

Bloch, Kurt. *German Interests and Politics in the Far East.* New York, 1939.

Bouscaren, Anthony T. *Soviet Foreign Policy: A Pattern of Persistence.* Philadelphia, 1961.

Borg, Dorothy. *American Policy and the Chinese Revolution, 1925–1928.* New York, 1947.

Brandt, Conrad. *Stalin's Failure in China, 1924–1927.* Cambridge, Mass., 1958.

Brandt, Conrad; Schwarts, Benjamin I.; and Fairbank, John K. *A Documentary History of Chinese Communism.* Cambridge, Mass., 1952.

Brown, Delmer M. *Nationalism in Japan: An Introductory Historical*

Analysis. Berkeley and Los Angeles, 1965.

——. "The Nature of Shintō"; paper read at the colloquium of the Center for Japanese and Korean Studies, University of California. Berkeley, May 18, 1966.

Buell, Raymond L. *The Washington Conference*. New York and London, 1922.

Bull, Hedley. "International Theory: The Case for the Classical Approach," *World Politics*, XVIII, 1966, pp. 361–367.

Bullock, Alan. *Hitler: A Study in Tyranny*. New York, 1961.

Cameron, Meribeth E.; Mahoney, Thomas H. D.; and McReynolds, George E. *China, Japan and the Powers*. New York, 1960.

Carr, E. H. *Britain, A Study of Foreign Policy from the Versailles Treaty to the Outbreak of War*. London, 1939.

Chang Kia-ngau. *China's Struggle for Railroad Development*. New York, 1943.

Chiang Chieh-shih Hsien-sheng Yen-shuo Chi 蔣介石先生演説集 (Collection of Chiang Kai-shek's speeches). Canton, 1927.

Ch'ien Tuan-sheng. *The Government and Politics of China*. Cambridge, Mass., 1950.

Chin-tai-shih Tzu-liao 近代史資料 (Documents of modern history), ed. Chung-kuo K'o-hsüeh-yüan 中国科学院 (China academy of science). Peking, 1954.

Chow Tse-tsung. *The May Fourth Movement: Intellectual Revolution in Modern China*. Cambridge, Mass., 1960.

Clyde, Paul H. *The Far East*, 3d ed. Englewood Cliffs, N. J., 1958.

Craig, Albert M. "Kido Kōin and Ōkubo Toshimichi: A Psycho-Social Analysis"; paper read at the colloquium of the Center for Japanese and Korean Studies, University of California. Berkeley, February 28, 1969.

Craig, Albert M., and Shively, Donald H., eds. *Personality in Japanese History*. Berkeley, 1971.

Craig, Gordon A., and Gilbert, Felix, eds. *The Diplomats, 1919–1939*. Princeton, 1953.

Dainihon Nōdō Kyōkai 大日本農道協会. *Kokutai no Hongi to Nōdō* 国体の本義と農道 (National polity and agrarianism). Tokyo, 1942.

Dallin, David. *The Rise of Russia in Asia*. New Haven, 1949.

Daniels, Roger. *The Politics of Prejudice: The Anti-Japanese Movement in California and the Struggle for Japanese Exclusion.* Berkeley, 1962.

De Bary, Wm. Theodore; Chan, Wing-tsit; and Watson, Burton, comps. *Sources of Chinese Tradition*; 2 vols. New York, 1968.

De Grazia, Sebastian. *The Political Community, A Study of Anomie.* Chicago, 1948.

Deutsch, Karl, and Edinger, Lewis. "Foreign Policy of the German Federal Republic," *Foreign Policy in World Politics*, ed. Roy C. Macridis. Englewood Cliffs, N. J., 1962, pp. 91–132.

De Vos, George, and Wagatsuma, Hiroshi. *Japan's Invisible Race: Caste in Culture and Personality.* Berkeley, 1967.

Doihara Kenji 土肥原賢二. *Kōdō no Shin-Seishin* 皇道の真精神 (The true spirit of the Imperial Way). Tokyo, 1939.

Dull, Paul S. "The Assassination of Chang Tso-lin," *Far Eastern Quarterly*, XI, No. 4 (August 1952), pp. 453–463.

Dulles, Foster R. *Forty Years of American-Japanese Relations.* New York, 1937.

Durkheim, Émile. *Suicide, A Study in Sociology*, trans. John A. Spaulding and George Simpson, ed. with an intro. George Simpson. Glencoe, Ill., 1962.

Duus, Peter. *Party Rivalry and Political Change in Taishō Japan.* Cambridge, Mass., 1968.

Earl, David M. *Emperor and Nation in Japan: Political Thinkers of the Tokugawa Period.* Seattle, 1964.

Eisenstadt, S. N. *Modernization: Protest and Change.* Englewood Cliffs, N. J., 1966.

Ellis, L. Ethan. *Frank B. Kellogg and American Foreign Relations, 1925–1929.* New Brunswick, N. J., 1961.

Etō Shinkichi 衛藤瀋吉. *Higashi Ajia Seiji-shi Kenkyū* 東アジア政治史研究 (A study of East Asian political history). Tokyo, 1968.

——. "Kei-Hō-sen Shadan Mondai no Gaikō Katei — Tanaka Gaikō to sono Haikei" 京奉線遮断問題の外交過程 — 田中外交とその背景 (Diplomatic process concerning the problem of intercepting the Peking-Mukden line — Tanaka diplomacy and its background), *Kindai Nihon no Seiji Shidō* 近代日本の政治指導 (Political leaderships in modern Japan); eds. Shinohara Hajime 篠原一 and Mitani Taichirō 三谷太一郎. Tokyo, 1965,

——. *Kindai Chūgoku Seiji-shi Kenkyū* 近代中国政治史研究 (A political history of modern China). Tokyo, 1968.

——. "Nikka Kinchō to Nihonjin" 日華緊張と日本人 (Sino-Japanese tension and the Japanese), *Chūgoku o meguru Kokusai Seiji*. See Banno.

Fairbank, John K.; Reischauer, Edwin O.; and Craig, Albert M. *East Asia: The Modern Transformation*. Boston, 1965.

Falconeri, Gennaro. "*Reactions to Revolution: Japanese Attitudes and Foreign Policy toward China, 1924–1927.*" Unpublished Ph. D. dissertation, University of Michigan, 1967 (Order No. 68–7591).

Feis, Herbert. *The Diplomacy of the Dollar: The First Era, 1919–1932.* Baltimore, 1950.

Feng Yü-hsiang. 馮玉祥. *Wo-te Sheng-huo* 我的生活 (My life); 3 vols. Chungking, 1944.

Fisher, Louis. *Soviets in World Affairs*; 2 vols. New York, 1930.

Fox, William T. R., ed. *Theoretical Aspects of International Relations*. Notre Dame, Ind., 1959.

Fu Ch'i-hsüeh 伝啓学. *Chung-kuo Wai-chiao Shi* 中国外交史 (A diplomatic history of China). Taipei, 1957.

Fujita Tōko 藤田東湖. "Hitachi Obi" 常陸帯, *Fujita Tōko Zenshū* 藤田東湖全集 (A complete collection of Fujita Tōko's works), ed. Takasu Yoshijirō 高須芳次郎 Tokyo, 1935, I, pp. 420–431.

Fukuchi Shigetaka 福地重孝. *Gunkoku Nihon no Keisei: Shizoku Ishiki no Tenkai to sono Shūmatsu* 軍国日本の形成，士族意識の展開とその終末 (The formation of militant nation, Japan: The development and decline of samurai consciousness). Tokyo, 1959.

——. *Shizoku to Samurai-Ishiki, Kindai Nihon o Okoserumono Horobosumono* 士族と士意識，近代日本を興せるもの亡ぼすもの (Samurai caste and samurai consciousness which established and destroyed modern Japan). Tokyo, 1956.

Fukuzawa Yukichi 福沢諭吉. *Bunmei-ron no Gairyaku* 文明論の概略 (A short treatise of civilization). Tokyo, 1953.

Furukawa Tetsushi 古川哲史. *Nihon Rinri Shisō-shi Kenkyū* 日本倫理思想史研究 (A study of Japanese ethical thought); 3 vols. Tokyo, 1957.

Gaimushō Hyakunenshi Hensan Iinkai 外務省百年史編纂委員会 (ed.). *Gaimushō no Hyakunen* 外務省の百年 (One-hundred-year history of the

Foreign Ministry of Japan); 2 vols. Tokyo, 1969.

Gaimushō Japan 日本国外務省 ed. *Beikoku tai-shi Keizai Seiryoku no Zembō* 米国対支経済勢力の全貌 (American economic influence in China). Tokyo, 1940.

——. *Nihon Gaikō Hyakunen Shōshi* 日本外交百年小史 (A short survey of one-hundred-year history of Japanese diplomacy). Tokyo, 1956.

Gondō Seikyō 権藤成卿 (Seikei). *Jichi Mimpan* 自治民範 (Self-government by the people). Tokyo, 1932.

——. *Kōmin Jichi Hongi* 皇民自治本義 (The fundamental principle of self-rule by the imperial subjects). Ashiya, 1921.

——. *Kummin Kyōji Ron* 君民共治論 (Co-operative rule of the emperor and his subjects). Tokyo, 1932.

——. *Nōson Jikyū Ron* 農村自救論 (Self-help for villages). Tokyo, 1932.

Gotō Shimpei 後藤新平. *Seiji no Rinrika* 政治の倫理化 (Moralization of politics). Tokyo, 1926.

Grew, Joseph C. *Ten Years in Japan*. New York, 1944.

——. *Turbulent Era: A Diplomatic Record of Forty Years, 1904–1945*; 2 vols. Boston, 1952.

Griswold, Whitney A. *The Far Eastern Policy of the United States*. New York, 1938.

Haas, Ernst B., and Whiting, Allen S. *Dynamics of International Relations*. New York, Toronto and London, 1956.

Hara Kei 原敬 (Satoshi). *Hara Kei Nikki* 原敬日記 (Hara Kei's diary), ed. Hara Keiichirō 原奎一郎; 9 vols. Tokyo, 1950–1951.

Harada Kumao 原田熊男. *Saionji Kō to Seikyoku* 西園寺公と政局 (Prince Saionji and Politics); 8 vols. Tokyo, 1952.

Harris, Townsend. *The Complete Journal of Townsend Harris*. Garden City, N. Y., 1930.

Harootunian, H. D. *Toward Restoration: The Growth of Political Consciousness in Tokugawa Japan*. Berkeley, 1970.

Hata Ikuhiko 秦郁彦. *Gun Fasshizumu Undō-shi* 軍ファッシズム運動史 (A history of the military fascist movement). Tokyo, 1962.

Hatano Kan'ichi 波多野乾一. *Chūgoku Kyōsantō-shi* 中国共産党史 (A history of the Chinese Communist Party); 10 vols. Tokyo, 1961.

Hayashi Gonsuke 林権助. *Waga Shichijū-nen o Kataru* 我が七十年を語る (Reminiscences of my seventy years). Tokyo, 1935.

Hidaka Rokurō 日高六郎 ed. *Kindai-shugi* 近代主義 (Modernism). Tokyo, 1965.

Hirano Reiji 平野零児. *Manshū no Imbōsha: Kōmoto Daisaku no Un-meiteki na Ashiato* 満洲の陰謀者：河本大作の運命的な足あと (A conspirator in Manchuria: fateful steps of Kōmoto Daisaku). Tokyo, 1959.

Holtom, Daniel C. *Modern Japan and Shinto Nationalism; A Study of Present Day Trends in Japanese Religions*. New York, 1963.

Hori Shigeru 保利茂 (Shika 史華). *Saishō to naru made, Tanaka Giichi* 宰相となる迄, 田中義一 (Tanaka Giichi until he became Premier). Tokyo, 1928.

Horie Yasuzō 堀江保蔵. *Nihon Keizai-shi* 日本経済史 (An economic history of Japan). Tokyo, 1942.

Horiuchi Tateki 堀内干城. *Chūgoku no Arashi no Nakade* 中国の嵐の中で (Amid the storms of China). Tokyo, 1950.

Hosokawa Ryūgen 細川隆元. *Tanaka Giichi* 田中義一. Tokyo, 1958.

Hsü, Immanuel C. Y. *China's Entrance into the Family of Nations: The Diplomatic Phase, 1858–1880*. Cambridge, Mass., 1960.

Hu Hua 胡華. *Chung-kuo Hsin-min-chu-chu-i Ko-ming-shi* 中国新民主主義革命史 (A history of China's new democratic revolution). Peking, 1950.

Hua Kang 華崗. *Chung-kuo Ta-ko-ming-shi* 中国大革命史 (A history of China's great revolution). Shanghai, 1932.

Hung Chün-p'ei 洪鈞培. *Kuo-min Cheng-fu Wai-chiao-shih* 国民政府外交史 (Diplomatic history of the Nationalist Government). Shanghai, 1930.

Husserl, Edmund. *Ideas: General Introduction to Pure Phenomenology*, trans. W. R. Boyce Gibson. New York, 1958.

Hyman, Herbert. *Political Socialization*, Glencoe, Ill., 1959.

Ichihashi, Yamato. *The Washington Conference and After*. Stanford, 1928.

Ide Kiwata 井出季和太. *Shina Kanzei Tokubetsu Kaigi no Keika* 支那関税特別会議の経過 (The report on the progress of Special Conference on the Chinese Customs Tariff). Taipei, 1927.

Ikei Masaru 池井優. "Dai-niji Hō-Choku Sensō to Nihon" 第二次奉直戦争と日本 (The second Fengtien-Chihli war and Japan), *Hōgaku Kenkyū* 法学研究 (Journal of jurisprudence); XXXVII, No. 3 (March 1964), pp. 48–75.

Imai Seiichi 今井清一. "Seitō Seiji to Shidehara Gaikō" 政党政治と幣

原外交 (Party politics and the Shidehara Diplomacy), *Rekishigaku Kenkyū* 歴史学研究 (Journal of historical studies); No. 219 (May 1958), pp. 20–26.

——. "Shidehara Gaikō ni okeru Seisaku Kettei" 幣原外交における政策決定 (Decision-making in the Shidehara Diplomacy), *Nempō Seijigaku* 年報政治学 (Annals of Japanese Political Science Association; 1959), pp. 92–112.

Imai Seiichi 今井清一 and Takahashi Masae 高橋正衛, eds. *Kokkashugi Undō* 国家主義運動 (Nationalist movements); 2 vols. Tokyo, 1963.

Inoo Tentaro 稲生典太郎. "Bakumatsu ni okeru Kōbu no Jōyaku Rongi" 幕末における公武の条約論議 (Discussions on treaties by bushi and court nobles toward the end of Tokugawa), *Nihon Gaikō-shi Kenkyū: Bakumatsu Ishin Jidai* 日本外交史研究 : 幕末維新時代 (Studies of Japanese diplomatic history, during the end of Tokugawa and the Restoration period), ed. Nihon Kokusai Seiji Gakkai 日本国際政治学会 Tokyo, 1960, pp. 83–96.

——. "Tanaka Jōsōbun o meguru Ni-san no Mondai" 「田中上奏文」をめぐる二, 三の問題 (A few problems concerning the 'Tanaka Memorandum'), *Nihon Gaikō-shi no Shomondai* 日本外交史の諸問題 (Various problems in Japanese diplomatic history), ed. Nihon Kokusai Seiji Gakkai 日本国際政治学会; I. Tokyo, 1964. pp. 73–87.

Inoue Kiyoshi 井上清 and Watanabe Tōru 渡辺徹 eds. *Kome Sōdō no Kenkyū* 米騒動の研究 (A study of rice riots); 5 vois. Tokyo, 1959–1962.

Inoue Tetsujirō 井上哲次郎 and Arima Sukemasa 有馬祐政, eds. *Bushidō Sōsho* 武士道叢書 (Bushidō library); 3 vols. Tokyo, 1905.

Inukai Ken 犬養健. *Yōsukō wa Ima mo Nagarete iru* 揚子江は今も流れている (Still flows the Yangtze River). Tokyo, 1960.

Iriye Akira. *After Imperialism: The Search for a New Order in the Far East.* Cambridge, Mass., 1965.

Isaacs, Harold. *The Tragedy of the Chinese Revolution.* Stanford, 1961.

Ishigami Ryōhei 石上良平. *Seitōshi-ron: Hara Kei Botsugo* 政党史論, 原敬歿後 (A history of a political party, Seiyūkai, since the death of Hara Kei). Tokyo, 1960.

Ishii Itarō 石射猪太郎. *Gaikō kan no Isshō* 外交官の一生 (A life of a diplomat). Tokyo, 1950.

Jansen, Marius B. ed. *Changing Japanese Attitudes toward Modernization.* Princeton, N. J., 1965.

——. "Changing Japanese Attitudes toward Modernization," *Changing Japanese Attitudes toward Modernization.* See Jansen, pp. 43–89.

——. *The Japanese and Sun Yat-sen.* Cambridge, Mass., 1954.

Japanese Foreign Ministry 日本国外務省. "Taishi Hōsaku An" 対支方策案 (Planned policy toward China), July 9, 1928. An unpublished document in the Document Office of the Japanese Foreign Ministry.

Kashima Morinosuke 鹿島守之助. *Nichi-Bei Gaikō-shi* 日米外交史 (Diplomatic relations between Japan and the United States). Tokyo, 1958.

Kajinishi Mitsuhaya 楫西光速 *et al. Nihon Shihon-shugi no Hatten* 日本資本主義の発展 (Development of capitalism in Japan). Tokyo, 1959.

Kamei Katsuichirō 亀井勝一郎, ed. *Kindaika to Dentō* 近代化と伝統 (Modernization and tradition). Tokyo, 1959.

Kamikawa Hikomatsu 神川彦松. "Nihon Gaikō e no Puroregomena" 日本外交へのプロレゴメナ (A prolegomena of Japanese diplomacy), *Nihon Gaikō no Bunseki* 日本外交の分析 (Analyses of Japanese diplomacy), ed. Nihon Kokusai Seiji Gakkai 日本国際政治学会. Tokyo, 1957, pp. 1–20.

Kao Ch'eng-yüan 高承元, ed. *Kuang-chou Wu-han Shih-ch'i Ko-ming Wai-chiao Wen-hsien* 広州武漢時期革命外交文献 (Documents of revolutionary diplomacy during the Canton and Wuhan periods). Shanghai, 1933.

Kardiner, Abram. *The Psychological Frontiers of Society.* New York, 1959.

Katō-haku Denki Hensan Iinkai 加藤伯伝記編纂委員会, ed. *Katō Takaaki* 加藤高明; 2 vols. Tokyo and Osaka, 1929.

Katō Hidetoshi 加藤秀俊. "Atarashii Sakariba: Asakusa to Sennichimae" 新しい盛り場, 浅草と千日前 (New mass amusement centers: Asakusa and Sennichimae), *Shōwa-shi no Shunkan.* See *Asahi Journal*, pp. 61–68.

——. "Ero guro nansensu" エロ・グロ・ナンセンス (Eroticism, grotesqueness and nonsense), *Shōwa-shi no Shukan.* See *Asahi Journal*, pp. 97–104.

Katsu Kaishū 勝海舟. "Rikugun Rekishi" 陸軍歴史 (A history of the army), *Kaishū Zenshū* 海舟全集 (A complete collection of Katsu Kaishū's works), ed. Kaishū Zenshū Kankō-kai 海舟全集刊行会, VI and VII. Tokyo, 1921.

Kawahara Jikichirō 川原次吉郎. *Katsura Tarō* 桂太郎. Tokyo, 1959.

Kawai Tsuguo 河合従雄. *Tanaka Giichi-den* 田中義一伝 (A biography of Tanaka Giichi). Tokyo, 1929.

Kawamura Tadao 河村只雄, ed. *Shisō Mondai Nempyō* 思想問題年表 (A chronological table of ideological problems). Tokyo, 1936.

Kazama Atsushi 風間阜. *Kinsei Chūgoku-shi* 近世中国史 (A history of modern China). Tokyo, 1937.

Kikuchi Gorō 菊地悟郎, ed. *Rikken Seiyūkai Hōkoku-shi* 立憲政友会報国史 (The history of Rikken Seiyūkai); 2 vols. Tokyo, 1931.

Kimura Seiji 木村靖二. *Nihon Nōgyō Kyōkō no Bunseki* 日本農業恐慌の分析 (An analysis of agrarian panic in Japan). Tokyo, 1948.

Kishimoto Eitarō 岸本英太郎. *Nihon Rōdō Undō-shi* 日本労働運動史 (A history of Japanese labor movement). Tokyo, 1952.

Kiya Ikusaburō 木舎幾三郎. *Seikai Gojūnen no Butai-ura* 政界五十年の舞台裏 (Behind the scenes of a fifty-year political world). Tokyo, 1965.

Kiyohara Sadao 清原貞雄. *Kokushi to Nihon Seishin no Kengen* 国史と日本精神の顕現 (National history and manifestation of Japanese spirits). Tokyo, 1942.

——. *Kokutairon-shi* 国体論史 (A history of *kokutai* treatises). Tokyo, 1939.

——. *Nihon no Shimei to Kokumin no Jikaku* 日本の使命と国民の自覚 (Awake to Japan's mission). Tokyo, 1937.

Kiyosawa Kiyoshi 清沢洌. *Nihon Gaikō-shi* 日本外交史 (A diplomatic history of Japan); 2 vols. Tokyo, 1942.

Kluchhohn, Clyde and Murray, Henry, ed. *Personality in Nature, Society and Culture*. New York, 1965.

Kodama Kōta 児玉幸多 *et al.*, eds. *Zusetsu Nihon Bunkashi Taikei: Taishō Shōwa Jidai* 図説日本文化史大系：大正昭和時代 (Illustrated Japanese cultural history: Taishō and Shōwa periods); XII. Tokyo, 1956.

Kokuryū-kai 黒竜会 ed. "Kogetsu-kai Sensō Sokushin Undō" 湖月会戦争促進運動 (Kogetsu-kai's promotion of war), *Tōa Senkaku Shishi Kiden*, I, pp. 726-738.

——. *Tōa Senkaku Shishi Kiden* 東亜先覚志士紀伝 (Records of pioneers in East Asia); 3 vols. Tokyo, 1966.

Kokusai Seiji Gakkai 国際政治学会 ed. *Taiheiyō Sensō e no Michi* 太平洋戦争への道 (The road to the Pacific War); 8 vols. Tokyo, 1962–1963.

Kōmoto Daisaku 河本大作. "Watakushi ga Chō Saku-rin o Koroshita" 私が張作霖を殺した (I killed Chang Tso-lin), *Bungei Shunjū*, XXXII, No. 12 (December 1954), pp. 194–201.

Kondō Misao 近藤操. *Katō Takaaki* 加藤高明. Tokyo, 1959.

Kōno Seizō 河野省三. *Kokutai Kannen no Shiteki Kenkyū* 国体観念の史的研究 (A historical study of the concept of national polity). Tokyo, 1943.

——. *Nihon Seishin Hattatsu-shi* 日本精神発達史 (A history of the development of Japanese spirits). Tokyo, 1939.

"Kuhara Fusanosuke-shi ni mono o Kiku Zadan-kai" 久原房之助氏にものを聞く座談会 (A conversation with Mr. Kuhara Fusanosuke), *Bungei Shunjū* (April 1932), pp. 168–184.

Kumagai Tatsujirō 熊谷辰次郎. *Dai-Nihon Seinendan-shi* 大日本青年団史 (A history of greater Japan youth association). Tokyo, 1943.

Kuo Mo-jo 郭沫若. "Pei-fa T'u-tz'u" 北伐途次 (The northern expedition), in his *Ko-ming Ch'un-ch'iu* 革命春秋 (History of the revolution), II, Shanghai, 1951.

Kuroda Kōshirō 黒田甲子郎 ed. *Gensui Terauchi Hakushaku Denki* 元帥寺内伯爵伝記 (General and Count Terauchi's biography). Tokyo, 1920.

Kuroda Toshio 黒田寿男 and Ikeda Tsuneo 池田恒雄. *Nihon Nōmin Kumiai Undō-shi* 日本農民組合運動史 (A history of Japanese farmer's union movement). Tokyo, 1949.

Lasswell, Harold D. *Psychopathology and Politics*. Chicago, 1930.

Li Chien-nung. *The Political History of China, 1840–1928*. Trans. Teng Ssu-yu and Jeremy Ingalls. New York, 1956.

Liu, F. F. *Military History of Modern China, 1924–1949*. Princeton, 1956.

Lockwood, William W. *The Economic Development of Japan*. Princeton, 1954.

Lu, David J. *From the Marco Polo Bridge to Pearl Harbor; Japan's*

Entry into World War II. Washington, D. C., 1961.

MacNair, H. F. and Lach, Donald F. *Modern Far Eastern International Relations.* Toronto, 1955.

Maeda Renzan 前田蓮山, ed. *Tokonami Takejirō-den* 床次竹二郎伝 (A biography of Tokonami Takejirō). Tokyo, 1939.

Maezawa Hiroaki 前沢広明, ed. *Nihon Kokkai Shichijū-nen-shi* 日本国会七十年史 (Seventy-year history of Japanese Diet); 2 vols. Tokyo, 1954.

Maruyama Masao. "Patterns of Individuation and the Case of Japan: A Conceptual Scheme," in Jansen, ed., *Changing Japanese Attitudes toward Modernization,* pp. 489–531.

——. *Thought and Behavior in Modern Japanese Politics,* ed. Ivan Morris. London, 1963.

Maruyama Masao 丸山真男; Hattori Shisō 服部之総; and Tōyama Shigeki. 遠山茂樹. *Son-Jō Shisō to Zettai-shugi* 尊攘思想と絶対主義 (The "revere-the-emperor-expel-the-barbarians" thought and absolutism). Tokyo, 1948.

Matsui Kiyoshi 松井清. *Nihon Bōeki-ron* 日本貿易論 (A treatise on Japan's trade). Tokyo, 1950.

——. *Kindai Nihon Bōeki-shi* 近代日本貿易史 (A history of modern Japanese trade), II and III. Tokyo, 1963.

Matsushita Yoshio 松下芳男. *Nihon Gumbatsu no Kōbō* 日本軍閥の興亡 (The rise and fall of Japanese military cliques). Tokyo, 1967.

——. *Nihon no Gumbatsu-zo* 日本の軍閥像 (Japanese military cliques). Tokyo, 1969.

——. *Nihon Riku-Kaigun Sōdō-shi* 日本陸海軍騒動史 (A history of disputes in the Japanese Army and Navy). Tokyo, 1966.

Maxon, Yale C. *Control of Japanese Foreign Policy: A Study of Civil-Military Rivalry, 1930–1945.* Berkeley and Los Angeles, 1957.

Mead, George H. *The Philosophy of the Act.* Chicago, 1964.

——. *On Social Psychology; Selected Papers.* Chicago, 1964.

——, ed. *Mind, Self and Society from the Standpoint of a Social Behaviorist.* Chicago, 1937.

Medlicott, William N. *British Foreign Policy Since Versailles, 1919–1939.* London, 1968.

Miller, David Hunter. *The Geneva Protocol.* New York, 1925.

Minami Hiroshi 南博. *Taishō Bunka* 大正文化 (Taishō culture). Tokyo, 1965.

Ministry of Education. *Kokutai no Hongi* (Cardinal principles of the national entity of Japan). Trans. John O. Gauntlett and with an intro. Robert K. Hall. Cambridge, Mass., 1949.

Mitani Taichirō 三谷太一郎. "Tenkan-ki, 1918–1921, no Gaikō Shidō — Hara Kei oyobi Tanaka Giichi o Chūshin to shite" 転換期，1918–1921，の外交指導—原敬および田中義一を中心として (Diplomatic leadership in a transitional period, 1918–1921 — Hara Kei and Tanaka Giichi), *Kindai Nihon no Seiji Shidō* 近代日本の政治指導 (Political leaderships in modern Japan), eds. Shinohara Hajime 篠原一 and Mitani Taichirō 三谷太一郎. Tokyo, 1964, pp. 293–374.

Mitarai Tatsuo 御手洗辰雄. *Yamagata Aritomo* 山県有朋. Tokyo, 1958.

Mitsukawa Kametarō 満川亀太郎. *Ubawaretaru Ajia* 奪われたる亜細亜 (Asia, deprived). Tokyo, 1921.

Miyake Setsurei 三宅雪嶺. "Tanaka Giichi-ron" 田中義一論 (Treatise on Tanaka Giichi). *Chūō Kōron*, June 1927, pp. 121–124.

Mori Kiichi 森喜一. *Rōdōsha no Seikatsu* 労働者の生活 (Laborers' life). Tokyo, 1963.

Morishima Morito 森島守人. *Imbō Ansatsu Guntō* 陰謀暗殺軍刀 (Conspiracies, assassinations, swords). Tokyo, 1951.

Morley, James W. *The Japanese Thrust into Siberia, 1918*. New York, 1957.

Morton, William F. "Sainan Jiken" 済南事件 (Tsinan Incident), *Nihon Gaikō-shi Kenkyū: Nitchū-Kankei no Tenkai* 日本外交史研究，日中関係の展開 (Studies of Japanese diplomacy: Sino-Japanese relations). Tokyo, 1961, pp. 103–118.

———. "The Tanaka Cabinet's China Policy, 1927–1929." Unpublished Ph. D. dissertation, Columbia University, 1969. (Order No. 70–17,037).

Morse, Hosea Ballou and MacNair, Harley F. *Far Eastern International Relations*. Boston, 1931.

Muraoka Tsunetsugu. *Studies in Shintō Thought*. Trans. D. M. Brown and James T. Araki. Tokyo, 1964.

Naikaku Kambō, Japan 内閣官房, ed. *Naikaku Seido Shichijū-nen-shi* 内閣制度七十年史 (Seventy-year history of the Cabinet). Tokyo, 1955.

Naitō Juntarō 内藤順太郎. *Zai-Shina Bōseki Sōgi* 在支那紡績争議

(Disputes at cotton mills in China). Tokyo, 1925.

Najita Tetsuo. *Hara Kei in the Politics of Compromise: 1905–1915.* Cambridge, Mass., 1967.

Nakamura Kikuo 中村菊男. "Tanaka Naikaku no Taika Gaikō" 田中内閣の対華外交 (Tanaka Cabinet's policy toward China), *Hōgaku Kenkyū* 法学研究 (Journal of jurisprudence), XXXI, No. 4 and 9 (April and September, 1958), pp. 1–13, 19–50.

Nakamura Ryūei 中村隆英 (Takahide). "Go-sanjū Jiken to Zaikabō" 五・卅事件と在華紡 (The May Thirtieth Incident and the Japanese cotton industry in China), *Kindai Chūgoku Kenkyū* 近代中国研究 (Studies in Modern China), VI. 1964, pp. 99–169.

Naramoto Tatsuya 奈良本辰也. *Yoshida Shōin* 吉田松陰. Tokyo, 1951.

Nashimoto Yūhei 梨本祐平. *Chūgoku no Naka no Nihonjin* 中国の中の日本人 (Japanese in China); 2 vols. Tokyo, 1958.

Nezu Masashi ねずまさし. "Shidehara Gaikō no Sai-hyōka" 幣原外交の再評価 (Reappraisal of Shidehara Diplomacy), in *Hihan Nihon Gendai-shi* 批判日本現代史 (A critical modern Japanese history). Tokyo, 1958, pp. 101–117.

Nihon Gaikō Gakkai 日本外交学会, ed. *Taiheiyō Sensō Gen'in-ron* 太平洋戦争原因論 (Treatises on the causes of the Pacific War). Tokyo, 1953.

Nihon Kokusai Seiji Gakkai 日本国際政治学会, ed. *Nihon Gaikō no Bunseki* 日本外交の分析 (Analyses of Japanese diplomacy). Tokyo, 1957.

——. *Nihon Gaikō-shi Kenkyū: Bakumatsu, Ishin Jidai* 日本外交史研究, 幕末維新時代 (Studies of Japanese diplomatic history, during the end of Tokugawa and the Restoration period). Tokyo, 1960.

——. *Nihon Gaikō-shi Kenkyū: Gaikō Shidōsha-ron* 日本外交史研究, 外交指導者論 (Studies of Japanese diplomatic history: Treatises on Japanese diplomatic leaderships). Tokyo, 1967.

——. *Nihon Gaikō-shi Kenkyū: Meiji Jidai* 日本外交史研究, 明治時代 (Studies of Japanese diplomatic history, during the Meiji period). Tokyo, 1957.

——. *Nihon Gaikō-shi Kenkyū: Taishō Jidai* 日本外交史研究, 大正時代 (Studies of Japanese diplomatic history, during the Taishō period). Tokyo, 1958.

Nikka Jitsugyō Kyōkai 日華実業協会, ed. *Shina Kindai no Seiji Keizai*

支那近代の政治経済 (Politics and economy of modern China). Tokyo, 1931.

Nitobe Inazō. *Bushidō, the Soul of Japan.* New York and London, 1905.

Ogata Sadako N. *Defiance in Manchuria: The Making of Japanese Foreign Policy, 1931–1932.* Berkeley and Los Angeles, 1964.

Ohara Keishi 小原敬士, ed. *Nichi-Bei Bunka Kōshō-shi* 日米文化交渉史 (History of Japanese-American cultural relations), II: *Tsūshō Sangyō-hen* 通商産業編 (trade and industry). Tokyo, 1954.

Ōhara Shakai Mondai Kenkyū-sho 大原社会問題研究所, ed. *Nihon Rōdō Nenkan* 日本労働年鑑. Tokyo, 1924–1932.

Ōhata Tokushirō 大畑篤四郎. *Kokusai Kankyō to Nihon Gaikō* 国際環境と日本外交 (International environments and Japanese diplomacy). Tokyo, 1966.

Oka Yoshitake 岡義武. *Kindai Nihon Seiji-shi* 近代日本政治史 (A political history of Modern Japan), I. Tokyo, 1962.

——. *Yamagata Aritomo* 山県有朋. Tokyo, 1958.

Okano Masujirō 岡野増次郎. *Wu P'ei-fu* 呉佩孚 Tokyo, 1937.

Ōkawa Shūmei 大川周明. *Fukkō Ajia no Shomondai* 復興亜細亜の諸問題 (Various problems of restored Asia). Tokyo, 1922.

——. *Nihon oyobi Nihonjin no Michi* 日本及日本人の道 (The way for Japan and the Japanese). Tokyo, 1930.

——. *Nihon Seishin Kenkyū* 日本精神研究 (A study of Japanese spirits). Tokyo, 1930.

Okazaki Jirō 岡崎次郎, Kajinishi Mitsuhaya 楫西光速, and Kuramochi Hiroshi 倉持博, eds. *Nihon Shihonshugi Hattatsu-shi Nempyō* 日本資本主義発達史年表 (The chronological table of the development of Japanese capitalism). Tokyo, 1949.

Ōkōchi Kazuo 大河内一男. *Nihon Shihonshugi to Rōdō Mondai* 日本資本主義と労働問題 (Capitalism and labor problems in Japan). Tokyo, 1947.

Ōmichi Hiroo 大道弘雄, ed. *Nihon Keizai Tōkei Sōkan* 日本経済統計総観 (A general survey of Japanese economic statistics). Osaka, 1930.

Ono Michio 小野道雄 *et al. Nihon Nōgyō Kyōkō Kenkyū* 日本農業恐慌研究 (A study of Japan's agrarian panic). Tokyo, 1932.

Ōshima Kiyoshi 大島清. *Nihon Kyōkō-shi-ron* 日本恐慌史論 (A treatise on the history of Japan's panics); 2 vols. Tokyo, 1952–1955.

Ōuchi Tsutomu 大内力. *Nihon Shihonshugi no Nōgyō Mondai* 日本資本主義の農業問題 (Agrarian problems in Japanese capitalism). Tokyo, 1948.

Oyamada Kennan 小山田剣南. "Tanaka Giichi-ron" (On Tanaka Giichi), *Nihon oyobi Nihonjin*, No. 81 (September 15, 1925), pp. 47–58.

Pollard, Robert T. *China's Foreign Relations, 1917–1931.* New York, 1933.

Pratt, Sir John. *War and Politics in China.* London, 1943.

Pusey, Merlo J. *Charles Evans Hughes*; 2 vols, New York, 1952.

Pyle, Kenneth B. *The New Generation in Meiji Japan: Problems of Cultural Identity, 1885–1895,* Stanford, 1969.

Raser, John R. "Personal Characteristics of Political Decision-Makers: A Literature Review," *Peace Research Society (International) Papers,* V. Philadelphia Conference, 1965, pp. 177–181.

Reischauer, Edwin O.; Fairbank, John K.; and Craig, Albert N. *East Asia: The Modern Transformation.* Boston, 1965.

Rekishigaku Kenkyū-Kai 歴史学研究会, ed. *Kindai Nihon no Keisei* 近代日本の形成 (The formation of modern Japan). Tokyo, 1959.

Remer, Charles F. *A Study of Chinese Boycotts,* Baltimore, 1935.

——. *Foreign Investments in China.* New York, 1933.

Riesman, David, *The Lonely Crowd, A Study of the Changing American Character.* New Haven, 1960.

Rosovsky, Henry, *Quantitative Japanese Economic History.* Berkeley, 1961.

Rōyama Masamichi 蠟山政道. *Seiji-shi* 政治史 (A political history). Tokyo, 1940.

Saigō Kōsaku 西郷鋼作. *Ishiwara Kanji* 石原莞爾. Tokyo, 1937.

Sasaki Tōitsu 佐々木到一. *Wuhan ka Nanking ka* 武漢乎南京乎 (Wuhan or Nanking?). Tokyo, 1927.

Satō Shunzō 佐藤俊三. *Shina no Kokunai Tōsō* 支那の国内闘争 (The internal struggle in China). Tokyo, 1941.

Sawamura Yasushi 沢村康. *Nōgyō Dantai-ron* 農業団体論 (A study of agrarian associations). Tokyo, 1936.

Scalapino, Robert A. *Democracy and the Party Movement in Prewar Japan.* Berkeley, 1962.

——. *The Japanese Communist Movement 1920–1966.* Berkeley, 1967.

Scheiner, Irwin. *Christian Converts and Social Protest in Meiji Japan.* Berkeley, 1970.

Schuts, Alfred. *The Phenomenology of the Social World*. Trans. George Walsh and Frederick Lehnert. Evanston, Ill., 1967.

Schwarts, Benjamin I. *Chinese Communism and the Rise of Mao*. Cambridge, Mass., 1964.

Shiba Kōkan 司馬江漢. "Shumparō Hikki" 春波楼筆記 (Memoirs at Shumparō), *Hyakka Setsurin* 百家説林 (Treatises of a hundred philosophers), ed. Yoshikawa Kōbunkan, I. Tokyo, 1905, pp. 1119–1187.

Shidehara Heiwa Bunko 幣原平和文庫. "Manshū Mondai" 満洲問題 (Manchurian problems). Unpublished documents.

——. "Shidehara Keizai Gaikō Shiryō" 幣原経済外交資料 (Materials on Shidehara's economic-oriented diplomacy). Unpublished materials.

——. "Shina Mondai Kankei" 支那問題関係 (Problems related to China). Unpublished materials.

——. "Shoka no Shidehara-kan" 諸家の幣原観 (Various people's views on Shidehara). Unpublished materials.

Shidehara Heiwa Zaidan 幣原平和財団, ed. *Shidehara Kijūrō* 幣原喜重郎. Tokyo, 1955.

Shidehara Kijūrō 幣原喜重郎. *Gaikō Gojūnen* 外交五十年 (Fifty years of diplomacy). Tokyo, 1951.

——. "Gaikō Kanken" 外交管見 (My view on diplomacy). At Shidehara Heiwa Bunko in the Library of Congress in Tokyo. Unpublished.

——. "Wasure e nu Hitobito" 忘れ得ぬ人々 (Unforgettable people), *Bungei Shunjū*. January 1951, pp. 54–65.

——. "Watakushi no Yōshō Jidai" 私の幼少時代 (My childhood), *The Yomouri Shimbun Gakkō-ban* 読売新聞学校版. November 27, 1950.

Shigemitsu Mamoru. *My Struggle for Peace*. Trans. Oswald White; ed. F. S. G. Peggott. New York, 1958.

——. 重光葵 *Shōwa no Dōran* 昭和の動乱 (Upheavals of Shōwa); 2 vols. Tokyo, 1952.

Shihō-shō Keiji-kyoku, Japan 司法省刑事局. *Wagakuni ni okeru Kyōsanshugi Undō-shi Gairon* 我国に於ける共産主義運動史概論 (An outline of the communist movement in Japan). Tokyo, 1939.

Shinobu Jumpei 信夫淳平. *Taishō Gaikō Jūgo-nen* 大正外交十五年 (The fifteen-year diplomatic history of the Taishō era). Tokyo, 1927.

Shinobu Seizaburō 信夫清三郎. *Taishō Seiji-shi* 大正政治史 (Taishō

political history); 4 vols. Tokyo, 1951–1952.

Shinohara Hajime 篠原— and Mitani Taichirō 三谷太一郎, eds. *Kindai Nihon no Seiji Shidō* 近代日本の政治指導 (Political leaderships in modern Japan). Tokyo, 1965.

Shioda Shōbei 塩田庄兵衛. *Nihon Rōdō Undō no Rekishi* 日本労働運動の歴史 (A history of the labor movement in Japan). Tokyo, 1966.

Shively, Donald H. "Nishimura Shigeki: A Confucian View of Modernization," *Changing Japanese Attitudes toward Modernization*. See Jansen, pp. 193–241.

Singer, David J. "The Level of Analysis Problem in International Relations," *World Politics*, XIV (1961), pp. 77–92.

——, ed. *Human Behavior and International Politics*. Chicago, 1965.

Snyder, Richard C.; Bruck, H. W.; and Sapin, Burton. *Foreign Policy Decision-Making: An Approach to the Study of International Politics*. Glencoe, Ill., 1962.

South Manchuria Railway Research Bureau 満鉄調査部, ed. *Man-Mō Jijō* 満蒙事情 (Manchurian and Mongolian affairs). Dairen, 1930–1931.

Sprout, Harold and Margerett. *Man-Milieu Relationship in the Context of International Politics*. Trans. W. R. Boyce Gibson. Princeton, 1956.

Storry, Richard. *The Double Patriots: A Study of Japanese Nationalism*. Boston, 1957.

Sullivan, Mark. *The Great Adventure at Washington*. New York, 1922.

Suma Yakichirō 須磨弥吉郎. *Gaikō Hiroku* 外交秘録 (Confidential diplomatic reminiscences). Tokyo, 1956.

Suzuki Yasuzō 鈴木安蔵, ed. *Manshū Jihen Zengo* 満洲事変前後 (Pre- and post-Manchurian incident). Tokyo, 1943.

Tabata Shinobu 田畑忍. "Kempō Kyū-jō no Hatsuansha, Shidehara Kijūrō" 憲法九条の発案者幣原喜重郎 (Shidehara Kijūrō, the originator of Article IX of the Constitution), in his *Teikō-ken* 抵抗権 (Right of resistance), ed. Kempō Kenkyūsho Shuppankai 憲法研究所出版会. Kyoto, 1965, pp. 352–356.

Tabohashi Kiyoshi 田保橋潔. *Kindai Nissen Kankei no Kenkyū* 近代日鮮関係の研究 (A study of recent Japanese-Korean relations), I. Seoul, 1940.

Taishi Kōrō-sha Denki Hensan-kai 対支功労者伝記編纂会 *Taishi Kaiko-roku* 対支回顧録 (Recollections of affairs related to China); 4 vols.

Tokyo, 1936.

Takagi Seiju 高木清寿 and Takagi Junko 高木珣子 *Tōa no Chichi Ishiwara Kanji* 東亜の父石原莞爾 (The father of Asia, Ishiwara Kanji). Tokyo, 1954.

Takahashi Masae 高橋正衛, ed. *Kokka-shugi Undō* 国家主義運動 (Nationalist movement). Tokyo, 1964.

Takeda Kiyoko 武田清子. *Dochaku to Haikyō* 土着と背教 (The indigenous and the pervert). Tokyo, 1968.

Takeuchi Tatsuji. *War and Diplomacy in the Japanese Empire.* New York, 1967.

Takizawa Makoto 滝沢誠. *Gondō Seikyō Oboegaki* 権藤成卿覚え書 (Notes on Gondō Seikyō). Nagaoka, 1968.

Tanaka Naikaku 田中内閣, ed. *Tanaka Naikaku* 田中内閣 (Tanaka cabinet). Tokyo, 1928.

Tanaka Giichi Denki Kankō-kai 田中義一伝記刊行会 *Tanaka Giichi Denki* 田中義一伝記 (A biography of Tanaka Giichi); 3 vols. Tokyo, 1958.

Tang, Peter S. H. *Russian and Soviet Policy in Manchuria and Outer Mongolia, 1911-1931.* Durham, N. C., 1959.

Tazaki Jingi 田崎仁義. *Kōdō Nihon to Ōdō Manshū* 皇道日本と王道満洲 (Japan and Manchuria under the Imperial Way). Tokyo, 1933.

Thompkins, Pauline. *American-Russian Relations in the Far East.* New York, 1949.

Togawa Isao 戸川猪佐武. *Shōwa Gaikō-shi* 昭和外交史 (A diplamatic history of the Shōwa period). Tokyo, 1962.

Tokutomi Iichirō 徳富猪一郎. *Gendai Nihon to Sekai no Ugoki* 現代日本と世界の動き (Present Japan and world affairs). Tokyo, 1921.

——. *Kōdō Nihon no Sekaika* 皇道日本の世界化 (Internationalization of Japan's Imperial Way). Tokyo, 1938.

——. *Nihon Teikoku no Ichi-Tenki* 日本帝国の一転機 (A turning point of the Japanese empire). Tokyo, 1929.

——, ed. *Kōshaku Yamagata Aritomo-den* 公爵山県有朋伝 (Prince Yamagata Aritomo's biography); 3 vols. Tokyo, 1933.

Tong, Hollington K. *Chiang Kai-shek: Soldier and Statesman*; vols. I and II. Shanghai, 1937.

Totten, George O. *The Social Democratic Movement in Prewar Japan.*

New Haven, 1966.

Tōyama Shigeki 遠山茂樹, ed. *Kindai Nihon no Seijika* 近代日本の政治家 (Statesmen of modern Japan). Tokyo, 1964.

Tōyama Shigeki 遠山茂樹; Imai Seiichi 今井清一; and Fujiwara Akira 藤原彰. *Shōwa-shi* 昭和史 (A history of the Shōwa era). Tokyo, 1959.

Tsuchiya Takao 土屋喬雄. *Zoku Nihon Keizai-shi Gaiyō* 続日本経済史概要 (A survey of Japanese economic history, continued). Tokyo, 1941.

Tsukui Tatsuo 津久井竜雄. *Nihonshugi Undō no Riron to Jissen* 日本主義運動の理論と実践 (Theory and practice of the Japanism movement). Tokyo, 1935.

Tsunoda Ryusaku; De Bary, Wm. Theodore; and Keene, Donald, eds. *Sources of Japanese Tradition*; 2 vols. New York, 1965.

Tsurumi Yūsuke 鶴見裕輔, ed. *Gotō Shimpei* 後藤新平; 4 vols. Tokyo, 1937–1938.

Tupper, Eleanor and McReynolds, George E. *Japan in American Public Opinion*. New York, 1937.

Uchida Naosaku 内田直作. "Sensō Boppatsu to Chūgoku no Tai-Nichi Boikotto Mondai" 戦争勃発と中国の対日ボイコット問題 (The outbreak of the Pacific War and the Chinese boycott of Japanese goods), *Taiheiyō Sensō Geninron*. See Nihon Gaikō Gakkai, pp. 575–604.

Uchiyama Masakuma 内山正熊. "Kasumigaseki Seitō Gaikō no Seiritsu" 霞ヶ関正統外交の成立 (The establishment of the orthodox Kasumigaseki diplomacy), *Nihon Gaikō no Shomondai* 日本外交史の諸問題 (Various problems of Japanese diplomatic history), II ed. Nihon Kokusai Seiji Gakkai. Tokyo, 1965, pp. 1–16.

Ugaki Kazunari 宇垣一成. *Ugaki Kazunari Nikki* 宇垣一成日記 (Ugaki Kazunari's diary). Tokyo, 1954.

Ujita Naoyoshi 宇治田直義. *Shidehara Kijūrō* 幣原喜重郎. Tokyo, 1958.

Usui Katsumi 臼井勝美. "Chō Sakurin Bakushi no Shinsō" 張作霖爆死の真相 (Truth of the assassination of Chang Tso-lin), *Himerareta Shōwa-shi* 秘められた昭和史 (Secret stories of the Shōwa period: a special issue of *Chisei* 知性 [Intellect]). Tokyo, 1956, pp. 26–28.

——. "Go-sanjū Jiken to Nihon" 五・卅事件と日本 (The May 30th incident and Japan), *Ajiya Kenkyū* アジヤ研究 (Studies of Asia).

October 1957, pp. 43–64.

——. "Shidehara Gaikō Oboegaki" 幣原外交覚書 (A note on the Shidehara Diplomacy), *Nihon Rekishi* 日本歴史 (Japanese history), No. 126 (December 1958), pp. 62–68.

——. "Shōwa Shoki no Chū-Nichi Kankei: Hokubatsu e no Kanshō," 昭和初期の中日関係, 北伐への干渉 (Sino-Japanese relations during the early Shōwa period: the intervention in the Northern Expedition), *Kokushi Ronshū* 国史論集 (Essays in Japanese history), II (Kyoto, 1959), pp. 1657–1672.

——. "Tanaka Gaikō ni tsuite no Oboegaki" 田中外交についての覚書 (A note on the Tanaka diplomacy), *Nihon Gaikō-shi Kenkyū: Shōwa Jidai*. See Nihon Kokusai Seiji Gakkai, pp. 26–35.

Van Straelen, Henricus. *Yoshida Shōin, Forerunner of the Meiji Restoration*. T'oung Pao monograph; Leiden, 1952.

Wakatsuki Reijirō 若槻礼次郎. *Kofūan Kaiko-roku* 古風庵回顧録 (Reminiscences of Kofūan). Tokyo, 1950.

Watsuji Tetsurō 和辻哲郎. *Nihon Seishin-shi Kenkyū* 日本精神史研究 (A study of the development of Japanese spirits); 2 vols. Tokyo, 1940.

Wang Tsi C. *The Youth Movement in China*. New York, 1928.

Ward, Robert E., ed. *Political Development in Modern Japan*. Princeton, 1968.

Ward, Robert E. and Rustow, Dankwart A., eds. *Political Modernization in Japan and Turkey*. Princeton, 1964.

Weber, Max. *From Max Weber: Essays in Sociology*. Trans. ed., and with an intro. H. H. Gerth and C. W. Mills. London, 1947.

Wheeler, Gerald E. "Isolated Japan: Anglo-American Diplomatic Cooperation, 1927–1936." *Pacific Historical Review*, XXX, No. 2 (May 1961), pp. 165–178.

Wibur, C. Martin and How, Julie Lien-ying. *Documents on Communism, Nationalism, and Soviet Advisers in China, 1918–1927*. New York, 1956.

Williams, William S. "China and Japan: A Challenge and a Choice of the 1920's" *Pacific Historical Review*, XXVI, No. 3 (August 1957), pp. 259–279.

Wolfers, Arnold. "The Actors in International Politics," *Theoretical Aspects of International Relations*, ed. William T. R. Fox. Notre

Dame, 1959, pp. 83–106.

Wright, Stanley F. *China's Struggle for Tariff Autonomy, 1843–1938.* Shanghai, 1938.

Yamaguchi Shigeji 山口重次. *Higeki no Shōgun Ishiwara Kanji* 悲劇の将軍石原莞爾 (A tragic general, Ishiwara Kanji). Tokyo, 1952.

Yamakawa Kikue 山川菊栄 and Yamakawa Shinsaku 山川振作, eds. *Yamakawa Hitoshi Zenshū* 山川均全集 (A complete collection of Yamakawa Hitoshi's works), V. Tokyo, 1968.

Yamamoto Jyōtarō-ō Denki Hensan-kai 山本条太郎翁伝記編纂会 (A biography of Yamamoto Jōtarō). Tokyo, 1942.

Yamaura Kan'ichi 山浦貫一, ed. *Tōa Shintaisei no Senku, Mori Kaku* 東亜新体制の先駆, 森恪 (A forerunner of the new order in East Asia, Mori Kaku). Tokyo, 1940.

Yamazaki Kazuyoshi 山崎一芳. *Kuhara Fusanosuke* 久原房之助. Tokyo, 1939.

Yanaga Chitoshi. *Japan since Perry.* New York, 1949.

Yanagida Kunio 柳田国男. *Meiji Taishō-shi: Sesōhen* 明治大正史, 世相編 (Meiji Taishō history: social features). Tokyo, 1931.

Yanaihara Tadao 矢内原忠雄, ed. *Gendai Nihon Shōshi* 現代日本小史 (A short history of modern Japan). Tokyo, 1953.

——. *Manshū Mondai* 満洲問題 (The Manchurian problem). Tokyo, 1934.

Yoshihashi Takehiko. *Conspiracy at Mukden: The Rise of the Japanese Military.* New Haven, 1963.

Yoshizawa Kenkichi 芳沢謙吉. *Gaikō Rokujū-nen* 外交六十年 (Sixty years of diplomacy). Tokyo, 1958.

Zener, Karl *et al*, eds. "Inter-Relationships between Perception and Personality: A Symposium," *Journal of Personality*, XVIII (1949), pp. 1–266.

Zimmern, Alfred. *The League of Nations and the Rule of Law, 1918–1935.* London, 1936.

INDEX

Marxism-Leninism, 40.
Marxist-oriented tenant unions, 63.
Matsudaira Masanao, 278n.
Matsui Iwane, 36n, 348, 370, 371.
Matsui Keishirō, 159n, 266, 296.
Matsuoka Yōsuke, 84n, 127, 170, 238, 281, 294, 306, 315.
Matsushima Licenced Quarter Incident. See Incident.
May Fifteenth Incident. See Incident.
May Fourth Movement. See movement(s).
May Thirtieth: Incident. See Incident; movement. See movement(s).
Meiji: Restoration, 11, 13, 26, 44, 54, 80n, 88, 90, 94, 95, 104, 106, 116n, 141, 142, 195, 361; Government, 26, 92, 93, 96, 141; Constitution, 27n, 76, 178; absolutism, 44, 59; Emperor, 44, 59, 178, 367; étatisme, 44; Japanism movement. See movement(s).
Meirinkan, 95.
meishu (the lord of Asia). See also Lord of East Asia.
Memorandum. See Tanaka Memorandum.
militant diplomacy. See diplomacy.
Military: Academy, 100, 101, 124, 128; University, 101.
mimpon-shugi, 45, 50, 51.
Minami Jirō, 294.
Minamoto no Yoshitsune, 180.
Minseitō, 166, 169, 326, 327, 353, 355.
Minseitō Government. See Government.
Mito: School, 26; rōnin, 106.
Mitsubishi: Company, 149, 150; Zaibatsu, 149, 364. See also Mitsui.
Mitsui: executive, 170; Mitsubishi Companies, 111.
Mitsukawa Kametarō, 75, 81n, 195, 197.
(Mito) Mitsukuni (Tokugawa Mitsukuni), 79.
Miyake Setsurei, 226.

"Mondō muyō", 369.
Monroe Doctrine, 152; Oriental, 334.
Moralization Campaign, 77. See also Rinrika Undō.
Mori Kaku, 35n, 75, 127, 131, 169, 195, 221n, 229, 238, 264, 284, 294, 295, 297, 300, 301, 304, 306, 315, 360.
Mōri Motoaki, 134.
Mori Takachika, 90.
Motono Ichirō, 153, 159n.
Motoori Norinaga, 97.
movement(s): (Meiji) Japanism, 14n, 26, 75n, 82n, 150; jōi (Expel the Barbarian), 31, 78, 90, 196; labor-socialist, 56n; farmers' union, 63n; new Japanism, 75; agrarian "Self-help", 79; anti-Japanese, 132, 169, 244, 292, 293, 298–300, 302, 334, 335, 342, 343, 345, 346, 350, 351; exclusionist, 157; May Fourth, 190; constitutional, 225; May Thirtieth, 241, 245, 263; anti-imperialist, 245, 246n, 305; anti-foreign, 264, 270, 280; Chinese labor, 285n; anti-Chang, 342.
Mutō Nobuyoshi, 209, 294, 296, 297, 341.
Mutsu Munemitsu, 145, 363, 364.

Nagai Matsuzō, 39, 222, 371.
Nagai Ryūtarō, 221n, 355.
Nagata Hidejirō, 80.
Nagata Tetsuzan, 169.
Nakano Ōye, 199.
Nakano Seigo, 68, 355.
Nanking Incident. See Incident.
Nanking Government. See Government.
National Anti-Imperialist Convention, 244.
National Anti-Japanese League, 351.
National Anti-Revolutionary League Army, 320.
National Convention Concerning China, 237.